WORD PICTURES
IN THE
NEW TESTAMENT

PASTOR RUSSELL McLEOD.

WORD PICTURES
IN THE
NEW TESTAMENT

BY

ARCHIBALD THOMAS ROBERTSON,
A. M., D. D. LL. D., Litt. D.,
PROFESSOR OF NEW TESTAMENT INTERPRETATION
IN THE
SOUTHERN BAPTIST THEOLOGICAL SEMINARY
OF
LOUISVILLE, KENTUCKY

VOLUME V
THE FOURTH GOSPEL
THE EPISTLE TO THE HEBREWS

BROADMAN PRESS
NASHVILLE, TENNESSEE

PRINTED IN THE UNITED STATES OF AMERICA

CONTENTS

THE FOURTH GOSPEL

		PAGE
CHAPTER	I	3
CHAPTER	II	33
CHAPTER	III	43
CHAPTER	IV	58
CHAPTER	V	78
CHAPTER	VI	96
CHAPTER	VII	117
CHAPTER	VIII	137
CHAPTER	IX	160
CHAPTER	X	173
CHAPTER	XI	192
CHAPTER	XII	213
CHAPTER	XIII	235
CHAPTER	XIV	248
CHAPTER	XV	257
CHAPTER	XVI	265
CHAPTER	XVII	274
CHAPTER	XVIII	283
CHAPTER	XIX	296
CHAPTER	XX	308
CHAPTER	XXI	318

THE EPISTLE TO THE HEBREWS

CHAPTER	I	334
CHAPTER	II	342
CHAPTER	III	353
CHAPTER	IV	360
CHAPTER	V	367
CHAPTER	VI	373

CONTENTS

		PAGE
CHAPTER	VII	380
CHAPTER	VIII	388
CHAPTER	IX	394
CHAPTER	X	406
CHAPTER	XI	418
CHAPTER	XII	432
CHAPTER	XIII	444

BY WAY OF INTRODUCTION

GREATEST OF BOOKS

The test of time has given the palm to the Fourth Gospel over all the books of the world. If Luke's Gospel is the most beautiful, John's Gospel is supreme in its height and depth and reach of thought. The picture of Christ here given is the one that has captured the mind and heart of mankind. It is not possible for a believer in Jesus Christ as the Son of God to be indifferent to modern critical views concerning the authorship and historical value of this Holy of Holies of the New Testament. Here we find *The Heart of Christ* (E. H. Sears), especially in chapters 14 to 17. If Jesus did not do or say these things, it is small consolation to be told that the book at least has symbolic and artistic value for the believer. The language of the Fourth Gospel has the clarity of a spring, but we are not able to sound the bottom of the depths. Lucidity and profundity challenge and charm us as we linger over it.

THE BELOVED DISCIPLE

The book claims to be written by "the disciple whom Jesus loved" (John 21:20) who is pointedly identified by a group of believers (apparently in Ephesus) as the writer: "This is the disciple which beareth witness of these things, and wrote these things: and we know that his witness is true" (21:24). This is the first criticism of the Fourth Gospel of which we have any record, made at the time when the book was first sent forth, made in a postscript to the epilogue or appendix. Possibly the book closed first with 20:31, but chapter 21 is in precisely the same style and was probably added before publication by the author. The

natural and obvious meaning of the language in 21:24 is
that the Beloved Disciple wrote the whole book. He is apparently still alive when this testimony to his authorship
is given. There are scholars who interpret it to mean that
the Beloved Disciple is responsible for the facts in the book
and not the actual writer, but that is a manifest strain-
ing of the language. There is in this verse no provision
made for a redactor as distinct from the witness as is
plausibly set forth by Dr. A. E. Garvie in *The Beloved
Disciple* (1922).

A Personal Witness

It is manifest all through the book that the writer is the
witness who is making the contribution of his personal
knowledge of the Lord Jesus Christ during his earthly ministry. In 1:14 he plainly says that "the Word became
flesh, and dwelt among us and we beheld his glory" (*etheasametha tēn doxan autou*). He here associates others with
him in this witness to the glory of the Word, but in 21:25
he employs the singular "I suppose" (*oimai*) in sharp distinction from the plural "we know" (*oidamen*) just before.
The writer is present in nearly all the scenes described. The
word witness (*martureō, marturia*) so common in this Gospel
(1:7, 8, 19; 3:11, 26, 33; 5:31; 12:17; 21:24, etc.) illustrates
well this point of view. In the Gospel of Luke we have the
work of one who was not a personal witness of Christ (Luke
1:1–4). In the Gospel of Matthew we possess either the
whole work of a personal follower and apostle or at least the
Logia of Matthew according to Papias preserved in it. In
Mark's Gospel we have as the basis the preaching of Simon
Peter as preserved by his interpreter John Mark. John's
Gospel claims to be the personal witness of "the disciple
whom Jesus loved" and as such deserves and has received
exceptional esteem. One may note all through the book
evidences of an eye-witness in the vivid details.

With a Home in Jerusalem

It is not only that the writer was a Jew who knew accurately places and events in Palestine, once denied though now universally admitted. The Beloved Disciple took the mother of Jesus "to his own home" (*eis ta idia*, 19:27) from the Cross when Jesus commended his mother to his care. But this Beloved Disciple had access to the palace of the high priest (18:15f.). Delff (*Das vierte Evangelium wiederhergestellt*, 1890) argues that this fact shows that the Beloved Disciple was not one of the twelve apostles, one of a priestly family of wealth in Jerusalem. He does seem to have had special information concerning what took place in the Sanhedrin (John 7:45–52; 11:47–53; 12:10ff.). But at once we are confronted with the difficulty of supposing one outside of the circle of the twelve on even more intimate terms with Jesus than the twelve themselves and who was even present at the last passover meal and reclined on the bosom of Jesus (13:23). Nor is this all, for he was one of the seven disciples by the Sea of Galilee (21:1ff.) when Peter speaks to Jesus about the "Beloved Disciple" (21:20).

Only One John of Ephesus

It is true that an ambiguous statement of Papias (*circa* A.D. 120) is contained in Eusebius where the phrase "the Elder John" (*ho presbuteros Iōannēs*) occurs. The most natural way to understand Papias is that he is referring to the Apostle John by this phrase as he describes the teachings of the apostles by "the words of the elders" just before. This interpretation of the allusion of Papias has been rendered almost certain by the work of Dom John Chapman, *John the Presbyter and the Fourth Gospel* (1911). Not before Eusebius is the error found of two Johns in Ephesus, one the apostle, the other the so-called Presbyter. "Papias is no witness for the admission of two Johns of Asia Minor.

Irenaeus, too, in any case, knows of but one John of Asia Minor. And this John was an eye-witness of our Lord's Life" (Bousset, *Die Offenbarumg des Joh.*, p. 38, translation of Nolloth, *The Fourth Evangelist*, p. 63, note). Let this be admitted and much becomes clear.

No Early Martyrdom for the Apostle John

In 1862 a fragment of the Chronicle of Georgius Hamartolus, a Byzantine monk of the ninth century, was published. It is the *Codex Coislinianus*, Paris, 305, which differs from the other manuscripts of this author in saying that John according to Papias was slain by the Jews (*hupo Ioudaiōn aneirethē*) while the other manuscripts say that John rested in peace (*en eirēnēi anepausato*). The passage also quotes Eusebius to the effect that John received Asia as his sphere of work and lived and died in Ephesus. This same George the Sinner misquotes Origen about the death of John for Origen really says that the Roman king condemned him to the Isle of Patmos, not to death. Another fragment of Philip of Side, apparently used by Georgius, makes the same erroneous reference to Papias. It is therefore a worthless legend growing out of the martyrdom promised James and John by Jesus (Mark 10:39 = Matt. 20:23) and realized by James first of all (Acts 12:1f.). John drank the cup in the exile to Patmos. The correction to Peter in John 21: 20-23 would have no meaning if the Apostle John had already been put to death.

The Author the Apostle John

Loisy (*Le Quatr. Évangile*, p. 132) says that if one takes literally what is given in the body of the Gospel of the Beloved Disciple he is bound to be one of the twelve. Loisy does not take it "literally." But why not? Are we to assume that the author of this greatest of books is playing a part or using a deliberate artifice to deceive? It may be asked why John does not use his own name instead of a *nom de plume*. Reference can be made to the Gospels of Matthew, Mark, and Luke, no one of which gives the author's name. One can see a reason for the turn here given since the book consists so largely of personal experiences of the author with Christ. He thus avoids the too frequent use of the personal pronoun and preserves the element of witness which marks the whole book. One by one the other twelve apostles disappear if we test their claims for the authorship. In the list of seven in chapter 21 it is easy to drop the names of Simon Peter, Thomas, and Nathanael. There are left two unnamed disciples and the sons of Zebedee (here alone mentioned, not even named, in the book). John in this Gospel always means the Baptist. Why does the author so uniformly slight the sons of Zebedee if not one of them himself? In the Acts Luke does not mention his own name nor that of Titus his brother, though so many other friends of Paul are named. If the Beloved Disciple is John the Apostle, the silence about James and himself is easily understood. James is ruled out because of his early death (Acts 12:1). The evidence in the Gospel points directly to the Apostle John as the author.

Early and Clear Witness to the Apostle John

Ignatius (*ad Philad.* vii. 1) about A.D. 110 says of the Spirit that "he knows whence he comes and whither he is going," a clear allusion to John 3:8. Polycarp (*ad Phil.* § 7) quotes I John 4:2, 3. Eusebius states that Papias quoted First John. Irenaeus is quoted by Eusebius (H. E. V, 20) as saying that he used as a boy to hear Polycarp tell "of his intercourse with John and the others who had seen the Lord." Irenaeus accepted all our Four Gospels. Tatian made his *Diatessaron* out of the Four Gospels alone. Theophilus of Antioch (*Ad Autol.* ii. 22) calls John the author of the Fourth Gospel. This was about A.D. 180. The Mura-

torian Canon near the close of the second century names
John as the author of the Fourth Gospel. Till after the
time of Origen no opposition to the Johannine authorship
appears outside of Marcion and the Alogi. No other New
Testament book has stronger external evidence.

THE USE OF THE SYNOPTIC GOSPELS

As the latest of the Gospels and by the oldest living
apostle, it is only natural that there should be an infrequent
use of the Synoptic Gospels. Outside of the events of Passion Week and the Resurrection period the Fourth Gospel
touches the Synoptic narrative in only one incident, that
of the Feeding of the Five Thousand and the walking on
the water. The author supplements the Synoptic record in
various ways. He mentions two passovers not given by the
other Gospels (John 2:23; 6:4) and another (5:1) may be
implied. Otherwise we could not know certainly that the
ministry of Jesus was more than a year in length. He adds
greatly to our knowledge of the first year of our Lord's
public ministry ("the year of obscurity," Stalker) without
which we should know little of this beginning (John 1:19–
4:45). The Synoptics give mainly the Galilean and Perean
and Judean ministry, but John adds a considerable Jerusalem ministry which is really demanded by allusions in the
Synoptics. The Prologue (John 1:1–18) relates the Incarnation to God's eternal purpose as in Col. 1:14–20 and Heb. 1:
1–3 and employs the language of the intellectuals of the
time (*Logos* — Word) to interpret Christ as the Incarnate
Son of God.

A DIFFERENT STYLE OF TEACHING

So different is it in fact that some men bluntly assert
that Jesus could not have spoken in the same fashion as
presented in the Synoptics and in the Fourth Gospel. Such
critics need to recall the Socrates of Xenophon's *Memora-*

bilia and of Plato's *Dialogues*. There is a difference beyond a doubt, but there is also some difference in the reports in the Synoptics. Jesus for the most part spoke in Aramaic, sometimes in Greek, as to the great crowds from around Palestine (the Sermon on the Mount, for instance). There is the Logia of Jesus (Q of criticism) preserved in the non-Markan portions of Matthew and Luke besides Mark, and the rest of Matthew and Luke. Certain natural individualities are preserved. The difference is greater in the Fourth Gospel, because John writes in the ripeness of age and in the richness of his long experience. He gives his reminiscences mellowed by long reflection and yet with rare dramatic power. The simplicity of the language leads many to think that they understand this Gospel when they fail to see the graphic pictures as in chapters 7 to 11. The book fairly throbs with life. There is, no doubt, a Johannine style here, but curiously enough there exists in the Logia (Q) a genuine Johannine passage written long before the Fourth Gospel (Matt. 11:25–30=Luke 10:21–24). The use of "the Father" and "the Son" is thoroughly Johannine. It is clear that Jesus used the Johannine type of teaching also. Perhaps critics do not make enough allowance for the versatility and variety in Jesus.

The Same Style in the Discourses

It is further objected that there is no difference in style between the discourses of Jesus in John's Gospel and his own narrative style. There is an element of truth in this criticism. There are passages where it is not easy to tell where discourse ends and narrative begins. See, for instance, John 3:16–21. Does the discourse of Jesus end with verse 15, 16, or 21? So in 12:44 to 50. Does John give here a resumé of Christ's teaching or a separate discourse? It is true also that John preserves in a vivid way the conversational style of Christ as in chapters 4, 6, 7, 8, 9. In the

Synoptic Gospels this element is not so striking, but we do not have to say that John has done as Shakespeare did with his characters. Each Gospel to a certain extent has the colouring of the author in reporting the words of Jesus. An element of this is inevitable unless men are mere automata, phonographs, or radios. But each Gospel preserves an accurate and vivid picture of Christ. We need all four pictures including that of John's Gospel for the whole view of Christ.

HISTORICAL VALUE OF THE FOURTH GOSPEL

It is just here that the chief attack is made on the Fourth Gospel even by some who admit the Johannine authorship. It is now assumed by some that the Fourth Gospel is not on a par with the Synoptics in historical reliability and some harmonies omit it entirely or place it separately at the close, though certainly Tatian used it with the Synoptics in his *Diatessaron*, the first harmony of the Gospels. Some even follow Schmiedel in seeing only a symbolic or parabolic character in the miracles in the Fourth Gospel, particularly in the narrative of the raising of Lazarus in chapter 11 which occurs here alone. But John makes this miracle play quite an important part in the culmination of events at the end. Clearly the author professes to be giving actual data largely out of his own experience and knowledge. It is objected by some that the Fourth Gospel gives an unnatural picture of Christ with Messianic claims at the very start. But the Synoptics give that same claim at the baptism and temptation, not to mention Luke's account of the Boy Jesus in the temple. The picture of the Jews as hostile to Jesus is said to be overdrawn in the Fourth Gospel. The answer to that appears in the Sermon on the Mount, the Sabbath miracles, the efforts of the Pharisees and lawyers to catch Jesus in his talk, the final denunciation in Matthew 23, all in the Synoptics. The opposition to Jesus grew steadily as he revealed himself more clearly. Some of the difficulties raised are gratuitous as in the early cleansing of the temple as if it could not have happened twice, confounding the draught of fishes in chapter 21 with that in Luke 5, making Mary of Bethany at the feast of a Simon in chapter 12 the same as the sinful woman at the feast of another Simon in Luke 7, making John's Gospel locate the last passover meal a day ahead instead of at the regular time as the Synoptics have it. Rightly interpreted these difficulties disappear. In simple truth, if one takes the Fourth Gospel at its face value, the personal recollections of the aged John phrased in his own way to supplement the narratives in the Synoptics, there is little left to give serious trouble. The Jerusalem ministry with the feasts is a case in point. The narrative of the call of the first disciples in chapter 1 is another. The author followed Simon in bringing also his own brother James to Jesus. John was present in the appearance of Christ before Annas, and Pilate. He was at the Cross when no other apostles were there. He took the mother of Jesus to his home and then returned to the Cross. He saw the piercing of the side of Jesus. He knew and saw the deed of Joseph of Arimathea and Nicodemus. E. H. Askwith has a most helpful discussion of this whole problem in *The Historical Value of the Fourth Gospel* (1910).

Like the Johannine Epistles

Critics of all classes agree that, whoever was the author of the Fourth Gospel, the same man wrote the First Epistle of John. There is the same inimitable style, the same vocabulary, the same theological outlook. Undoubtedly the same author wrote also Second and Third John, for, brief as they are, they exhibit the same characteristics. In Second and Third John the author describes himself as "the Elder" (*ho presbuteros*), which fact has led some to argue for the mythical "Presbyter John" as the author in place of the Apostle John and so of First John and the Fourth Gospel. It is argued that the Apostle John would have termed himself "the Apostle John" after the fashion of Paul. But the example of the Apostle Peter disposes of that argument, for in addressing the elders (I Peter 5:1) he calls himself "your fellow-elder" (*ho sunpresbuteros*). In the Epistles John opposes Gnosticism both of the Docetic type which denied the actual humanity of Jesus as in I John 1:1–4 and the Cerinthian type which denied the identity of the man Jesus and the *aeon* Christ which came on Jesus at his baptism and left him at his death on the Cross as in I John 2:22. One of the many stories told about John is his abhorrence of Cerinthus when found in the same public bath with him. As Westcott shows, the Epistles of John prove his actual humanity while assuming his deity, whereas the Fourth Gospel proves his deity while assuming his humanity.

But Different from the Apocalypse

It should be said at once that the Johannine authorship of the Fourth Gospel does not depend on that of the Apocalypse. In fact, some men hold to the Johannine authorship of the Apocalypse who deny that of the Gospel while some hold directly the opposite view. Some deny the Johannine authorship of both Gospel and Apocalypse, while the majority hold to the Johannine authorship of Gospel, Epistles, and Apocalypse as was the general rule till after the time of Origen. The author of the Apocalypse claims to be John (1:4, 9; 22:8), though what John he does not say. Denial of the existence of a "Presbyter John" naturally leads one to think of the Apostle John. Origen says that John, the brother of James, was banished to the Isle of Patmos where he saw the Apocalypse. There is undoubted radical difference in language between the Apocalypse and the other Johannine books which will receive discussion when the

Apocalypse is reached. Westcott explained these differences as due to the early date of the Apocalypse in the reign of Vespasian before John had become master of the Greek language. Even J. H. Moulton (*Prolegomena*, p. 9, note 4) says bluntly: "If its date was 95 A.D., the author cannot have written the fourth Gospel only a short time after." Or before, he would say. But the date of the Apocalypse seems definitely to belong to the reign of Domitian. So one ventures to call attention to the statement in Acts 4:13 where Peter and John are described as *agrammatoi kai idiōtai* (unlettered and private or unschooled men). It is curious also that it is precisely in II Peter and the Apocalypse that we have so many grammatical solecisms and peculiarities. We know that the Fourth Gospel was reviewed by a group of John's friends in Ephesus, while he was apparently alone in the Isle of Patmos. The excitement of the visions would naturally increase the uncouth vernacular of the Apocalypse so much like that in the Greek papyri as seen in Milligan's *Greek Papyri*, for instance. This being true, one is able, in spite of Moulton's dictum, to hold to the Johannine authorship of both Gospel and Apocalypse and not far apart in date.

The Unity of the Gospel

This has been attacked in various ways in spite of the identity of style throughout. There are clearly three parts in the Gospel: the Prologue, 1:1–18, the Body of the Book, 1:19–20:31, the Epilogue, 21. But there is no evidence that the Prologue was added by another hand, even though the use of Logos (Word) for Christ does not occur thereafter. This high conception of Christ dominates the whole book. Some argue that the Epilogue was added by some one else than John, but here again there is no proof and no real reason for the supposition. It is possible, as already stated, that John stopped at 20:31 and then added 21 before sending the book forth after his friends added 21:24 as their endorsement of the volume. Some scholars claim that they detect various displacements in the arrangement of the material, but such subjective criticism is never convincing. There are undoubtedly long gaps in the narrative as between chapters 5 and 6, but John is not giving a continuous narrative, but only a supplementary account assuming knowledge of the Synoptics. It is held that editorial comments by redactors can be detected here and there. Perhaps, and perhaps not. The unity of this great book stands even if that be true.

ORIGINAL LANGUAGE OF THE BOOK

The late Dr. C. F. Burney of Oxford wrote a volume called, *The Aramaic Origin of the Fourth Gospel* (1922) in which he tried to prove that the Fourth Gospel is really the first in time and was originally written in Aramaic. The theory excited some interest, but did not convince either Aramaic or Greek scholars to an appreciable extent. Some of the examples cited are plausible and some quite fanciful. This theory cannot be appealed to in any serious interpretation of the Fourth Gospel. The author was beyond doubt a Jew, but he wrote in the *Koiné* Greek of his time that is comparatively free from crude Semiticisms, perhaps due in part to the help of the friends in Ephesus.

THE PURPOSE OF THE BOOK

He tells us himself in 20:30f. He has made a selection of the many signs wrought by Jesus for an obvious purpose: "But these are written, that ye may believe that Jesus is the Christ, the Son of God; and that believing ye may have life in his name." This is the high and noble purpose plainly stated by the author. The book is thus confessedly apologetic and this fact ruins it with the critics who demand a dull and dry chronicle of events without plan or purpose in a book of history. Such a book would not be read and would be of little value if written. Each of the Synoptics is written with a purpose and every history or biography worth reading is written with a purpose. It is one thing to have a purpose in writing, but quite another to suppress or distort facts in order to create the impression that one wishes. This John did not do. He has given us his deliberate, mature, tested view of Jesus Christ as shown to him while alive and as proven since his resurrection. He writes to win others to like faith in Christ.

John's Portrait of Christ

No one questions that the Fourth Gospel asserts the deity of Christ. It is in the Prologue at the very start: "And the Word was God" (1:1) and in the correct text of 1:18, "God only begotten" (*theos monogenēs*). It occurs repeatedly in the book as in the witness of the Baptist: "This is the Son of God" (1:34). It is in the charge of the Pharisees (5:18) and the claim of Christ himself (5:20–23; 6:48; 8:12, 58; 11:25; 14:9; 17:5) with the full and frank conviction of the author in 20:31. He has made good his purpose. He has proven that Jesus of Nazareth is the Son of God. With some critics this purpose has vitiated the entire book. The effort has been made to show that Paul, Peter, the Epistle to the Hebrews, the Synoptics give a lower view of Christ without the term *theos* applied to him. In particular it was once argued that Q, the Logia of Jesus, used by Matthew and Luke (the non-Markan portions in both Matthew and Luke), gives a reduced picture of Jesus as on a lower plane than God, the Arian or Ritschlian view at any rate as answering for God to us though not God in actual nature. But in the Logia of Jesus we find the same essential picture of Jesus Christ as the Son of God and the Son of Man as I have shown in my *The Christ of the Logia* (1924). The only way to get rid of the deity of Christ in the New Testament is to throw overboard all the books in it as legendary or reflections of late theological development away from the original picture. The very earliest picture drawn of Christ that has been preserved to us, that in the Logia of Jesus (drawn W. M. Ramsay believes before Christ's crucifixion), is in essential agreement with the fully drawn portrait in the Fourth Gospel. Each picture in the Four Gospels adds touches of its own, but the features are the same, those of the God-Man Jesus Christ, the Saviour of the world. The brilliant blind preacher of Edinburgh, George Matheson, sees this clearly (*Studies in the Portrait of the Messiah*, 1900; *St. John's Portrait of Christ*, 1910).

A BRIEF BIBLIOGRAPHY OF RECENT LITERATURE (SINCE 1880)

ABBOT, EZRA, *On the Authorship of the Fourth Gospel* (1880).

ABBOT, PEABODY, and LIGHTFOOT, *The Fourth Gospel* (1891).

ABBOTT, E. A., *Johannine Vocabulary* (1905).

————, *Johannine Grammar* (1906).

APPEL, *Die Echtheit des Johannesevangeliums* (1915).

ASKWITH, E. H., *The Historical Value of the Fourth Gospel* (1910).

BACON, B. W., *The Fourth Gospel in Research and Debate* (1910).

BALDENSPERGER, W., *Der Prolog des vierten Evangeliums* (1898).

BARTH, K., *The Gospel of John and the Synoptic Gospels* (1907).

BAUER, W., *Das Johannes-Evangelium.* 2 Aufl. (1925).

BELZER, *Das Evangelium des heiligen Johannes* (1905).

BERNARD, J. H., *Gospel according to St. John* (2 vols., 1929), in Int. Crit. Comm.

BERT, *Das Evangelium des Johannes* (1922).

BLASS, F., *Evangelium secundum Johannem* (1902).

Brooke, A. E., *The Historical Value of the Fourth Gospel* (Cambridge Biblical Essays, pp. 289 to 328. 1909).

Burch, Vacher, *The Structure and Message of St. John's Gospel* (1928).

Burney, C. F., *The Aramaic Origin of the Fourth Gospel* (1922).

Calmes, L'Évangile selon S. Jean (1904).

Candler, W. A., *Practical Studies in the Gospel of John* (3 vols., 1912–15).

Carpenter, J. Estlin, *The Johannine Writings* (1927).

Chapman, Dom John, *John the Presbyter and the Fourth Gospel* (1911).

Charnwood, Lord, *According to St. John* (1925).

Clemen, C., *Die Entstehung des Johannesevangeliums* (1912).

D'Alma, *La Controverse du quatrième évangile* (1908).

———, *Philo et le quatrième évangile* (1911).

Dausch, *Das Johannesevangelium* (1909).

Delff, H., *Das vierte Evangelium wiederhergestellt* (1890).

———, *Neue Beiträge zur Kritik und Erklärung des vierten Evangeliums* (1890).

Dods, M., *Expositor's Bible* (2 vols., 1891).

———, *Expositor's Greek Testament* (1897).

Drummond, James, *An Inquiry into the Character and Authorship of the Fourth Gospel* (1904).

Evans, H. H., *St. John the Author of the Fourth Gospel* (1888).

Ewald, P., *Das Hauptproblem der Evangelienfrage und der Weg zu seiner Lösung* (1890).

Fouard, S., *Jean et la fin de l'âge apostolique* (1904).

Gardner, P., *The Ephesian Gospel* (1915).

Garvie, A. E., *The Beloved Disciple* (1922).

Göbel, *Die Reden des Herrn nach Johannes* (2 vols., 1906, 1910).

Godet, F., *Comm. on the Gospel of St. John* (Tr., 2 vols., 1886–90).

Goguel, M., *Les sources du recit Johannique de la Passion* (1910).

GOGUEL, M., *Le quatrième évangile* (1924).

GORDON, S. D., *Quiet Talks on St. John's Gospel.*

GORE, C., *Exposition of the Gospel of John* (1920).

GREEN, A. V., *The Ephesian Canonical Writings* (1910).

GREGORY, C. R., *Wellhausen und Johannes* (1910).

GRILL, J., *Untersuchungen über die Entstehung des vierten Evangeliums* (1902).

GUMBEL, *Das Johannesevangelium Eine Ergänzung des Lukas ev.* (1911).

HARRIS, J. RENDEL, *The Origin of the Prologue to St. John's Gospel* (1917).

HAYES, D. A., *John and His Writings* (1917).

HOERNLE, E. S., *The Record of the Loved Disciple* etc. (1913).

HOLLAND, H. S., *The Philosophy of Faith and the Fourth Gospel* (1919).

———, *The Fourth Gospel* (1923).

HOLTZMANN, H. J., *Evangelium, Briefe, und Offenbarung des Johannes.* 3 Aufl. (1908).

HOLTZMANN, *Hand-Comm.* 3 Aufl. von Bauer (1908).

HOVEY, A. H., *In American Comm.* (1885).

HOWARD, W. F., *The Fourth Gospel in Recent Criticism and Interpretation* (1931).

IVERACH, JAMES, *Gospel of John* (Int. Stand. Bible Encycl.).

JACKSON, H. L., *The Fourth Gospel and Some Recent German Criticism* (1906).

———, *The Problem of the Fourth Gospel* (1918).

JOHNSTON, J. S., *The Philosophy of the Fourth Gospel* (1909).

KEISKER, *The Inner Witness of the Fourth Gospel* (1922).

KREYENBÜHL, *Neue Lösung der Johanneischen Frage* (1905).

LARFIELD, *Die beide Johannes von Ephesus* (1914).

LEATHES, STANLEY, *The Witness of St. John to Christ.*

LEPIN, *L'origine du quatrième évangile* (1907; 1927).

———, *La valeur historique du quatrième évangile* (1910).

LEWIS, F. G., *The Irenaeus Testimony to the Fourth Gospel* (1908).

LEWIS, F. G., *Disarrangements in the Fourth Gospel* (1910).
LIGHTFOOT, J. B., *Biblical Essays* (pages 1 to 198; I–III, 1893).
LLOYD, J. P. D., *The Son of Thunder* (1932).
LOISY, A., *Le quatrième évangile* (1903).
LOWRIE, *The Doctrine of John* (1899).
LYMAN, MARY ELY, *The Fourth Gospel and the Life of Today* (1931).
MANSON, W., *The Incarnate Glory* (1923).
MAURICE, F. D., *The Gospel of St. John* (1906).
McGREGOR, G. H., *The Moffatt Commentary* (1930).
MONTGOMERY, J. A., *The Origin of the Gospel According to St. John* (1923).
MOUSE, *Johannes und Paulus* (1915).
MUIRHEAD, L. A., *The Message of the Fourth Gospel* (1925).
NOLLOTH, C. F., *The Fourth Evangelist* (1925).
NUNN, H. P. V., *The Son of Zebedee and the Fourth Gospel* (1927).
ORR, JAMES, *The Authenticity of St. John's Gospel Deduced from Internal Evidence*.
OVERBECK, *Das Johannesevangelium* (1911).
PLUMMER, A., *Cambridge Greek Testament* (1913).
REVILLE, J., *Le quatrième évangile* (1901).
REYNOLDS, H. R., *Gospel of John* (Hastings, D. B., 1899).
RICHMOND, W., *The Gospel of the Rejection* (1906).
ROBERTSON, A. T., *The Divinity of Christ in the Gospel of John* (1916).
ROBINSON, A., *The Historical Character of St. John's Gospel* (1929).
ROBINSON, B. W., *The Gospel of John* (1925).
SANDAY, W., *Criticism of the Fourth Gospel* (1905).
SCHLATTER, *Die Sprache und Heimath des vierten Evangelisten* (1903).
SCHMIEDEL, P. W., *The Johannine Writings* (1908).

Scott, E. F., *The Fourth Gospel: Its Purpose and Theology* (1906).

Scott, E. F., *The Historical and Religious Value of the Fourth Gospel* (1903).

Scott-Moncrieff, C. E., St. *John, Apostle, Evangelist and Prophet* (1909).

Selbie, W. B., *Belief and Life: Studies in the Thought of the Fourth Gospel* (1916).

Smith, J. R., *The Teaching of the Fourth Gospel* (1903).

Smith, P. V., *The Fourth Gospel: Its Historical Importance* (1926).

Speer, R. E., *The Greatest Book in the World* (1915).

Spitta, F., *Das Johannesevangelium als Quelle der Geschichte Jesu* (1910).

Stange, *Die Eigenart des Johanneischen Produktion* (1914).

Stanton, V. H., *The Fourth Gospel* (Part III of Gospels as Hist. Documents, 1921).

Stevens, G. B., *The Johannine Theology* (1898).

Strachan, R. H., *Gospel of John* (Hastings, D C G 1906).

————, *The Fourth Gospel: Its Significance and Environment* (1917).

————, *The Fourth Evangelist: Dramatist or Historian* (1925).

Tillmann, Fritz, *Das Johannesevangelium Uebersetzt und Erklärt* (1931).

Vedder, H. C., *The Johannine Writings and the Johannine Problems* (1917).

Warschauer, J., *The Problem of the Fourth Gospel.*

Watkins, W. H., *Modern Criticism Considered in its Relation to the Fourth Gospel* (1890).

Watson, H. A., *The Mysticism of St. John's Gospel* (1916).

Wearing, *The World View of the Fourth Gospel* (1918).

Weiss, B., *Meyer Komm.* 9 Aufl. (1902).

————, *Das Johannesevangelium als einheitliches Werk* (1911).

WELLHAUSEN, J., *Das Evangelium Johannis* (1908).
WENDT, H. H., *The Gospel according to St. John: An Inquiry into its Genesis and Historical Value* (1911).
————, *Die Schichten im vierten Evangelium* (1911).
WESTCOTT, B. F., *The Gospel according to St. John* (2 vols., 1908).
WHITELAW, *The Gospel of John* (1888).
WINDISCH, H., *Johannes und die Synoptiker* (1927).
WORSLEY, *The Fourth Gospel and the Synoptists* (1911).
WREDE, W., *Charakter und Tendenz des Johannesevangelium* (1903).
ZAHN, TH., *Das Evangelium Johannis* (1908). 6 Aufl. (1921).

THE FOURTH GOSPEL

BY THE APOSTLE JOHN ABOUT A.D. 90

CHAPTER I

1. *In the beginning (en archēi)*. *Archē* is definite, though anarthrous like our at home, in town, and the similar Hebrew *be reshith* in Gen. 1:1. But Westcott notes that here John carries our thoughts beyond the beginning of creation in time to eternity. There is no argument here to prove the existence of God any more than in Genesis. It is simply assumed. Either God exists and is the Creator of the universe as scientists like Eddington and Jeans assume or matter is eternal or it has come out of nothing. *Was (ēn)*. Three times in this sentence John uses this imperfect of *eimi* to be which conveys no idea of origin for God or for the Logos, simply continuous existence. Quite a different verb (*egeneto*, became) appears in verse 14 for the beginning of the Incarnation of the Logos. See the distinction sharply drawn in 8:58 "before Abraham came (*genesthai*) I am" (*eimi*, timeless existence). *The Word (ho logos)*. *Logos* is from *legō*, old word in Homer to lay by, to collect, to put words side by side, to speak, to express an opinion. *Logos* is common for reason as well as speech. Heraclitus used it for the principle which controls the universe. The Stoics employed it for the soul of the world (*anima mundi*) and Marcus Aurelius used *spermatikos logos* for the generative principle in nature. The Hebrew *memra* was used in the Targums for the manifestation of God like the Angel of Jehovah and the Wisdom of God in Prov. 8:23. Dr. J. Rendel Harris thinks that there was a lost wisdom book that combined phrases in Proverbs and in the Wisdom of Solomon which John used for his Prologue (*The Origin of the Prologue to St. John*, p. 43) which he has undertaken to reproduce. At any rate John's standpoint is that of the Old

3

Testament and not that of the Stoics nor even of Philo who uses the term *Logos*, but not John's conception of personal pre-existence. The term *Logos* is applied to Christ only in John 1:1, 14 and Rev. 19:13 and I John 1:1 "concerning the Word of life" (an incidental argument for identity of authorship). There is a possible personification of "the Word of God" in Heb. 4:12. But the personal pre-existence of Christ is taught by Paul (II Cor. 8:9; Phil. 2:6f.; Col. 1:17) and in Heb. 1:2f. and in John 17:5. This term suits John's purpose better than *sophia* (wisdom) and is his answer to the Gnostics who either denied the actual humanity of Christ (Docetic Gnostics) or who separated the *aeon* Christ from the man Jesus (Cerinthian Gnostics). The pre-existent Logos "became flesh" (*sarx egeneto*, verse 14) and by this phrase John answered both heresies at once. *With God* (*pros ton theon*). Though existing eternally with God the Logos was in perfect fellowship with God. *Pros* with the accusative presents a plane of equality and intimacy, face to face with each other. In I John 2:1 we have a like use of *pros:* "We have a Paraclete with the Father" (*paraklēton echomen pros ton patera*). See *prosōpon pros prosōpon* (face to face, I Cor. 13:12), a triple use of *pros*. There is a papyrus example of *pros* in this sense *to gnōston tēs pros allēlous sunētheias*, "the knowledge of our intimacy with one another" (M. & M., *Vocabulary*) which answers the claim of Rendel Harris, *Origin of Prologue*, p. 8) that the use of *pros* here and in Mark 6:3 is a mere Aramaism. It is not a classic idiom, but this is *Koiné*, not old Attic. In John 17:5 John has *para soi* the more common idiom. *And the Word was God* (*kai theos ēn ho logos*). By exact and careful language John denied Sabellianism by not saying *ho theos ēn ho logos*. That would mean that all of God was expressed in *ho logos* and the terms would be interchangeable, each having the article. The subject is made plain by the article (*ho logos*) and the predicate without it (*theos*) just as in John 4:24 *pneuma ho theos* can only mean "God is spirit," not "spirit is God." So in I John 4:16 *ho theos agapē estin* can only mean "God is love," not "love is God" as a so-called Christian scientist would confusedly say. For the article with the predicate see Robertson, *Grammar*, pp. 767f. So in John 1:14 *ho Logos sarx egeneto*, "the Word became flesh," not "the flesh became Word." Luther argues that here John disposes of Arianism also because the Logos was eternally God, fellowship of Father and Son, what Origen called the Eternal Generation of the Son (each necessary to the other). Thus in the Trinity we see personal fellowship on an equality.

2. *The same (houtos).* "This one," the Logos of verse 1, repeated for clarity, characteristic of John's style. He links together into one phrase two of the ideas already stated separately, "in the beginning he was with God," "afterwards in time he came to be with man" (Marcus Dods). Thus John clearly states of the Logos Pre-existence before Incarnation, Personality, Deity.

3. *All things (panta).* The philosophical phrase was *ta panta* (the all things) as we have it in I Cor. 8:6; Rom. 11:36; Col. 1:16. In verse 10 John uses *ho kosmos* (the orderly universe) for the whole. *Were made (egeneto).* Second aorist middle indicative of *ginomai*, the constative aorist covering the creative activity looked at as one event in contrast with the continuous existence of *ēn* in verses 1 and 2. All things "came into being." Creation is thus presented as a becoming (*ginomai*) in contrast with being (*eimi*). *By him (di' autou).* By means of him as the intermediate agent in the work of creation. The Logos is John's explanation of the creation of the universe. The author of Hebrews (1:2) names God's Son as the one "through whom he made the ages." Paul pointedly asserts that "the all things were created in him" (Christ) and "the all things stand created through him and unto him" (Col. 1:16). Hence it is not a peculiar doctrine that John here enunciates. In I Cor. 8:6, Paul distinguishes

between the Father as the primary source (*ex hou*) of the all things and the Son as the intermediate agent as here (*di' hou*). *Without him* (*chōris autou*). Old adverbial preposition with the ablative as in Phil. 2:14, "apart from." John adds the negative statement for completion, another note of his style as in John 1:20 and I John 1:5. Thus John excludes two heresies (Bernard) that matter is eternal and that angels or aeons had a share in creation. *Not anything* (*oude hen*). "Not even one thing." Bernard thinks the entire Prologue is a hymn and divides it into strophes. That is by no means certain. It is doubtful also whether the relative clause "that hath been made" (*ho gegonen*) is a part of this sentence or begins a new one as Westcott and Hort print it. The verb is second perfect active indicative of *ginomai*. Westcott observes that the ancient scholars before Chrysostom all began a new sentence with *ho gegonen*. The early uncials had no punctuation.

4. *In him was life* (*en autōi zōē ēn*). That which has come into being (verse 3) in the Logos was life. The power that creates and sustains life in the universe is the Logos. This is what Paul means by the perfect passive verb *ektistai* (stands created) in Col. 1:16. This is also the claim of Jesus to Martha (John 11:25). This is the idea in Heb. 1:3 "bearing (upholding) the all things by the word of his power." Once this language might have been termed unscientific, but not so now after the spiritual interpretation of the physical world by Eddington and Jeans. Usually in John *zōē* means spiritual life, but here the term is unlimited and includes all life; only it is not *bios* (manner of life), but the very principle or essence of life. That is spiritual behind the physical and to this great scientists today agree. It is also personal intelligence and power. Some of the western documents have *estin* here instead of *ēn* to bring out clearly the timelessness of this phrase of the work of the *Logos*. *And the life was the light of men* (*kai hē zōē ēn to phōs tōn anthrōpōn*). Here

the article with both *zōē* and *phōs* makes them interchangeable. "The light was the life of men" is also true. That statement is curiously like the view of some physicists who find in electricity (both light and power) the nearest equivalent to life in its ultimate physical form. Later Jesus will call himself the light of the world (John 8:12). John is fond of these words life and light in Gospel, Epistles, Revelation. He here combines them to picture his conception of the Pre-incarnate Logos in his relation to the race. He was and is the Life of men (*tōn anthrōpōn*, generic use of the article) and the Light of men. John asserts this relation of the Logos to the race of men in particular before the Incarnation.

5. *Shineth* (*phainei*). Linear present active indicative of *phainō*, old verb from *phaō*, to shine (*phaos*, *phōs*). "The light keeps on giving light." *In the darkness* (*en tēi skotiāi*). Late word for the common *skotos* (kin to *skia*, shadow). An evident allusion to the darkness brought on by sin. In II Peter 2:17 we have *ho zophos tou skotou* (the blackness of darkness). The Logos, the only real moral light, keeps on shining both in the Pre-incarnate state and after the Incarnation. John is fond of *skotia* (*skotos*) for moral darkness from sin and *phōs* (*phōtizō*, *phainō*) for the light that is in Christ alone. In I John 2:8 he proclaims that "the darkness is passing by and the true light is already shining." The Gnostics often employed these words and John takes them and puts them in the proper place. *Apprehended it not* (*auto ou katelaben*). Second aorist active indicative of *katalambanō*, old verb to lay hold of, to seize. This very phrase occurs in John 12:35 (*hina mē skotia humas katalabēi*) "that darkness overtake you not," the metaphor of night following day and in I Thess. 5:4 the same idiom (*hina katalabēi*) is used of day overtaking one as a thief. This is the view of Origen and appears also in II Macc. 8:18. The same word appears in Aleph D in John 6:17 *katelabe de autous hē skotia* ("but darkness overtook them," came down on them). Hence, in

spite of the Vulgate *comprehenderunt*, "overtook" or "overcame" seems to be the idea here. The light kept on shining
in spite of the darkness that was worse than a London fog as
the Old Testament and archaeological discoveries in Egypt,
Assyria, Babylonia, Persia, Crete, Asia Minor show.
6. *There came a man* (*egeneto anthrōpos*). Definite event
in the long darkness, same verb in verse 3. *Sent* (*apestalmenos*). Perfect passive participle of *apostellō*, to send.
From God (*para theou*). From the side of (*para*) God (ablative
case *theou*). *Whose name* (*onoma autōi*). "Name to him,"
nominative parenthetic and dative (Robertson, *Grammar*,
p. 460). *John* (*Iōanēs*). One *n* in Westcott and Hort. In
the giving of the name see Luke 1:59 to 63, Hellenized form
of Jonathan, Joanan (Gift of God), used always of the Baptist
in this Gospel which never mentions the name of John son
of Zebedee (the sons of Zebedee once, 21:2).
7. *For witness* (*eis marturian*). Old word from *martureō*
(from *martus*), both more common in John's writings than
the rest of the N.T. This the purpose of the Baptist's ministry. *That he might bear witness* (*hina marturēsēi*). Final
clause with *hina* and aorist active subjunctive of *martureō*
to make clearer *eis marturian*. *Of the light* (*peri tou phōtos*).
"Concerning the light." The light was shining and men with
blinded eyes were not seeing the light (John 1:26), blinded
by the god of this world still (II Cor. 4:4). John had his
own eyes opened so that he saw and told what he saw. That
is the mission of every preacher of Christ. But he must
first have his own eyes opened. *That all might believe* (*hina
pisteusōsin*). Final clause with *hina* and first aorist active
subjunctive of *pisteuō*, ingressive aorist "come to believe."
This is one of John's great words (about 100 times), "with
nine times the frequency with which it is used by the Synoptists" (Bernard). And yet *pistis*, so common in Paul, John
uses only in I John 5:4 and four times in the Apocalypse
where *pisteuō* does not occur at all. Here it is used absolutely

as in John 1:50, etc. *Through him (di' autou)*. As the intermediate agent in winning men to believe in Christ (the
Logos) as the Light and the Life of men. This is likewise
the purpose of the author of this book (21:31). The preacher
is merely the herald to point men to Christ.

8. *He (ekeinos)*. "That one," i.e. John. He was a light
(John 5:35) as all believers are (Matt. 5:14), but not "the
light" *(to phōs)*. *But came (all')*. No verb in the Greek, to
be supplied by repeating *ēlthen* of verse 7. See similar ellipses
in 9:3; 13:18; 15:25. In Johannine fashion we have the final
hina clause of verse 7 repeated.

9. *There was (ēn)*. Imperfect indicative. Emphatic position at the beginning of the sentence and so probably not
periphrastic conjugation with *erchomenon* (coming) near the
end, though that is possible. *The true light (to phōs to alēthinon)*. "The light the genuine," not a false light of wreckers
of ships, but the dependable light that guides to the harbor
of safety. This true light had been on hand all the time in
the darkness (*ēn* imperfect, linear action) before John came.
Even the light (not in the Greek). Added in the English to
make plain this interpretation. *Lighteth every man (phōtizei
panta.anthrōpon)*. Old verb (from *phōs*) to give light as in
Rev. 22:5 and Luke 11:35f. The Quakers appeal to this
phrase for their belief that to every man there is given an
inner light that is a sufficient guide, the Quaker's text it is
called. But it may only mean that all the real light that
men receive comes from Christ, not necessarily that each
one receives a special revelation. *Coming (erchomenon)*. This
present middle participle of *erchomai* can be taken with
anthrōpon just before (accusative masculine singular), "every
man as he comes into the world." It can also be construed
with *phōs* (nominative neuter singular). This idea occurs
in John 3:19; 11:27; 12:46. In the two last passages the
phrase is used of the Messiah which makes it probable here.
But even so the light presented in 11:27; 12:46 is that of the

Incarnate Messiah, not the Pre-incarnate Logos. Here *kosmos* rather than *panta* occurs in the sense of the orderly universe as often in this Gospel. See Eph. 1:4.

10. *He was in the world* (*en tōi kosmōi ēn*). Imperfect tense of continuous existence in the universe before the Incarnation as in verses 1 and 2. *Was made by him* (*di' autou egeneto*). "Through him." Same statement here of "the world" (*ho kosmos*) as that made in verse 3 of *panta*. *Knew him not* (*auton ouk egnō*). Second aorist active indicative of common verb *ginōskō*, what Gildersleeve called a negative aorist, refused or failed to recognize him, his world that he had created and that was held together by him (Col. 1:16). Not only did the world fail to know the Pre-incarnate Logos, but it failed to recognize him when he became Incarnate (John 1:26). Two examples in this sentence of John's fondness for *kai* as in verses 1, 4, 5, 14, the paratactic rather than the hypotactic construction, like the common Hebrew use of *wav*.

11. *Unto his own* (*eis ta idia*). Neuter plural, "unto his own things," the very idiom used in 19:27 when the Beloved Disciple took the mother of Jesus "to his own home." The world was "the own home" of the Logos who had made it. See also 16:32; Acts 21:6. *They that were his own* (*hoi idioi*). In the narrower sense, "his intimates," "his own family," "his own friends" as in 13:1. Jesus later said that a prophet is not without honour save in his own country (Mark 6:4; John 4:44), and the town of Nazareth where he lived rejected him (Luke 4:28f.; Matt. 13:58). Probably here *hoi idioi* means the Jewish people, the chosen people to whom Christ was sent first (Matt. 15:24), but in a wider sense the whole world is included in *hoi idioi*. Conder's *The Hebrew Tragedy* emphasizes the pathos of the situation that the house of Israel refused to welcome the Messiah when he did come, like a larger and sadder Enoch Arden experience. *Received him not* (*auton ou parelabon*). Second aorist active indica-

tive of *paralambanō*, old verb to take to one's side, common verb to welcome, the very verb used by Jesus in 14:3 of the welcome to his Father's house. Cf. *katelaben* in verse 5. Israel slew the Heir (Heb. 1:2) when he came, like the wicked husbandmen (Luke 20:14).

12. *As many as received him (hosoi elabon auton).* Effective aorist active indicative of *lambanō* "as many as did receive him," in contrast with *hoi idioi* just before, exceptional action on the part of the disciples and other believers. *To them (autois).* Dative case explanatory of the relative clause preceding, an anacoluthon common in John 27 times as against 21 in the Synoptists. This is a common Aramaic idiom and is urged by Burney (*Aramaic Origin*, etc., p. 64) for his theory of an Aramaic original of the Fourth Gospel. *The right (exousian).* In 5:27 *edōken* (first aorist active indicative of *didōmi*) *exousian* means authority but includes power (*dunamis*). Here it is more the notion of privilege or right. *To become (genesthai).* Second aorist middle of *ginomai*, to become what they were not before. *Children of God (tekna theou).* In the full spiritual sense, not as mere offspring of God true of all men (Acts 17:28). Paul's phrase *huioi theou* (Gal. 3:26) for believers, used also by Jesus of the pure in heart (Matt. 5:9), does not occur in John's Gospel (but in Rev. 21:7). It is possible that John prefers *ta tekna tou theou* for the spiritual children of God whether Jew or Gentile (John 11:52) because of the community of nature (*teknon* from root *tek-*, to beget). But one cannot follow Westcott in insisting on "adoption" as Paul's reason for the use of *huioi* since Jesus uses *huioi theou* in Matt. 5:9. Clearly the idea of regeneration is involved here as in John 3:3. *Even to them that believe (tois pisteuousin).* No "even" in the Greek, merely explanatory apposition with *autois*, dative case of the articular present active participle of *pisteuō*. *On his name (eis to onoma).* Bernard notes *pisteuō eis* 35 times in John, to put trust in or on. See also 2:23; 3:38 for

pisteuō eis to onoma autou. This common use of *onoma* for
the person is an Aramaism, but it occurs also in the vernacular papyri and *eis to onoma* is particularly common in the
payment of debts (Moulton and Milligan's *Vocabulary*).
See Acts 1:15 for *onomata* for persons.

13. *Which were born* (*hoi egennēthēsan*). First aorist passive
indicative of *gennaō*, to beget, "who were begotten." By
spiritual generation (of God, *ek theou*), not by physical (*ex
haimatōn*, plural as common in classics and O.T., though why
it is not clear unless blood of both father and mother; *ek
thelēmatos sarkos*, from sexual desire; *ek thelēmatos andros*,
from the will of the male). But *b* of the old Latin reads
qui natus est and makes it refer to Christ and so expressly
teach the Virgin Birth of Jesus. Likewise Irenaeus reads
qui natus est as does Tertullian who argues that *qui nati sunt*
(*hoi egennēthēsan*) is an invention of the Valentinian Gnostics.
Blass (*Philology of the Gospels*, p. 234) opposes this reading,
but all the old Greek uncials read *hoi egennēthēsan* and it
must be accepted. The Virgin Birth is doubtless implied
in verse 14, but it is not stated in verse 13.

14. *And the Word became flesh* (*kai ho logos sarx egeneto*).
See verse 3 for this verb and note its use for the historic
event of the Incarnation rather than *ēn* of verse 1. Note
also the absence of the article with the predicate substantive
sarx, so that it cannot mean "the flesh became the Word."
The Pre-existence of the Logos has already been plainly
stated and argued. John does not here say that the Logos
entered into a man or dwelt in a man or filled a man. One
is at liberty to see an allusion to the birth narratives in
Matt. 1:16–25 and Luke 1:28–38, if he wishes, since John
clearly had the Synoptics before him and chiefly supplemented them in his narrative. In fact, one is also at liberty
to ask what intelligent meaning can one give to John's
language here apart from the Virgin Birth? What ordinary
mother or father ever speaks of a child "becoming flesh"?

For the Incarnation see also II Cor. 8:9; Gal. 4:4; Rom. 1:3; 8:3; Phil. 2:7f.; I Tim. 3:16; Heb. 2:14. "To explain the exact significance of *egeneto* in this sentence is beyond the powers of any interpreter" (Bernard). Unless, indeed, as seems plain, John is referring to the Virgin Birth as recorded in Matthew and Luke. "The Logos of philosophy is, John declares, the Jesus of history" (Bernard). Thus John asserts the deity and the real humanity of Christ. He answers the Docetic Gnostics who denied his humanity. *Dwelt among us* (*eskēnōsen en hēmin*). First aorist ingressive aorist active indicative of *skēnoō*, old verb, to pitch one's tent or tabernacle (*skēnos* or *skēnē*), in N.T. only here and Rev. 7·15; 12:12; 13:6; 21:3. In Revelation it is used of God tabernacling with men and here of the Logos tabernacling, God's Shekinah glory here among us in the person of his Son. *We beheld his glory* (*etheasametha tēn doxan autou*). First aorist middle indicative of *theaomai* (from *thea*, spectacle). The personal experience of John and of others who did recognize Jesus as the Shekinah glory (*doxa*) of God as James, the brother of Jesus, so describes him (James 2:1). John employs *theaomai* again in 1:32 (the Baptist beholding the Spirit coming down as a dove) and 1:38 of the Baptist gazing in rapture at Jesus. So also 4:35; 11:45; I John 1:1f.; 4:12, 14. By this word John insists that in the human Jesus he beheld the Shekinah glory of God who was and is the Logos who existed before with God. By this plural John speaks for himself and all those who saw in Jesus what he did. *As of the only begotten from the Father* (*hōs monogenous para patros*). Strictly, "as of an only born from a father," since there is no article with *monogenous* or with *patros*. In John 3:16 and I John 4:9 we have *ton monogenē* referring to Christ. This is the first use in the Gospel of *patēr* of God in relation to the Logos. *Monogenēs* (only born rather than only begotten) here refers to the eternal relationship of the Logos (as in 1:18) rather than to the Incarnation. It dis-

tinguishes thus between the Logos and the believers as
children (*tekna*) of God. The word is used of human rela-
tionships as in Luke 7:12; 8:42; 9:38. It occurs also in the
LXX and Heb. 11:17, but elsewhere in N.T. only in John's
writings. It is an old word in Greek literature. It is not
clear whether the words *para patros* (from the Father) are
to be connected with *monogenous* (cf. 6:46; 7:29, etc.) or
with *doxan* (cf. 5:41, 44). John clearly means to say that
"the manifested glory of the Word was as it were the glory
of the Eternal Father shared with His only Son" (Bernard).
Cf. 8:54; 14:9; 17:5. *Full* (*plērēs*). Probably indeclinable
accusative adjective agreeing with *doxan* (or genitive with
monogenous) of which we have papyri examples (Robertson,
Grammar, p. 275). As nominative *plērēs* can agree with the
subject of *eskēnōsen*. *Of grace and truth* (*charitos kai alētheias*).
Curiously this great word *charis* (grace), so common with
Paul, does not occur in John's Gospel save in 1:14, 16, 17,
though *alētheia* (truth) is one of the keywords in the Fourth
Gospel and in I John, occurring 25 times in the Gospel and
20 in the Johannine Epistles, 7 times in the Synoptics and
not at all in Revelation (Bernard). In 1:17 these two words
picture the Gospel in Christ in contrast with the law of
Moses. See Epistles of Paul for origin and use of both words.

15. *Beareth witness* (*marturei*). Historical (dramatic) present indicative of this characteristic word in John (cf. 1:17f.).
See 1:32, 34 for historical examples of John's witness to
Christ. This sentence is a parenthesis in Westcott and
Hort's text, though the Revised Version makes a parenthesis
of most of verse 14. The witness of John is adduced in proof
of the glory full of grace and truth already claimed for the
Incarnate Logos. *Crieth* (*kekragen*). Second perfect active
indicative of *krazō*, old verb for loud crying, repeated in
dramatic form again for emphasis recalling the wonderful
Voice in the wilderness which the Beloved Disciple can still
hear echoing through the years. *This was* (*houtos ēn*). Im-

perfect indicative where John throws the tense back in past time when he looked forward to the coming of the Messiah as in Acts 3:10 where we should prefer "is" (*estin*). Gildersleeve (*Syntax*, p. 96) calls this the "imperfect of sudden appreciation of the real state of things." *Of whom I said* (*hon eipon*). But B C and a corrector of Aleph (Westcott and Hort) have *ho eipōn* "the one who said," a parenthetical explanation about the Baptist, not the words of the Baptist about Christ. *After me* (*opisō mou*). See also 1:27. Later in time John means. He described "the Coming One" (*ho erchomenos*) before he saw Jesus. The language of John here is precisely that in Matt. 3:11 *ho opisō mou erchomenos* (cf. Mark 1:7). The Beloved Disciple had heard the Baptist say these very words, but he also had the Synoptic Gospels. *Is become* (*gegonen*). Second perfect active indicative of *ginomai*. It is already an actual fact when the Baptist is speaking. *Before me* (*emprosthen mou*). In rank and dignity, the Baptist means, *ho ischuroteros mou* "the one mightier than I" (Mark 1:7) and *ischuroteros mou* "mightier than I" (Matt. 3:11). In John 3:28 *emprosthen ekeinou* (before him, the Christ) does mean priority in time, but not here. This superior dignity of the Messiah John proudly recognizes always (John 3:25–30). *For he was before me* (*hoti prōtos mou ēn*). Paradox, but clear. He had always been (*ēn* imperfect) before John in his Pre-incarnate state, but "after" John in time of the Incarnation, but always ahead of John in rank immediately on his Incarnation. *Prōtos mou* (superlative with ablative) occurs here when only two are compared as is common in the vernacular *Koiné*. So the Beloved Disciple came first (*prōtos*) to the tomb, ahead of Peter (20:4). So also *prōton humōn* in 15:18 means "before you" as if it were *proteron humōn*. Verse 30 repeats these words almost exactly.

16. *For* (*hoti*). Correct text (Aleph B C D L) and not *kai* (and) of the Textus Receptus. Explanatory reason for

verse 14. *Of his fulness (ek tou plērōmatos)*. The only instance of *plērōma* in John's writings, though five times of
Christ in Paul's Epistles (Col. 1:19; 2:9; Eph. 1:23; 3:19;
4:13). See Col. 1:19 for discussion of these terms of the
Gnostics that Paul employs for all the attributes of God
summed up in Christ (Col. 2:9) and so used here by John
of the Incarnate Logos. *We all (hēmeis pantes)*. John is
facing the same Gnostic depreciation of Christ of which
Paul writes in Colossians. So here John appeals to all his
own contemporaries as participants with him in the fulness
of the Logos. *Received (elabomen)*. Second aorist active indicative of *lambanō*, a wider experience than beholding *(etheasametha*, verse 14) and one that all believers may have.
Grace for grace (charin anti charitos). The point is in *anti*,
a preposition disappearing in the *Koiné* and here only in
John. It is in the locative case of *anta* (end), "at the end,"
and was used of exchange in sale. See Luke 11:11, *anti
ichthuos ophin*, "a serpent for a fish," Heb. 12:2 where
"joy" and "cross" are balanced against each other. Here
the picture is "grace" taking the place of "grace" like the
manna fresh each morning, new grace for the new day and
the new service.

17. *Was given (edothē)*. First aorist passive indicative of
didōmi. By Moses (dia Mōuseōs). "Through Moses" as the
intermediate agent of God. *Came (egeneto)*. The historical
event, the beginning of Christianity. *By Jesus Christ (dia
Iēsou Christou)*. "Through Jesus Christ," the intermediate
agent of God the Father. Here in plain terms John identifies
the Pre-incarnate Logos with Jesus of Nazareth, the Messiah.
The full historical name "Jesus Christ" is here for the first
time in John. See also 17:3 and four times in I John and
five times in Revelation. Without Christ there would have
been no Christianity. John's theology is here pictured by
the words "grace and truth" (*hē charis kai hē alētheia*), each
with the article and each supplementary to the other. It is

grace in contrast with law as Paul sets forth in Galatians and Romans. Paul had made grace "a Christian commonplace" (Bernard) before John wrote. It is truth as opposed to Gnostic and all other heresy as Paul shows in Colossians and Ephesians. The two words aptly describe two aspects of the Logos and John drops the use of *Logos* and *charis*, but clings to *alētheia* (see 8:32 for the freedom brought by truth), though the ideas in these three words run all through his Gospel.

18. *No man hath seen God at any time* (*theon oudeis heōraken pōpote*). "God no one has ever seen." Perfect active indicative of *horaō*. Seen with the human physical eye, John means. God is invisible (Ex. 33:20; Deut. 4:12). Paul calls God *aoratos* (Col. 1:15; I Tim. 1:17). John repeats the idea in John 5:37; 6:46. And yet in 14:7 Jesus claims that the one who sees him has seen the Father as here. *The only begotten Son* (*ho monogenēs huios*). This is the reading of the Textus Receptus and is intelligible after *hōs monogenous para patros* in verse 14. But the best old Greek manuscripts (Aleph B C L) read *monogenēs theos* (God only begotten) which is undoubtedly the true text. Probably some scribe changed it to *ho monogenēs huios* to obviate the blunt statement of the deity of Christ and to make it like 3:16. But there is an inner harmony in the reading of the old uncials. The Logos is plainly called *theos* in verse 1. The Incarnation is stated in verse 14, where he is also termed *monogenēs*. He was that before the Incarnation. So he is "God only begotten," "the Eternal Generation of the Son" of Origen's phrase. *Which is in the bosom of the Father* (*ho ōn eis ton kolpon tou patros*). The eternal relation of the Son with the Father like *pros ton theon* in verse 1. In 3:13 there is some evidence for *ho ōn en tōi ouranōi* used by Christ of himself while still on earth. The mystic sense here is that the Son is qualified to reveal the Father as Logos (both the Father in Idea and Expression) by reason of the continual fellowship

with the Father. *He (ekinos)*. Emphatic pronoun referring to the Son. *Hath declared him (exēgēsato)*. First aorist (effective) middle indicative of *exēgeomai*, old verb to lead out, to draw out in narrative, to recount. Here only in John, though once in Luke's Gospel (24:35) and four times in Acts (10:8; 15:12; 14; 21:19). This word fitly closes the Prologue in which the Logos is pictured in marvellous fashion as the Word of God in human flesh, the Son of God with the Glory of God in him, showing men who God is and what he is.

19. *And this is the witness of John (kai hautē estin hē marturia tou Iōanou)*. He had twice already alluded to it (verses 7f., 15) and now he proceeds to give it as the most important item to add after the Prologue. Just as the author assumes the birth narratives of Matthew and Luke, so he assumes the Synoptic accounts of the baptism of Jesus by John, but adds various details of great interest and value between the baptism and the Galilean ministry, filling out thus our knowledge of this first year of the Lord's ministry in various parts of Palestine. The story in John proceeds along the same lines as in the Synoptics. There is increasing unfolding of Christ to the disciples with increasing hostility on the part of the Jews till the final consummation in Jerusalem. *When the Jews sent unto him (hote apesteilan pros auton hoi Ioudaioi)*. John, writing in Ephesus near the close of the first century long after the destruction of Jerusalem, constantly uses the phrase "the Jews" as descriptive of the people as distinct from the Gentile world and from the followers of Christ (at first Jews also). Often he uses it of the Jewish leaders and rulers in particular who soon took a hostile attitude toward both John and Jesus. Here it is the Jews from Jerusalem who sent (*apesteilan*, first aorist active indicative of *apostellō*). *Priests and Levites (hiereis kai Leueitas)*. Sadducees these were. Down below in verse 24 the author explains that it was the Pharisees who sent the Sadducees. The Synoptics throw a flood of light on this

circumstance, for in Matt. 3:7 we are told that the Baptist called the Pharisees and Sadducees "offspring of vipers" (=Luke 3:7). Popular interest in John grew till people were wondering "in their hearts concerning John whether haply he were the Christ" (Luke 3:15). So the Sanhedrin finally sent a committee to John to get his own view of himself, but the Pharisees saw to it that Sadducees were sent. *To ask him* (*hina erōtēsōsin auton*). Final *hina* and the first aorist active subjunctive of *erōtaō*, old verb to ask a question as here and often in the *Koiné* to ask for something (John 14:16) like *aiteō*. *Who art thou?* (*su tis ei;*). Direct question preserved and note proleptic position of *su*, "Thou, who art thou?" The committee from the Sanhedrin put the question sharply up to John to define his claims concerning the Messiah.

20. *And he confessed* (*kai hōmologēsen*). The continued paratactic use of *kai* (and) and the first aorist active indicative of *homologeō*, old verb from *homologos* (*homon, legō*, to say the same thing), to confess, in the Synoptics (Matt. 10:32) as here. *And denied not* (*kai ouk ērnēsato*). Negative statement of same thing in Johannine fashion, first aorist middle indicative of *arneomai*, another Synoptic and Pauline word (Matt. 10:33; II Tim. 2:12). He did not contradict or refuse to say who he was. *And he confessed* (*kai hōmologēsen*). Thoroughly Johannine again in the paratactic repetition. *I am not the Christ* (*Egō ouk eimi ho Christos*). Direct quotation again with recitative *hoti* before it like our modern quotation marks. "I am not the Messiah," he means by *ho Christos* (the Anointed One). Evidently it was not a new question as Luke had already shown (Luke 3:15).

21. *And they asked him* (*kai erōtēsan auton*). Here the paratactic *kai* is like the transitional *oun* (then). *What then?* (*Ti oun;*). Argumentative *oun* like Paul's *ti oun* in Rom. 6:15. *Quid ergo? Art thou Elijah?* (*Su Elias ei;*). The next inevitable question since Elijah had been understood to be the forerunner of the Messiah from Mal. 4:5. In Mark 9:11f.

Jesus will identify John with the Elijah of Malachi's prophecy. Why then does John here flatly deny it? Because the expectation was that Elijah would return in person. This John denies. Jesus only asserts that John was Elijah in spirit. Elijah in person they had just seen on the Mount of Transfiguration. *He saith* (*legei*). Vivid dramatic present. *I am not* (*ouk eimi*). Short and blunt denial. *Art thou the prophet?* (*ho prophētēs ei su;*). "The prophet art thou?" This question followed naturally the previous denials. Moses (Deut. 18:15) had spoken of a prophet like unto himself. Christians interpreted this prophet to be the Messiah (Acts 3:22; 7:37), but the Jews thought him another forerunner of the Messiah (John 7:40). It is not clear in John 6:15 whether the people identified the expected prophet with the Messiah, though apparently so. Even the Baptist later became puzzled in prison whether Jesus himself was the true Messiah or just one of the forerunners (Luke 7:19). People wondered about Jesus himself whether he was the Messiah or just one of the looked for prophets (Mark 8:28; Matt. 16:14). *And he answered* (*kai apekrithē*). First aorist passive (deponent passive, sense of voice gone) indicative of *apokrinomai*, to give a decision from myself, to reply. *No* (*Ou*). Shortest possible denial.

22. *They said therefore* (*eipan oun*). Second aorist active indicative of defective verb *eipon* with *a* instead of usual *o*. Note *oun*, inferential here as in verse 21 though often merely transitional in John. *Who art thou?* (*Tis ei;*). Same question as at first (verse 19), but briefer. *That we give answer* (*hina apokrisin dōmen*). Final use of *hina* with second aorist active subjunctive of *didōmi* with *apokrisin* from *apokrinomai*, above, old substantive as in Luke 2:47. *To those that sent* (*tois pempsasin*). Dative case plural of the articular participle first aorist active of *pempō*. *What sayest thou of thyself?* (*Ti legeis peri seautou;*). This time they opened wide the door without giving any hint at all.

23. *He said (ephē).* Common imperfect active (or second aorist active) of *phēmi*, to say, old defective verb. *I am the voice of one crying in the wilderness* (*Egō phōnē boōntos en tēi erēmōi*). For his answer John quotes Isa. 40:3. The Synoptics (Mark 1:3 = Matt. 3:3 = Luke 3:4) quote this language from Isaiah as descriptive of John, but do not say that he also applied it to himself. There is no reason to think that he did not do so. John also refers to Isaiah as the author of the words and also of the message, "*Make straight the way of the Lord*" (*Euthunate tēn hodon tou kuriou*). By this language (*euthunō* in N.T. only here and James 3:4, first aorist active imperative here) John identifies himself to the committee as the forerunner of the Messiah. The early writers note the differences between the use of *Logos* (Word) for the Messiah and *phōnē* (Voice) for John.

24. *They had been sent (apestalmenoi ēsan).* Periphrastic past perfect passive of *apostellō*. *From the Pharisees (ek tōn Pharisaiōn).* As the source (*ek*) of the committee of Sadducees (verse 19).

25. *Why then baptizest thou?* (*Ti oun baptizeis;*). In view of his repeated denials (three here mentioned). *If thou art not (ei su ouk ei).* Condition of first class. They did not interpret his claim to be "the voice" to be important enough to justify the ordinance of baptism. Abrahams (*Studies in Pharisaism and the Gospels*) shows that proselyte baptism was probably practised before John's time, but its use by John was treating the Jews as if they were themselves Gentiles.

26. *In the midst of you standeth (mesos humōn stēkei).* Adjective as in 19:18, not *en mesōi humōn*. Present active indicative of late verb *stēkō* from perfect stem *hestēka*. John had already baptized Jesus and recognized him as the Messiah. *Whom ye know not (hon humeis ouk oidate).* This was the tragedy of the situation (1:11). Apparently this startling declaration excited no further inquiry from the committee.

27. *Coming after me* (*opisō mou erchomenos*). No article (*ho*) in Aleph B. John as the forerunner of the Messiah has preceded him in time, but not in rank as he instantly adds. *The latchet of whose shoe I am not worthy to unloose* (*hou ouk eimi axios hina lusō autou ton himanta tou hupodēmatos*). Literally, "of whom I am not worthy that I unloose the latchet (see Mark 1:7 for *himas*) of his sandal (see Matt. 3:11 for *hupodēma*, bound under the foot)." Only use of *axios* with *hina* in John, though used by Paul in this saying of the Baptist (Acts 13:25), *hikanos hina* in Matt. 3:8, but *hikanos lusai* (aorist active infinitive instead of *lusō*, aorist active subjunctive) in Mark 1:7 (=Luke 3:16) and *bastasai* in Matt. 3:11.

28. *In Bethany beyond Jordan* (*en Bēthaniāi peran tou Iordanou*). Undoubtedly the correct text, not "in Bethabara" as Origen suggested instead of "in Bethany" of all the known Greek manuscripts under the mistaken notion that the only Bethany was that near Jerusalem. *Was baptizing* (*ēn baptizōn*). Periphrastic imperfect, common idiom in John.

29. *On the morrow* (*tēi epaurion*). Locative case with *hēmērāi* (day) understood after the adverb *epaurion*. "Second day of this spiritual diary" (Bernard) from verse 19. *Seeth Jesus coming* (*blepei ton Iēsoun erchomenon*). Dramatic historical present indicative (*blepei*) with vivid present middle participle (*erchomenon*). Graphic picture. *Behold the Lamb of God* (*ide ho amnos tou theou*). Exclamation *ide* like *idou*, not verb, and so nominative *amnos*. Common idiom in John (1:36; 3:26, etc.). For "the Lamb of God" see I Cor. 5:7 (cf. John 19:36) and I Peter 1:19. The passage in Isa. 53:6f. is directly applied to Christ by Philip in Acts 8:32. See also Matt. 8:17; I Peter 2:22f.; Heb. 9:28. But the Jews did not look for a suffering Messiah (John 12:34) nor did the disciples at first (Mark 9:32; Luke 24:21). But was it not possible for John, the Forerunner of the Messiah, to have a prophetic insight concerning the Messiah as the

Paschal Lamb, already in Isaiah 53, even if the rabbis did
not see it there? Symeon had it dimly (Luke 2:35), but
John more clearly. So Westcott rightly. Bernard is unwilling
to believe that John the Baptist had more insight on this
point than current Judaism. Then why and how did he recognize Jesus as Messiah at all? Certainly the Baptist did not
have to be as ignorant as the rabbis. *Which taketh away the
sin of the world* (*ho airōn tēn hamartian tou kosmou*). Note
singular *hamartian* not plural *hamartias* (I John 3:5) where
same verb *airō*, to bear away, is used. The future work of
the Lamb of God here described in present tense as in I John
1:7 about the blood of Christ. He is the Lamb of God for
the world, not just for Jews.

30. *Of whom* (*huper hou*). Not *peri*, but *huper*. "On behalf
of whom." John points to Jesus as he speaks: "This is he."
There he is. See verse 15 for discussion of these words of
John.

31. *And I knew him not* (*kágō ouk ēidein auton*). Repeated
in verse 33. Second past perfect of *oida* as imperfect. He
had predicted the Messiah and described him before he met
him and baptized him. See the Synoptics for that story.
Whether John knew Jesus personally before the baptism
we do not know. *But that he should be made manifest to Israel*
(*all' hina phanerōthēi tōi Israēl*). Final clause with *hina* and
first aorist passive subjunctive of *phaneroō*. The purpose of
John's ministry was to manifest to Israel with their spiritual
privileges (1:49) the presence of the Messiah. Hence he was
baptizing in water those who confessed their sins, he means,
as in Mark 1:5. The Synoptic account is presupposed all
along here.

32. *Bare witness* (*emarturēsen*). First aorist active indicative of *martureō*. Another specimen of John's witness to the
Messiah (1:7, 15, 19, 29, 35, 36). *I have beheld* (*tetheamai*).
Perfect middle indicative of *theaomai*, the realization of the
promise of the sign (verse 33) by which he should recognize

the Messiah. As a matter of fact, we know that he so recognized Jesus as Messiah when he came for baptism before the Holy Spirit came (Matt. 3:14ff.). But this sight of the Spirit descending as a dove upon Jesus at his baptism (Mark 1:10 = Matt. 3:16 = Luke 3:22) became permanent proof to him. John's allusion assumes the Synoptic record. The Semites regarded the dove as a symbol of the Spirit.

33. *He said* (*ekeinos eipen*). Explicit and emphatic pronoun as in verse 8, referring to God as the one who sent John (verse 6). *With the Holy Spirit* (*en pneumati hagiōi*). "In the Holy Spirit." Here again one needs the background of the Synoptics for the contrast between John's baptism in water (John 1:26) and that of the Messiah in the Holy Spirit (Mark 1:8 = Matt. 3:11 = Luke 3:16).

34. *I have seen* (*heōraka*). Present perfect active of *horaō*. John repeats the statement of verse 32 (*tetheamai*). *Have borne witness* (*memarturēka*). Perfect active indicative of *martureō* for which verb see 32. *This is the Son of God* (*ho huios tou theou*). The Baptist saw the Spirit come on Jesus at his baptism and undoubtedly heard the Father's voice hail him as "My Beloved Son" (Mark 1:11 = Matt. 3:17 = Luke 3:22). Nathanael uses it as a Messianic title (John 1:49) as does Martha (11:27). The Synoptics use it also of Christ (Mark 3:11; Matt. 14:33; Luke 22:70). Caiaphas employs it to Christ as a Messianic title (Matt. 26:63) and Jesus confessed under oath that he was (verse 64), thus applying the term to himself as he does in John's Gospel (5:25; 10:36; 11:4) and by implication (the Father, the Son) in Matt. 11:27(= Luke 10:22). Hence in the Synoptics also Jesus calls himself the Son of God. The phrase means more than just Messiah and expresses the peculiar relation of the Son to the Father (John 3:18; 5:25; 17:5; 19:7; 20:31) like that of the Logos with God in 1:1.

35. *Again on the morrow* (*tēi epaurion palin*). Third day since verse 19. *Was standing* (*histēkei*). Past perfect of

histēmi, intransitive, and used as imperfect in sense. See same form in 7:37. *Two (duo)*. One was Andrew (verse 40), the other the Beloved Disciple (the Apostle John), who records this incident with happy memories.

36. *He looked (emblepsas)*. First aorist active participle of *emblepō*, antecedent action before *legei* (says). *As he walked (peripatounti)*. Present active participle in dative case after *emblepsas* and like *erchomenon* in verse 29 vividly pictures the rapture of John in this vision of Jesus, so far as we know the third and last glimpse of Jesus by John (the baptism, verse 29, and here). *Saith (legei)*. Historical present, change from *histēkei* before. He repeats part of the tribute in verse 29.

37. *Heard him speak (ēkousan autou lalountos)*. First active indicative of *akouō* and present active participle of *laleō* in genitive case agreeing with *autou*, object of *akouō*. "Heard him speaking" (kind of indirect discourse). John had disciples (*mathētai*, learners, from *manthanō*, to learn). *They followed Jesus (ēkolouthēsan tōi Iēsou)*. Associative instrumental case after verb (first aorist active indicative, ingressive aorist, of *akoloutheō*). These two disciples of the Baptist (Andrew and John) took him at his word and acted on it. John the Baptist had predicted and portrayed the Messiah, had baptized him, had interpreted him, and now for the second time had identified him.

38. *Turned (strapheis)*. Second aorist passive participle of *strephō*, vividly picturing the sudden act of Jesus on hearing their steps behind him. *Beheld (theasamenos)*. First aorist middle participle of *theaomai* (verse 32). Both participles here express antecedent action to *legei* (saith). *Following (akolothountas)*. Present active participle of *akoloutheō* (verse 37). It was Christ's first experience of this kind and the two came from the Baptist to Jesus. *What seek ye? (Ti zēteite;)*. Not "whom" (*tina* 18:4; 20:15), but "what purpose have you." The first words of Jesus preserved in

this Gospel. See Luke 2:49; Matt. 3:15 for words spoken
before this and Mark 1:15 for Mark's first report in the
Galilean ministry. *Rabbi* (*Rabbei*). Aramaic title for
"Teacher" which John here translates by *Didaskale* as he
is writing late and for general readers. Luke, a Greek
Christian, does not use it, but John recalls his first use of
this term to Jesus and explains it. Matthew has it only in
the greeting of Judas to the Master (Matt. 26:25, 49) and
Mark once by Judas (Mark 14:45) and twice by Peter
(9:5; 11:21). John's Gospel has the disciples at first addressing Jesus by Rabbi while others address him by *Kurie*
(Lord or Sir) as in 4:11, 49; 5:7. Peter uses *Kurie* in 6:68.
In the end the disciples usually say *Kurie* (13:6, 25, etc.),
but Mary Magdalene says *Rabbounei* (20:16). *Being interpreted* (*methermēmeuomenon*). Present passive participle, of
methermēneuō, late compound of *meta* and *hermēneuō*, to explain (John 1:42), old word from *Hermes*, the god of speech
(hermeneutics). John often explains Aramaic words (1:38,
41, 42; 4:25; 9:7, etc.). *Where abidest thou?* (*Pou meneis;*).
They wished a place for quiet converse with Jesus.

39. *Come and ye shall see* (*erchesthe kai opsesthe*). Polite
invitation and definite promise (future middle indicative
opsesthe from *horaō*, correct text, not imperative *idete*).
Where he abode (*pou menei*). Indirect question preserving
the present active indicative after secondary tense (*eidan*,
saw) according to regular Greek idiom. Same verb *menō* as in
38. *With him* (*par' autōi*). "By his side," "beside him."
That day (*tēn hēmeran ekeinēn*). Accusative of extent of
time, all during that day. *About the tenth hour* (*hōra hōs
dekatē*). Roman time and so ten o'clock in the morning.
John in Ephesus at the close of the century naturally uses
Roman time. See 20:19 "evening on that day," clearly
Roman time. Thus also John 19:14 (sixth hour, morning)
and Mark 15:25 (third hour, nine A.M.) suit. To his latest
day John never forgot the hour when first he met Jesus.

40. *Andrew* (*Andreas*). Explained by John as one of the two disciples of the Baptist and identified as the brother of the famous Simon Peter (cf. also 6:8; 12:22). The more formal call of Andrew and Simon, James and John, comes later (Mark 1:16ff. = Matt. 4:18ff. = Luke 3:1–11). *That heard John speak* (*tōn akousantōn para Iōanou*). "That heard from John," a classical idiom (*para* with ablative after *akouō*) seen also in 6:45; 7:51; 8:26, 40; 15:15.

41. *He findeth first* (*heuriskei houtos prōton*). "This one finds (vivid dramatic present) first" (*prōton*). *Prōton* (adverb supported by Aleph' A B fam. 13) means that Andrew sought "his own brother Simon" (*ton adelphon ton idion Simōna*) before he did anything else. But Aleph L W read *prōtos* (nominative adjective) which means that Andrew was the first who went after his brother implying that John also went after his brother James. Some old Latin manuscripts (b, e, r apparently), have *mane* for Greek *prōi* (early in the morning). Bernard thinks that this is the true reading as it allows more time for Andrew to bring Simon to Jesus. Probably *prōton* is correct, but even so John likely brought also his brother James after Andrew's example. *We have found the Messiah* (*Heurēkamen ton Messian*). First aorist active indicative of *heuriskō*. Andrew and John had made the greatest discovery of the ages, far beyond gold or diamond mines. The Baptist had told about him. "We have seen him." *Which is* (*ho estin*). Same explanatory neuter relative as in verse 38, "which word is." This Aramaic title Messiah is preserved in the N.T. only here and 4:25, elsewhere translated into *Christos*, Anointed One, from *chriō*, to anoint. See on Matt. 1:1 for discussion.

42. *Looked upon him* (*emblepsas autōi*). See verse 36 for same word and form of John's eager gaze at Jesus. Luke uses this word of Jesus when Peter denied him (Luke 22:61). *He brought him* (*ēgagen auton*). Effective second aorist active indicative of *agō* as if Andrew had to overcome some resistance on Simon's part. *Thou shalt be called Cephas (su klēthēsei Kēphās)*. Apparently before Simon spoke. We do not know whether Jesus had seen Simon before or not, but he at once gives him a nickname that will characterize him some day, though not yet, when he makes the noble confession (Matt. 16:17f.), and Jesus will say, "Thou art Peter." Here the future passive indicative of *kaleō* is only prophecy. The Aramaic *Cēphās* (rock) is only applied to Simon in John except by Paul (I Cor. 1:12; Gal. 1:18, etc.). But the Greek *Petros* is used by all. In the ancient Greek *petra* was used for the massive ledge of rock like Stone Mountain while *petros* was a detached fragment of the ledge, though itself large. This distinction may exist in Matt. 16:17f., except that Jesus probably used Aramaic which would not have such a distinction.

43. *On the morrow (tēi epaurion)*. The fourth of the days from verse 19. *He findeth Philip (heuriskei Philippon)*. Vivid dramatic present as in 41, though *ēthelēsen* (was minded, wished) is aorist active indicative. Apparently not an accidental finding, possibly due to the efforts of Andrew and Peter. Both Andrew and Philip have Greek names. *Follow me (akolouthei moi)*. Present active imperative, a direct challenge to Philip. Often Jesus uses this verb to win disciples (Mark 2:14; Matt. 8:22; 9:21; 19:21; Luke 9:59; John 21:19). Already Jesus had four personal followers (Andrew and Simon, John and James). He has begun his work.

44. *From Bēthsaida (apo Bēthsaida)*. Same expression in 12:21 with the added words "of Galilee," which locates it in Galilee, not in Iturea. There were two Bethsaidas, one called Bethsaida Julias in Iturea (that in Luke 9:10) or the Eastern Bethsaida, the other the Western Bethsaida in Galilee (Mark 6:45), perhaps somewhere near Capernaum. This is the town of Andrew and Peter and Philip. Hence Philip would be inclined to follow the example of his townsmen.

45. *Philip findeth* (*heuriskei Philippos*). Dramatic present again. Philip carries on the work. One wins one. If that glorious beginning had only kept on! Now it takes a hundred to win one. *Nathaniel* (*ton Nathanaēl*). It is a Hebrew name meaning "God has given" like the Greek *Theodore* (Gift of God). He was from Cana of Galilee (John 21:2), not far from Bethsaida and so known to Philip. His name does not occur in the Synoptics while Bartholomew (a patronymic, *Bar Tholmai*) does not appear in John. They are almost certainly two names of the same man. Philip uses *heurēkamen* (verse 41) also to Nathanael and so unites himself with the circle of believers, but instead of *Messian* describes him "of whom (*hon* accusative with *egrapsen*) Moses in the law (Deut. 18:15) and the prophets (so the whole O.T. as in Luke 24:27, 44) did write." *Jesus of Nazareth the son of Joseph* (*Iēsoun huion tou Iōsēph ton apo Nazaret*). More exactly, "Jesus, son of Joseph, the one from Nazareth." Jesus passed as son (no article in the Greek) of Joseph, though John has just described him as "God-only Begotten" in verse 18, but certainly Philip could not know this. Bernard terms this part "the irony of St. John" for he is sure that his readers will agree with him as to the real deity of Jesus Christ. These details were probably meant to interest Nathanael.

46. *Can any good thing come out of Nazareth?* (*Ek Nazaret dunatai ti agathon einai;*). Literally, "Out of Nazareth can anything good be." There is a tinge of scorn in the question as if Nazareth (note position at beginning of sentence) had a bad name. Town rivalry may account to some extent for it since Cana (home of Nathanael) was near Nazareth. Clearly he had never heard of Jesus. The best thing in all the world came out of Nazareth, but Philip does not argue the point. A saying had arisen that no prophet comes out of Galilee (John 7:52), untrue like many such sayings. *Come and see* (*erchou kai ide*). Present middle imperative (come on) and second active imperative (and see at once).

Philip followed the method of Jesus with Andrew and John (verse 39), probably without knowing it. Wise is the one who knows how to deal with the sceptic.

47. *Behold* (*ide*). Here an exclamation (see 1:29) as often like *idou*. *An Israelite indeed* (*alēthōs Israēleitēs*). "Truly an Israelite," one living up to the covenant name, Israel at its best (Rom. 2:29), without the guile (*dolos*, deceit, bait for fish, from *deleazō*, to catch with bait) that Jacob once had of which Isaac complained (Gen. 27:35, *dolos*, here in LXX). The servant of Jehovah was to be without guile (Isa. 53:9).

48. *Whence knowest thou me?* (*Pothen me ginōskeis;*). Nathanael is astonished at this tribute, at any knowledge about himself by Jesus. He had overheard Christ's comment and longed to know its source. *Before Philip called thee* (*Pro tou se Philippon phōnēsai*). Idiomatic Greek, *pro* and the ablative case of the articular aorist active infinitive (*tou phōnēsai*, from *phōneō*, to call) with *se* as the object and *Philippon*, the accusative of general reference, "before the calling thee as to Philip." *When thou wast under the fig tree* (*onta hupo tēn sukēn*). "Being under the fig tree," accusative present participle agreeing with *se*. The fig tree was a familiar object in Palestine, probably in leaf at this time, the accusative with *hupo* may suggest that Nathanael had withdrawn there for prayer. Note genitive with *hupokatō* in verse 50. Jesus saw Nathanael's heart as well as his mere presence there. He saw him in his worship and so knew him.

49. *Thou art the Son of God* (*su ei ho huios tou theou*). Whether Nathanael had heard the Baptist say this of Jesus (1:34) we do not know, apparently not, but Nathanael was a student of the Old Testament as Philip implied (1:45) and was quick to put together his knowledge, the statement of Philip, and the manifest supernatural knowledge of Jesus as just shown. There is no reason for toning down the noble confession of Nathanael in the light of Christ's claim in verse 51. Cf. the confession of Peter in 6:69 and Matt. 16:16

and Martha's in John 11:27. Nathanael goes further. *Thou art King of Israel (Basileus ei tou Israēl).* To us this seems an anti-climax, but not so to Nathanael for both are Messianic titles in Psalm 2 and Jesus is greeted in the Triumphal Entry as the King of Israel (John 12:13).

50. *Answered and said (apekrithē kai eipen).* This redundant use of both verbs (cf. 1:26) occurs in the Synoptics also and in the LXX also. It is Aramaic also and vernacular. It is not proof of an Aramaic original as Burney argues *(Aramaic Origin,* etc., p. 53). *Because (hoti).* Causal use of *hoti* at beginning of the sentence as in 14:19; 15:19; 16:6. The second *hoti* before *eidon* (I saw) is either declarative (that) or merely recitative (either makes sense here). *Thou shalt see greater things than these (meizō toutōn opsēi).* Perhaps volitive future middle indicative of *horaō* (though merely futuristic is possible as with *opsesthe* in 51) ablative case of *toutōn* after the comparative adjective *meizō.* The wonder of Nathanael no doubt grew as Jesus went on.

51. *Verily, Verily (Amēn, amēn).* Hebrew word transliterated into Greek and then into English, our "amen." John always repeats it, not singly as in the Synoptics, and only in the words of Jesus, an illustration of Christ's authoritative manner of speaking as shown also by *legō humin* (I say unto you). Note plural *humin* though *autōi* just before is singular (to him). Jesus addresses thus others besides Nathanael. *The heaven opened (ton ouranon aneōigota).* Second perfect active participle of *anoigō* with double reduplication, standing open. The words remind one of what took place at the baptism of Jesus (Matt. 3:16 = Luke 3:21), but the immediate reference is to the opened heaven as the symbol of free intercourse between God and man (Isa. 64:1) and as it was later illustrated in the death of Stephen (Acts 7:56). There is a quotation from Gen. 28:12f., Jacob's vision at Bethel. That was a dream to Jacob, but Christ is himself the bond of fellowship between heaven and earth, between God and

man, for Jesus is both "the Son of God" as Nathanael said and "the Son of Man" (*epi ton huion tou anthrōpou*) as Jesus here calls himself. God and man meet in Christ. He is the true Jacob's Ladder. "I am the Way," Jesus will say. He is more than King of Israel, he is the Son of Man (the race). So quickly has this Gospel brought out in the witness of the Baptist, the faith of the first disciples, the claims of Jesus Christ, the fully developed picture of the Logos who is both God and man, moving among men and winning them to his service. At the close of the ministry Christ will tell Caiaphas that he will see the Son of Man sitting at the right hand of power and coming with the clouds of heaven (Mark 14:62). Here at the start Jesus is conscious of the final culmination and in apocalyptic eschatological language that we do not fully understand he sets forth the dignity and majesty of his Person.

CHAPTER II

1. *The third day* (*tēi hēmerāi tēi tritēi*). "On the day the third" (locative case), from the start to Galilee when Philip was found (1:43), seven days since 1:19. *There was a marriage* (*gamos egeneto*). "A wedding (or marriage festival) took place." See on Matt. 22:8. *In Cana of Galilee* (*en Kana tēs Galilaias*). This town, the home of Nathanael (21:2), is only mentioned again in 4:46 as the home of the nobleman. There was a Cana in Coele-Syria. It is usually located at *Kefr Kenna* (3½ miles from Nazareth), though *Ain Kana* and *Khirbet Kana* are also possible. Bernard thinks that it was probably on Wednesday afternoon the fourth day of the week (usual day for marriage of virgins), when the party of Jesus arrived. *And the mother of Jesus was there* (*kai ēn hē mētēr tou Iēsou ekei*). When they arrived. John does not mention her name, probably because already well known in the Synoptics. Probably Joseph was already dead. Mary may have been kin to the family where the wedding took place, an intimate friend clearly.

2. *Jesus also was bidden* (*eklēthē kai ho Iēsous*). First aorist passive indicative of *kaleō*, "was also invited" as well as his mother and because of her presence, possibly at her suggestion. *And his disciples* (*kai hoi mathētai*). Included in the invitation and probably all of them acquaintances of the family. See on 1:35 for this word applied to John's followers. This group of six already won form the nucleus of the great host of "learners" through the ages who will follow Jesus as Teacher and Lord and Saviour. The term is sometimes restricted to the twelve apostles, but more often has a wider circle in view as in John 6:61, 66; 20:30.

33

3. *When the wine failed* (*husterēsantos oinou*). Genitive absolute with first aorist active participle of *hustereō*, old verb from *husteros*, late or lacking. See same use in Mark 10:21. A longer Western paraphrase occurs in some manuscripts. It was an embarrassing circumstance, especially to Mary, if partly due to the arrival of the seven guests. *They have no wine* (*Oinon ouk echousin*). The statement of the fact was in itself a hint and a request. But why made by the mother of Jesus and why to Jesus? She would not, of course, make it to the host. Mary feels some kind of responsibility and exercises some kind of authority for reasons not known to us. Mary had treasured in her heart the wonders connected with the birth of Jesus (Luke 2:19, 51). The ministry of the Baptist had stirred her hopes afresh. Had she not told Jesus all that she knew before he went to the Jordan to be baptized of John? This group of disciples meant to her that Jesus had begun his Messianic work. So she dares propose the miracle to him.

4. *Woman* (*gunai*). Vocative case of *gunē*, and with no idea of censure as is plain from its use by Jesus in 19:26. But the use of *gunai* instead of *mēter* (Mother) does show her she can no longer exercise maternal authority and not at all in his Messianic work. That is always a difficult lesson for mothers and fathers to learn, when to let go. *What have I to do with thee?* (*Ti emoi kai soi;*). There are a number of examples of this ethical dative in the LXX (Judges 11:12; II Sam. 16:10; I Kings 17:18; II Kings 3:13; II Chron. 35:21) and in the N.T. (Mark 1:24; 5:7; Matt. 8:29; 27:19; Luke 8:28). Some divergence of thought is usually indicated. Literally the phrase means, "What is it to me and to thee?" In this instance F. C. Burkitt (*Journal of Theol. Studies*, July, 1912) interprets it to mean, "What is it to us?" That is certainly possible and suits the next clause also. *Mine hour is not yet come* (*oupō hēkei hē hōra mou*). This phrase marks a crisis whenever it occurs, especially of his death

(7:30; 8:20; 12:23; 13:1; 17:1). Here apparently it means
the hour for public manifestation of the Messiahship, though
a narrower sense would be for Christ's intervention about
the failure of the wine. The Fourth Gospel is written on
the plane of eternity (W. M. Ramsay) and that standpoint
exists here in this first sign of the Messiah.

5. *Unto the servants* (*tois diakonois*). See on Matt. 20:26 for
this word (our "deacon," but not that sense here). *Whatsoever
he saith unto you, do it* (*Hoti an legei humin poiēsate*). Indefinite relative sentence (*hoti an* and present active subjunctive,
general statement) with aorist active imperative of *poieō* for
instant execution. Mary took comfort in the "not yet" (*oupō*)
and recognized the right of Jesus as Messiah to independence
of her, but evidently expected him to carry out her suggestion
ultimately as he did. This mother knew her Son.

6. *Waterpots* (*hudriai*). Old word from *hudōr* (water) and
used in papyri for pots or pans for holding money or bread
as well as water. These stone (*lithinai* as in II Cor. 3:3) jars
full of water were kept handy (*set there, keimenai*, present
middle participle of *keimai*) at a feast for ceremonial cleansing of the hands (II Kings 3:11; Mark 7:3), "after the Jews'
manner of purifying" (*kata ton katharismon tōn Ioudaiōn*).
See Mark 1:44 and Luke 2:22 for the word *katharismos* (from
katharizō) which fact also raised a controversy with disciples
of John because of his baptizing (John 3:25). *Containing*
(*chōrousai*). Present active participle feminine plural of
chōreō, old verb from *chōros*, place, space, having space or
room for. *Two or three firkins apiece* (*ana metrētas duo ē treis*).
The word *metrētēs*, from *metreō*, to measure, simply means
"measurer," an amphora for measuring liquids (in Demosthenes, Aristotle, Polybius), the Hebrew *bath* (II Chron. 4:5),
here only in N.T., about 8½ English gallons. Each *hudria*
thus held about 20 gallons. This common distributive use of
ana occurs here only in this Gospel, but is in Rev. 4:8. In John
4:28 a much smaller *hudria* was used for carrying water.

7. *Fill* (*gemisate*). Effective first aorist active imperative of *gemizō*, to fill full. *With water* (*hudatos*). Genitive case of material. *Up to the brim* (*heōs anō*). "Up to the top." See *heōs katō* (Matt. 27:51) for "down to the bottom." No room left in the waterpots now full of water.

8. *Draw out now* (*Antlēsate nun*). First aorist active imperative of *antleō*, from *ho antlos*, bilge water, or the hold where the bilge water settles (so in Homer). The verb occurs in John 4:7, 15, for drawing water from the well, and Westcott so interprets it here, but needlessly so, since the servants seem bidden to draw from the large water-jars now full of water. Apparently the water was still water when it came out of the jars (verse 9), but was changed to wine before reaching the guests. The water in the jars remained water. *Unto the ruler of the feast* (*tōi architriklinōi*). Dative case. The *triklinos* was a room (*oikos*) with three couches (*klinē*) for the feast. The *architriklinos* was originally the superintendent of the dining-room who arranged the couches and tasted the food, not the toast-master (*sumposiarchēs*). *And they bare it* (*hoi de ēnegkan*). Second aorist active indicative of *pherō*. Apparently not knowing at first that they bore wine.

9. *Tasted* (*egeusato*). First aorist middle indicative of *geuomai*. As it was his function to do. *The water now become wine* (*to hudōr oinon gegenēmenon*). Accusative case, though the genitive also occurs with *geuomai*. Perfect passive participle of *ginomai* and *oinon*, predicative accusative. The tablemaster knew nothing of the miracle, "whence it was" (*pothen estin*, indirect question retaining present indicative). The servants knew the source of the water, but not the power that made the wine. *Calleth the bridegroom* (*phōnei ton numphion*). As apparently responsible for the supply of the wine (*thou hast kept tetērēkas*). See Matt. 9:15 for *numphios*. *When men have drunk freely* (*hotan methusthōsin*). Indefinite temporal clause with *hotan* and first aorist passive

subjunctive of *methuskō*. The verb does not mean that these guests are now drunk, but that this is a common custom to put "the worse" (*ton elassō*, the less, the inferior) wine last. It is real wine that is meant by *oinos* here. Unlike the Baptist Jesus mingled in the social life of the time, was even abused for it (Matt. 11:19=Luke 7:34). But this fact does not mean that today Jesus would approve the modern liquor trade with its damnable influences. The law of love expounded by Paul in I Cor. 8 to 10 and in Rom. 14 and 15 teaches modern Christians to be willing gladly to give up what they see causes so many to stumble into sin.

11. *This beginning of his signs did Jesus* (*tautēn epoiēsen archēn tōn sēmeiōn ho Iēsous*). Rather, "this Jesus did as a beginning of his signs," for there is no article between *tautēn* and *archēn*. "We have now passed from the 'witness' of the Baptist to the 'witness' of the works of Jesus" (Bernard). This is John's favourite word "signs" rather than wonders (*terata*) or powers (*dunameis*) for the works (*erga*) of Jesus. *Sēmeion* is an old word from *sēmainō*, to give a sign (12:33). He selects eight in his Gospel by which to prove the deity of Christ (20:30) of which this is the first. *Manifested his glory* (*ephanerōsen tēn doxan autou*). First aorist (effective) active indicative of *phaneroō*, that glory of which John spoke in 1:14. *Believed on him* (*episteusan eis auton*). First aorist active indicative of *pisteuō*, to believe, to put trust in, so common in John. These six disciples (learners) had already believed in Jesus as the Messiah (1:35-51). Now their faith was greatly strengthened. So it will be all through this Gospel. Jesus will increasingly reveal himself while the disciples will grow in knowledge and trust and the Jews will become increasingly hostile till the culmination.

12. *He went down to Capernaum* (*katebē eis Kapharnaoum autos*). Second aorist active indicative of *katabainō*. Cana was on higher ground. This brief stay (*not many days, ou pollas hēmeras*) in this important city (Tell Hum) on the

north shore of Galilee was with Christ's mother, brothers (apparently friendly at first) and the six disciples, all in the fresh glow of the glory manifested at Cana. Surely Mary's heart was full.

13. *The passover of the Jews* (*to pascha tōn Ioudaiōn*). The Synoptics do not give "of the Jews," but John is writing after the destruction of the temple and for Gentile readers. John mentions the passovers in Christ's ministry outside of the one when Christ was crucified, this one and one in 6:4. There may be another (5:1), but we do not know. But for John we should not know that Christ's ministry was much over a year in length.

14. *Those that sold* (*tous pōlountas*). Present active articular participle of *pōleō*, to sell. They were in the Court of the Gentiles within the temple precinct (*en tōi hierōi*), but not in the *naos* or temple proper. The sacrifices required animals (oxen, *boas*, sheep, *probata*, doves, *peristeras*) and "changers of money" (*kermatistas*, from *kermatizō*, to cut into small pieces, to change money, only here in N.T., late and rare). Probably their very presence in his Father's house angered Jesus. The Synoptics (Mark 11:15-17 = Matt. 21:12f. = Luke 10:45f.) record a similar incident the day after the Triumphal Entry. If there was only one, it would seem more natural at the close. But why could it not occur at the beginning also? Here it is an obvious protest by Christ at the beginning of his ministry as in the Synoptics it is an indignant outcry against the desecration. The cessation was only temporary in both instances.

15. *A scourge of cords* (*phragellion ek schoiniōn*). The Latin *flagellum*. In papyri, here only in N.T. and note Latin *l* becomes *r* in *Koiné*. *Schoinion* is a diminutive of *schoinos* (a rush), old word for rope, in N.T. only here and Acts 27:32. *Cast out* (*exebalen*). Second aorist active indicative of *ekballō*. It is not said that Jesus smote the sheep and oxen (note *te kai*, both and), for a flourish of the scourge would answer.

He poured out (execheen). Second aorist active indicative of *ekcheō*, to pour out. *The changers' money (tōn kollubistōn ta kermata)*. "The small pieces of money (*kermata*, cut in pieces, change) of the bankers (*kollubistēs* from *kollubos*, clipped, late word see on Matt. 21:12)." Perhaps he took up the boxes and emptied the money. *Overthrew their tables (tas trapezas anetrepsen)*. First aorist active indicative of *anatrepō*, to turn up, though some MSS. have *anestrepsen* from *anastrephō*, also to turn up.

16. *Take these things hence (Arate tauta enteuthen)*. First aorist active imperative of *airō*. Probably the doves were in baskets or cages and so had to be taken out by the traders. *Make not my Father's house a house of merchandise (mē poieite ton oikon tou patros mou oikon emporiou)*. "Stop making," it means, *mē* and the present active imperative. They had made it a market-house (*emporiou*, here only in N.T., old word from *emporos*, merchant, one who goes on a journey for traffic, a drummer). Note the clear-cut Messianic claim here (My Father as in Luke 2:49). Jerome says: "A certain fiery and starry light shone from his eyes and the majesty of Godhead gleamed in His face."

17. *Remembered (emnēsthēsan)*. First aorist passive indicative of *mimnēskō*, to remind, "were reminded." Westcott notes the double effect of this act as is true of Christ's words and deeds all through John's Gospel. The disciples are helped, the traders are angered. *That it is written (hoti gegrammenon estin)*. Periphrastic perfect passive indicative of *graphō* retained in indirect discourse (assertion). *The zeal of thine house (ho zēlos tou oikou sou)*. Objective genitive. "The zeal for thy house." *Shall eat me up (kataphagetai me)*. Future middle indicative of *katesthiō*, defective verb, to eat down ("up" we say), perfective use of *kata-*. This future *phagomai* is from the second aorist *ephagon*. It is a quotation from Psa. 69:9, frequently quoted in the N.T.

18. *What sign shewest thou unto us?* (*Ti sēmeion dei-knueis hēmin;*). They may have heard of the "sign" at Cana or not, but they have rallied a bit on the out-side of the temple area and demand proof for his Messi-anic assumption of authority over the temple worship. These traders had paid the Sadducees and Pharisees in the Sanhedrin for the concession as traffickers which they en-joyed. They were within their technical rights in this question.

19. *Destroy this temple* (*lusate ton naon touton*). First aorist active imperative of *luō*, to loosen or destroy. It is the permissive imperative, not a command to do it. Note also *naos*, not *hieron*, the sanctuary, symbol of God's *naos*, in our hearts (I Cor. 3:16f.). There is much confusion about this language since Jesus added: "And in three days I will raise it up" (*kai en trisin hēmerais egerō auton*). Those who heard Jesus, including the disciples till after the resurrec-tion (verse 22), understood the reference to be to Herod's temple. Certainly that is the obvious way to take it. But Jesus often spoke in parables and even in enigmas. He may have spoken of the literal temple as a parable for his own body which of course they would not understand, least of all the resurrection in three days.

20. *Forty and six years was this temple in building* (*Tes-serakonta kai hex etesin oikodomēthē ho naos houtos*). "Within forty and six years (associative instrumental case) was built (first aorist passive indicative, constative or summary use of the aorist, of *oikodomeō*, without augment) this temple." As a matter of fact, it was not yet finished, so distrustful had the Jews been of Herod. *And wilt thou?* (*kai su;*). An evident sneer in the use of *su* (thou, an unknown upstart from Galilee, of the peasant class, not one of the Sanhedrin, not one of the ecclesiastics or even architects).

21. *But he spake of the temple of his body* (*ekeinos de elegen peri tou naou tou sōmatos autou*). Emphatic he (*ekeinos*)

and imperfect tense (he had been speaking). This is John's view as he looks back at it, not what he understood when Jesus spoke the words.

22. *When therefore he was raised from the dead* (*Hote oun ēgerthē ek nekrōn*). First aorist passive indicative of *egeirō*, to raise up. And not at first then, but only slowly after the disciples themselves were convinced. Then "they believed the Scripture" (*episteusan tēi graphēi*). They "believed" again. Dative case *graphēi*. Probably Psa. 16:10 is meant (Acts 2:31; 13:35). *And the word which Jesus had said* (*kai tōi logōi hon eipen*). Dative case *logōi* also, but *hon* (relative) is not attracted to the dative. Clearly then John interprets Jesus to have a parabolic reference to his death and resurrection by his language in 2:19. There are those who bluntly say that John was mistaken. I prefer to say that these scholars are mistaken. Even Bernard considers it "hardly possible" that John interprets Jesus rightly in 1:21. "Had he meant that, He would have spoken with less ambiguity." But how do we know that Jesus wished to be understood clearly at this time? Certainly no one understood Christ when he spoke the words. The language of Jesus is recalled and perverted at his trial as "I will destroy" (Mark 14:58), "I can destroy" (Matt. 26:61), neither of which he said.

23. *In Jerusalem* (*en tois Ierosolumois*). The form *Ierosoluma* as in 2:13 always in this Gospel and in Mark, and usually in Matthew, though *Ierousalēm* only in Revelation, and both forms by Luke and Paul. *During the feast* (*en tēi heortēi*). The feast of unleavened bread followed for seven days right after the passover (one day strictly), though *to pascha* is used either for the passover meal or for the whole eight days. *Believed on his name* (*episteusan eis to onoma autou*). See on 1:12 for this phrase. Only one has to watch for the real import of *pisteuō*. *Beholding his signs* (*theōrountes autou ta sēmeia*). Present active participle (causal use) of *theōreō*. *Which he did* (*ha epoiei*). "Which he was doing"

(imperfect tense). He did his first sign in Cana, but now he was doing many in Jerusalem. Already Jesus had become the cynosure of all eyes in Jerusalem at this first visit in his ministry.

24. *But Jesus did not trust himself to them* (*autos de Iēsous ouk episteuen hauton autois*). "But Jesus himself kept on refusing (negative imperfect) to trust himself to them." The double use of *pisteuō* here is shown by Acts 8:13 where Simon Magus "believed" (*episteusen*) and was baptized, but was unsaved. He merely believed that he wanted what Philip had. *For that he knew all men* (*dia to auton ginōskein pantas*). Causal use of *dia* and the accusative case of the articular infinitive *to ginōskein* (because of the knowing) with the object of the infinitive (*pantas*, all men) and the accusative of general reference (*auton*, as to himself).

25. *And because he needed not* (*kai hoti chreian eichen*). Imperfect active, "and because he did not have need." *That any one should bear witness concerning man* (*hina tis marturēsei peri tou anthrōpou*). Non-final use of *hina* with first aorist active subjunctive of *martureō* and the generic article (*peri tou anthrōpou*) concerning mankind as in the next clause also. *For he himself knew* (*autos gar eginōsken*). Imperfect active, "for he himself kept on knowing" as he did from the start. *What was in man* (*ti ēn en tōi anthrōpōi*). Indirect question with *estin* of the direct changed to the imperfect *ēn*, a rare idiom in the *Koiné*. This supernatural knowledge of man is a mark of deity. Some men of genius can read men better than others, but not in the sense meant here.

CHAPTER III

1. *Now* (*de*). So often in John *de* is explanatory and transitional, not adversative. Nicodemus is an instance of Christ's knowledge of men (2:25) and of one to whom he did trust himself unlike those in 2:24. As a Pharisee "he belonged to that party which with all its bigotry contained a salt of true patriotism and could rear such cultured and high-toned men as Gamaliel and Paul" (Marcus Dods). *Named Nicodemus* (*Nikodēmos onoma*). Same construction as in 1:6, "Nicodemus name to him." So Rev. 6:8. It is a Greek name and occurs in Josephus (*Ant.* XIV. iii. 2) as the name of an ambassador from Aristobulus to Pompey. Only in John in N.T. (here, 7:50; 19:39). He was a Pharisee, a member of the Sanhedrin, and wealthy. There is no evidence that he was the young ruler of Luke 18:18 because of *archōn* (ruler) here.

2. *The same* (*houtos*). "This one." *By night* (*nuktos*). Genitive of time. That he came at all is remarkable, not because there was any danger as was true at a later period, but because of his own prominence. He wished to avoid comment by other members of the Sanhedrin and others. Jesus had already provoked the opposition of the ecclesiastics by his assumption of Messianic authority over the temple. There is no ground for assigning this incident to a later period, for it suits perfectly here. Jesus was already in the public eye (2:23) and the interest of Nicodemus was real and yet he wished to be cautious. *Rabbi* (*Rabbei*). See on 1:38. Technically Jesus was not an acknowledged Rabbi of the schools, but Nicodemus does recognize him as such and calls him "My Master" just as Andrew and John did (1:38). It was a long step for Nicodemus as a Pharisee

43

to take, for the Pharisees had closely scrutinized the credentials of the Baptist in 1:19–24 (Milligan and Moulton's *Comm.*). *We know (oidamen).* Second perfect indicative first person plural. He seems to speak for others of his class as the blind man does in 9:31. Westcott thinks that Nicodemus has been influenced partly by the report of the commission sent to the Baptist (1:19–27). *Thou art a teacher come from God (apo theou eleluthas didaskalos).* "Thou hast come from God as a teacher." Second perfect active indicative of *erchomai* and predicative nominative *didaskalos*. This is the explanation of Nicodemus for coming to Jesus, obscure Galilean peasant as he seemed, evidence that satisfied one of the leaders in Pharisaism. *Can do (dunatai poiein).* "Can go on doing" (present active infinitive of *poieo* and so linear). *These signs that thou doest (tauta ta semeia ha su poieis).* Those mentioned in 2:23 that convinced so many in the crowd and that now appeal to the scholar. Note *su* (thou) as quite out of the ordinary. The scorn of Jesus by the rulers held many back to the end (John 12:42), but Nicodemus dares to feel his way. *Except God be with him (ean me ei ho theos met' autou).* Condition of the third class, presented as a probability, not as a definite fact. He wanted to know more of the teaching accredited thus by God. Jesus went about doing good because God was with him, Peter says (Acts 10:38).

3. *Except a man be born anew (ean me tis gennethei anothen).* Another condition of the third class, undetermined but with prospect of determination. First aorist passive subjunctive of *gennao*. *Anothen.* Originally "from above" (Mark 15:38), then "from heaven" (John 3:31), then "from the first" (Luke 1:3), and then "again" (*palin anothen*, Gal. 4:9). Which is the meaning here? The puzzle of Nicodemus shows (*deuteron*, verse 4) that he took it as "again," a second birth from the womb. The Vulgate translates it by *renatus fuerit denuo*. But the misapprehension of Nicodemus does

not prove the meaning of Jesus. In the other passages in
John (3:31; 19:11, 23) the meaning is "from above" (*desu-
per*) and usually so in the Synoptics. It is a second birth,
to be sure, regeneration, but· a birth from above by the
Spirit. *He cannot see the kingdom of God* (*ou dunatai idein
tēn basileian tou theou*). To participate in it as in Luke 9:27.
For this use of *idein* (second aroist active infinitive of
horaō) see John 8:51; Rev. 18:7.

4. *Being old* (*gerōn ōn*). Nicodemus was probably familiar
with the notion of re-birth for proselytes to Judaism for the
Gentiles, but not with the idea that a Jew had to be reborn.
But "this stupid misunderstanding" (Bernard) of the meaning of Jesus is precisely what John represents Nicodemus
as making. How "old" Nicodemus was we do not know,
but surely too old to be the young ruler of Luke 18:18 as
Bacon holds. The blunder of Nicodemus is emphasized by
the second question with the *mē* expecting the negative
answer. The use of *deuteron* adds to the grotesqueness
of his blunder. The learned Pharisee is as jejune in spiritual insight as the veriest tyro. This is not an unheard of
phenomenon.

5. *Of water and the Spirit* (*ex hudatos kai pneumatos*).
Nicodemus had failed utterly to grasp the idea of the spiritual
birth as essential to entrance into the Kingdom of God.
He knew only Jews as members of that kingdom, the political kingdom of Pharisaic hope which was to make all the
world Jewish (Pharisaic) under the King Messiah. Why
does Jesus add *ex hudatos* here? In verse 3 we have "*anōthen*"
(from above) which is repeated in verse 7, while in verse 8
we have only *ek tou pneumatos* (of the Spirit) in the best
manuscripts. Many theories exist. One view makes baptism,
referred to by *ex hudatos* (coming up out of water), essential
to the birth of the Spirit, as the means of obtaining the new
birth of the Spirit. If so, why is water mentioned only once
in the three demands of Jesus (3, 5, 7)? Calvin makes water

and Spirit refer to the one act (the cleansing work of the Spirit). Some insist on the language in verse 6 as meaning the birth of the flesh coming in a sac of water in contrast to the birth of the Spirit. One wonders after all what was the precise purpose of Jesus with Nicodemus, the Pharisaic ceremonialist, who had failed to grasp the idea of spiritual birth which is a commonplace to us. By using water (the symbol before the thing signified) first and adding Spirit, he may have hoped to turn the mind of Nicodemus away from mere physical birth and, by pointing to the baptism of John on confession of sin which the Pharisees had rejected, to turn his attention to the birth from above by the Spirit. That is to say the mention of "water" here may have been for the purpose of helping Nicodemus without laying down a fundamental principle of salvation as being by means of baptism. Bernard holds that the words *hudatos kai* (water and) do not belong to the words of Jesus, but "are a gloss, added to bring the saying of Jesus into harmony with the belief and practice of a later generation." Here Jesus uses *eiselthein* (enter) instead of *idein* (see) of verse 3, but with the same essential idea (participation in the kingdom).

6. *That which is born* (*to gegennēmenon*). Perfect passive articular participle. The sharp contrast between flesh (*sarx*) and Spirit (*pneuma*), drawn already in 1:13, serves to remind Nicodemus of the crudity of his question in 3:4 about a second physical birth.

7. *Marvel not* (*mē thaumasēis*). "Do not begin to wonder" (ingressive first aorist active subjunctive with *mē*), as clearly Nicodemus had done. In John the word *thaumazō* usually means "unintelligent wonder" (Bernard). *Ye must be born anew* (*dei humas gennēthēnai anōthen*). Jesus repeats the point in verse 3 (*dei* and the infinitive instead of *ean mē* and the subjunctive) with *anōthen* (from above) only and not *ex hudatos*.

8. *The wind* (*to pneuma*). In Greek *pneuma* means either
wind or spirit as *spiritus* does in Latin (so also in Hebrew
and Syriac). Wycliff follows the Latin and keeps spirit
here and Marcus Dods argues for it. The word *pneuma*
occurs 370 times in the N.T. and never means wind elsewhere
except in a quotation from the O.T. (Heb. 1:7 from Psa.
104:4), though common in the LXX. On the other hand
pneō (bloweth, *pnei*) occurs five times elsewhere in the N.T.
and always of the wind (like John 6:18). So *phōnē* can be
either sound (as of wind) or voice (as of the Spirit). In
simple truth either sense of *pneuma* can be taken here as
one wills. Tholuck thinks that the night-wind swept through
the narrow street as Jesus spoke. In either case the etymol-
ogy of *pneuma* is "wind" from *pneō*, to blow. The Spirit
is the use of *pneuma* as metaphor. Certainly the conclusion
"of the Spirit" is a direct reference to the Holy Spirit who
works his own way beyond our comprehension even as men
even yet do not know the law of the wind.

9. *How?* (*Pōs;*). Nicodemus is not helped either by the
use of *hudōr* or *pneuma* to understand *dei gennēthēnai anōthen*
(the necessity of the birth from above or regeneration). He
falls back into his "stupid misunderstanding." There are
none so dull as those who will not see. Preoccupation prevents insight. Literally one must often empty his mind to
receive new truth.

10. *The teacher of Israel* (*ho didaskalos tou Israēl*). The
well-known or the authorized (the accepted) teacher of the
Israel of God. Note both articles. *And understandest not
these things?* (*kai tauta ou ginōskeis;*). After being told by
Jesus and after so propitious a start. His Pharisaic theology
had made him almost proof against spiritual apprehension.
It was outside of his groove (rote, rut, rot, the three terrible
r's of mere traditionalism).

11. *We speak that we do know* (*ho oidamen laloumen*).
Jesus simply claims knowledge of what he has tried to make

plain to the famous Rabbi without success. John uses *laleō*
some 60 times, half of them by Jesus, very little distinction
existing between the use of *laleō* and *legō* in John. Originally
laleō referred to the chatter of birds. Note John's frequent
use of *amēn amēn* and *legō* (double emphasis). *And bear
witness of that we have seen (kai ho heōrakamen marturoumen)*.
The same use of neuter singular relative *ho* as before. Perfect active indicative of *horaō*. He is not a dreamer, guesser,
or speculator. He is bearing witness from personal knowledge, strange as this may seem to Nicodemus. *And ye receive not our witness (kai tēn marturian hēmōn ou lambanete)*.
This is the tragedy of the matter as John has shown (1:11, 26)
and as will continue to be true even today. Jesus probably
associates here with himself ("we") those who have personal experience of grace and so are qualified as witnesses.
Note the plural in I John 1:1f. Bernard thinks that John
has here read into the words of Jesus the convictions of a
later age, a serious charge to make.

12. *If I told (ei eipon)*. Condition of the first class, assumed to be true. *Earthly things (ta epigeia)*. Things upon
the earth like *ta epi tēs gēs* (Col. 3:2), not things of an earthly
nature or worldly or sinful. The work of the kingdom of God
including the new birth which Nicodemus did not understand belongs to *ta epigeia*. *If I tell you heavenly things (ean
eipō humin ta epourania)*. Condition of the third class, undetermined. What will Nicodemus do in that case? By
ta epourania Jesus means the things that take place in
heaven like the deep secrets of the purpose of God in the
matter of redemption such as the necessity of the lifting up
of Christ as shown in verse 14. Both Godet and Westcott
note that the two types of teaching here pointed out by
Jesus (the earthly, the heavenly) correspond in general to
the difference between the Synoptics (the earthly) and the
Fourth Gospel (the heavenly), a difference noted here in
the Fourth Gospel as shown by Jesus himself. Hence the

one should not be pitted against the other. There are speci-
mens of the heavenly in the Synoptics as in Matt. 11:25ff.
and Luke 10:18ff.

13. *But he that descended out of heaven (ei mē ho ek tou
ouranou katabas).* The Incarnation of the Pre-existent Son of
God who was in heaven before he came down and so knows
what he is telling about "the heavenly things." There is
no allusion to the Ascension which came later. This high
conception of Christ runs all through the Gospel and is
often in Christ's own words as here. *Which is in heaven
(ho ōn en tōi ouranōi).* This phrase is added by some manuscripts, not by Aleph B L W 33, and, if genuine, would merely
emphasize the timeless existence of God's Son who is in
heaven even while on earth. Probably a gloss. But "the
Son of man" is genuine. He is the one who has come down
out of heaven.

14. *Moses lifted up the serpent (Mōusēs hupsōsen ton
ophin).* Reference to Numb. 21:7ff. where Moses set the
brazen serpent upon the standard that those who believed
might look and live. Jesus draws a vivid parallel between
the act of Moses and the Cross on which he himself (the
Son of man) "must" (*dei*, one of the heavenly things) "be
lifted up" (*hupsōthēnai*, first aorist passive infinitive of
hupsoō, a word not used about the brazen serpent). In
John *hupsoō* always refers to the Cross (8:28; 12:32, 34),
though to the Ascension in Acts (2:33; 5:31). Jesus is
complimenting the standing and intelligence of Nicodemus
as "the teacher of Israel" by telling him this great truth
and fact that lies at the basis of the work of the kingdom of
God (the atoning death of Christ on the Cross).

15. *That whosoever believeth may in him have eternal life
(hina pas ho pisteuōn en autōi echēi zōēn aiōnion).* Final use
of *hina* with present active subjunctive of *echō*, that he may
keep on having eternal life (a frequent phrase in John, always in John *aiōnios* occurs with *zōē*, 16 times in the Gospel,

6 in I John, ageless or endless life, beginning now and lasting forever). It is more than endless, for it is sharing in the life of God in Christ (5:26; 17:3; I John 5:12). So here *en autōi* (in him) is taken with *echēi* rather than with *pisteuōn*. The interview with Nicodemus apparently closes with verse 15. In verses 16 to 21 we have past tenses constantly as is natural for the reflection of John, but unnatural for Jesus speaking. There are phrases like the Prologue (verse 19 and 1:9–11). "Only begotten" does not occur elsewhere in the words of Jesus, but is in 1:14, 18; I John 4:9. John often puts in explanatory comments (1:16–18; 12:37–41).

16. *For so* (*houtōs gar*). This use of *gar* is quite in John's style in introducing his comments (2:25; 4:8; 5:13, etc.). This "Little Gospel" as it is often called, this "comfortable word" (the Anglican Liturgy), while not a quotation from Jesus is a just and marvellous interpretation of the mission and message of our Lord. In verses 16 to 21 John recapitulates in summary fashion the teaching of Jesus to Nicodemus. *Loved* (*ēgapēsen*). First aorist active indicative of *agapaō*, the noble word so common in the Gospels for the highest form of love, used here as often in John (14:23; 17:23; I John 3:1; 4:10) of God's love for man (cf. II Thess. 2:16; Rom. 5:8; Eph. 2:4). In 21:15 John presents a distinction between *agapaō* and *phileō*. *Agapaō* is used also for love of men for men (13:34), for Jesus (8:42), for God (I John 4:10). *The world* (*ton kosmon*). The whole cosmos of men, including Gentiles, the whole human race. This universal aspect of God's love appears also in II Cor. 5:19; Rom. 5:8. *That he gave* (*hōste edōken*). The usual classical construction with *hōste* and the indicative (first aorist active) practical result, the only example in the N.T. save that in Gal. 2:13. Elsewhere *hōste* with the infinitive occurs for actual result (Matt. 13:32) as well as purpose (Matt. 10:1), though even this is rare. *His only begotten Son* (*ton huion ton monogenē*). "The Son the only begotten." For this word see on 1:14, 18

and also 3:18. The rest of the sentence, the purpose clause with *hina-echēi* precisely reproduces the close of 3:15 save that *eis auton* takes the place of *en autōi* (see 1:12) and goes certainly with *pisteuōn* (not with *echēi* as *en autōi* in verse 15) and the added clause "should not perish but" (*mē apolētai alla*, second aorist middle subjunctive, intransitive, of *apollumi*, to destroy). The same contrast between "perish" and "eternal life" (for this world and the next) appears also in 10-28. On "perish" see also 17:12.

17. *For God sent not the Son* (*ou gar apesteilen ho theos ton huion*). Explanation (*gar*) of God's sending the Son into the world. First aorist active indicative of *apostellō*. John uses both *apostellō* from which comes *apostolos* (3:34; 5:36, 38, etc.) and *pempō* (4:34; 5:23, 24, 30, etc.) for God's sending the Son and *pempō* more frequently, but with no real difference in meaning. All the Gospels use *ho huios* in the absolute sense in contrast with the Father (Mark 13:32; Matt. 11:27; Luke 10:22). *To judge* (*hina krinēi*). Final clause with *hina* and the present (or aorist) active subjunctive of *krinō*. The Messiah does judge the world as Jesus taught (Matt. 25:31f.; John 5:27), but this was not the primary or the only purpose of his coming. See on Matt. 7:1 for *krinō*, to pick out, select, approve, condemn, used so often and in so many varying contexts in the N.T. *But that the world should be saved through him* (*all hina sōthēi ho kosmos di' autou*). First aorist passive subjunctive of *sōzō*, the common verb to save (from *sōs*, safe and sound), from which *sōtēr* (Saviour) comes (the Saviour of the world, 4:42; I John 4:14) and *sōtēria* (salvation, 4:22 here only in John). The verb *sōzō* is often used for physical health (Mark 5:28), but here of the spiritual salvation as in 5:34.

18. *Is not judged* (*ou krinetai*). Present passive indicative. Trust in Christ prevents condemnation, for he takes our place and pays the penalty for sin for all who put their case in his hands (Rom. 8:32f.). The believer in Christ as

Saviour does not come into judgment (John 5:24). *Hath been judged already* (*ēdē kekritai*). Perfect passive indicative of *krinō*. Judgment has already been passed on the one who refuses to believe in Christ as the Saviour sent by the Father, the man who is not willing to come to Christ for life (5:40). *Because he hath not believed* (*hoti mē pepisteuken*). Perfect active indicative of *pisteuō*, has taken a permanent attitude of refusal. Here *hoti mē* states the reason subjectively as the judgment of the Judge in any such case (*ho mē pisteuōn* already mentioned) while in I John 5:10 *hoti ou pepisteuken* gives the reason objectively (*ou* instead of *mē*) conceived as an actual case and no longer hypothetical. See 1:12 for *eis to onoma* with *pisteuō* (believing on the name) and 1:14 for *monogenous* (only begotten) and also 3:16.

19. *And this is the judgment* (*hautē de estin hē krisis*). A thoroughly Johannine phrase for sequence of thought (15:12; 17:3; I John 1:5; 5:11, 14; III John 6). It is more precisely the process of judging (*kri-sis*) rather than the result (*kri-ma*) of the judgment. "It is no arbitrary sentence, but the working out of a moral law" (Bernard). *The light is come* (*to phōs elēluthen*). Second perfect active indicative of *erchomai*, a permanent result as already explained in the Prologue concerning the Incarnation (1:4, 5, 9, 11). Jesus is the Light of the world. *Loved darkness* (*ēgapēsan to skotos*). Job (24:13) spoke of men rebelling against the light. Here *to skotos*, common word for moral and spiritual darkness (I Thess. 5:5), though *hē skotia* in John 1:5. "Darkness" is common in John as a metaphor for the state of sinners (8:12; 12:35, 46; I John 1:6; 2:8, 9, 11). Jesus himself is the only moral and spiritual light of the world (8:12) as he dared claim to his enemies. The pathos of it all is that men fall in love with the darkness of sin and rebel against the light like denizens of the underworld, "for their works were evil (*ponēra*)." When the light appears, they scatter to their holes and dens. *Ponēros* (from *ponos*, toil, *poneō*, to toil)

is used of the deeds of the world by Jesus (7:7). In the end
the god of this world blinds men's eyes so that they do not
see the light (II Cor. 4:4). The fish in the Mammoth Cave
have no longer eyes, but only sockets where eyes used to
be. The evil one has a powerful grip on the world (I John
5:19).

20. *That doeth ill* (*ho phaula prassōn*). The word *phau-
los* means first worthless and then wicked (usually so in
N.T.) and both senses occur in the papyri. In 5:29 see
contrast between *agatha poieō* (doing good things) and *phaula
prassō* (practising evil things). *Hateth the light* (*misei to
phōs*). Hence talks against it, ridicules Christ, Christianity,
churches, preachers, etc. Does it in talk, magazines, books,
in a supercilious tone of sheer ignorance. *Cometh not to the
light* (*ouk erchetai pros to phōs*). The light hurts his eyes,
reveals his own wickedness, makes him thoroughly uncom-
fortable. Hence he does not read the Bible, he does not
come to church, he does not pray. He goes on in deeper
darkness. *Lest his works should be reproved* (*hina mē elegch-
thēi ta erga autou*). Negative final clause (*hina mē*) with
first aorist passive subjunctive of *elegchō*, old word to correct
a fault, to reprove, to convict. See also 8:46; 16:8. To escape
this unpleasant process the evil man cuts out Christ.

21. *That doeth the truth* (*ho poiōn tēn alētheian*). See I
John 1:6 for this striking phrase. *Comes to the light* (*erchetai
pros to phōs*). Is drawn by the light, spiritual heliotropes,
not driven from it. *That may be made manifest* (*hina phanerōthēi*). Final *hina* with first aorist passive subjunctive of
phaneroō. *They have been wrought in God* (*en theōi estin
eirgasmena*). Periphrastic perfect passive indicative of
ergazomai. He does not claim that they are perfect, only
that they have been wrought in the sphere of and in the
power of God. Hence he wants the light turned on.

22. *After these things* (*meta tauta*). Transition after the
interview with Nicodemus. For the phrase see 5:1; 6:1;

7:1. *Into the land of Judea* (*eis tēn Ioudaian gēn*). Into the country districts outside of Jerusalem. The only example of this phrase in the N.T., but "the region of Judea" (*hē Ioudaia chōra*) in Mark 1:5. *He tarried* (*dietriben*). Descriptive imperfect active of *diatribō*, old verb to rub between or hard, to spend time (Acts 14:3). *Baptized* (*ebaptizen*). Imperfect active of *baptizō*. "He was baptizing." The six disciples were with him and in 4:2 John explains that Jesus did the baptizing through the disciples.

23. *John was also baptizing* (*ēn de kai ho Iōanēs baptizōn*). Periphrastic imperfect picturing the continued activity of the Baptist simultaneous with the growing work of Jesus. There was no real rivalry except in people's minds. *In Aenon near to Salim* (*en Ainōn eggus tou Saleim*). It is not clearly known where this place was. Eusebius locates it in the Jordan valley south of Beisan west of the river where are many springs (fountains, eyes). There is a place called Salim east of Shechem in Samaria with a village called 'Aimen, but with no water there. There may have been water there then, of course. *Because there was much water there* (*hoti hudata polla ēn ekei*). "Because many waters were there." Not for drinking, but for baptizing. "Therefore even in summer baptism by immersion could be continued" (Marcus Dods). *And they came, and were baptized* (*kai pareginonto kai ebaptizonto*). Imperfects both, one middle and the other passive, graphically picturing the long procession of pilgrims who came to John confessing their sins and receiving baptism at his hands.

24. *For John had not yet been cast into prison* (*oupō gar ēn beblēmenos eis tēn phulakēn Iōanēs*). Periphrastic past perfect indicative of *ballō* explaining (*gar*) why John was still baptizing, the reason for the imprisonment having been given by Luke (3:19f.).

25. *A questioning* (*zētēsis*). Old word from *zēteō*. See Acts 15:2 for the word where also *zētēma* (question) occurs. *Zētēsis* (process of inquiry) means a meticulous dispute

(I Tim. 6:4). *With a Jew (meta Ioudaiou)*. So correct text, not *Ioudaiōn* (Jews). Probably some Jew resented John's baptism of Jesus as implying impurity or that they were like Gentiles (cf. proselyte baptism). *About purifying (peri katharismou)*. See 2:6 for the word. The committee from the Sanhedrin had challenged John's right to baptize (1:25). The Jews had various kinds of baptisms or dippings (Heb. 6:2), "baptisms of cups and pots and brazen vessels" (Mark 6:4). The disciples of John came to him with the dispute (the first known baptismal controversy, on the meaning of the ceremony) and with a complaint.

26. *Rabbi (Rabbei)*. Greeting John just like Jesus (1:38; 3:2). *Beyond Jordan (peran tou Iordanou)*. Evident reference to John's witness to Jesus told in 1:29–34. *To whom thou hast borne witness (hōi su memarturēkas)*. Note avoidance of calling the name of Jesus. Perfect active indicative of *martureō* so common in John (1:7, etc.). These disciples of John are clearly jealous of Jesus as a rival of John and they distinctly blame John for his endorsement of one who is already eclipsing him in popularity. *The same baptizeth (houtos baptizei)*. "This one is baptizing." Not personally (4:2), as John did, but through his six disciples. *And all men come to him (kai pantes erchontai pros auton)*. Linear present middle indicative, "are coming." The sight of the growing crowds with Jesus and the dwindling crowds with John stirred John's followers to keenest jealousy. What a life-like picture of ministerial jealousy in all ages.

27. *Except it have been given him from heaven (ean mē ei dedomenon autōi ek tou ouranou)*. See the same idiom in John 6:65 (cf. 19:11). Condition of third class, undetermined with prospect of determination, *ean mē* with the periphrastic perfect passive subjunctive of *didōmi*. The perfect tense is rare in the subjunctive and an exact rendering into English is awkward, "unless it be granted him from heaven." See I Cor. 4:7 where Paul says the same thing.

28. *I said (eipon)*. As in 1:20, 23. He had always put
Jesus ahead of him as the Messiah (1:15). *Before him (emprosthen ekeinou)*. "Before that one" (Jesus) as his forerunner simply. *I am sent (apestalmenos eimi)*. Periphrastic
perfect passive indicative of *apostellō*.

29. *The bridegroom (numphios)*. Predicate nominative
without article. Both *numphē* (bride) and *numphios* are old
and common words. Jesus will use this metaphor of himself
as the Bridegroom (Mark 2:19) and Paul develops it (II
Cor. 11:2; Eph. 5:23–32) and so in Revelation (19:7; 21:2).
John is only like the *paranymph (paranumphios)* or "the
friend of the bridegroom." His office is to bring groom and
bride together. So he stands expectant (*hestēkōs*, second
perfect active participle of *histēmi*) and listens (*akouōn*,
present active participle of *akouō*) with joy (*rejoiceth greatly,
charāi chairei*, "with joy rejoices") to the music of the
bridegroom's voice. *This my joy therefore is fulfilled (hautē
oun hē chara peplērōtai)*. Perfect passive indicative of
pleroō, stands filled like a cup to the brim with joy.

30. *Must (dei)*. It has to be (see 3:14). He is to go on
growing (present active infinitive *auxanein*) while I go on
decreasing (present passive infinitive *elattousthai*, from comparative *elattōn*, less). These are the last words that we have
from John till the despondent message from the dungeon in
Machaerus whether Jesus is after all the Messiah (Matt.
11:2 = Luke 7:19). He went on to imprisonment, suspense,
martyrdom, while Jesus grew in popular favour till he had
his *via dolorosa*. "These last words of St. John are the fulness
of religious sacrifice and fitly close his work" (Westcott).

31. *Is above all (epanō pantōn)*. Ablative case with the
compound preposition *epanō*. See the same idea in Rom. 9:5.
Here we have the comments of Evangelist (John) concerning the last words of John in verse 30 which place Jesus
above himself. He is above all men, not alone above the
Baptist. Bernard follows those who treat verses 31 to 36

as dislocated and put them after verse 21 (the interview with Nicodemus), but they suit better here. *Of the earth (ek tēs gēs).* John is fond of this use of *ek* for origin and source of character as in 1:46; I John 4:5. Jesus is the one that comes out of heaven (*ho ek tou ouranou erchomenos*) as he has shown in 1:1–18. Hence he is "above all."

32. *What he hath seen and heard (ho heōraken kai ēkousen).* Perfect active indicative followed by aorist active indicative, because, as Westcott shows, the first belongs to the very existence of the Son and the latter to his mission. There is no confusion of tenses here. *No man (oudeis).* There were crowds coming to Jesus, but they do not really accept him as Saviour and Lord (1:11; 2:24). It is superficial as time will show. But "no one" is not to be pressed too far, for it is the rhetorical use.

33. *Hath set his seal (esphragisen).* First aorist active indicative of *sphragizō* for which verb see Matt. 27:66. The metaphor of sealing is a common one for giving attestation as in 6:27. The one who accepts the witness of Jesus attests that Jesus speaks the message of God.

34. *The words of God (ta rēmata tou theou).* God sent his Son (3:17) and he speaks God's words. *By measure (ek metrou).* That is God has put no limit to the Spirit's relation to the Son. God has given the Holy Spirit in his fulness to Christ and to no one else in that sense.

35. *Hath given all things into his hand (panta dedōken en tēi cheiri autou).* John makes the same statement about Jesus in 13:3 (using *eis tas cheiras* instead of *en tēi cheiri*). Jesus makes the same claim in 5:19–30; Matt. 11:27; 28:18.

36. *Hath eternal life (echei zōēn aiōnion).* Has it here and now and for eternity. *That obeyeth not (ho apeithōn).* "He that is disobedient to the Son." Jesus is the test of human life as Simeon said he would be (Luke 2:34f.). This verb does not occur again in John's Gospel.

CHAPTER IV

1. *When therefore* (*Hōs oun*). Reference to 3:22f. the work of the Baptist and the jealousy of his disciples. *Oun* is very common in John's Gospel in such transitions. *The Lord* (*ho Kurios*). So the best manuscripts (Neutral Alexandrian), though the Western class has *ho Iēsous*. Mark usually has *ho Iēsous* and Luke often *ho Kurios*. In the narrative portion of John we have usually *ho Iēsous*, but *ho Kurios* in five passages (4:1; 6:23; 11:2; 20:20; 21:12). There is no reason why John should not apply *ho Kurios* to Jesus in the narrative sections as well as Luke. Bernard argues that these are "explanatory glosses," not in the first draft of the Gospel. But why? When John wrote his Gospel he certainly held Jesus to be *Kurios* (Lord) as Luke did earlier when he wrote both Gospel and Acts. This is hypercriticism. *Knew* (*egnō*). Second aorist active indicative of *ginōskō*. The Pharisees knew this obvious fact. It was easy for Jesus to know the attitude of the Pharisees about it (2:24). Already the Pharisees are suspicious of Jesus. *How that* (*hoti*). Declarative *hoti* (indirect assertion). *Was making and baptizing more disciples than John* (*pleionas mathētas poiei kai baptizei ē Iōanēs*). Present active indicative in both verbs retained in indirect discourse. Recall the tremendous success of John's early ministry (Mark 1:5 = Matt. 3:5 = Luke 3:7, 15) in order to see the significance of this statement that Jesus had forged ahead of him in popular favour. Already the Pharisees had turned violently against John who had called them broods of vipers. It is most likely that they drew John out about the marriage of Herod Antipas and got him involved directly with the tetrarch so as to have him cast into prison (Luke 3:19f.). Josephus (*Ant.* XVIII.

58

v. 2) gives a public reason for this act of Herod Antipas, the fear that John would "raise a rebellion," probably the public reason for his private vengeance as given by Luke. Apparently John was cast into prison, though recently still free (John 3:24), before Jesus left for Galilee. The Pharisees, with John out of the way, turn to Jesus with envy and hate.

2. *Although Jesus himself baptized not, but his disciples* (*kaitoige Iēsous autos ouk ebaptizen all' hoi mathētai autou*). Parenthetical explanation that applies also to 3:22. Imperfect tense means that it was not the habit of Jesus. This is the only N.T. instance of *kaitoige* (and yet indeed), compound conjunction (*kaitoi* in Acts 14:17; Heb. 4:3) with intensive particle *ge* added. This is the last mention of baptism under the direction of Jesus till the Great Commission (Matt. 28:19). It is possible that Jesus stopped the baptizing because of the excitement and the issue raised about his Messianic claims till after his resurrection when he enjoined it upon his disciples as a rite of public enlistment in his service.

3. *Left Judea* (*aphēken tēn Ioudaian*). Unusual use of *aphiēmi*. First (*Kappa*) aorist active indicative. Originally the word means to send away, to dismiss, to forsake, to forgive, to allow. Jesus uses it in this sense in 16:28. Evidently because Jesus did not wish to bring the coming conflict with the Pharisees to an issue yet. So he mainly avoids Jerusalem and Judea now till the end. Each time hereafter that Jesus appears in Jerusalem and Judea before the last visit there is an open breach with the Pharisees who attack him (John 5:1-47; 7:14-10:21; 10:22-42; 11:17-53). *Again into Galilee* (*palin eis tēn Galilaian*). Reference to 2:1-12. The Synoptics tell nothing of this early work in Perea (John 1:19-51), Galilee, or Judea (2:13-4:2). John supplements their records purposely.

4. *He must needs pass through Samaria* (*Edei de auton dierchesthai dia tēs Samarias*). Imperfect indicative of the

impersonal verb *dei* with subject infinitive (*dierchesthai*) and accusative of general reference (*auton*). Note repetition of *dia*. It was only necessary to pass through Samaria in going directly north from Judea to Galilee. In coming south from Galilee travellers usually crossed over the Jordan and came down through Perea to avoid the hostility of the Samaritans towards people who passed through their land to go to Jerusalem. Jesus once met this bitterness on going to the feast of tabernacles (Luke 9:51–56).

5. *So he cometh* (*erchetai oun*). Vivid present middle indicative and transitional *oun*. *Sychar* (*Suchar*). There is a dispute whether this is just a variation of Shechem as meaning "drunken-town" (Isa. 28:1) or "lying-town" (Hab. 2:18) or is a separate village near Shechem (Neapolis, Nablous) as the Talmud and Eusebius indicate. Apparently the present village Askar corresponds well with the site. The use of *polin* (city) does not mean that it was a large town. Mark and John use it freely for small places. *Parcel of ground* (*chōriou*). Old use of this diminutive of *chōros* or *chōra*, a piece of ground. *That Jacob gave to his son Joseph* (*ho edōken Iakōb tōi Iōsēph tōi huiōi autou*). See Gen. 33:19; 48:22. Relative *ho* is not attracted to case of *chōriou*. First aorist active indicative *edōken*.

6. *Jacob's well* (*pēgē tou Iakōb*). "A spring of Jacob" (here and verse 14), but *phrear* (well, pit, cistern) in verses 11 and 12. It is really a cistern 100 feet deep dug by a stranger apparently in a land of abundant springs (Gen. 26:19). *Wearied* (*kekopiakōs*). Perfect active participle of *kopiaō*, a state of weariness. The verb means to toil excessively (Luke 5:5). John emphasizes the human emotions of Jesus (1:14; 11:3, 33, 35, 38, 41f.; 12:27; 13:21; 19:28). *With his journey* (*ek tēs hodoiporias*). As a result (*ek*) of the journey. Old compound word from *hodoporos* (wayfarer), in N.T. only here and II Cor. 11:26. *Sat* (*ekathezeto*). Imperfect (descriptive) middle of *kathezomai*, "was sitting." *Thus* (*houtōs*).

Probably "thus wearied," graphic picture. *By the well (epi tēi pēgēi)*. Literally, "upon the curbstone of the well." *Sixth hour (hōs hektē)*. Roman time, about 6 P.M., the usual time for drawing water.

7. *There cometh (erchetai)*. Vivid historical present as in verse 5. *A woman of Samaria (gunē ek tēs Samarias)*. The country, not the city which was two hours away. *To draw water (antlēsai hudōr)*. First aorist active infinitive of purpose of *antleō* for which see 2:8f. Cf. Rebecca in Gen. 24:11, 17. *Give me to drink (dos moi pein)*. Second aorist active imperative of *didōmi* and second aorist active infinitive (object of *dos*) of *pinō*, shortened form of *piein*. A polite request.

8. *For (gar)*. Explanation of the reason for asking her. *Were gone away (apelēlutheisan)*. Past perfect of *aperchomai*, to go off. They had already gone before she came. To Sychar (5, 39). *To buy food (hina trophas agorasōsin)*. *Hina* in purpose clause with first aorist active subjunctive of *agorazō*, old verb from *agora* (marketplace). See Matt. 21:12. *Trophē* (nourishment) is old word from *trephō*, to nourish (Matt. 3:4). "Victuals" (plural).

9. *The Samaritan woman (hē gunē hē Samareitis)*. Different idiom from that in 7, "the woman the Samaritan." The Samaritans were a mixture by intermarriage of the Jews left in the land (II Chron. 30:6, 10; 34:9) with colonists from Babylon and other regions sent by Shalmaneser. They had had a temple of their own on Mt. Gerizim and still worshipped there. *Thou being a Jew (su Ioudaios ōn)*. Race antipathy was all the keener because the Samaritans were half Jews. *Drink (pein)*. Same infinitive form as in 7 and the object of *aiteis* (askest). *Of me (par' emou)*. "From me," ablative case with *para*. *For Jews have no dealings with Samaritans (ou gar sunchrōntai Ioudaioi Samareitais)*. Explanatory (gar) parenthesis of the woman's astonishment. Associative instrumental case with *sunchrōntai* (present middle indicative of

sunchraomai, compound in literary *Koiné*, here only in N.T.). The woman's astonishment is ironical according to Bernard. At any rate the disciples had to buy food in a Samaritan village and they were travelling through Samaria. Perhaps she was surprised that Jesus would drink out of her waterpot. The Western class omit this explanatory parenthesis of the author.

10. *Answered and said* (*apekrithē kai eipen*). As often (redundant) in John. The first aorist passive (*apekrithē*) is deponent, no longer passive in sense. *If thou knewest* (*ei ēideis*). Condition of second class, determined as unfulfilled, *ei* and past perfect *ēideis* (used as imperfect) in condition and *an*, and aorist active indicative in conclusion (*an ēitēsas kai an edōken*, note repetition of *an*, not always done). *The gift of God* (*tēn dōrean tou theou*). Naturally the gift mentioned in 3:16 (Westcott), the inexpressible gift (II Cor. 9:15). Some take it to refer to the living water below, but that is another allusion (metaphor) to 3:16. See Eph. 4:7 for Paul's use of both *charis* and *dōrea* (from *didōmi*, to give). *Who it is* (*tis estin*). She only knew that he was a Jew. This Messianic self-consciousness of Jesus is plain in John, but it is early in the Synoptics also. *Living water* (*hudōr zōn*). Running water like a spring or well supplied by springs. This Jacob's Well was filled by water from rains percolating through, a sort of cistern, good water, but not equal to a real spring which was always preferred (Gen. 26:19; Lev. 14:5; Numb. 19:17). Jesus, of course, is symbolically referring to himself as the Living Water though he does not say it in plain words as he does about the Living Bread (6:51). The phrase "the fountain of life" occurs in Prov. 13:14. Jesus supplies the water of life (John 7:39). Cf. Rev. 7:17; 22:1.

11. *Sir* (*Kurie*). So it has to mean here in the mouth of the Samaritan woman, not Lord. *Thou hast nothing to draw with and the well is deep* (*oute antlēma echeis kai to phrear estin*

bathu). This broken construction of *oute-kai* (neither — and) occurs in N.T. elsewhere only in III John 10. *Antlēma* (from *antleō*, to draw) is a late word for that which is drawn, then (Plutarch) for the act of drawing, and then for the rope as here to draw with. This well (*phrear*) is 100 feet deep and Jesus had no rope. The bucket of skin ("with three cross sticks at the mouth to keep it open," Vincent) was kept at the well to be let down by a goat's hair rope. *That living water* (*to hudōr to zōn*). "The water the living," with the article referring to the language of Jesus in verse 10. She is still thinking only of literal water.

12. *Art thou* (*Mē su ei*). Expecting a negative answer. *Greater than our father Jacob* (*meizōn ei tou patros hēmōn Iakōb*). Ablative case *patros* after the comparative adjective *meizōn* (positive *megas*). The Samaritans claimed descent from Jacob through Joseph (tribes of Ephraim and Manasseh). *Cattle* (*thremmata*). Old word from *trephō*, to nourish, nursling, child, flock, cattle. Only here in N.T.

13. *Every one that drinketh* (*pas ho pinōn*). Present active articular participle with *pas*, parallel to the indefinite relative with the second aorist active subjunctive (*hos an piēi*) in verse 14. With this difference in the tenses used (*pinōn*, keep on drinking, *piēi*, once for all). Note *ek* and the ablative both times, out of the water. Jesus pointed to the well ("this water").

14. *That I shall give him* (*hou egō dōsō autōi*). Relative *hou* attracted to the case (genitive) of the antecedent (*hudatos*). Future active indicative of *didōmi*. *Shall never thirst* (*ou mē dipsēsei eis ton aiona*). The double negative *ou mē* is used with either the future indicative as here or the aorist subjunctive, the strongest possible negative. See both constructions (*ou mē peinasei* and *ou me dipsēsei*) in John 6:35. Jesus has not answered the woman's question save by the necessary implication here that he is superior to Jacob. *A well of water springing up unto eternal life* (*pēgē hudatos*

hallomenou eis zōēn aiōnion). "Spring (or fountain) of water leaping (bubbling up) unto life eternal." Present middle participle of *hallomai*, old verb, in N.T. only here and Acts 3:8; 14:10. The woman's curiosity is keenly excited about this new kind of water.

15. *Sir* (*Kurie*). Not yet "Lord" for her. See verse 11. *This water* (*touto to hudōr*). This peculiar kind of water. She did not grasp the last phrase "unto life eternal," and speaks half ironically of "this water." *That I thirst not* (*hina mē dipsō*). Final clause with *hina*, alluding to the words of Jesus, water that will prevent thirst. *Neither come* (*mēde dierchōmai*). Carrying on the negative purpose with present middle subjunctive, "nor keep on coming" as she has to do once or twice every day. She is evidently puzzled and yet attracted.

16. *Go, call thy husband* (*Hupage phōnēson sou ton andra*). Two imperatives (present active, first aorist active). Had she started to leave after her perplexed reply? Her frequent trips to the well were partly for her husband. We may not have all the conversation preserved, but clearly Jesus by this sudden sharp turn gives the woman a conviction of sin and guilt without which she cannot understand his use of water as a metaphor for eternal life.

17. *I have no husband* (*ouk echō andra*). The Greek *anēr* means either "man" or "husband." She had her "man," but he was not a legal "husband." Her language veils her deceit. *Thou saidst well* (*kalōs eipes*). Jesus saw through the double sense of her language and read her heart as he only can do, a supernatural gift of which John often speaks (1:48; 2:24f.; 5:20). *For thou hast had five husbands* (*pente gar andras esches*). "For thou didst have five men." Second aorist (constative) active indicative of *echō*. *Is not thy husband* (*ouk estin sou anēr*). In the full and legal sense of *anēr*, not a mere "man." *This hast thou said truly* (*touto alēthes eirēkas*). "This a true thing thou hast said." Note absence

of article with *alēthes* (predicate accusative). Perfect active indicative *eirēkas* here, not aorist *eipes* (verse 17).

19. *Sir* (*Kurie*). So still. *I perceive* (*theōrō*). "I am beginning to perceive" from what you say, your knowledge of my private life (verse 29). See 2:23 for *theōreō* which John's Gospel has 23 times, of bodily sight (20:6, 14), of mental contemplation (12:45; 14:17). See both *theōreō* and *optomai* in 1:51 and 16:16. *That thou art a prophet* (*hoti prophētēs ei su*). "That a prophet art thou" (emphasis on "thou"). She felt that this was the explanation of his knowledge of her life and she wanted to change the subject at once to the outstanding theological dispute.

20. *In this mountain* (*en tōi orei toutōi*). Jacob's Well is at the foot of Mount Gerizim toward which she pointed. Sanballat erected a temple on this mountain which was destroyed by John Hyrcanus B.C. 129. Abraham (Gen. 12:7) and Jacob (Gen. 33:20) set up altars at Shechem. On Gerizim were proclaimed the blessings recorded in Deut. 28. The Samaritan Pentateuch records an altar set up on Gerizim that is on Ebal (over 200 feet higher than Gerizim) in the Hebrew (Deut. 27:4). The Samaritans held that Abraham offered up Isaac on Gerizim. The Samaritans kept up this worship on this mountain and a handful do it still. *And ye say* (*kai humeis legete*). Emphasis on *humeis* (ye). Ye Jews. *Ought to worship* (*proskunein dei*). "Must worship," as of necessity (*dei*). The woman felt that by raising this theological wrangle she would turn the attention of Jesus away from herself and perhaps get some light on the famous controversy. *Proskuneō* in John is always worship, not just respect.

21. *Believe me* (*pisteue moi*). Correct text. Present active imperative. Unique phrase in place of the common *amēn amēn* (verily, verily). *The hour cometh* (*erchetai hōra*). "There is coming an hour." The same idiom occurs also in John 4:34; 5:25, 28; 16:2, 25, 32. *Neither in this mountain nor in*

Jerusalem (oute en tōi orei toutōi oute en Ierosolumois). The
worship of God will be emancipated from bondage to place.
Both Jews and Samaritans are wrong as to the "necessity"
(dei). "These ancient rivalries will disappear when the
spirituality of true religion is fully realized." Jesus told
this sinful woman one of his greatest truths.

22. *That which ye know not (ho ouk oidate)*. Cf. Acts 17:23.
"You know whom to worship, but you do not know him"
(Westcott). The Samaritans rejected the prophets and the
Psalms and so cut themselves off from the fuller knowledge
of God. *We (hēmeis)*. We Jews. Jesus is a Jew as he fully
recognizes (Matt. 15:24). *That which we know (ho oidamen)*.
Neuter singular relative as before. The Jews, as the chosen
people, had fuller revelations of God (Psa. 147:19f.; Rom.
9:3–5). But even so the Jews as a whole failed to recognize
God in Christ (1:11, 26; 7:28). *For salvation is from the Jews
(hoti hē sōtēria ek tōn Ioudaiōn estin)*. "The salvation," the
Messianic salvation which had long been the hope and guiding star of the chosen people (Luke 1:69, 71, 77; Acts 13:26,
47). It was for the whole world (John 3:17), but it comes
"out of" *(ek)* the Jews. This tremendous fact should never
be forgotten, however unworthy the Jews may have proved
of their privilege. The Messiah, God's Son, was a Jew.

23. *And now is (kai nun estin)*. See this same phrase
in 5:25. This item could not be added in verse 21 for local
worship was not abolished, but spiritual independence of
place was called for at once. So contrast 5:25 and 28, 16:25
and 32. *The true worshippers (hoi alēthinoi proskunētai)*.
See 1:9 for *alēthinos* (genuine). *Proskunētēs* is a late word
from *proskuneō*, to bow the knee, to worship, occurs here
only in N.T., but is found in one pre-Christian inscription
(Deissmann, *Light*, etc., p. 101) and in one of the 3rd century A.D. (Moulton & Milligan, *Vocabulary*). *In spirit and
truth (en pneumati kai alētheiāi)*. This is what matters, not
where, but how (in reality, in the spirit of man, the highest

part of man, and so in truth). All this is according to the Holy
Spirit (Rom. 8:5) who is the Spirit of truth (John 16:13).
Here Jesus has said the final word on worship, one needed today. *Seeketh* (*zētei*). The Father has revealed himself in the
Son who is the truth (John 14:6,9). It does matter whether we
have a true conception of God whom we worship. *To be his
worshippers* (*tous proskunountas auton*). Rather, "seeks such
as those who worship him" (predicate accusative articular
participle in apposition with *toioutous* (such). John pictures
the Father as seeking worshippers, a doctrine running all
through the Gospel (3:16; 6:44; 15:16 and I John 4:10).

24. *God is a Spirit* (*pneuma ho theos*). More precisely,
"God is Spirit" as "God is Light" (I John 1:5), "God is
Love" (I John 4:8). In neither case can we read Spirit is
God, Light is God, Love is God. The non-corporeality of
God is clearly stated and the personality of God also. All
this is put in three words for the first time. *Must* (*dei*).
Here is the real necessity (*dei*), not the one used by the
woman about the right place of worship (verse 20).

25. *Messiah cometh* (*Messias erchetai*). Hebrew word in
N.T. only here and 1:41 and explained by *Christos* in both
places. The Samaritans looked for a Messiah, a prophet
like Moses (Deut. 18:18). Simon Magus gave himself out
in Samaria as some great one and had a large following
(Acts 8:9). Pilate quelled an uprising in Samaria over a
fanatical Messianic claimant (Josephus, *Ant.* XVIII. iv. 1).
When he is come (*hotan elthēi ekeinos*). "Whenever that
one comes." Indefinite temporal clause with *hotan* (*hote, an*)
and the second aorist active subjunctive. Wistfully she
turns to this dim hope as a bare possibility about this
strange "prophet." *He will declare unto us all things* (*anaggelei hēmin hapanta*). Future active indicative of *anaggellō*,
old and common verb to announce fully (*ana*, up and down).
See also 16:13. Perhaps here is light on the knowledge of
her life by Jesus as well as about the way to worship God.

26. *I that speak unto thee am he* (*Egō eimi ho lalōn soi*).
"I am he, the one speaking to thee." In plain language
Jesus now declares that he is the Messiah as he does to the
blind man (John 9:37).

27. *Upon this* (*epi toutōi*). This idiom only here in N.T.
At this juncture. Apparently the woman left at once when
the disciples came. *They marvelled* (*ethaumazon*). Imperfect
active describing the astonishment of the disciples as they
watched Jesus talking with a woman. *Was speaking* (*elalei*).
As in 2:25, so here the tense is changed in indirect discourse
from *lalei* to *elalei*, an unusual idiom in Greek. However,
hoti here may be "because" and then the imperfect is regular. It is not "with the woman" (*meta tēs gunaikos*), but
simply "with a woman" (*meta gunaikos*). There was a
rabbinical precept: "Let no one talk with a woman in the
street, no, not with his own wife" (Lightfoot, *Hor, Hebr.* iii.
287). The disciples held Jesus to be a rabbi and felt that
he was acting in a way beneath his dignity. *Yet no man said*
(*oudeis mentoi eipen*). John remembers through the years
their amazement and also their reverence for Jesus and un-
willingness to reflect upon him.

28. *Left her waterpot* (*aphēken tēn hudrian*). First aorist
active indicative of *aphiēmi*, ingressive aorist, in her excitement and embarrassment. It was too large for speed anyhow (2:6). *And says* (*kai legei*). Graphic historic present
indicative again.

29. *All things that ever I did* (*panta ha epoiēsa*). *Ha*, not
hosa (as many as), no "ever" in the Greek. But a guilty
conscience (verse 18f.) led her to exaggerate a bit. *Can this
be the Christ?* (*mēti houtos estin ho Christos;*). She is already
convinced herself (verses 26f.), but she puts the question
in a hesitant form to avoid arousing opposition. With a
woman's intuition she avoided *ouk* and uses *mēti*. She does
not take sides, but piques their curiosity.

30. *They went out* (*exēlthon*). Second aorist (effective)

indicative of *exerchomai*, at once and in a rush. *And were coming to him (kai ērchonto pros auton).* Imperfect middle, graphically picturing the long procession as they approached Jesus.

31. *In the meanwhile (en tōi metaxu).* Supply *kairoi* or *chronoi.* See *to metaxu Sabbaton*, "the next Sabbath" (Acts 13:42) and *en tōi metaxu* (Luke 8:1). *Metaxu* means between. *Prayed him (ērōtōn auton).* Imperfect active, "kept beseeching him." For this late (*Koinē*) use of *erōtaō*, to beseech, instead of the usual sense to question see also verses 40 and 47. Their concern for the comfort of Jesus overcame their surprise about the woman.

32. *Meat (brōsin).* Originally the act of eating (Rom. 14:17) from *bibrōskō*, but soon and commonly as that which is eaten like *brōma* once in John (verse 34). So here and 6:27, 55. Cf. vernacular English "good eating," "good eats." *I . . . ye (egō . . . humeis).* Emphatic contrast. Spiritual food Jesus had.

33. *Hath any man brought him aught to eat? (Mē tis ēnegken autōi phagein;).* Negative answer expected (*mē*). "Did any one bring him (something) to eat?" During our absence, they mean. Second aorist active indicative of *pherō (ēnegken)* and second aorist active infinitive of *esthiō (phagein)*, defective verbs both of them. See 4:7 for like infinitive construction (*dos pein*).

34. *To do the will (hina poiēsō to thelēma).* Non-final use of *hina* and the first aorist active subjunctive as subject or predicate nominative as in 6:29; 15:8; 17:3. The Messianic consciousness of Jesus is clear and steady (5:30; 6:38). He never doubted that the Father sent him. *And to accomplish his work (kai teleiōsō autou to ergon).* *Hina* understood with *teleiōsō* in like idiom, first aorist active subjunctive of *teleioō* (from *teleios*), to bring to an end. See 5:36. In 17:4 (the Intercessory Prayer) he will say that he has done (*teleiōsas*) this task which the Father gave him to do. On the Cross

Jesus will cry *Tetelestai* (It is finished). He will carry through the Father's programme (John 3:16). That is his "food." He had been doing that in winning the woman to God.

35. *Say not ye?* (*Ouch humeis legete;*). It is not possible to tell whether Jesus is alluding to a rural proverb of which nothing is known about there being four months from seedtime to harvest (a longer time than four months in fact) or whether he means that it was then actually four months to harvest. In the latter sense, since harvest began about the middle of April, it would be December when Jesus spoke. *There are yet four months* (*eti tetramēnos estin*). The use of *eti* (yet) and the fact that the space between seedtime and harvest is longer than four months (*tetra*, Aeolic for *tessara*, and *mēn*, month) argue against the proverb idea. *And then cometh the harvest* (*kai ho therismos erchetai*). "And the harvest (*therismos*, from *therizō*, rare in Greek writers) comes." The possible Iambic verse here is purely accidental as in 5:14. *Lift up your eyes* (*eparate tous ophthalmous humōn*). First aorist active imperative of *epairō*. Deliberate looking as in John 6:5 where *theaomai* also is used as here. *Fields* (*chōras*). Cultivated or ploughed ground as in Luke 21:21. *White* (*leukai*). Ripened grain like grey hair (Matt. 5:36). *Already unto harvest* (*pros therismon ēdē*). Probably *ēdē* (already) goes with verse 36. The Samaritans could already be seen approaching and they were the field "white for harvest." This is the meaning of Christ's parable. If it is the spring of the year and Christ can point to the ripened grain, the parable is all the plainer, but it is not dependent on this detail. Recall the parable of the sower in Matthew 13.

36. *Already he that reapeth receiveth wages* (*ēdē ho therizōn misthon lambanei*). The spiritual harvester can gather his harvest without waiting four months. Jesus is reaping a harvest right now by the conversion of this woman. The labourer is worthy of his hire (Luke 10:7; II Tim. 2:6). John does not use *misthos* (reward) again, but *karpos* (15:2–16),

"fruit for life eternal" (cf. 4:14). *That he that soweth and he that reapeth may rejoice together* (*hina ho speirōn homou chairēi kai ho therizōn*). Final use of *hina* with present active subjunctive of *chairō*, to rejoice, in the singular with *ho speirōn* (the sower) and to be repeated with *ho therizōn* (the reaper). The adverb *homou* (together) elsewhere in N.T. only 20:4; 21:2; Acts 2:1. Usually considerable time passes between the sowing and the reaping as in verse 35. Amos (9:13) spoke of the time when "the ploughman shall overtake the reaper" and that has happened here with the joy of the harvest time (Isa. 9:3). Jesus the Sower and the disciples as the reapers are here rejoicing simultaneously.

37. *For herein* (*en gar toutōi*). In this relation between the sower and the reaper. *The saying* (*ho logos*). Like I Tim. 1:15; 3:1, etc. Probably a proverb that is particularly true (*alēthinos* for which see 1:9) in the spiritual realm. *One soweth, and another reapeth* (*allos estin ho speirōn kai allos ho therizōn*). "One is the sower and another the reaper." It is sad when the sower misses the joy of reaping (Job 31:8) and has only the sowing in tears (Psa. 126:5f.). This may be the punishment for sin (Deut. 28:30; Micah 6:15). Sometimes one reaps where he has not sown (Deut. 6:11; Josh. 24:13). It is the prerogative of the Master to reap (Matt. 25:26f.), but Jesus here lets the disciples share his joy.

38. *I sent* (*egō apesteila*). Emphatic use of *egō* and first aorist active indicative of *apostellō* common in John for to send. *Whereon ye have not laboured* (*ho ouch humeis kekopiakate*). Perfect active indicative of *kopiaō* for which see 4:6. So also *kekopiakasin* in next line. The disciples had done no sowing here in Sychar, only Jesus and the woman. *Others* (*alloi:* Jesus, the Baptist, the prophets). *And ye* (*kai humeis*). Emphatic contrast. *Have entered* (*eiselēluthate*). Perfect active indicative of *eiserchomai*. *Into their labour* (*eis ton kopon autōn*). Into the fruit and blessed results of their toil (*kopos*). This is always true as seen in Acts 8:5–7, 14f.

39. *Because of the saying of the woman who testified* (*dia ton logon tēs gunaikos marturousēs*). She bore her witness clearly and with discretion. She told enough to bring her neighbours to Christ. They knew her evil life and she frankly confessed Christ's rebuke to her. She had her share in this harvest. How timid and cowardly we often are today in not giving our testimony for Christ to our neighbour.

40. *Two days* (*duo hēmeras*). Accusative of extent of time. They wanted to cultivate the acquaintance of Jesus. So he remained in Sychar in a continuous revival, a most unexpected experience when one recalls the feeling between the Jews and the Samaritans (4:9). The reaping went on gloriously.

41. *Many more* (*polloi pleious*). "More by much" (instrumental case *polloi*) in comparison with just "many" (*polloi*) of verse 39. Jesus was reaping more rapidly than the woman did. But all were rejoicing that so many "believed" (*episteusan*, really believed).

42. *Not because of thy speaking* (*ouketi dia tēn sēn lalian*). "No longer because of thy talk," good and effective as that was. *Lalia* (cf. *laleō*) is talk, talkativeness, mode of speech, one's vernacular, used by Jesus of his own speech (John 8:43). *We have heard* (*akēkoamen*). Perfect active indicative of *akouō*, their abiding experience. *For ourselves* (*autoi*). Just "ourselves." *The Saviour of the world* (*ho sōtēr tou kosmou*). See Matt. 1:21 for *sōsei* used of Jesus by the angel Gabriel. John applies the term *sōtēr* to Jesus again in I John 4:14. Jesus had said to the woman that salvation is of the Jews (verse 22). He clearly told the Samaritans during these two days that he was the Messiah as he had done to the woman (verse 26) and explained that to mean Saviour of Samaritans as well as Jews. Sanday thinks that probably John puts this epithet of Saviour in the mouth of the Samaritans, but adds: "At the same time it is possible that such an epithet might be employed by them merely as synonymous

with Messiah." But why "merely"? Was it not natural for
these Samaritans who took Jesus as their "Saviour," Jew
as he was, to enlarge the idea to the whole world? Bernard
has this amazing statement on John 4:42: "That in the
first century Messiah was given the title *sōtēr* is not proven."
The use of "saviour and god" for Ptolemy in the third
century B.C. is well known. "The ample materials collected
by Magic show that the full title of honour, Saviour of the
world, with which St. John adorns the Master, was bestowed
with sundry variations in the Greek expression on Julius
Caesar, Augustus, Claudius, Vespasian, Titus, Trajan, Ha-
drian, and other Emperors in inscriptions in the Hellenistic
East" (Deissmann, *Light, etc.*, p. 364). Perhaps Bernard
means that the Jews did not call Messiah Saviour. But what
of it? The Romans so termed their emperors and the New
Testament so calls Christ (Luke 2:11; John 4:42; Acts 5:31;
13:23; Phil. 3:20; Eph. 5:23; Titus 1:4; 2:13; 3:6; II Tim.
1:10; II Peter 1:1, 11; 2:20; 3:2, 18). All these are writings
of the first century A.D. The Samaritan villagers rise to the
conception that he was the Saviour of the world.

43. *After the two days* (*Meta tas duo hēmeras*). Those in
verse 40. *Into Galilee* (*eis tēn Galilaian*). As he had started
to do (verse 3) before the interruption at Sychar.

44. *For Jesus himself testified* (*autos gar Iēsous emarturēsen*). John's explanation of the conduct of Jesus by
quoting a proverb often used by Jesus (Mark 6:4; Matt.
13:57; Luke 4:24 in reference to Nazareth), but not necessarily used by Jesus on this occasion. A similar proverb has
been found in Plutarch, Pliny, Seneca. *A prophet hath no
honour in his own country* (*prophētēs en tēi idiāi patridi timēn
ouk echei*). What is meant by *patridi*? In the Synoptics
(Luke 4:24; Mark 6:4; Matt. 13:57) the reference is to
Nazareth where he was twice rejected. But what has John
in mind in quoting it here? He probably knew the quotations in the Synoptics. Does John refer to Judea by "his own

country"? If so, the application hardly fits for he had already explained that Jesus was leaving Judea because he was too popular there (4:1-3). If he means Galilee, he immediately mentions the cordial welcome accorded Jesus there (verse 45). But even so this is probably John's meaning for he is speaking of the motive of Jesus in going into Galilee where he had not yet laboured and where he apparently had no such fame as in Judea and now in Samaria.

45. *So when* (*hote oun*). Transitional use of *oun*, sequence, not consequence. *Received him* (*edexanto auton*). First aorist middle of *dechomai*, "welcomed him." Jesus had evidently anticipated a quiet arrival. *Having seen* (*heōrakotes*). Perfect active participle of *horaō*. Note *theōrountes* in 2:23 about this very thing at the feast in Jerusalem. The miracles of Jesus at that first passover made a stir. *For they also went* (*kai autoi gar ēlthon*). The Samaritans did not go and so Jesus was a new figure to them, but the Galileans, as orthodox Jews, did go and so were predisposed in his favour.

46. *Again* (*palin*). A second time. *Unto Cana* (*eis tēn Kana*). Note article, "the Cana of Galilee" already mentioned in 2:1. *Where he made the water wine* (*hopou epoiēsen to hudōr oinon*). That outstanding first miracle would still be remembered in Cana and would indicate that Jesus had some friends there. *Nobleman* (*basilikos*). One connected with the king (*basileus*), whether by blood or by office. Probably here it is one of the courtiers of Herod the tetrarch of Galilee, Chuzas (Luke 8:3), Manaen (Acts 13:1), or some one else. Some of the manuscripts used *basiliskos*, a petty king, a diminutive of *basileus*. *Was sick* (*ēsthenei*). Imperfect active of *astheneō* (*a* privative and *sthenos*, without strength, Matt. 25:36), continued sick. *At Capernaum* (*en Kapharnaoum*). Some miles from Cana near where the Jordan enters the Sea of Galilee.

47. *When he heard* (*akousas*). First aorist active participle
of *akouō*. The news spread rapidly about Jesus. *Was come*
(*hēkei*). Present active indicative of *hēkō*, one of the perfective presents, retained in indirect discourse. He had heard
the people talk about the miracles in Jerusalem and the
first one in Cana. *Went and besought* (*apēlthen kai ērōta*).
Ingressive aorist indicative (went off at once) and imperfect
active (*ērōta*, began to beg and kept it up). *That he would
come down* (*hina katabēi*, *hina* and second aorist active subjunctive of *katabainō*, come down at once) *and heal his son*
(*kai iasētai autou ton huion*, *hina* construction, sub-final use
or object clause, with first aorist middle subjunctive of
iaomai, completely heal). *For he was at the point of death*
(*ēmellen gar apothnēskein*). Reason (*gar*) for the urgency.
Imperfect active of *mellō* with present active infinitive old
and common verb for what is about to be and it is used with
the infinitive present as here, the aorist infinitive (Rev.
13:16), or the future infinitive (Acts 11:28). The idiom is used
of the impending death of Jesus (John 11:51; 12:33; 18:32).

48. *Except ye see* (*ean mē idēte*). Condition of the third
class (*ean mē*, negative, with second aorist active subjunctive
of *horaō*). Jesus is not discounting his "signs and wonders"
(*sēmeia kai terata*, both words together here only in John,
though common in N.T. as in Matt. 24:24; Mark 13:22
Acts 2:19, 22, 43; II Thess 2:9; Heb. 2:4), though he does
seem disappointed that he is in Galilee regarded as a mere
miracle worker. *Ye will in no wise believe* (*ou mē pisteusēte*).
Strong double negative with aorist active subjunctive of
pisteuō, picturing the stubborn refusal of people to believe
in Christ without miracles.

49. *Sir* (*Kurie*). See 1:38. *Come down* (*katabēthi*). Second
aorist active imperative, tense and tone of urgency. *Ere my
child die* (*prin apothanein to paidion mou*). Regular idiom
with *prin* in positive clause, second aorist active infinitive of
apothnēskō and accusative of general reference, "before dying

as to my child." Bengel notes that he only thought Jesus had power before death as even Martha and Mary felt at first (11:21, 32). But the father's heart goes out to Jesus.

50. *Thy son liveth* (*ho huios sou zēi*). "Thy son is living," and will not now die, Jesus means. Words too good and gracious to be true. His son is healed without Jesus even going to Capernaum, "absent treatment" so to speak, but without the cure being absent. *Believed the word* (*episteusen tōi logōi*). Instantaneous faith (aorist active indicative), trusted the word (dative case *logōi*). *Went his way* (*eporeueto*). Inchoative imperfect middle, "started on his way," acted on his faith.

51. *As he was now going down* (*ēdē autou katabainontos*). Genitive absolute in spite of the fact that *autōi* (associative instrumental case with *hupēntēsan* aorist active indicative of *hupantaō*) is near. *That his son lived* (*hoti ho pais autou zēi*). Present active indicative preserved in indirect discourse (cf. the words of Jesus in verse 50). Note *pais* here (only example in John), *huios* in 50, *paidion* (diminutive of tenderness) in 49.

52. *Inquired* (*eputheto*). Second aorist middle indicative of *punthanomai*. *Began to mend* (*kompsoteron eschen*). Second aorist ingressive active indicative of *echō* (took a turn, got better) and comparative of adverb *kompsōs*. Arrian (*Epictetus* iii. 10.13) has *kompsōs echeis* from a physician, "Thou hast it fine," "Thou art doing finely." The papyri give several similar examples. *Kompsōs* (neat) is from *komeō*, to take care of. *At the seventh hour* (*hōran hebdomēn*). The accusative case without a preposition as in Rev. 3:3, though we have *peri hōran enatēn* (about the ninth hour) in Acts 10:3. See the accusative also in Ex. 9:18 *tautēn tēn hōran aurion* (tomorrow about this hour). The accusative has the notion of extension and can be thus loosely used. It can even mean here "during the seventh hour." In verse 53 the locative is more exact, "at that hour" (*en ekeinēi tēi hōrāi*). The seventh hour would be (Roman time) seven P.M.

53. *So the father knew* (*egnō oun ho patēr*). Second aorist active indicative of *ginōskō*. Inferential use of *oun*. *Himself believed* (*episteusen autos*). Not just the word of Jesus (verse 50), but complete faith in Jesus himself as the Messiah, absolute use of *pisteuō* as in 1:7. *And his whole house* (*kai hē oikia autou*). All his family, the first example of a whole family believing in Jesus like the later case of Crispus (Acts 18:8).

54. *The second sign that* (*deuteron sēmeion*). No article, simply predicate accusative, "This again a second sign did Jesus having come out of Judea into Galilee." The first one was also in Cana (2:1ff.), but many were wrought in Jerusalem also (2:23).

CHAPTER V

1. *After these things (meta tauta).* John is fond of this vague phrase (3:22; 6:1). He does not mean that this incident follows immediately. He is supplementing the Synoptic Gospels and does not attempt a full story of the work of Jesus. Some scholars needlessly put chapter 5 after chapter 6 because in chapter 6 Jesus is in Galilee as at the end of chapter 4. But surely it is not incongruous to think of Jesus making a visit to Jerusalem before the events in chapter 6 which undoubtedly come within a year of the end (6:4). *A feast of the Jews (heortē tōn Ioudaiōn).* Some manuscripts have the article (hē) "the feast" which would naturally mean the passover. As a matter of fact there is no way of telling what feast it was which Jesus here attended. Even if it was not the passover, there may well be another passover not mentioned besides the three named by John (2:13, 23;6:4:12:1). *Went up (anebē).* Second aorist active indicative of *anabainō.* It was up towards Jerusalem from every direction save from Hebron.

2. *There is (estin).* Bengel argues that this proves a date before the destruction of Jerusalem, but it is probably only John's vivid memory. *By the sheep gate (epi tēi probatikēi).* Supply *pulēi* (gate) which occurs with the adjective *probatikē* (pertaining to sheep, *probata*) in Neh. 3:1, 22. *A pool (kolumbēthra).* A diving or swimming pool (from *kolumbaō*, to swim, Acts 27:43), old word, only here in N.T. *Which is called (hē epilegomenē).* "The surnamed" (present passive participle, only N.T. example except Acts 15:40 first aorist middle participle *epilexamenos*). *In Hebrew (Ebraisti).* "In Aramaic" strictly as in 19:13, 17, 20; 20:16; Rev. 9:11; 16:16. *Bethesda (Bethesda,* or House of Mercy. So A C Syr cu).

78

Aleph D L 33 have *Bethzatha* or House of the Olive, while B W Vulg. Memph. have *Bethsaida*. *Having five porches* (*pente stoas echousa*). *Stoa* was a covered colonnade where people can gather from which Stoic comes (Acts 17:18). See John 10:23; Acts 3:11. Schick in 1888 found twin pools north of the temple near the fortress of Antonia one of which has five porches. It is not, however, certain that this pool existed before A.D. 70 when the temple was destroyed (Sanday, *Sacred Sites of the Gospels*, p. 55). Some have identified it with the Pool of Siloam (9:7), though John distinguishes them. There is also the Virgin's Well, called the Gusher, because it periodically bubbles over from a natural spring, a kind of natural siphon. This is south of the temple in the Valley of Kedron and quite possibly the real site.

3. *In these* (*en tautais*). In these five porches. *Lay* (*katekeito*). Imperfect middle of *katakeimai*, to lie down, singular number because *plēthos* (multitude) is a collective substantive. *Withered* (*xērōn*). Old adjective *xēros* for dry, wasted as the hand (Matt. 12:10). The oldest and best manuscripts omit what the Textus Receptus adds here "waiting for the moving of the water" (*ekdechomenon tēn tou hudatos kinēsin*), a Western and Syrian addition to throw light on the word *tarachthēi* (is troubled) in verse 7.

4. All of this verse is wanting in the oldest and best manuscripts like Aleph B C D W 33 Old Syriac, Coptic versions, Latin Vulgate. It is undoubtedly added, like the clause in verse 3, to make clearer the statement in verse 7. Tertullian is the earliest writer to mention it. The Jews explained the healing virtues of the intermittent spring by the ministry of angels. But the periodicity of such angelic visits makes it difficult to believe. It is a relief to many to know that the verse is spurious.

5. *Which had been thirty and eight years* (*triakonta kai oktō etē echōn*). Literally, "having thirty and eight years," "having spent thirty and eight years."

6. *Knew that he had been a long time* (*gnous hoti polun ēdē chronon echei*). How Jesus "knew" (*gnous*, second aorist active participle of *ginōskō*) we are not told, whether supernatural knowledge (2:24f.) or observation or overhearing people's comments. In *ēdē echei* we have a progressive present active indicative, "he has already been having much time" (*chronon*, accusative of extent of time). *Wouldest thou be made whole?* (*Theleis hugiēs genesthai;*). "Dost thou wish to become whole?" Predicate nominative *hugiēs* with *genesthai* (second aorist middle infinitive). It was a pertinent and sympathetic question.

7. *When the water is troubled* (*hotan tarachthēi to hudōr*). Indefinite temporal clause with *hotan* and the first aorist passive subjunctive of *tarassō*, old verb to agitate (Matt. 2:3). The popular belief was that, at each outflow of this intermittent spring, there was healing power in the water for the first one getting in. *To put me into the pool* (*hina balēi me eis tēn kolumbēthran*). Final use of *hina* and the second aorist active subjunctive of *ballō*, "that he throw me in" quickly before any one else. For this use of *ballō* see Mark 7:30; Luke 16:20. *But while I am coming* (*en hōi de erchomai*). Temporal use of the relative, "in which time" (*chronōi* or *kairōi* understood). *Egō* (I) is emphatic.

8. *Arise, take up thy bed, and walk* (*Egeire, āron ton krabatton sou kai peripatei*). Present active imperative of *egeirō*, a sort of exclamation, like our "Get up." The first active imperative (*āron* of *airō*) means to pick up the pallet, and then "go on walking" (present active imperative of *peripateō*). For *krabatton* (pallet) see Mark 2:2-12; 6:55; Acts 5:15; 9:33.

9. *Took up his bed and walked* (*ēre ton krabatton autou kai periepatei*). The same distinction in tenses in the same verbs preserved, punctiliar action in *ēre* (first aorist active of *airō*, took it up at once) and linear act (imperfect active of *peripateō*, went on walking). *The sabbath on that day* (*sabbaton*

en ekeinēi tēi hēmerāi). The first of the violations of the Sabbath rules of the Jews by Jesus in Jerusalem that led to so much bitterness (cf. 9:14, 16). This controversy will spread to Galilee on Christ's return there (Mark 2:23–3:6 =· Matt. 12:1–14 = Luke 6:1–11).

10. *Unto him that was cured* (*tōi tetherapeumenōi*). Perfect passive articular participle of *therapeuō* (only example in John), "to the healed man." See Matt. 8:7. *To take up thy bed* (*ārai ton krabatton*). The very words of Jesus (verse 8), only infinitive (first aorist active). Carrying burdens was considered unlawful on the Sabbath (Ex. 23:12; Neh. 13:19; Jer. 17:21). Stoning was the rabbinical punishment. The healing of the man was a minor detail.

11. *But he answered* (*hos de apekrithē*). Demonstrative *hos* (But this one) and deponent use of *apekrithē* (first aorist passive indicative of *apokrinomai* with no passive force). *The same* (*ekeinos*). "That one," emphatic demonstrative as often in John (1:18, 33; 9:37; 10:1, etc.). The man did not know who Jesus was nor even his name. He quotes the very words of Jesus. *Whole* (*hugiē*). Predicate accusative agreeing with *me* (me).

12. *Who is the man?* (*Tis estin ho anthrōpos;*). Contemptuous expression, "Who is the fellow?" They ask about the command to violate the Sabbath, not about the healing.

13. *He that was healed* (*ho iatheis*). First aorist passive articular participle of *iaomai* (John's usual word). *Who it was* (*tis estin*). Present tense preserved in indirect question. *Had conveyed himself away* (*exeneusen*). First aorist active indicative of *ekneō*, old verb to swim out, to slip out, or from *ekneuō*, to turn out, to turn the head to one side (to one side with which compare *eneneuon*, they nodded, Luke 1:62). Either of these verbs can explain the form here. The aorist tense simply states an antecedent action without being a pastperfect. *A multitude being in the place* (*ochlou ontos en tōi topōi*). Genitive absolute and the reason for Christ's departure.

14. *Findeth him* (*heuriskei auton*). Dramatic present as in
1:45, possibly after search as in 9:35. *Sin no more* (*mēketi
hamartane*). "No longer go on sinning." Present active
imperative with *mēketi*, a clear implication that disease was
due to personal sin as is so often the case. Jesus used the
same words to the woman taken in adultery in the spurious
passage (John 8:11). He had suffered for 38 years. All sickness is not due to personal sin (9:3), but much is and nature
is a hard paymaster. Jesus is here living up to his name
(Matt. 1:21). *Lest a worse thing befall thee* (*hina mē cheiron
soi ti genētai*). Negative final clause with second aorist
middle subjunctive of *ginomai*. *Cheiron* is comparative of
kakos, bad. Worse than the illness of 38 years, bad as that
is. He will now be sinning against knowledge.

15. *Went away and told* (*apēlthen kai eipen*). Both aorist
active indicatives. Instead of giving heed to the warning of
Jesus about his own sins he went off and told the Jews that
now he knew who the man was who had commanded him
to take up his bed on the Sabbath Day, to clear himself
with the ecclesiastics and escape a possible stoning. *That
it was Jesus* (*hoti Iēsous estin*). Present indicative preserved
in indirect discourse. The man was either ungrateful and
wilfully betrayed Jesus or he was incompetent and did not
know that he was bringing trouble on his benefactor. In
either case one has small respect for him.

16. *Persecute* (*ediōkon*). Inchoative imperfect, "began to
persecute" and kept it up. They took this occasion as one
excuse (*dia touto*, because of this). They disliked Jesus when
here first (2:18) and were suspicious of his popularity (4:1).
Now they have cause for an open breach. *Because he did*
(*hoti epoiei*). Imperfect active, not just this one act, but he
was becoming a regular Sabbath-breaker. The Pharisees
will watch his conduct on the Sabbath henceforth (Mark
2:23; 3:2).

17. *Answered* (*apekrinato*). Regular aorist middle indica-

tive of *apokrinomai*, in John here only and verse 19, elsewhere *apekrithē* as in verse 11. *My Father* (*ho patēr mou*). Not "our Father," claim to peculiar relation to the Father. *Worketh even until now* (*heōs arti ergazetai*). Linear present middle indicative, "keeps on working until now" without a break on the Sabbath. Philo points out this fact of the continuous activity of God. Justin Martyr, Origen and others note this fact about God. He made the Sabbath for man's blessing, but cannot observe it himself. *And I work* (*kágō ergazomai*). Jesus puts himself on a par with God's activity and thus justifies his healing on the Sabbath.

18. *Sought the more* (*mallon ezētoun*). Imperfect active of *zēteō*, graphic picture of increased and untiring effort "to kill him" (*auton apokteinai*, first aorist active, to kill him off and be done with him). John repeats this clause "they sought to kill him" in 7:1, 19, 25; 8:37, 40. Their own blood was up on this Sabbath issue and they bend every energy to put Jesus to death. If this is a passover, this bitter anger, murderous wrath, will go on and grow for two years. *Not only brake the Sabbath* (*ou monon elue to sabbaton*). Imperfect active of *luō*. He was now a common and regular Sabbath-breaker. *Luō* means to loosen, to set at naught. The papyri give examples of *luō* in this sense like *luein ta penthē* (to break the period of mourning). This was the first grudge against Jesus, but his defence had made the offence worse and had given them a far graver charge. *But also called God his own Father* (*alla kai patera idion elege ton theon*). "His own" (*idion*) in a sense not true of others. That is precisely what Jesus meant by "My Father." See Rom. 8:32 for *ho idios huios*, "his own Son." *Making himself equal with God* (*ison heauton poiōn tōi theōi*). *Isos* is an old common adjective (in papyri also) and means *equal*. In Phil. 2:6 Paul calls the Pre-incarnate Christ *isa theōi*, "equal to God" (plural *isa*, attributes of God). Bernard thinks that Jesus would not claim to be *isos theōi* because in John 14:28 he

says: "The Father is greater than I." And yet he says in
14:7 that the one who sees him sees in him the Father.
Certainly the Jews understood Jesus to claim equality with
the Father in nature and privilege and power as also in 10:33;
19:7. Besides, if the Jews misunderstood Jesus on this
point, it was open and easy for him to deny it and to
clear up the misapprehension. This is precisely what he
does not do. On the contrary Jesus gives a powerful
apologetic in defence of his claim to equality with the Father
(verses 19–47).

19. *The Son* (*ho huios*). The absolute use of the Son in
relation to the Father admitting the charge in verse 18 and
defending his equality with the Father. *Can do nothing by
himself* (*ou dunatai poiein aph'heautou ouden*). True in a
sense of every man, but in a much deeper sense of Christ
because of the intimate relation between him and the Father.
See this same point in 5:30; 7:28; 8:28; 14:10. Jesus had
already made it in 5:17. Now he repeats and defends it.
But what he seeth the Father doing (*an mē ti blepēi ton patera
poiounta*). Rather, "unless he sees the Father doing something." Negative condition (*an mē = ean mē*, if not, unless)
of third class with present (habit) subjunctive (*blepēi*) and
present active participle (*poiounta*). It is a supreme example
of a son copying the spirit and work of a father. In his work
on earth the Son sees continually what the Father is doing.
In healing this poor man he was doing what the Father
wishes him to do. *For what things soever he doeth, these the
Son also doeth in like manner* (*ha gar an ekeinos poiēi tauta
kai ho huios homoiōs poiei*). Indefinite relative clause with
an and the present active subjunctive (*poiēi*). Note *ekeinos*,
emphatic demonstrative, that one, referring to the Father.
This sublime claim on the part of Jesus will exasperate his
enemies still more.

20. *Loveth* (*philei*). In 3:35 we have *agapāi* from *agapaō*,
evidently one verb expressing as noble a love as the other.

Sometimes a distinction (21:17) is made, but not here, unless
phileō presents the notion of intimate friendship (*philos*,
friend), fellowship, the affectionate side, while *agapaō* (Latin
diligo) is more the intelligent choice. But John uses both
verbs for the mystery of love of the Father for the Son.
Greater works than these (*meizona toutōn erga*). *Toutōn* is
ablative case after the comparative *meizona* (from *megas*,
great). John often uses *erga* for the miracles of Christ
(5:36; 7:3, 21; 10:25, 32, 38, etc.). It is the Father who does
these works (14:10). There is more to follow. Even the
disciples will surpass what Christ is doing in the extent of
the work (14:12). *Deixei* is future active indicative of *deiknumi*, to show. See also 10:32. *That ye may marvel* (*hina
humeis thaumazēte*). Purpose clause with *hina* and present
active subjunctive of *thaumazō*. Wonder belongs to child-
hood and to men of knowledge. Modern science has increased the occasion for wonder. Clement of Alexandria has
a saying of Jesus: "He that wonders shall reign, and he that
reigns shall rest."

21. *Quickeneth whom he will* (*hous thelei zōopoiei*). Present
active indicative of *zōopoieō* (from *zōopoios*, making alive),
common in Paul (I Cor. 15:45, etc.). As yet, so far as we
know, Jesus had not raised the dead, but he claims the power
to do it on a par with the power of the Father. The raising
of the son of the widow of Nain (Luke 7:11–17) is not far
ahead, followed by the message to the Baptist which speaks
of this same power (Luke 7:22 = Matt. 11:5), and the raising
of Jairus' daughter (Matt. 9:18, 22–26). Jesus exercises
this power on those "whom he wills." Christ has power to
quicken both body and soul.

22. *He hath given all judgement unto the Son* (*tēn krisin
pāsan dedōken tōi huiōi*). Perfect active indicative of *didōmi*,
state of completion (as in 3:35; 6:27, 29; 10:29, etc.). See
this prerogative claimed for Christ already in 3:17. See the
picture of Christ as Judge of men in Matt. 25:31–46.

23. *That all may honour the Son* (*hina pantes timōsin ton huion*). Purpose clause with *hina* and present active subjunctive of *timaō* (may keep on honouring the Son). *He that honoureth not the Son* (*ho mē timōn ton huion*). Articular present active participle of *timaō* with negative *mē*. Jesus claims here the same right to worship from men that the Father has. Dishonouring Jesus is dishonouring the Father who sent him (8:49; 12:26; 15:23; I John 2:23). See also Luke 10:16. There is small comfort here for those who praise Jesus as teacher and yet deny his claims to worship. The Gospel of John carries this high place for Christ throughout, but so do the other Gospels (even Q, the Logia of Jesus) and the rest of the New Testament.

24. *Hath eternal life* (*echei zōēn aiōnion*). Has now this spiritual life which is endless. See 3:36. In verses 24 and 25 Jesus speaks of spiritual life and spiritual death. In this passage (21 to 29) Jesus speaks now of physical life and death, now of spiritual, and one must notice carefully the quick transition. In Rev. 20:14 we have the phrase "the second death" with which language compare Rev. 20:4–6. *But hath passed out of death into life* (*alla metabebēken ek tou thanatou eis tēn zōēn*). Perfect active indicative of *metabainō*, to pass from one place or state to another. Out of spiritual death into spiritual life and so no judgement (*krisis*).

25. *And now is* (*kai nun estin*). See 4:23 for this phrase. Not the future resurrection in verse 28, but the spiritual resurrection here and now. *The dead* (*hoi nekroi*). The spiritually dead, dead in trespasses and sins (Eph. 2:1, 5; 5:14). *Shall hear the voice of the Son of God* (*akousousin tēs phōnēs tou huiou tou theou*). Note three genitives (*phōnēs* after *akousousin*, *huiou* with *phōnēs*, *theou* with *huiou*). Note three articles (correlation of the article) and that Jesus here calls himself "the Son of God" as in 10:36; 11:4. *Shall live* (*zēsousin*). Future active indicative, shall come to life spiritually.

26. *In himself* (*en heautōi*).   The Living God possesses life wholly in himself and so he has bestowed this power of life to the Son as already stated in the Prologue of the Logos (1:3).   For "gave" (*edōken*, timeless aorist active indicative) see also 3:35; 17:2, 24.   The particles "as" (*hōsper*) and "so" (*houtōs*) mark here the fact, not the degree (Westcott).

27. *Because he is the Son of man* (*hoti huios anthrōpou estin*).   Rather, "because he is a son of man" (note absence of articles and so not as the Messiah), because the judge of men must partake of human nature himself (Westcott). Bernard insists that John is here giving his own reflections rather than the words of Jesus and uses *huios anthrōpou* in the same sense as *ho huios tou anthrōpou* (always in the Gospels used by Jesus of himself).   But that in my opinion is a wrong view since we have here ostensibly certainly the words of Jesus himself.   So in Rev. 1:13 and 4:14 *huion anthrōpou* means "a son of man."

28. *In the tombs* (*en tois mnēmeiois*).   *Taphos* (grave) presents the notion of burial (*thaptō*, to bury) as in Matt. 23:27, *mnēmeion* (from *mnaomai*, *mimnēskō*, to remind) is a memorial (sepulchre as a monument).   Jesus claims not only the power of life (spiritual) and of judgement, but of power to quicken the actual dead at the Last Day.   They will hear his voice and come out (*ekporeusontai*, future middle indicative of *ekporeuomai*).   A general judgement and a general bodily resurrection we have here for both good and bad as in Matt. 25:46; Acts 24:15; II Cor. 5:10 and as often implied in the words of Jesus (Matt. 5:29f.; 10:28; Luke 11:32).   In John 6:39 Jesus asserts that he will raise up the righteous.

29. *Unto the resurrection of life* (*eis anastasin zōēs*).   *Anastasis* is an old word (Aeschylus) from *anistēmi*, to raise up, to arise.   This combination occurs nowhere else in the N.T. nor does "the resurrection of judgement" (*eis anastasin kriseōs*), but in Luke 14:14 there is the similar phrase "in

the resurrection of the just" (*en tēi anastasei tōn dikaiōn*).
Only there note both articles. Here without the articles it
can mean "to a resurrection of life" and "to a resurrection
of judgement," though the result is practically the same.
There are two resurrections as to result, one to life, one to
judgement. See both in Dan. 12:2.

30. *I* (*Egō*). The discourse returns to the first person after
using "the Son" since verse 19. Here Jesus repeats in the
first person (as in 8:28) the statement made in verse 19
about the Son. In John *emautou* is used by Jesus 16 times
and not at all by Jesus in the Synoptics. It occurs in the
Synoptics only in Matt. 8:8 = Luke 7:7f. *Righteous* (*dikaia*).
As all judgements should be. The reason is plain (*hoti*, because), the guiding principle with the Son being the will of
the Father who sent him and made him Judge. Judges
often have difficulty in knowing what is law and what is
right, but the Son's task as Judge is simple enough, the will
of the Father which he knows (verse 20).

31. *If I bear witness of myself* (*Ean egō marturō peri
emautou*). Condition of third class, undetermined with
prospect of determination (*ean* and present active subjunctive of *martureō*). The emphasis is on *egō* (I alone with no
other witness). *Is not true* (*ouk estin alēthēs*). In law the
testimony of a witness is not received in his own case (Jewish, Greek, Roman law). See Deut. 19:15 and the allusion
to it by Jesus in Matt. 18:16. See also II Cor. 13:1; I Tim.
5:19. And yet in 8:12 to 19 Jesus claims that his witness
concerning himself is true because the Father gives confirmation of his message. The Father and the Son are the two
witnesses (8:17). It is a paradox and yet true. But here
Jesus yields to the rabbinical demand for proof outside of
himself. He has the witness of another (the Father, 5:32, 37),
the witness of the Baptist (5:33), the witness of the works of
Jesus (5:36), the witness of the Scriptures (5:39), the witness
of Moses in particular (5:45).

32. *Another* (*allos*). The Father, not the Baptist who is mentioned in verse 33. This continual witness of the Father (*ho marturōn*, who is bearing witness, and *marturei*, present active indicative) is mentioned again in verses 36 to 38 as in 8:17.

33. *Ye have sent* (*humeis apestalkate*). Emphatic use of *humeis* (ye) and perfect active indicative of *apostellō*, official and permanent fact and so the witness of the Baptist has to be recognized as trustworthy by the Sanhedrin. The reference is to the committee in 1:19 to 28. *He hath borne witness* (*memarturēken*). Perfect active indicative of *martureō* showing the permanent and abiding value of John's testimony to Christ as in 1:34; 3:26; 5:37. So also 19:35 of the testimony concerning Christ's death. This was the purpose of the Baptist's mission (1:7).

34. *But the witness which I receive* (*Egō de ou tēn marturian lambanō*). "But I do not receive the witness" simply from a man (like John). The *egō* (I) in sharp contrast with *humeis* (ye) of verse 33. Jesus complained of Nicodemus for not accepting his witness (3:11). Cf. also 3:32. In I John 5:9 the witness of God is greater than that of men and this Jesus has. *That ye may be saved* (*hina humeis sōthēte*). Final clause with *hina* and first aorist passive subjunctive of *sōzō*. This was the purpose of Christ's coming, that the world might be saved (3:17).

35. *He* (*ekeinos*). "That one" (John of 33). Common demonstrative (that one) in John to point out the subject. Used in 1:8 of the Baptist as here. John was now in prison and so Christ uses *ēn* (was). His active ministry is over. *The lamp* (*ho luchnos*). The lamp in the room (Mark 4:21). Old word for lamp or candle as in Matt. 5:15. Used of Christ (the Lamb) as the Lamp of the New Jerusalem (Rev. 21:23). *Lampas* (Matt. 25:1, 3, etc.) is a torch whose wick is fed with oil. The Baptist was not the Light (*to phōs*, 1:8), but a lamp shining in the darkness. "When the Light comes,

the lamp is no longer needed" (Bernard). *"Non Lux iste, sed lucerna."* Jesus by his own claim is the Light of the World (8:12; 9:5; 12:46). And yet all believers are in a sense "the light of the world" (Matt. 5:14) since the world gets the Light of Christ through us. *That burneth* (*ho kaiomenos*). See Matt. 5:15 for this verb used with *luchnos* (lighting a candle or lamp). The lamp that is lit and is burning (present passive participle of *kaiō*, and so is consumed). *And shineth* (*kai phainōn*). See 1:4 for this verb used of the Logos shining in the darkness. Cf. I John 2:8. John was giving light as he burned for those in darkness like these Jews. *And ye were willing* (*humeis de ethelēsate*). "But ye became willing." Ingressive aorist active indicative of *thelō*. Reference again to 1:19. Cf. also for the temporary popularity of the Baptist Mark 1:5; Matt. 3:5; 11:7; 21:26. The Jews were attracted to John "like moths to a candle" (Bernard). *To rejoice* (*agalliathēnai*). First aorist passive infinitive of *agalliaomai*, late word for *agallomai* for which see Matt. 5:12. "They were attracted by his brightness, not by his warmth" (Bengel). Even so the brightness of John's shining did not really enlighten their minds. "The interest in the Baptist was a frivolous, superficial, and short-lived excitement" (Vincent). It was only "for an hour" (*pros hōran*) when they turned against him.

36. *But the witness which I have is greater than that of John* (*Egō de echō tēn marturian meizō tou Iōanou*). Literally, "But I have the witness greater than John's." *Meizō* (*meizona*) is predicate accusative and *Iōanou* is ablative of comparison after *meizō*. Good as the witness of John is, Christ has superior testimony. *To accomplish* (*hina teleiōsō*). Final clause with *hina* and first aorist active subjunctive of *teleioō*, the same idiom in 4:34. Jesus felt keenly the task laid on him by the Father (cf. 3:35) and claimed at the end that he had performed it (17:4; 19:30). Jesus held that the highest form of faith did not require these "works" (*erga*) as in 2:23; 10:38; 14:11. But these "works" bear the seal

of the Father's approval (5:20, 36; 10:25) and to reject their witness is wrong (10:25; 10:37f.; 15:24). *The very works* (*auta ta erga*). "The works themselves," repeating *ta erga* just before for vernacular emphasis. *Hath sent me* (*me apestalken*). Perfect active indicative of *apostellō*, the permanence of the mission. Cf. 3:17. The continuance of the witness is emphasized in 5:32; 8:18.

37. *He hath borne witness* (*ekeinos memarturēken*). *Ekeinos* (that one; cf. 5:35, 38), not *autos*. Perfect active indicative of *martureō*, the direct witness of the Father, besides the indirect witness of the works. Jesus is not speaking of the voice of the Father at his baptism (Mark 1:11), the transfiguration (Mark 9:7), nor even at the time of the visit of the Greeks (John 12:28). This last voice was heard by many who thought it was thunder or an angel. The language of Jesus refers to the witness of the Father in the heart of the believers as is made plain in I John 5:9 and 10. God's witness does not come by audible "voice" (*phōnēn*) nor visible "form" (*eidos*). Cf. 1:18; 6:46; I John 4:12. *Akēkoate* is perfect active indicative of *akouō*, to hear, and *heōrakate* is perfect active indicative of *horaō*, to see. It is a permanent state of failure to hear and see God. The experience of Jacob in Peniel (Gen. 32:30) was unusual, but Jesus will say that those who have seen him have seen the Father (John 14:9), but here he means the Father's "voice" and "form" as distinct from the Son.

38. *And* (*kai*). "And yet" as in 1:10 and 5:40 below. *His word abiding in you* (*ton logon autou en humin menonta*). But God's word had come to them through the centuries by the prophets. For the phrase see 10:35; 15:3; 17:6; I John 1:10; 2:14. *Him ye believe not* (*toutōi humeis ou pisteuete*). "This one" (*toutōi*, dative case with *pisteuete*) in emphatic relation to preceding "he" (*ekeinos*, God). Jesus has given them God's word, but they reject both Jesus and God's word (John 14:9).

39. *Ye search (eraunāte)*. Proper spelling as the papyri show rather than *ereunāte*, the old form (from *ereuna*, search) as in 7:52. The form here can be either present active indicative second person plural or the present active imperative second person plural. Only the context can decide. Either makes sense here, but the reason given "because ye think" (*hoti humeis dokeite*, clearly indicative), supports the indicative rather than the imperative. Besides, Jesus is arguing on the basis of their use of "the Scriptures" (*tas graphas*). The plural with the article refers to the well-known collection in the Old Testament (Matt. 21:42; Luke 24:27). Elsewhere in John the singular refers to a particular passage (2:22; 7:38; 10:35). *In them ye have eternal life (en autais zōēn aiōnion echein)*. Indirect assertion after *dokeite* without "ye" expressed either as nominative (*humeis*) or accusative (*humas*). Bernard holds that in John *dokeō* always indicates a mistaken opinion (5:45; 11:13, 31; 13:29; 16:20; 20:15). Certainly the rabbis did make a mechanical use of the letter of Scripture as a means of salvation. *These are they (ekeinai eisin hai)*. The true value of the Scriptures is in their witness to Christ (of me, *peri emou*). Luke (24:27, 45) gives this same claim of Jesus, and yet some critics fail to find the Messiah in the Old Testament. But Jesus did.

40. *And ye will not come to me (kai ou thelete elthein pros me)*. "And yet" (*kai*) as often in John. "This is the tragedy of the rejection of Messiah by the Messianic race" (Bernard). See John 1:11 and Matt. 23:37 (*kai ouk ēthelēsate*, and ye would not). Men loved darkness rather than light (John 3:19). *That ye may have life (hina zōēn echēte)*. Life in its simplest form as in 3:36 (cf. 3:16). This is the purpose of John in writing the Fourth Gospel (20:31). There is life only in Christ Jesus.

41. *Glory from men (doxan para anthrōpōn)*. Mere honour and praise Jesus does not expect from men (verse 34). This

is not wounded pride, for ambition is not Christ's motive. He is unlike the Jews (5:44; 12:43; Matt. 6:1f.) and seeks not his own glory, but the glory and fellowship of the Father (1:14; 2:11; 7:18). Paul did not seek glory from men (I Thess. 2:6).

42. *But I know you* (*alla egnōka humas*). Perfect active indicative of *ginōskō*, "I have come to know and still know," the knowledge of personal experience (2:24f.). *The love o' God* (*tēn agapēn tou theou*). Objective genitive, "the love toward God." See Luke 11:42 for this phrase in the same sense (only other instance in the Gospels, but common in I John (2:5; 3:17; 4:7, 9; 5:3) and in II Thess. 3:5; II Cor. 13:14; Rom. 5:5. The sense of God's love for man occurs in I John 3:1; 4:9, 10, 16 and in John 15:9f. of Christ's love for man. These rabbis did not love God and hence did not love Christ.

43. *In my Father's name* (*en tōi onomati tou patros mou*). Seven times Jesus in John speaks of the "Name" of the Father (5:43; 10:25; 12:28; 17:6, 11, 12, 26). See 1:12 for use of *onoma* (Luke 1:49). *And ye receive me not* (*kai ou lambanete me*). "And yet ye do not receive me," as in verse 40, "the Gospel of the Rejection" (1:11; 3:11, 32; 12:37) often applied to the Fourth Gospel. *If another come* (*ean allos elthēi*). Condition of third class (*ean* and second aorist active subjunctive of *erchomai*). Note *allos*, not *heteros*, like *allon Iēsoun* in II Cor. 11:4. Similar prophecies occur in Mark 13:6, 22 (= Matt. 24:5, 24), all general in character like Antichrist in II Thess. 2:8–12. There is no occasion for a reference to any individual like Barcochba (about A.D. 134) as Pfleiderer and Schmiedel hold. These Messianic upstarts all come "in their own name" and always find a following. *Him ye will receive* (*ekeinon lēmpsesthe*). "That one," whoever he is, as Jesus said. Future active indicative of *lambanō*. Credulous about the false Messiahs, incredulous about Christ.

44. *How can ye believe?* (*pōs dunasthe humeis pisteusai;*).
Emphasis on "ye" (*humeis*), ye being what ye are. They
were not true Jews (Rom. 2:29; Esther 9:28) who cared for
the glory of God, but they prefer the praise of men (Matt.
6:1f.; 23:5) like the Pharisees who feared to confess Christ
(John 12:43). *From the only God* (*para tou monou theou*).
B and W omit *theou* which is certainly meant even if not
genuine here. See 17:3; Rom. 16:27; I Tim. 6:15f.

45. *Think not* (*mē dokeite*). Prohibition with *mē* and the
present imperative. See on verse 39 for *dokeō* for mistaken
opinions in John. *I will accuse you* (*egō katēgorēsō humōn*).
Emphasis on *egō* (I). Future active indicative of *katēgoreō*
(*kata*, against, *agoreuō*, to speak in the assembly *agora*, to
bring an accusation in court, a public accusation). See
Rom. 3:9 for *proaitiaomai* for making previous charge and
Luke 16:1 for *diaballō*, a secret malicious accusation, and
Rom. 8:33 for *egkaleō*, for public charge, not necessarily
before tribunal. *Even Moses* (*Mōusēs*). No "even" in the
Greek. *On whom ye have set your hope* (*eis hon humeis
ēlpikate*). Perfect active indicative of *elpizō*, state of repose
in Moses. Only example of *elpizō* in John. See II Cor. 1:10
for use of *eis* with *elpizō* instead of the usual *epi* (I Tim.
4:10).

46. *Ye would believe me* (*episteuete an emoi*). Conclusion
of condition of second class (determined as unfulfilled) with
imperfect indicative in both protasis and apodosis and *an* in
apodosis. This was a home-thrust, proving that they did
not really believe Moses. *For he wrote of me* (*peri gar emou
ekeinos egrapsen*). Deut. 18:18f. is quoted by Peter (Acts
3:22) as a prophecy of Christ and also by Stephen in Acts
7:37. See also John 3:14 about the brazen serpent and 8:56
about Abraham foreseeing Christ's day. Jesus does here
say that Moses wrote concerning him.

47. *His writings* (*tois ekeinou grammasin*). Dative case
with *pistuete*. See Luke 16:31 for a like argument. The

authority of Moses was the greatest of all for Jews. There
is a contrast also between *writings* (*grammasin*, from *graphō*,
to write) and *words* (*rēmasin*, from *eipon*). *Gramma* may
mean the mere letter as opposed to spirit (II Cor. 3:6;
Rom. 2:27, 29; 7:6), a debtor's bond (Luke 16:6f.), letters
or learning (John 7:15; Acts 26:24) like *agrammatoi* for
unlearned (Acts 4:13), merely written characters (Luke
23:38; II Cor. 3:7; Gal. 6:11), official communications (Acts
28:21), once *hiera grammata* for the sacred writings (II Tim.
3:15) instead of the more usual *hai hagiai graphai*. *Graphē*
is used also for a single passage (Mark 12:10), but *biblion*
for a book or roll (Luke 4:17) or *biblos* (Luke 20:42). Jesus
clearly states the fact that Moses wrote portions of the Old
Testament, what portions he does not say. See also Luke
24:27, 44 for the same idea. There was no answer from the
rabbis to this conclusion of Christ. The scribes (*hoi grammateis*) made copies according to the letter (*kata to gramma*).

CHAPTER VI

1. *After these things* (*meta tauta*). A common, but indefinite, note of time in John (3:22; 5:1; 6:1; 7:1). The phrase does not mean immediate sequence of events. As a matter of fact, a whole year may intervene between the events of chapter 5 in Jerusalem and those in chapter 6 in Galilee. There is no sufficient reason for believing that chapter 6 originally preceded chapter 5. The feeding of the five thousand is the only event before the last visit to Jerusalem recorded in all Four Gospels (Mark 6:30–44 = Matt. 14:13–21 = Luke 9:10–17 = John 6:1–13). The disciples have returned from the tour of Galilee and report to Jesus. It was the passover time (John 6:4) just a year before the end. *To the other side of the Sea of Galilee* (*peran tēs thalassēs tēs Galilaias*). The name given in Mark and Matthew. It is called Gennesaret in Luke 5:1 and "Sea of Tiberias" in John 21:1. Here "of Tiberias" (*tēs Tiberiados*) is added as further description. Herod Antipas A.D. 22 built Tiberias to the west of the Sea of Galilee and made it his capital. See verse 23 for this city. Luke (9:10) explains that it was the eastern Bethsaida (Julias) to which Jesus took the disciples, not the western Bethsaida of Mark 6:45 in Galilee.

2. *Followed* (*ēkolouthei*). Descriptive imperfect active, picturing the crowd, but without the details of the boat for Christ and the rapid race of the crowd on foot (Mark 6:32f. = Matt. 14:13f.). *They beheld* (*etheōroun*). Imperfect active of *theōreō*. They had been beholding the signs which Jesus had been doing (*epoiei*, imperfect again) for a long time (2:23), most of which John has not given (Mark 1:29f.; 2:1; 3:1; 6:5). The people were eager to hear Jesus again

(Luke 9:11) and to get the benefit of his healing power "on them that were sick" (*epi tōn asthenountōn*, the weak or feeble, without strength, *a* privative and *sthenos*, strength).

3. *Into the mountain* (*eis to oros*). From the level of the Jordan valley up into the high hill on the eastern side. Mark (6:46) and Matthew (14:23) mention that after the miracle Jesus went further up into the mountain to pray. *Sat* (*ekathēto*). Imperfect middle of *kathēmai*, was sitting, a picture of repose.

4. *The feast of the Jews* (*hē heortē tōn Ioudaiōn*). Here used of the passover (*to pascha*) as in 7:2 of the tabernacles. This is probably the third passover in Christ's ministry (2:13 and one unmentioned unless 5:1 be it). In 2:13, here, and 11:55 (the last one) the adverb *eggus* (near) is used. John is fond of notes of time. Jesus failed to go to this passover because of the hostility in Jerusalem (7:1).

5. *Lifting up his eyes* (*eparas tous ophthalmous*). First aorist active participle of *epairō*. See the same phrase in 4:35 where it is also followed by *theaomai*; 11:41; 17:1; Luke 6:20. Here it is particularly expressive as Jesus looked down from the mountain on the approaching multitude. *Cometh unto him* (*erchetai pros auton*). Present middle indicative, "is coming to him." The same *ochlos polus* (here *polus ochlos*) of verse 2 that had followed Jesus around the head of the lake. *Whence are we to buy?* (*Pothen agorasōmen;*). Deliberative subjunctive (aorist active). John passes by the earlier teaching and healing of the Synoptics (Mark 6:34f. =Matt. 14:14f. =Luke 9:11f.) till mid-afternoon. In John also Jesus takes up the matter of feeding the multitude with Philip (from the other Bethsaida, 1:44) whereas in the Synoptics the disciples raise the problem with Jesus. So the disciples raise the problem in the feeding of the four thousand (Mark 8:4 =Matt. 15:33). See Numb. 11:13-22 (about Moses) and II Kings 4:42f. (about Elisha). *Bread* (*artous*). "Loaves" (plural) as in Matt. 4:3. *That these*

may eat (*hina phagōsin houtoi*). Purpose clause with *hina* and the second aorist active subjunctive of *esthiō* (defective verb).

6. *To prove him* (*peirazōn auton*). Present active participle of *peirazō*, testing him, not here in bad sense of tempting as so often (Matt. 4:1). *What he would do* (*ti ēmellen poiein*). Indirect question with change of tense to imperfect. As in 2:25 so here John explains why Jesus put the question to Philip.

7. *Two hundred pennyworth of bread* (*diakosiōn dēnariōn artoi*). "Loaves of two hundred denarii." The Roman coin originally for ten asses (afterwards sixteen), about 16⅔ cents. The denarius was the usual pay for a day's labour (Matt. 20:2, 9, 13). This item in Mark 6:37, but not in Matthew or Luke. *That every one may take a little* (*hina hekastos brachu labēi*). Final clause with *hina* and second aorist active subjunctive of *lambanō*. This detail in John alone.

8. *One of* (*heis ek*). So in 12:4; 13:23 and Mark 13:1 without *ek*. *Simon Peter's brother* (*ho adelphos Simōnos Petrou*). So described in 1:40. The great distinction of Andrew was precisely this that he brought Simon to Christ. Philip and Andrew appear together again in 12:20–22, but in the Synoptics he is distinguished only in Mark 13:3. In the Muratorian Fragment Andrew received the revelation for John to write the Fourth Gospel.

9. *A lad here* (*paidarion hōde*). Old word, diminutive of *pais*, here only in N.T., not genuine in Matt. 11:16. How he came to have this small supply we do not know. *Barley* (*krithinous*). Adjective, here and verse 13 only in N.T., in the papyri, from *krithē*, barley (Rev. 6:6). Considered an inferior sort of bread. *Fishes* (*opsaria*). Late diminutive of *opson*, common in papyri and inscriptions for delicacies with bread like fish. In N.T. only here, verse 11, and 21:9–13. Synoptics have *ichthuas*.

10. *Sit down* (*anapesein*). Literally, "fall back," lie down, recline. Second aorist active infinitive of *anapiptō*. *Much grass* (*chortos polus*). Old word for pasture, green grass (Mark 6:39) or hay (I Cor. 3:12). It was spring (John 6:4) and plenty of green grass on the hillside. *The men* (*hoi andres*). Word for men as distinct from women, expressly stated in Matt. 14:21. *In number* (*ton arithmon*). Adverbial accusative (of general reference). *About* (*hōs*). General estimate, though they were arranged in orderly groups by hundreds and fifties, "in ranks" like "garden beds" (*prasiai,* Mark 6:40).

11. *The loaves* (*tous artous*). Those of verse 9. *Having given thanks* (*eucharistēsas*). The usual grace before meals (Deut. 8:10). The Synoptics use "blessed" *eulogēsen* (Mark 6:41 = Matt. 14:19 = Luke 9:16). *He distributed* (*diedōken*). First aorist active indicative of *diadidōmi*, old verb to give to several (*dia*, between). *To them that were set down* (*tois anakeimenois*). Present middle participle (dative case) of *anakeimai*, old verb to recline like *anapesein* in verse 10. *As much as they would* (*hoson ēthelon*). Imperfect active of *thelō*, "as much as they wished."

12. *And when they were filled* (*hōs de eneplēsthēsan*). First aorist (effective) passive indicative of *empimplēmi*, old verb to fill in, to fill up, to fill completely. They were all satisfied. The Synoptics have *echortasthēsan* like John 6:26 (*echortasthēte*). *Gather up* (*sunagagete*). Second aorist active imperative of *sunagō*, to gather together. *Broken pieces* (*klasmata*). From *klaō*, to break. Not crumbs or scraps on the ground, but pieces broken by Jesus (Mark 6:41) and not consumed. *Be lost* (*apolētai*). Second aorist middle subjunctive of *apollumi* with *hina* in purpose clause. Only in John. There was to be no wastefulness in Christ's munificence. The Jews had a custom of leaving something for those that served.

13. *Twelve baskets* (*dōdeka kophinous*). One for each of

the apostles. What about the lad? Stout wicker baskets (coffins, Wycliff) in distinction from the soft and frail *sphurides* used at the feeding of the four thousand (Mark 8:8 = Matt. 15:37). Here all the Gospels (Mark 6:43 = Matt. 14:20 = Luke 9:17 = John 6:13) use *kophinoi*. The same distinction between *kophinoi* and *sphurides* is preserved in the allusion to the incidents by Jesus in Mark 8:19 and 20 and Matt. 16:9 and 10. *Unto them that had eaten* (*tois bebrōkosin*). Articular perfect active participle (dative case) of *bibrōskō*, old verb to eat, only here in N.T., though often in LXX.

14. *Saw the sign which he did* (*idontes ha epoiēsen sēmeia*). "Signs" oldest MSS. have. This sign added to those already wrought (verse 2). Cf. 2:23; 3:2. *They said* (*elegon*). Inchoative imperfect, began to say. *Of a truth* (*alēthōs*). Common adverb (from *alēthēs*) in John (7:40). *The prophet that cometh* (*ho prophētēs ho erchomenos*). There was a popular expectation about the prophet of Deut. 18:15 as being the Messiah (John 1:21; 11:27). The phrase is peculiar to John, but the idea is in Acts (3:22; 7:37). The people are on the tiptoe of expectation and believe that Jesus is the political Messiah of Pharisaic hope.

15. *Perceiving* (*gnous*). Second aorist active participle of *ginōskō*. It was not hard for Christ to read the mind of this excited mob. *They were about* (*mellousin*). Present active indicative of *mellō*. Probably the leaders were already starting. *Take him by force* (*harpazein*). Present active infinitive of *harpazō*, old verb for violent seizing (Matt. 11:12; 13:19). There was a movement to start a revolution against Roman rule in Palestine by proclaiming Jesus King and driving away Pilate. *To make him king* (*hina poiēsōsin basilea*). Purpose clause with *hina* and the first aorist active subjunctive of *poieō* with *basilea* as predicate accusative. It was a crisis that called for quick action. *Himself alone* (*autos monos*). At first he had the disciples

with him (verse 3). But he sent them hurriedly by boat to
the western side (Mark 6:45f.=Matt. 14:22f.) because
clearly the apostles were sympathetic with the revolutionary
impulse of the crowd. Then Jesus sent the multitudes away
also and went up into the mountain alone. He was alone in
every sense, for no one but the Father understood him at
this stage, not even his own disciples. He went up to pray
(Mark 6:46=Matt. 14:23).

16. *When evening came* (*hōs opsia egeneto*). "The late
hour" (*hōra* understood), and so in late Greek the adjective
is used as a substantive. It is late evening (real evening),
not the early evening in mid-afternoon (Matt. 14:15). The
disciples were in no hurry to start back to Bethsaida in
Galilee (Mark 6:45), Capernaum in John (6:17).

17. *Were going* (*ērchonto*). Picturesque imperfect. *It was
now dark* (*skotia ēdē egegonei*). Past perfect active of *ginomai*.
While they were going, "darkness had already come." *And
Jesus had not yet come to them* (*kai ouk elēluthei pros autous
ho Iēsous*). Another past perfect active of *erchomai* with
negative *oupō*. Darkness had come, but Jesus had not
come, while they were going over the sea. The tenses in
these verses are very graphic.

18. *And the sea was rising* (*hē te thalassa diegeireto*). Imperfect (without augment) passive of *diegeirō*, late compound
to wake up thoroughly, to arouse. *By reason of a great wind
that blew* (*anemou megalou pneontos*). Genitive absolute
with present active participle of *pneō*, to blow, "a great
wind blowing."

19. *When therefore they had rowed* (*elēlakotes oun*). Perfect
active participle of *elaunō*, old verb to march (Xenophon),
to drive (James 3:4), to row (Mark 6:48). *Furlongs* (*sta-
dious*). Stadia, accusative of extent of space, a little over
halfway across, "in the midst of the sea" (Mark 6:47).
It was about forty stadia (six miles) across. *They behold*
(*theōrousin*). Graphic dramatic present active indicative of

theōreō, vividly preserving the emotions of the disciples. *Walking (peripatounta)*. Present active participle in the accusative case agreeing with *Iēsoun*. *Drawing nigh unto the boat (eggus tou ploiou ginomenon)*. Present middle participle of *ginomai* describing the process. "Coming near the boat." They behold Jesus slipping closer and closer to them on the water. *They were afraid (ephobēthēsan)*. Ingressive aorist passive indicative of *phobeomai*, "they became afraid." Sudden change to the regular historical sequence.

20. *Be not afraid (mē phobeisthe)*. Prohibition with *mē* and present middle imperative of *phobeomai*. So in Mark 6:50 (=Matt. 14:27). John does not tell that the disciples thought Jesus was an apparition (Mark 6:49=Matt. 14:26), nor does he give the account of Peter walking on the water (Matt. 14:28–31).

21. *They were willing therefore (ēthelon oun)*. Inchoative imperfect, "they began to be willing." This does not contradict Mark 6:51 as Bernard thinks. Both Jesus and Peter climbed into the boat. *Whither they were going (eis hēn hupēgon)*. Progressive imperfect active, "to which land they had been going" (intransitive use of *hupagō*, to lead under, to go under or away as in verse 67; 7:33; 12:11, 18:8.

22. *Which stood (ho hestēkōs)*. Perfect active (intransitive) participle of *histēmi*, to put, to stand. Jesus had sent the multitudes away the evening before (Mark 6:45=Matt. 14:22), but evidently some did not go very far, still lingering in excitement on the eastern side of the lake next morning. *Boat (ploiarion)*. Diminutive of *ploion*, little boat (Mark 3:9). *Entered not with (ou suneisēlthen)*. Second aorist active of the double compound verb *suneiserchomai*, followed by associative instrumental case *mathētais*. *Went away alone (monoi apēlthon)*. Second aorist active indicative of *aperchomai*, to go away or off. *Monoi* is predicate nominative. These people noted these three items.

23. *Howbeit* (*alla*). Verse 23 is really an explanatory parenthesis in this long sentence. Tiberias, capital of Herod Antipas, diagonally across the lake, is only mentioned in John in the N.T. (6:1, 23; 21:1). *Boats* (*ploia*). Called "little boats" (*ploiaria*) in verse 24.

24. *When the multitude therefore saw* (*hote oun eiden ho ochlos*). Resumption and clarification of the complicated statements of verse 22. *That Jesus was not there* (*hoti Iēsous ouk estin ekei*). Present indicative retained in indirect discourse. They still did not understand how Jesus had crossed over, but they acted on the basis of the plain fact. *They themselves got into* (*enebēsan autoi eis*). Second aorist active indicative of *embainō* followed by *eis* (both *en* and *eis* together as often in N.T.). *Seeking Jesus* (*zētountes ton Iēsoun*). Present active participle of *zēteō*. They had a double motive apart from the curiosity explained in verse 22. They had clearly not given up the impulse of the evening before to make Jesus king (6:15) and they had hopes of still another bountiful repast at the hands of Jesus as he said (6:26).

25. *When they found him* (*heurontes auton*). Second aorist active participle of *heuriskō*. Found him after search and in the synagogue as John explains (verse 59) in Capernaum, perhaps that very synagogue built by a centurion (Luke 7:5). *Rabbi* (*Rabbei*). See on 1:38 for this courteous title. *When camest thou hither?* (*pote hōde gegonas;*). Second perfect active indicative of *ginomai*. "When hast thou come?" We sought you anxiously on the other side of the lake and could not see how you came across (verses 22–24).

26. *Not because ye saw signs* (*ouch hoti eidete sēmeia*). Second aorist active indicative of the defective verb *horaō*. They had seen the "signs" wrought by Jesus (verse 2), but this one had led to wild fanaticism (verse 14) and complete failure to grasp the spiritual lessons. *But because ye ate of the loaves* (*all' hoti ephagete ek tōn artōn*). Second aorist active indicative of *esthiō*, defective verb. *Ye were filled* (*echortas-*

thēte).   First aorist passive indicative of *chortazō*, from *chortos* (grass) as in verse 10, to eat grass, then to eat anything, to satisfy hunger.   They were more concerned with hungry stomachs than with hungry souls.   It was a sharp and deserved rebuke.

27. *Work not for (mē ergazesthe).*   Prohibition with *mē* and present middle imperative of *ergazomai*, old verb from *ergon*, work. *The meat (tēn brōsin).*   The act of eating (Rom. 14:17), corrosion (Matt. 6:19), the thing eaten as here (II Cor. 9:10). See on John 4:32. *Which perisheth (tēn apollumenēn).* Present middle participle of *apollumi*.   They were already hungry again. *Unto eternal life (eis zōēn aiōnion).*   Mystical metaphor quite beyond this crowd hungry only for more loaves and fishes.   Bernard thinks that John has here put together various sayings of Christ to make one discourse, a gratuitous interpretation. *Will give (dōsei).*   Future active indicative of *didōmi*.   The outcome is still future and will be decided by their attitude towards the Son of man (verse 51). *For him the Father, even God, hath sealed (touton gar ho patēr esphragisen ho theos).*   Literally, "For this one the Father sealed, God."   First aorist active indicative of *sphragizō*, to seal.   See elsewhere in John 3:33 (attestation by man).   Sealing by God is rare in N.T. (II Cor. 1:22; Eph. 1:13; 4:30).   It is not clear to what item, if any single one, John refers when the Father set his seal of approval on the Son.   It was done at his baptism when the Holy Spirit came upon him and the Father spoke to him. Cf. 5:37.

28. *What must we do? (Ti poiōmen;).*   Present active deliberative subjunctive of *poieō*, "What are we to do as a habit?"   For the aorist subjunctive (*poiēsōmen*) in a like question for a single act see Luke 3:10.   For the present indicative (*poioumen*) of inquiry concerning actual conduct see John 11:47 (what are we doing?). *That we may work the works of God (hina ergazōmetha ta erga tou theou).*   Final clause with *hina* and the present middle subjunctive, "that

we may go on working the works of God." There may have
been an element of vague sincerity in this question in spite of
their supercilious attitude.

29. *The work of God that ye believe (to ergon tou theou hina
pisteuēte).* In I Thess. 1:3 Paul speaks of "your work of
faith" (*humōn tou ergou tēs pisteōs).* So here Jesus terms belief in him as the work of God. These Jews were thinking of
various deeds of the Pharisaic type and rules. Jesus turns
their minds to the central fact. "This simple formula con-
tains the complete solution of the relation of faith and
works" (Westcott). Note the present active subjunctive
pisteuēte, "that ye may keep on believing." *On him whom he
hath sent (eis hon apesteilen ekeinos).* The pronominal antecedent (*eis touton hon*) is omitted and the preposition *eis*
is retained with the relative *hon* really the direct object of
apesteilen (sent). Note *ekeinos* for God (emphatic he).

30. *For a sign (sēmeion).* Predicate accusative, as a sign,
with *ti* (what). As if the sign of the day before was without
value. Jesus had said that they did not understand his signs
(verse 26). *That we may see, and believe thee (hina idōmen kai
pisteusōmen).* Purpose clause with *hina* and the second
aorist (ingressive) active subjunctive of *horaō* and the first
aorist (ingressive) active subjunctive of *pisteuō,* "that we
may come to see and come to have faith in thee." It is hard
to have patience with this superficial and almost sneering
mob. *What workest thou? (Ti ergazēi;).* They not simply
depreciate the miracle of the day before, but set up a standard for Jesus.

31. *Ate the manna (to manna ephagon).* The rabbis quoted
Psa. 72:16 to prove that the Messiah, when he comes, will
outdo Moses with manna from heaven. Jesus was claiming
to be the Messiah and able to give bread for eternal life
(verse 27). Lightfoot (*Biblical Essays,* p. 152) says: "The
key to the understanding of the whole situation is an acquaintance with the national expectation of the greater

Moses." They quote to Jesus Ex. 16:15 (of. Numb. 11:7; 21:5; Deut. 8:3). Their plea is that Moses gave us bread "from heaven" (*ek tou ouranou*). Can Jesus equal that deed of Moses?

32. *It was not Moses that gave you* (*ou Mōusēs edōken humin*). "Not Moses gave you." Blunt and pointed denial (aorist active indicative of *didōmi*) that Moses was the giver of the bread from heaven (the manna). Moses was not superior to Christ on this score. *But my Father* (*all ho patēr mou*). Not "our Father," but same claim as in 5:17f. Which caused so much anger in Jerusalem. *Gives* (*didōsin*). Present active indicative, not aorist (*edōken*). Continual process. *The true bread out of heaven* (*ton arton ek tou ouranou ton alēthinon*). "The bread out of heaven" as the manna and more "the genuine bread" of which that was merely a type. On *alēthinos* see 1:9; 4:23.

33. *The bread of God* (*ho artos tou theou*). All bread is of God (Matt. 6:11). The manna came down from heaven (Numb. 11:9) as does this bread (*ho katabainōn*). Refers to the bread (*ho artos*, masculine). Bernard notes that this phrase (coming down) is used seven times in this discourse (33, 38, 41, 42, 50, 51, 58). *Giveth life* (*zōēn didous*). Chrysostom observes that the manna gave nourishment (*trophē*), but not life (*zōē*). This is a most astounding statement to the crowd.

34. *Lord* (*Kurie*). Used now instead of *Rabbi* (26) though how much the people meant by it is not clear. *Evermore give us this bread* (*pantote dos hēmin ton arton touton*). Second aorist active imperative second singular like *dos* in Matt. 6:11 (urgent petition). What kind of bread do they mean? The Jewish commentaries and Philo speak of the manna as typifying heavenly bread for the soul. Paul in I Cor. 10:3 seems to refer to the manna as "spiritual food." Like the woman at the well (4:15) they long "always" to have "this bread," a perpetual supply. It is probably to this crowd as the water in 4:15 was to the woman.

35. *I am the bread of life* (*Egō eimi ho artos tēs zōēs*). This sublime sentence was startling in the extreme to the crowd. Philo does compare the manna to the *theios logos* in an allegorical sense, but this language is far removed from Philo's vagueness. In the Synoptics (Mark 14:22 = Matt. 26:26 = Luke 22:19) Jesus uses bread (*artos*) as the symbol of his body in the Lord's Supper, but here Jesus offers himself in place of the loaves and fishes which they had come to seek (24, 26). He is the bread of life in two senses: it has life in itself, the living bread (51), and it gives life to others like the water of life, the tree of life. John often has Jesus saying "I am" (*egō eimi*). As also in 6:41, 48, 51; 8:12; 10:7, 9, 11, 14; 11:25; 14:6; 15:1, 5. *He that cometh to me* (*ho erchomenos pros eme*). The first act of the soul in approaching Jesus. See also verse 37. *Shall not hunger* (*ou mē peinasēi*). Strong double negative *ou mē* with first aorist (ingressive) active subjunctive, "shall not become hungry." *He that believeth on me* (*ho pisteuōn eis eme*). The continuous relation of trust after coming like *pisteuēte* (present tense) in verse 29. See both verbs used together also in 7:37f. *Shall never thirst* (*ou mē dipsēsei pōpote*). So the old MSS. the future active indicative instead of the aorist subjunctive as above, an even stronger form of negation with *pōpote* (1:18) added.

36. *That ye have seen me* (*hoti kai heōrakate me*). It is not certain that *me* is genuine. If not, Jesus may refer to verse 26. If genuine, some other saying is referred to that we do not have. Note *kai* (also or even). *And yet believe not* (*kai ou pisteuete*). Use of *kai* = and yet.

37. *All that* (*pān ho*). Collective use of the neuter singular, classic idiom, seen also in 6:39; 17:2, 24; I John 5:4. Perhaps the notion of unity like *hen* in 17:21 underlies this use of *pān ho*. *Giveth me* (*didōsin moi*). For the idea that the disciples are given to the Son see also 6:39, 65; 10:29; 17:2, 6, 9, 12, 24; 18:9. *I will in no wise cast out* (*ou mē ekbalō exō*).

Strong double negation as in verse 35 with second aorist active subjunctive of *ballō*. Definite promise of Jesus to welcome the one who comes.

38. *I am come down* (*katabebēka*). Perfect active indicative of *katabainō*. See on 33 for frequent use of this phrase by Jesus. Here *apo* is correct rather than *ek* with *tou ouranou*. *Not to do* (*ouch hina poiō*). "Not that I keep on doing" (final clause with *hina* and present active subjunctive of *poieō*). *But the will* (*alla to thelēma*). Supply *hina poiō* after *alla*, "but that I keep on doing." This is the fulness of joy for Jesus, to do his Father's will (4:34; 5:30).

39. *That of all that which* (*hina pān ho*). Literally, "That all which" (see verse 37 for *pān ho*), but there is a sharp anacoluthon with *pān* left as *nominativus pendens*. *I should lose nothing* (*mē apolesō ex autou*). Construed with *hina*, "that I shall not lose anything of it." *Apolesō*, from *apollumi*, can be either future active indicative or first aorist active subjunctive as is true also of *anastēsō* (from *anistēmi*), "I shall raise up." *At the last day* (*tēi eschatēi hēmerāi*). Locative case without *en*. Only in John, but four times here (39, 40, 44, 54) "with the majesty of a solemn refrain." In 7:37 it is the last day of the feast of tabernacles, but in 11:24 and 12:48 of the day of judgment as here. Christ is the Agent of the general resurrection in 5:28 as in I Cor. 15:22 while here only the resurrection of the righteous is mentioned.

40. *Should have eternal life* (*echēi zōēn aiōnion*). Present active subjunctive with *hina*, "that he may keep on having eternal life" as in 3:15, 36. *Beholdeth* (*theōrōn*). With the eye of faith as in 12:45. *And I will raise him up* (*kai anastēsō*). Future active indicative (volitive future, promise) as in 54.

41. *Murmured* (*egogguzon*). Imperfect active of the onomatopoetic verb *gogguzō*, late verb in LXX (murmuring against Moses), papyri (vernacular), like the cooing of doves

or the buzzing of bees. These Galilean Jews are puzzled over what Jesus had said (verses 33, 35) about his being the bread of God come down from heaven.

42. *How doth he now say?* (*Pōs nun legei;*). They knew Jesus as the son of Joseph and Mary. They cannot comprehend his claim to be from heaven. This lofty claim puzzles sceptics today.

43. *Murmur not* (*mē gogguzete*). Prohibition with *mē* and the present active imperative, "stop murmuring" (the very word of verse 41). There was a rising tide of protest.

44. *Except the Father draw him* (*ean mē helkusēi auton*). Negative condition of third class with *ean mē* and first aorist active subjunctive of *helkuō*, older form *helkō*, to drag like a net (John 21:6), or sword (18:10), or men (Acts 16:19), to draw by moral power (12:32), as in Jer. 31:3. *Surō*, the other word to drag (Acts 8:3; 14:19) is not used of Christ's drawing power. The same point is repeated in verse 65. The approach of the soul to God is initiated by God, the other side of verse 37. See Rom. 8:7 for the same doctrine and use of *oude dunatai* like *oudeis dunatai* here.

45. *Taught of God* (*didaktoi theou*). A free quotation from Isa. 54:13 with this phrase in the LXX. There is here the ablative case *theou* with the passive verbal adjective *didaktoi* (Robertson, *Grammar*, p. 516). In I Thess. 4:9 we have the compound verbal *theodidaktoi*. The same use of *didaktos* with the ablative occurs in I Cor. 2:13. *And hath learned* (*kai mathōn*). Second aorist active participle of *manthanō*. It is not enough to hear God's voice. He must heed it and learn it and do it. This is a voluntary response. This one inevitably comes to Christ.

46. *This one has seen the Father* (*houtos heōraken ton patera*). Perfect active indicative of *horaō*. With the eyes no one has seen God (1:18) save the Son who is "from God" in origin (1:1, 14; 7:29; 16:27; 17:8). The only way for others to see God is to see Christ (14:9).

47. *He that believeth* (*ho pisteuōn*). This is the way to see God in Christ.

48. *I am the bread of life* (*egō eimi ho artos tēs zōēs*). Jesus repeats the astounding words of verse 35 after fuller explanation. The believer in Christ has eternal life because he gives himself to him.

49. *And they died* (*kai apethanon*). Physical death. The manna did not prevent death. But this new manna will prevent spiritual death.

50. *That a man may eat thereof, and not die* (*hina tis ex autou phagēi kai mē apothanēi*). Purpose clause with *hina* and the second aorist active subjunctive of *esthiō* and *apothnēskō*. The wonder and the glory of it all, but quite beyond the insight of this motley crowd.

51. *The living bread* (*ho artos ho zōn*). "The bread the living." Repetition of the claim in 35, 41, 48, but with a slight change from *zōēs* to *zōn* (present active participle of *zaō*). It is alive and can give life. See 4:10 for living water. In Rev. 1:17 Jesus calls himself the Living One (*ho zōn*). *For ever* (*eis ton aiōna*). Eternally like *aiōnion* with *zōēn* in 47. *I shall give* (*egō dōsō*). Emphasis on *egō* (I). Superior so to Moses. *Is my flesh* (*hē sarx mou estin*). See on 1:14 for *sarx* the Incarnation. This new idea creates far more difficulty to the hearers who cannot grasp Christ's idea of self-sacrifice. *For the life of the world* (*huper tēs tou kosmou zōēs*). Over, in behalf of, *huper* means, and in some connexions instead of as in 11:50. See 1:30 for the Baptist's picture of Christ as the Lamb of God that taketh away the sin of the world. See also 3:17; 4:42; I John 3:16; Matt. 20:28; Gal. 3:13; II Cor. 5:14f.; Rom. 5:8. Jesus has here presented to this Galilean multitude the central fact of his atoning death for the spiritual life of the world.

52. *Strove* (*emachonto*). Imperfect (inchoative) middle of *machomai*, to fight in armed combat (Acts 7:26), then to wage a war of words as here and II Tim. 2:24. They were

already murmuring (41), now they began bitter strife with one another over the last words of Jesus (43–51), some probably seeing a spiritual meaning in them. There was division of opinion about Jesus in Jerusalem also later (7:12, 40; 9:16; 10:19). *How can?* (*Pōs dunatai;*). The very idiom used by Nicodemus in 3:4, 9. Here scornful disbelief. *This man* (*houtos*). Contemptuous use pictured in verse 42. *His flesh to eat* (*tēn sarka autou phagein*). As if we were cannibals! Some MSS. do not have *autou*, but the meaning is clear. The mystical appropriation of Christ by the believer (Gal. 2:20; Eph. 3:17) they could not comprehend, though some apparently were against this literal interpretation of "flesh" (*sarx*).

53. *Except ye eat* (*ean mē phagēte*). Negative condition of third class with second aorist active subjunctive of *esthiō*. Jesus repeats the statement in verses 50 and 51. Note change of *mou* (my) in verse 51 to *tou huiou tou anthrōpou* with same idea. *And drink his blood* (*kai piēte autou to haima*). Same condition with second aorist active subjunctive of *pinō*. This addition makes the demand of Jesus seem to these Jews more impossible than before if taken in a baldly literal sense. The only possible meaning is the spiritual appropriation of Jesus Christ by faith (verse 47), for "ye have not life in yourselves" (*ouk echete zōēn en heautois*). Life is found only in Christ.

54. *He that eateth* (*ho trōgōn*). Present active participle for continual or habitual eating like *pisteuete* in verse 29. The verb *trōgō* is an old one for eating fruit or vegetables and the feeding of animals. In the N.T. it occurs only in John 6:54, 56, 58; 13:18; Matt. 24:38. Elsewhere in the Gospels always *esthiō* or *ephagon* (defective verb with *esthiō*). No distinction is made here between *ephagon* (48, 50, 52, 53, 58) and *trōgō* (54, 56, 57, 58). Some men understand Jesus here to be speaking of the Lord's Supper by prophetic forecast or rather they think that John has put into the

mouth of Jesus the sacramental conception of Christianity by making participation in the bread and wine the means of securing eternal life. To me that is a violent misinterpretation of the Gospel and an utter misrepresentation of Christ. It is a grossly literal interpretation of the mystical symbolism of the language of Jesus which these Jews also misunderstood. Christ uses bold imagery to picture spiritual appropriation of himself who is to give his life-blood for the life of the world (51). It would have been hopeless confusion for these Jews if Jesus had used the symbolism of the Lord's Supper. It would be real dishonesty for John to use this discourse as a propaganda for sacramentalism. The language of Jesus can only have a spiritual meaning as he unfolds himself as the true manna.

55. *Meat indeed* (*alēthēs brōsis*). So the best MSS., "true food." See on 4:32 for *brōsis* as equal to *brōma* (a thing eaten). *Drink indeed* (*alēthēs posis*). Correct text, "true drink." For *posis* see Rom. 14:17; Col. 2:16 (only N.T. examples).

56. *Abideth in me and I in him* (*en emoi menei kágō en autōi*). Added to the phrase in 54 in the place of *echei zōēn aiōnion* (has eternal life). The verb *menō* (to abide) expresses continual mystical fellowship between Christ and the believer as in 15:4–7; I John 2:6, 27, 28; 3:6, 24; 4:12, 16. There is, of course, no reference to the Lord's Supper (Eucharist), but simply to mystical fellowship with Christ.

57. *The living Father* (*ho zōn patēr*). Nowhere else in the N.T., but see 5:26 and "the living God" (Matt. 16:16; II Cor. 6:16). The Father is the source of life and so "I live because of the Father" (*kágō zō dia ton patera*). *He that eateth me* (*ho trōgōn me*). Still bolder putting of the mystical appropriation of Christ (51, 53, 54, 56). *Because of me* (*di' eme*). The same idea appears in 14:19: "Because I live ye shall live also." See 11:25. Jesus Christ is our ground of

hope and guarantee of immortality. Life is in Christ. There
is no real difficulty in this use of *dia* with the accusative as
with *dia ton patera* just before. It occurs also in 15:3. As
the Father is the fount of life to Christ, so Christ is the
fount of life to us. See I John 4:9 where *dia* is used with
the genitive (*di' autou*) as the intermediate agent, not the
ground or reason as here.

58. *This is the bread* (*houtos estin ho artos*). Summary
and final explanation of the true manna (from verse 32 on)
as being Jesus Christ himself.

59. *In the synagogue* (*en sunagōgēi*). Definite like our
in church, though article absent. Only use of the word in
John except 18:20. "Among the ruins at *Tell Hum*, the probable site of Capernaum, have been found among the remains
of a synagogue a block of stone perhaps the lintel, carved
with a pot of manna, and with a pattern of vine leaves and
clusters of grapes" (Vincent).

60. *A hard saying* (*sklēros*). "This saying is a hard one."
Old adjective, rough, harsh, dried hard (from *skellō*, to dry),
probably the last saying of Jesus that he was the bread of
life come down from heaven and they were to eat him. It
is to be hoped that none of the twelve joined the many
disciples in this complaint. *Hear it* (*autou akouein*). Or
"hear him," hear with acceptation. For *akouō* with the
genitive see 10:3, 16, 27.

61. *Knowing in himself* (*eidōs en heautōi*). Second perfect
active participle of *oida*. See 2:25 for this supernatural insight into men's minds. *Murmured* (*gogguzousin*). Present
active indicative retained in indirect discourse. See 41 for
gogguzō. *At this* (*peri toutou*). "Concerning this word."
Cause to stumble (*skandalizei*). Common Synoptic verb
from *skandalon* for which see Matt. 5:29. In John again
only in 16:1.

62. *What then if ye should behold* (*ean oun theōrēte*). No
"what" in the Greek. Condition of third class with *ean*

and present active subjunctive, "if ye then behold." *Ascending* (*anabainonta*). Present active participle picturing the process. *Where he was before* (*hopou ēn to proteron*). Neuter articular adjective as adverb (accusative of general reference, at the former time as in 9:8 and Gal. 3:13). Clear statement of Christ's pre-existence in his own words as in 3:13 and 17:5 (cf. 1:1-18).

63. *That quickeneth* (*to zōopoioun*). Articular present active participle of *zōopoieō* for which see 5:21. For the contrast between *pneuma* (spirit) and *sarx* (flesh) see already 3:6. *The words* (*ta rēmata*). Those in this discourse (I have just spoken, *lelalēka*), for they are the words of God (3:34; 8:47; 17:8). No wonder they "are spirit and are life" (*pneuma estin kai zōē estin*). The breath of God and the life of God is in these words of Jesus. Never man spoke like Jesus (7:46). There is life in his words today.

64. *That believe not* (*hoi ou pisteuousin*). Failure to believe kills the life in the words of Jesus. *Knew from the beginning* (*ēidei ex archēs*). In the N.T. we have *ex archēs* only here and 16:4, but *ap' archēs* in apparently the same sense as here in 15:27; I John 2:7, 24; 3:11 and see Luke 1:2; I John 1:1. From the first Jesus distinguished between real trust in him and mere lip service (2:24; 8:31), two senses of *pisteuō*. *Were* (*eisin*). Present active indicative retained in indirect discourse. *And who it was that should betray him* (*kai tis estin ho paradōsōn*). Same use of *estin* and note article and future active participle of *paradidōmi*, to hand over, to betray. John does not say here that Jesus knew that Judas would betray him when he chose him as one of the twelve, least of all that he chose him for that purpose. What he does say is that Jesus was not taken by surprise and soon saw signs of treason in Judas. The same verb is used of John's arrest in Matt. 4:12. Once Judas is termed traitor (*prodotēs*) in Luke 6:16. Judas had gifts and was given his opportunity. He did not have to betray Jesus.

65. *Except it be given him of the Father* (*ean mē ēi dedo-menon autōi ek tou patros*). Condition of third class with *ean mē* and periphrastic perfect passive subjunctive of *di-dōmi*. Precisely the same point as in verse 44 where we have *helkusēi* instead of *ēi dedomenon*. The impulse to faith comes from God. Jesus does not expect all to believe and seems to imply that Judas did not truly believe.

66. *Upon this* (*ek toutou*). Same idiom in 19:12. "Out of this saying or circumstance." Jesus drew the line of cleavage between the true and the false believers. *Went back* (*apēlthon eis ta opisō*). Aorist (ingressive) active indicative of *aperchomai* with *eis ta opisō*, "to the rear" (the behind things) as in 18:6. *Walked no more with him* (*ouketi met' autou periepatoun*). Imperfect active of *peripateō*. The crisis had come. These half-hearted seekers after the loaves and fishes and political power turned abruptly from Jesus, walked out of the synagogue with a deal of bluster and were walking with Jesus no more. Jesus had completely disillusioned these hungry camp-followers who did not care for spiritual manna that consisted in intimate appropriation of the life of Jesus as God's Son.

67. *Would ye also go away?* (*Mē kai humeis thelete hupagein;*). Jesus puts it with the negative answer (*mē*) expected. See 21:5 where Jesus also uses *mē* in a question. Judas must have shown some sympathy with the disappointed and disappearing crowds. But he kept still. There was possibly restlessness on the part of the other apostles.

68. *Lord, to whom shall we go?* (*Kurie, pros tina apeleus-ometha;*). Peter is the spokesman as usual and his words mean that, if such a thought as desertion crossed their minds when the crowd left, they dismissed it instantly. They had made their choice. They accepted these very words of Jesus that had caused the defection as "the words of eternal life."

69. *We have believed* (*hēmeis pepisteukamen*). Perfect active indicative of *pisteuō*, "We have come to believe and still believe" (verse 29). *And know* (*kai egnōkamen*). Same tense of *ginōskō*, "We have come to know and still know." *Thou art the Holy One of God* (*su ei ho hagios tou theou*). Bernard follows those who believe that this is John's report of the same confession given by the Synoptics (Mark 8:27f. = Matt. 16:13–20 = Luke 9:18f.), an utterly unjustifiable conclusion. The details are wholly different. Here in the synagogue in Capernaum, there on Mt. Hermon near Caesarea Philippi. What earthly difficulty is there in supposing that Peter could make a noble confession twice? That is to my mind a wooden conception of the apostles in their growing apprehension of Christ.

70. *And one of you is a devil* (*kai ex humōn heis diabolos estin*). Jesus does not say that Judas was a devil when he chose him, but that he is one now. In 13:2 and 27 John speaks of the devil entering Judas. How soon the plan to betray Jesus first entered the heart of Judas we do not know (12:4). One wonders if the words of Jesus here did not cut Judas to the quick.

71. *Of Simon Iscariot* (*Simōnos Iskariōtou*). So his father was named Iscariot also, a man of Kerioth (possibly in Judah, Josh. 15:25, possibly in Moab, Jer. 48:24), not in Galilee. Judas was the only one of the twelve not a Galilean. The rest of the verse is like 12:4. *One of the twelve* (*heis ek tōn dōdeka*). The eternal horror of the thing.

CHAPTER VII

1. *After these things* (*meta tauta*). John's favourite general note of the order of events. Bernard conceives that the events in 7:1-14 follow 7:15-24 and both follow chapter 5, not chapter 6, a wholly needless readjustment of the narrative to suit a preconceived theory. John simply supplements the narrative in the Synoptics at points deemed important. He now skips the period of withdrawal from Galilee of about six months (from passover to tabernacles). *Walked* (*periepatei*). Imperfect active, a literal picture of the itinerant ministry of Jesus. He has returned to Galilee from the region of Caesarea Philippi. He had been avoiding Galilee as well as Judea for six months. *For he would not walk in Judea* (*ou gar ēthelen en tēi Ioudaiāi*). Imperfect active of *thelō* picturing the attitude of refusal to work in Judea after the events in chapter 5 (perhaps a year and a half before). *Sought to kill* (*ezētoun apokteinai*). Imperfect active again, progressive attitude, had been seeking to kill him as shown in 5:18 where the same words occur.

2. *The feast of tabernacles* (*hē skēnopēgia*). Only New Testament example of this word (*skēnē*, tent, *pēgnumi*, to fasten as in Heb. 8:2). Technical name of this feast (Deut. 16:13; Lev. 23:34, 43). It began on the 15th of the month Tisri (end of September) and lasted seven days and finally eight days in post-exilic times (Neh. 8:18). It was one of the chief feasts of the Jews.

3. *His brethren* (*hoi adelphoi autou*). "His brothers" (half-brothers actually), who "were not believing on him" (*oude episteuon eis auton*) as stated in verse 5. They were hostile to the Messianic assumptions of Jesus, a natural attitude as one can well see, though at first they were

117

friendly (2:12). *Depart hence* (*metabēthi enteuthen*). Second
aorist active imperative of *metabainō*, to pass to another
place (5:24; 13:1). It was impertinence on their part. *That
thy disciples also may behold* (*hina kai hoi mathētai sou
theōrēsousin*). Final clause with *hina* and the future active
indicative of *theōreō*. Jesus had many disciples in Judea at
the start (2:23; 4:1) and had left it because of the jealousy of
the Pharisees over his success (4:3). The brothers may have
heard of the great defection in the synagogue in Capernaum
(6:66), but the advice is clearly ironical. *Which thou doest*
(*ha poieis*). To what works they refer by this language we
do not know. But Jesus had been away from Galilee for
some months and from Judea for a year and a half. Perhaps
the brothers of Jesus may actually have been eager to rush
Jesus into the hostile atmosphere of Jerusalem again.

4. *In secret* (*en kruptōi*). See Matt. 6:4, 6 for this phrase.
Openly (*en parrēsiāi*). "In public" (*pān, rēsis*, telling it all).
See on Matt. 8:32. Common in John (7:13, 26; 10:24;
16:25, 29; 18:20; here again contrasted with *en kruptōi*).
It is wise advice in the abstract that a public teacher must
allow inspection of his deeds, but the motive is evil. They
might get Jesus into trouble. *If thou doest these things* (*ei
tauta poieis*). This condition of the first class assumes the
reality of the deeds of Jesus, but the use of the condition
at all throws doubt on it all as in Matt. 4:3, 6. *Manifest
thyself* (*phanerōson seauton*). First aorist active imperative
of *phaneroō*. *To the world* (*tōi kosmōi*). Not just to "thy
disciples," but to the public at large as at the feast of tabernacles. See 8:26; 14:22 for this use of *kosmos*.

5. *For even his brethren did not believe on him* (*oude gar
hoi adelphoi autou episteuon eis auton*). Literally, "For not
even were his brothers believing on him." Imperfect tense
of *pisteuō* with sad picture of the persistent refusal of the
brothers of Jesus to believe in his Messianic assumptions,
after the two rejections in Capernaum (Luke 4:16-31; Mark

6:1–6 = Matt. 13:54–58), and also after the blasphemous accusation of being in league with Beelzebub when the mother
and brothers came to take Jesus home (Mark 3:31–35 =
Matt. 12:46–50 = Luke 8:19–21). The brothers here are
sarcastic.

6. *My time is not yet come* (*ho kairos ho emos oupō parestin*).
Only use with verse 8 of *kairos* in this Gospel, elsewhere
chronos (John 5:6) or more often *hōra* (2:4) "the predestined
hour" (Bernard). Here *kairos* is the fitting or proper occasion for Christ's manifesting himself publicly to the authorities as Messiah as in verse 8. At the feast of tabernacles
Jesus did make such public claims (7:29, 33; 8:12, 28, 38,
42, 58). *Parestin* is present active indicative of *pareimi*,
old compound, to be by, to be present. The brothers of
Jesus had the regular Jewish obligation to go up to the feast,
but the precise day was a matter of indifference to them.

7. *Cannot hate* (*ou dunatai misein*). Because of "the law
of moral correspondence" (Westcott), often in John for
"inherent impossibility" (Vincent). The brothers of Jesus
here belong to the unbelieving world (*kosmos*) which is unable to love Jesus (15:18, 23, 24) and which Jesus had already exposed ("testify," *marturō*, 5:42, 45). This unbelieving "world" resented the exposure (3:19, cf. 18:37).

8. *Go ye up to the feast* (*humeis anabēte eis tēn heortēn*).
The emphatic word by position is *humeis* (ye) in contrast
with *egō* (I). Second aorist active imperative of *anabainō*,
old and common verb for going up to the feast (2:13) or
anywhere. Take your own advice (7:3). *I go not up yet*
(*egō oupō anabainō*). So Westcott and Hort after B W L
(Neutral) while *ou* (not) is read by Aleph D, African Latin,
Vulgate, Coptic (Western). Some of the early Greek Fathers
were puzzled over the reading *ouk* (I go not up) as contra-
dictory to verse 10 wherein it is stated that Jesus did go up.
Almost certainly *ouk* (not) is correct and is not really con-
tradictory when one notes in verse 10 that the manner of

Christ's going up is precisely the opposite of the advice of the brothers in verses 3 and 4. "Not yet" (*oupō*) is genuine before "fulfilled" (*peplērōtai*, perfect passive indicative of *pleroō*). One may think, if he will, that Jesus changed his plans after these words, but that is unnecessary. He simply refused to fall in with his brothers' sneering proposal for a grand Messianic procession with the caravan on the way to the feast. He will do that on the journey to the last passover.

9. *He abode still in Galilee* (*emeinen en tēi Galilaiāi*). No "still" (*eti*) in the Greek text. The constative aorist active indicative *emeinen* covers a period of some days.

10. *Were gone up* (*anebēsan*). Second aorist active indicative of *anabainō*, not past perfect though the action is antecedent in fact to the following *tote anebē*. The Greek does not always draw the precise distinction between the merely punctiliar (aorist) antecedent action and the past perfect (2:9; 4:45). *He also* (*tote autos*). As well as the brothers. *Not publicly* (*ou phanerōs*). Against their advice in verse 4, using *phanerōson* (the very same word stem). *But as it were in secret* (*alla hōs en kruptōi*). "Not with the usual caravan of pilgrims" (Bernard). Just the opposite of their advice in verse 4 with the same phrase *en phanerōi*. Plainly Jesus purposely went contrary to the insincere counsel of his brothers as to the manner of his Messianic manifestation. This secrecy concerned solely the journey to Jerusalem, not his public teaching there .after his arrival (7:26, 28; 18:20).

11. *The Jews* (*hoi Ioudaioi*). The hostile leaders in Jerusalem, not the Galilean crowds (7:12) nor the populace in Jerusalem (7:25). *Sought* (*ezētoun*). Imperfect active of *zēteō*, "were seeking," picture of the attitude of the Jewish leaders toward Jesus who had not yet appeared in public at the feast. In fact he had avoided Jerusalem since the collision in chapter 5. The leaders clearly wished to attack him. *Where is he?* (*pou estin ekeinos;*). "Where is that one?

(emphatic use of *ekeinos* as in 1:8; 9:12). Jesus had been at two feasts during his ministry (passover in 2:12ff.; possibly another passover in 5:1), but he had avoided the preceding passover (6:4; 7:1). The leaders in Jerusalem had kept in touch with Christ's work in Galilee. They anticipate a crisis in Jerusalem.

12. *Much murmuring (goggusmos polus)*. This Ionic onomatopoetic word is from *gogguzō* for which verb see 6:41, 61; 7:32, for secret displeasure (Acts 6:1) or querulous discontent (Phil. 2:14). *Among the multitudes (en tois ochlois)*. "The multitudes" literally, plural here only in John. These different groups were visitors from Galilee and elsewhere and were divided in their opinion of Jesus as the Galileans had already become (6:66). *A good man (agathos)*. Pure in motive. See Mark 10:17f.; Rom. 5:7 (absolute sense of God). Superior to *dikaios*. Jesus had champions in these scattered groups in the temple courts. *Not so, but he leadeth the multitude astray (ou, alla planāi ton ochlon)*. Sharp clash in the crowd. Present active indicative of *planaō*, to go astray (Matt. 18:12f.), like our "planets," to lead others astray (Matt. 24:4, 5, 11, etc.). In the end the rulers will call Jesus "that deceiver" (*ekeinos ho planos*, Matt. 27:63). The Jewish leaders have a following among the crowds as is seen (7:31f.).

13. *Howbeit (mentoi)*. See 4:27 for this compound particle (*men, toi*), by way of exception, but yet. *Spake (elalei)*. Imperfect active of *laleō*, "was speaking," picturing the whispering or secret talk (*no man openly, oudeis parrēsiāi*). Best MSS. do not have *en* here with *parrēsiāi* (locative or instrumental case of manner) as in 7:26; 10:24; 11:54, but *en* genuine in 7:4; Col. 2:15. This adverbial use of *parrēsiāi* is common enough (Mark 8:37). *For fear of the Jews (dia ton phobon tōn Ioudaiōn)*. Objective genitive. The crowds really feared the Jewish leaders and evidently did not wish to involve Jesus or themselves. See the same phrase and attitude on the part of the disciples in 19:38; 20:19.

14. *But when it was now in the midst of the feast (ēdē de tēs heortēs mesousēs).* Literally, "But feast being already midway." Genitive absolute, present active participle, of *mesoō*, old verb from *mesos*, in LXX, here only in N.T. The feast of tabernacles was originally seven days, but a last day (verse 37; Lev. 23:36) was added, making eight in all. *And taught (kai edidasken).* Imperfect active of *didaskō*, probably inchoative, "began to teach." He went up (*anebē*, effective aorist, arrived). The leaders had asked (verse 11) where Jesus was. There he was now before their very eyes.

15. *Marvelled (ethaumazon).* Picturesque imperfect active of *thaumazō*, "were wondering." After all the bluster of the rulers (verse 13) here was Jesus teaching without interruption. *Knoweth letters (grammata oiden).* Second perfect active indicative used as present. *Grammata,* old word from *graphō*, to write, is originally the letters formed (Gal. 6:11), then a letter or epistle (Acts 28:21), then the sacred Scriptures (John 5:47; II Tim. 3:15), then learning like Latin *litterae* and English letters (Acts 26:24; John 7:15). "The marvel was that Jesus showed Himself familiar with the literary methods of the time, which were supposed to be confined to the scholars of the popular teachers" (Westcott). *Having never learned (mē memathēkōs).* Perfect active participle of *manthanō* with *mē,* the usual negative (subjective) with the participle. It is not the wisdom of Jesus that disconcerted the Jewish leaders, but his learning (Marcus Dods). And yet Jesus had not attended either of the rabbinical theological schools in Jerusalem (Hillel, Shammai). He was not a rabbi in the technical sense, only a carpenter, and yet he surpassed the professional rabbis in the use of their own methods of debate. It is sometimes true today that unschooled men in various walks of life forge ahead of men of lesser gifts with school training. See the like puzzle of the Sanhedrin concerning Peter and John (Acts 4:13). This is not an argument against education,

but it takes more than education to make a real man. Probably this sneer at Jesus came from some of the teachers in the Jerusalem seminaries. "Christ was in the eyes of the Jews a merely self-taught enthusiast" (Westcott).

16. *Mine* (*emē*). Possessive pronoun, "not mine in origin." Jesus denies that he is self-taught, though not a schoolman. *But his that sent me* (*alla tou pempsantos me*). Genitive case of the articular participle (first aorist active of *pempō*). His teaching is not self-originated nor is it the product of the schools (see the Talmud in contrast with the New Testament). Jesus often in John uses this idiom of "the one who sent me" of the Father (4:34; 5:23, 24, 30, 37; 6:38–40, 44; 7:16, 18, 28, etc.). The bold claim is here made by Jesus that his teaching is superior in character and source to that of the rabbis.

17. *If any man willeth to do* (*ean tis thelēi poiein*). Condition of third class with *ean* and present active subjunctive *thelēi* not used as a mere auxiliary verb for the future "will do," but with full force of *thelō*, to will, to wish. See the same use of *thelō* in 5:40 "and yet ye are not willing to come" (*kai ou thelete elthein*). *He shall know* (*gnōsetai*). Future middle indicative of *ginōskō*. Experimental knowledge from willingness to do God's will. See this same point by Jesus in 5:46; 18:37. There must be moral harmony between man's purpose and God's will. "If there be no sympathy there can be no understanding" (Westcott). Atheists of all types have no point of contact for approach to the knowledge of Christ. This fact does not prove the non-existence of God, but simply their own isolation. They are out of tune with the Infinite. For those who love God it is also true that obedience to God's will brings richer knowledge of God. Agnostic and atheistic critics are disqualified·by Jesus as witnesses to his claims. *Of God* (*ek tou theou*). Out of God as source. *From myself* (*ap' emautou*). Instead of from God.

18. *From himself* (*aph' heautou*). This kind of teacher is self-taught, pushes his own ideas, presses his own claims for position and glory, "blows his own horn" as we say. Jesus is the other type of teacher, seeks the glory of the one who sent him, whose herald and ambassador he is. *The same* (*houtos*). "This one." *Unrighteousness* (*adikia*). Old word from *adikos* (*a* privative and *dikē*). Here in contrast with "true" (*alēthēs*). See II Thess. 2:10 and I Cor. 13:6 for the deceit of unrighteousness in contrast with truth as here.

19. *And yet* (*kai*). Clear use of *kai* in the adversative sense of "and yet" or "but." They marvelled at Christ's "ignorance" and boasted of their own knowledge of the law of Moses. And yet they violated that law by not practising it. *Why seek ye to kill me?* (*Ti me zēteite apokteinai;*). A sudden and startling question as an illustration of their failure to do the law of Moses. Jesus had previously known (5:39, 45–47) that the Jews really rejected the teaching of Moses while professing to believe it. On that very occasion they had sought to kill him (5:18), the very language used here. Apparently he had not been to Jerusalem since then. He undoubtedly alludes to their conduct then and charges them with the same purpose now.

20. *The multitude* (*ho ochlos*). Outside of Jerusalem (the Galilean crowd as in verses 11f.) and so unfamiliar with the effort to kill Jesus recorded in 5:18. It is important in this chapter to distinguish clearly the several groups like the Jewish leaders (7:13, 15, 25, 26, 30, 32, etc.), the multitude from Galilee and elsewhere (10–13, 20, 31, 40, 49), the common people of Jerusalem (25), the Roman soldiers (45f.). *Thou hast a devil* (*daimonion echeis*). "Demon," of course, as always in the Gospels. These pilgrims make the same charge against Jesus made long ago by the Pharisees in Jerusalem in explanation of the difference between John and Jesus (Matt. 11:18 = Luke 7:33). It is an easy way to

make a fling like that. "He is a monomaniac labouring under a hallucination that people wish to kill him" (Dods).

21. *One work* (*hen ergon*). Direct allusion to the healing of the impotent man when in Jerusalem before (5:1ff.). He had wrought others before (2:23; 4:45), but this one on the Sabbath caused the rulers to try to kill Jesus (5:18). Some wondered then, others had murder in their hearts. This crowd here is ignorant.

22. *For this cause* (*dia touto*). Some would take this phrase with the preceding verb *thaumazete* (ye marvel for this cause). *Hath given* (*dedōken*). Present active indicative of *didōmi* (permanent state). *Not that it is of Moses, but of the fathers* (*ouch hoti ek tou Mōuseōs estin all' ek tōn paterōn*). A parenthesis to explain that circumcision is older in origin than Moses. *And on the sabbath ye circumcise* (*kai en sabbatōi peritemnete*). Adversative use of *kai* = and yet as in 19. That is to say, the Jews keep one law (circumcision) by violating another (on the Sabbath, the charge against him in chapter 5, healing on the Sabbath).

23. *That the law of Moses may not be broken* (*hina mē luthēi ho nomos Mōuseōs*). Purpose clause with negative *mē* and first aorist passive subjunctive of *luō*. They are punctilious about their Sabbath rules and about circumcision on the eighth day. When they clash, they drop the Sabbath rule and circumcise. *Are ye wroth with me?* (*emoi cholāte;*). Old word from *cholē* (bile, gall), possibly from *chloē* or *chlōros* (yellowish green). Only here in N.T. So to be mad. With dative. Vivid picture of bitter spleen against Jesus for healing a man on the sabbath when they circumcise on the Sabbath. *A man every whit whole* (*holon anthrōpon hugiē*). Literally, "a whole (*holon*) man (all the man) sound (*hugiē*, well)," not just one member of the body mended.

24. *According to appearance* (*kat' opsin*). And so, superficially. See 11:44. Also not "righteous" (*dikaian*) judgment.

25. *Some therefore of them of Jerusalem* (*oun tines ek tōn Ierosolumeitōn*). The people of the city in contrast to the multitude of pilgrims at the feast. They form a separate group. The word is made from *Ierosoluma* and occurs in Josephus and IV Maccabees. In N.T. only here and Mark 1:5. These Jerusalem people knew better than the pilgrims the designs of the rulers (Vincent). *Is not this?* (*ouch houtos estin;*). Expecting affirmative answer. Clearly they were not as familiar with the appearance of Jesus as the Galilean multitude (Dods). *They seek* (*zētousin*). The plural refers to the group of leaders already present (7:15) to whom the Jerusalem crowd probably pointed. They knew of their threats to kill Jesus (5:18).

26. *They say nothing unto him* (*ouden autoi legousin*). But only make sneering comments about him (7:16) in spite of his speaking "openly" (*parrēsiāi*, for which word see 7:13 and 18:20) before all. It was sarcasm about the leaders, though an element of surprise on the part of "these shrewd townsmen" (Bernard) may have existed also. *Can it be that the rulers indeed know* (*mē pote alēthōs egnōsin hoi archontes*). Negative answer expected by *mē pote* and yet there is ridicule of the rulers in the form of the question. See a like use of *mē pote* in Luke 3:15, though nowhere else in John. *Egnōsan* (second aorist ingressive active indicative of *ginōskō*) may refer to the examination of Jesus by these rulers in 5:19ff. and means, "Did they come to know or find out" (and so hold now)? *That this is the Christ* (*hoti houtos estin ho Christos*). The Messiah of Jewish hope.

27. *Howbeit* (*alla*). Clearly adversative here. *This man* (*touton*). Possibly contemptuous use of *houtos* as may be true in 25 and 26. *Whence he is* (*pothen estin*). The Galilean Jews knew the family of Jesus (6:42), but they knew Jesus only as from Nazareth, not as born in Bethlehem (verse 42). *When the Christ cometh* (*ho Christos hotan erchētai*). Prolepsis of *ho Christos* and indefinite temporal clause with *hotan* and

the present middle subjunctive *erchētai* rather than the more usual second aorist active *elthēi* as in verse 31, a trifle more picturesque. This is a piece of popular theology. "Three things come wholly unexpected — Messiah, a godsend, and a scorpion" (*Sanhedrin* 97a). The rulers knew the birthplace to be Bethlehem (7:42; Matt. 2:5f.), but some even expected the Messiah to drop suddenly from the skies as Satan proposed to Jesus to fall down from the pinnacle of the temple. The Jews generally expected a sudden emergence of the Messiah from concealment with an anointing by Elijah (*Apoc. of Bar.* XXIX. 3; II Esdr. 7:28; 13:32; Justin Martyr, *Tryph.* 110).

28. *And I am not come of myself* (*kai ap' emautou ouk elēlutha*). *Kai* here = "and yet." Jesus repeats the claim of verse 17 and also in 5:30; 8:28; 12:49; 14:10. *Whom ye know not* (*hon humeis ouk oidate*). Jesus passes by a controversy over the piece of popular theology to point out their ignorance of God the Father who sent him. He tersely agrees that they know something of him. Jesus says of these Jews that they know not God as in 8:19, 55.

29. *I know him* (*egō oida auton*). In contrast to the ignorance of these people. See the same words in 8:55 and the same claim in 17:25; Matt. 11:27 = Luke 10:22 (the Johannine aërolite). "These three words contain the unique claim of Jesus, which is pressed all through the chapters of controversy with the Jews" (Bernard). Jesus is the Interpreter of God to men (John 1:18). *And he sent me* (*kākeinos me apesteilen*). First aorist active indicative of *apostellō*, the very verb used of Jesus when he sent forth the twelve (Matt. 10:5) and used by Jesus again of himself in John 17:3. He is the Father's Apostle to men.

30. *They sought therefore* (*ezētoun oun*). Imperfect active of *zēteō*, inchoative or conative, they began to seek. Either makes sense. The subject is naturally some of the Jerusalemites (Westcott) rather than some of the leaders (Bernard).

To take him (*auton piasai*).   First aorist active infinitive,
Doric form from *piazō*, from the usual *piezō*, occasionally so
in the papyri, but *piazō* always in N.T. except Luke 6:38.
And (*kai*).   Here = "but."   *Laid his hand* (*epebalen tēn
cheira*).   Second aorist active indicative of *epiballō*, to cast
upon. Old and common idiom for arresting one to make him
a prisoner (Matt. 26:50). See repetition in verse 44. *His
hour* (*hē hōra autou*). In 13:1 we read that "the hour" had
come, but that was "not yet" (*oupō*). "John is at pains to
point out at every point that the persecution and death of
Jesus followed a predestined course" (Bernard), as in 2:4;
7:6, 8; 8:10; 10:39; 13:1, etc. *Was not yet come* (*oupō elēluthei*). Past perfect active of *erchomai*, as John looks back on
the story.

31. *When the Christ shall come* (*ho Christos hotan elthēi*).
Proleptic position of *ho Christos* again as in 27, but *elthēi*
with *hotan* rather than *erchetai*, calling more attention to the
consummation (whenever he does come). *Will he do?* (*mē
poiēsei;*).   Future active indicative of *poieō* with *mē* (negative answer expected). Jesus had won a large portion of the
pilgrims (*ek tou ochlou polloi*) either before this day or during
this controversy. The use of *episteusan* (ingressive aorist
active) looks as if many came to believe at this point. These
pilgrims had watched closely the proceedings. *Than those
which* (*hōn*). One must supply the unexpressed antecedent
toutōn in the ablative case after *pleiona* (more). Then the
neuter plural accusative relative *ha* (referring to *sēmeia*
signs) is attracted to the ablative case of the pronominal
antecedent *toutōn* (now dropped out). *Hath done* (*epoiēsen*).
First aorist active indicative of *poieō*, a timeless constative
aorist summing up all the miracles of Jesus so far.

32. *The Pharisees* (*hoi Pharisaioi*). This group of the
Jewish rulers (7:11, 15, 25f.) was particularly hostile to
Christ, though already the Sadducees had become critical
(Matt. 16:6) and they join here (*hoi archiereis*, the chief

priests being Sadducees) in determining to silence Jesus by bringing him before the Sanhedrin. They had heard the whispered talk about Jesus before he arrived (7:12f.) and still more now. *Heard the multitude murmuring (ēkousan tou ochlou gogguzontos)*. First aorist active indicative of *akouō* with the genitive case and the descriptive participle of the vivid onomatopoetic verb *gogguzō* (verse 12) now grown louder like the hum of bees. It was the defence of Jesus by a portion of the crowd (7:31) that irritated the Pharisees. Here the Pharisees take the initiative and enlist the Sadducees in the Sanhedrin (for this combination see 7:45; 11:47, 57; Matt. 21:45; 27:62, the organized court) to send "officers" (*hupēretas*) "to take him" (*hina piasōsin auton*, final clause with *hina* and first aorist active subjunctive of *piazō* for which verb see verse 30). For *hupēretas* (temple police here) see verse 45; 18:3, 12, 22; 19:6; Acts 5:22, 26. For the word see Matt. 5:25; Luke 1:2, "an under rower" (*hupo, eretēs*), any assistant.

33. *Yet a little while (eti chronon mikron)*. Accusative of extent of time. It was only six months to the last passover of Christ's ministry and he knew that the end was near. *I go unto him that sent me (hupagō pros ton pempsanta me)*. See the same words in 16:5. *Hupagō*, old compound (*hupo, agō*), has the notion of withdrawing (literally, go under). See 16:7–10 for three words for going common in John (*poreuomai*, go for a purpose, *aperchomai*, to go away, *hupagō*, to withdraw personally). *Hupagō* often in John of going to the Father or God (8:14, 21; 13:3, 33, 36; 14:4, 5, 28; 15:16; 16:4, 7, 10, 17). See 6:21. It was enigmatic language to the hearers.

34. *And shall not find me (kai ouch heurēsete me)*. Future active indicative of *heuriskō*. Jesus had said: "Seek and ye shall find" (Matt. 7:7), but this will be too late. Now they were seeking (verse 30) to kill Jesus, then they will seek deliverance, but too late. *Where I am (hopou eimi egō)*.

No conflict with verse 33, but the essential eternal spiritual home of Christ "in absolute, eternal being and fellowship with the Father" (Vincent). *Ye cannot come* (*humeis ou dunasthe elthein*). This fellowship was beyond the comprehension of these hostile Jews. See the same idea in 7:36 by the Jews; 8:21 to the Jews and then to the disciples with the addition of "now" (*arti*, 13:33, *nun* in 36).

35. *Among themselves* (*pros heautous*). These Jewish leaders of verse 32 talk among themselves about what Jesus said in a spirit of contempt (this man or fellow, *houtos*). *That* (*hoti*). Almost result like *hoti* in Matt. 8:27. *Will he go?* (*mē mellei poreuesthai;*). Negative answer expected in an ironical question, "Is he about to go?" *Unto the Dispersion among the Greeks* (*eis tēn diasporan tōn Hellēnōn*). Objective genitive *tōn Hellēnōn* (of the Greeks) translated here "among," because it is the Dispersion of Jews among the Greeks. *Diaspora* is from *diaspeirō*, to scatter apart (Acts 8:1, 4). It occurs in Plutarch and is common in the LXX, in the N.T. only here, James 1:1; I Peter 1:1. There were millions of these scattered Jews. *And teach the Greeks* (*kai didaskein tous Hellēnas*). Confessing his failure to teach the Jews in Palestine, "thus ignorantly anticipating the course Christianity took; what seemed unlikely and impossible to them became actual" (Dods).

36. *What is this word?* (*Tis estin ho logos houtos;*). Puzzled and uneasy over this unintelligible saying. Even Peter is distressed over it later (13:37).

37. *Now on the last day* (*en de tēi eschatēi hēmerāi*). The eighth day which was "an holy convocation," kept as a Sabbath (Lev. 33:36), apparently observed as a memorial of the entrance into Canaan, hence "the great day of the feast" (*tēi megalēi tēs heortēs*). *Stood and cried* (*histēkei kai ekrasen*). Past perfect active of *histēmi* used as imperfect and intransitive and first aorist active of *krazō*. Picture Jesus standing (linear) and suddenly crying out (punctiliar). *If any man*

thirst (ean tis dipsāi). Third class condition with *ean* and present active subjunctive of *dipsaō*, "if any one is thirsty." On each of the seven preceding days water was drawn in a golden pitcher from the pool of Siloam and carried in procession to the temple and offered by the priests as the singers chanted Isa. 12:3: "With joy shall ye draw water out of the wells of salvation." "It is uncertain whether the libations were made upon the eighth day. If they were not made, the significant cessation of the striking rite on this one day of the feast would give a still more fitting occasion for the words" (Westcott).

38. *He that believeth on me (ho pisteuōn eis eme)*. Nominative absolute as is not uncommon. *The scripture (hē graphē)*. No precise passage can be quoted, though similar idea in several (Isa. 55:1; 58:11; Zech. 13:1; 14:8; Ezek. 47:1; Joel 3:18). Chrysostom confines it to Isa. 28:16 by punctuation (only the nominative absolute as the Scripture). *Out of his belly shall flow rivers of living water (potamoi ek tēs koilias autou reusousin hudatos zōntos)*. Some ancient Western writers connect *pinetō* of verse 37 with *ho pisteuōn* in verse 38. By this arrangement *autou (his)* with *koilias* is made to refer to Christ, not to the believer. Burney argues that *koilia* is a mistranslation of the Aramaic (fountain, not belly) and that the reference is to Ezek. 47:1. C. C. Torrey refers to Zech. 14:8. But the Eastern writers refer *autou* (his) to the believer who not only quenches in Christ his own thirst, but becomes a source of new streams for others (John 4:14). It is a difficult question and Westcott finally changed his view and held *autou* to refer to Christ. *Reusousin* is future active indicative of *reō*, old verb, to flow, here only in the N.T.

39. *Which (hou)*. Genitive by attraction of the relative *ho* (accusative singular object of *lambanein*) to the case of *tou pneumatos* (the Spirit) the antecedent. But it is purely grammatical gender (neuter *ho* because of *pneuma*) which

we do not have in English. Even here one should say "whom," not which, of the Spirit of God. *Were to receive* (*emellon lambanein*). Imperfect active of *mellō* with the present active infinitive *lambanein*, to receive, one of the three constructions with *mellō* (present, aorist, or future infinitive). Literally, "whom they were about to receive," a clear reference to the great pentecost. *For the Spirit was not yet given* (*oupō gar ēn pneuma*). No verb for "given" in the Greek. The reference is not to the existence of the Spirit, but to the dispensation of the Spirit. This same use of *eimi* like *pareimi* (to be present) appears in Acts 19:2 of the Spirit's activity. John, writing at the close of the century, inserts this comment and interpretation of the language of Jesus as an allusion to the coming of the Holy Spirit at pentecost (the Promise of the Father). *Because Jesus was not yet glorified* (*hoti Iēsous oupō edoxasthē*). Reason for the previous statement, the pentecostal outpouring following the death of Jesus here called "glorified" (*edoxasthē*, first aorist passive indicative of *doxazō*), used later of the death of Jesus (12:16), even by Jesus himself (12:23; 13:31).

40. *Some of the multitude* (*ek tou ochlou*). *Tines* (some) to be supplied, a common Greek idiom. *Of a truth* (*alēthōs*). "Truly." See 1:47. *The prophet* (*ho prophētēs*). The one promised to Moses (Deut. 18:15) and long expected. See on John 1:21. Proof of the deep impression made by Jesus.

41. *This is the Christ* (*houtos estin ho Christos*). These went further and dared to call Jesus the Messiah and not merely the prophet who might not be the Messiah. They said it openly. *What* (*gar*). These denied that Jesus was the Messiah and gave as their reason (*gar*, for) the fact that he came from Galilee. The use of *mē* expects a negative answer.

42. *The scripture* (*hē graphē*). The reference is to Micah 5:2, the very passage quoted by the chief priests and scribes in response to Herod's inquiry (Matt. 2:6). This ignorance

of the fact that Jesus was actually born in Bethlehem belongs to the Jews, not to John the author of the Gospel.

43. *A division (schisma).* A clear split. See Matt. 9:16 for the word from *schizō*, to rend. Used again in John 9:16; 10:19.

44. *Would have taken him (ēthelon piāsai auton).* Imperfect active of *thelō* and first aorist active infinitive of *piazō*, "were wishing to seize him." See verse 30 for a like impulse and restraint, there *epebalen ep' auton*, here *ebalen ep' auton* (simple verb, not compound).

45. *Why did ye not bring him? (Dia ti ouk ēgagete auton;).* Second aorist active indicative of *agō*. Indignant outburst of the Sanhedrin (both Sadducees and Pharisees) at the failure of the (*tous*, note article here referring to verse 32) temple police to arrest Jesus. "Apparently they were sitting in expectation of immediately questioning him" (Dods). They were stunned at this outcome.

46. *Never man so spake (oudepote elalēsen houtōs anthrōpos).* Police officers are not usually carried away by public speech. They had fallen under the power of Jesus "as the Galilean peasants had been impressed" (Bernard) in verses 28f. It was the words of Jesus that had so gripped these officers, not his works (15:24). It was most disconcerting to the Sanhedrin.

47. *Are ye also led astray? (Mē kai humeis peplanēsthe;).* The Pharisees took the lead in this scornful sneer at the officers. The use of *mē* formally expects a negative answer as in 4:29, but the Pharisees really believed it. See also 6:67. The verb form is perfect passive indicative of *planaō*, for which see verse 12 with perhaps an allusion to that phase of opinion.

48. *Hath any of the rulers believed on him? (Mē tis ek tōn archontōn episteusen eis auton;).* Negative answer sharply expected. First aorist active indicative of *pisteuō*. "Did any one of the rulers believe on him?" "What right have

subordinates to have a mind of their own?" (Dods). These police were employed by the temple authorities (rulers). "Power was slipping through their fingers" (Dods) and that was the secret of their hostility to Jesus. *Or of the Pharisees* (*ē ek tōn Pharisaiōn*). A wider circle and the most orthodox of all.

49. *This multitude* (*ho ochlos houtos*). The Pharisees had a scorn for the *amhaaretz* or "people of the earth" (cf. our "clod-hoppers") as is seen in rabbinic literature. It was some of the *ochlos* (multitude at the feast especially from Galilee) who had shown sympathy with Jesus (7:12, 28f.). *Which knoweth not the law* (*ho mē ginoskōn*). Present active articular participle of *ginōskō* with *mē* usual negative of the participle in the *Koiné*. "No brutish man is sin-fearing, nor is one of the people of the earth pious" (*Aboth*, II. 6). See the amazement of the Sanhedrin at Peter and John in Acts 4:13 as "unlettered and private men" (*agrammatoi kai idiōtai*). No wonder the common people (*ochlos*) heard Jesus gladly (Mark 12:37). The rabbis scouted and scorned them. *Are accursed* (*eparatoi eisin*). Construction according to sense (plural verb and adjective with collective singular *ochlos*). *Eparatoi* is old verbal adjective from *eparaomai*, to call down curses upon, here only in the N.T.

50. *Nicodemus* (*Nikodēmos*). Not heard from since chapter 3 when he timidly came to Jesus by night. Now he boldly protests against the injustice of condemning Jesus unheard. He appears once more (and only in John) in 19:39 with Joseph of Arimathea as a secret disciple of Jesus. He is a Pharisee and a member of the Sanhedrin and his present act is courageous. *Saith* (*legei*). Dramatic present active indicative as in 2:3. *Before* (*proteron*). This is genuine, a reference to the visit in chapter 3, but *nuktos* (by night) is not genuine here. *Being one of them* (*heis ōn ex autōn*). As a member of the Sanhedrin he takes up the challenge in verse 48. He is both ruler and Pharisee.

51. *Doth our law judge a man?* (*mē ho nomos hēmōn krinei ton anthrōpon;*). Negative answer expected and "the man," not "a man." These exponents of the law (verse 49) were really violating the law of criminal procedure (Ex. 23:1; Deut. 1:16). Probably Nicodemus knew that his protest was useless, but he could at least show his colours and score the point of justice in Christ's behalf. *Except it first hear from himself* (*ean mē akousēi prōton par' autou*). Third-class negative condition with *ean mē* and first aorist active subjunctive of *akouō*. That is common justice in all law, to hear a man's side of the case ("from him," *par' autou*). *And know what he doeth* (*kai gnōi ti poiei*). Continuation of the same condition with second aorist active subjunctive of *ginōskō* with indirect question and present active indicative (*ti poiei*). There was no legal answer to the point of Nicodemus.

52. *Art thou also of Galilee?* (*Mē kai su ek tēs Galilaias ei;*). Formally negative answer expected by *mē*, but really they mean to imply that Nicodemus from local feeling or prejudice has lined himself up with this Galilean mob (*ochlos*) of sympathizers with Jesus and is like Jesus himself a Galilean. "These aristocrats of Jerusalem had a scornful contempt for the rural Galileans" (Bernard). *That out of Galilee ariseth no prophet* (*hoti ek tēs Galilaias prophētēs ouk egeiretai*). As a matter of fact Jonah, Hosea, Nahum, possibly also Elijah, Elisha, and Amos were from Galilee. It was simply the rage of the Sanhedrin against Jesus regardless of the facts. Westcott suggests that they may have reference to the future, but that is a mere excuse for them.

53. This verse and through 8:12 (the passage concerning the woman taken in adultery) is certainly not a genuine part of John's Gospel. The oldest and best MSS. (Aleph A B C L W) do not have it. It first appears in Codex Bezae. Some MSS. put it at the close of John's Gospel and some place it in Luke. It is probably a true story for it is like

Jesus, but it does not belong to John's Gospel. The Canterbury Version on which we are commenting puts the passage in brackets. Westcott and Hort place it at the end of the Gospel. With this explanation we shall proceed. *They went* (*eporeuthēsan*). First aorist passive indicative of *poreuomai* used as a deponent verb without passive idea. In this context the verb has to refer to the Sanhedrin with a rather pointless contrast to Jesus.

CHAPTER VIII

1. *But Jesus went* (*Iēsous de eporeuthē*). Same deponent use of *poreuomai* as in 7:53 and in contrast to the Sanhedrin's conduct, though it seems "pointless" (Dods). Apparently Jesus was lodging in the home of Mary, Martha, and Lazarus.

2. *Early in the morning* (*orthrou*). Genitive of time, *orthros* meaning daybreak, old word, not in John, though in Luke 24:1; Acts 5:21. John uses *prōi* (18:28; 20:1; 21:4). *He came again into the temple* (*palin paregeneto eis to hieron*). If the paragraph is genuine, the time is the next day after the eighth and last day of the feast. If not genuine, there is no way of telling the time of this apparently true incident. *And all the people came unto him* (*kai pās ho laos ērcheto pros auton*). Imperfect middle of *erchomai* picturing the enthusiasm of the whole (*pās*) crowd now as opposed to the divisions in chapter 7. *Taught* (*edidasken*). Imperfect active of *didaskō*. He took his seat (*kathisas*, ingressive active participle of *kathizō*) as was customary for Jesus and began to teach (inchoative imperfect). So the picture.

3. *The scribes and the Pharisees* (*hoi grammateis kai hoi Pharisaioi*). John does not mention "scribes," though this combination (note two articles) is common enough in the Synoptics (Luke 5:30; 6:7, etc.). *Bring* (*agousin*). Vivid dramatic present active indicative of *agō*. Dods calls this "in itself an unlawful thing to do" since they had a court for the trial of such a case. Their purpose is to entrap Jesus. *Taken in adultery* (*epi moicheiāi kateilemmenēn*). Perfect passive participle of *katalambanō*, old compound to seize (Mark 9:18), to catch, to overtake (John 12:35), to overcome (or overtake) in 1:5. *Having set her in the midst* (*stē-*

137

santes autēn en mesōi). First aorist active (transitive) participle of *histēmi*. Here all could see her and what Jesus did with such a case. They knew his proneness to forgive sinners.

4. *Hath been taken* (*kateilēptai*). Perfect passive indicative of *katalambanō* (see verse 3), caught and still guilty. *In adultery* (*moicheuomenē*). Present passive participle of *moicheuō*, "herself suffering adultery" (Matt. 5:32). Used of married people. Not in John. *In the very act* (*ep' autophōrōi*). Old adjective (*autophōros*, *autos*, self, and *phōr*, thief) caught in the act of theft, then extended to any crime in which one is caught. Old idiom, but not elsewhere in the Greek Bible. One example in a Berlin papyrus.

5. *Commanded* (*eneteilato*). First aorist middle indicative of *entellō*, old verb to enjoin (Matt. 4:6). *To stone such* (*tas toiautas lithazein*). Present active infinitive of *lithazō* (from *lithos*), from Aristotle on. Stoning was specified for the case of a betrothed woman guilty of adultery (Deut. 22:23f.) and for a priest's daughter if guilty. In other cases just death was commanded (Lev. 20:10; Deut. 22:22). The Talmud prescribes strangulation. This case may have strictly come within the regulation as a betrothed virgin. *What then sayest thou of her?* (*su oun ti legeis;*). "Thou then, what dost thou say?" This was the whole point, to catch Jesus, not to punish the woman.

6. *Tempting him* (*peirazontes auton*). Evil sense of this present active participle of *peirazō*, as so often (Mark 8:11; 10:2, etc.). *That they might have whereof to accuse him* (*hina echōsin katēgorein autou*). Purpose clause with *hina* and present active subjunctive of *echō*. This laying of traps for Jesus was a common practice of his enemies (Luke 11:16, etc.). Note present active infinitive of *katēgoreō* (see Matt. 12:10 for the verb) to go on accusing (with genitive *autou*). It was now a habit with these rabbis. *Stooped down* (*katō kupsas*). First aorist active participle of *kuptō*, old verb to bow the head, to bend forward, in N.T. only here and

verse 8 and Mark 1:7. The use of *katō* (down) gives a vivid touch to the picture. *With his finger* (*tōi daktulōi*). Instrumental case of *daktulos* for which see Matt. 23:4. *Wrote on the ground* (*kategraphen eis tēn gēn*). Imperfect active of *katagraphō*, old compound, here only in N.T., to draw, to delineate, to write down, apparently inchoative, began to write on the sand as every one has done sometimes. The only mention of writing by Jesus and the use of *katagraphō* leaves it uncertain whether he was writing words or drawing pictures or making signs. If we only knew what he wrote! Certainly Jesus knew how to write. And yet more books have been written about this one who wrote nothing that is preserved than any other person or subject in human history. There is a tradition that Jesus wrote down the names and sins of these accusers. That is not likely. They were written on their hearts. Jesus alone on this occasion showed embarrassment over this woman's sin.

7. *When they continued asking* (*hōs epemenon erōtōntes*). Imperfect active indicative of *epimenō* (waiting in addition or still, *epi*, old verb) with supplementary active participle of *erōtaō*, to question. See same construction in Acts 12:16. The verb *epimenō* does not occur in John. They saw that Jesus seemed embarrassed, but did not know that it was as much because of "the brazen hardness of the prosecutors" as because of the shame of the deed. *He lifted himself up* (*anekupsen*). First aorist active indicative of *anakuptō*, the opposite of *katakuptō*, to bend down (verse 8) or of *katō kuptō* (verse 6). *He that is without sin* (*ho anamartētos*). Verbal adjective (*an* privative and *hamartētos* from *hamartanō*), old word, either one who has not sinned as here and Deut. 29:19 or one who cannot sin, not in the N.T. *Among you* (*humōn*). Objective genitive. *First cast* (*prōtos baletō*). The nominative *prōtos* means first before others, be the first to cast, not cast before he does something else. See 20:4. The verb is second aorist imperative of *ballō*, old verb

to fling or cast. Jesus thus picks out the executioner in the case.

8. *Again he stooped down* (*palin katakupsas*). First aorist active participle of *katakuptō*, old and rare verb (in Epictetus II, 16. 22) instead of *katō kupsas* in verse 6. *With his finger* (*tōi daktulōi*). Not genuine, only in D and Western class. *Wrote on the ground* (*egraphen eis tēn gēn*). Imperfect active of the simplex *graphō*, not *katagraphō*. The second picture of Jesus writing on the ground.

9. *Went out* (*exērchonto*). Inchoative imperfect. Graphic picture. *One by one* (*heis kath' heis*). Not a Johannine phrase, but in Mark 14:19 where also the second nominative is retained as if *kath'* (*kata*) is regarded as a mere adverb and not as a preposition. *Beginning from the eldest* (*arxamenoi apo tōn presbuterōn*). "From the elder (comparative form, common in *Koinē* as superlative) men," as was natural for they had more sins of this sort which they recalled. "They are summoned to judge themselves rather than the woman" (Dods). *Was left alone* (*kateleiphthē monos*). First aorist effective passive indicative of *kataleipō*, to leave behind, with predicate nominative *monos*. "Jesus was left behind alone." *And the woman, where she was, in the midst* (*kai hē gunē en mesōi ousa*). The woman was left behind also "being in the midst" as they had placed her (verse 3) before they were conscience stricken and left.

10. *Lifted up himself* (*anakupsas*). First aorist active participle of *anakuptō* as in verse 7. *Where are they?* (*Pou eisin;*). Jesus had kept on writing on the ground as the accusers had slipped away one by one. *Did no man condemn thee?* (*oudeis se katekrinen;*). First aorist active indicative of *katakrinō*, old and common verb to give judgment against (down on) one, but not in John. No one dared to cast a stone at the woman on Christ's terms.

11. *No man, Lord* (*Oudeis, Kurie*). "No one, Sir." She makes no excuse for her sin. Does she recognize Jesus as

"Lord"? *Neither do I condemn thee (Oude egō se katakrinō).*
Jesus does not condone her sin. See 8:15 for "I do not judge
(condemn) any one." But he does give the poor woman
another chance. *Henceforth sin no more (apo tou nun mēketi
hamartane).* See also 5:14 where this same language is used
to the impotent man. It literally means (prohibition with
present active imperative): "Henceforth no longer go on
sinning." One can only hope that the. woman was really
changed in heart and life. Jesus clearly felt that even a
wicked woman can be saved.

12. *Again therefore (palin oun).* This language fits in
better with 7:52 than with 8:11. Just suppose Jesus is in
the temple on the following day. *Unto them (autois).* The
Pharisees and crowds in the temple after the feast was past.
I am the light of the world (egō eimi to phōs tou kosmou). Jesus
had called his followers "the light of the world" (Matt.
5:14), but that was light reflected from him. Already Jesus
(the Logos) had been called the true light of men (1:9;3:19).
The Psalmist calls God his Light (27:1). So Isa. 60:19. At
the feast of tabernacles in the Court of the Women where
Jesus was on this day (8:20) there were brilliant candelabra
and there was the memory of the pillar of cloud by day and
of fire by night. But with all this background this supreme
and exclusive claim of Jesus (repeated in 9:5) to being the
light of the whole world (of Gentiles as well as of Jews)
startled the Pharisees and challenged their opposition. *Shall
have the light of life (hexei to phōs tēs zōēs).* The light which
springs from and issues in life (Westcott). Cf. 6:33, 51 about
Jesus being the Bread of Life. In this sublime claim we
come to a decisive place. It will not do to praise Jesus and
deny his deity. Only as the Son of God can we justify and
accept this language which otherwise is mere conceit and
froth.

13. *Of thyself (peri seautou).* This technical objection
was according to the rules of evidence among the rabbis.

"No man can give witness for himself" (*Mishnah, Ketub.*
11. 9). Hence, they say, "not true" (*ouk alēthes*), not
pertinent. "They were still in the region of pedantic rules
and external tests." In John 5:31 Jesus acknowledged this
technical need of further witness outside of his own claims
(19–30) and proceeded to give it (32–47) in the testimony of
the Baptist, of the Father, of his works, of the Scriptures,
and of Moses in particular.

14. *Even if* (*kån*). That is *kai ean*, a condition of the
third class with the present active subjunctive *marturō*.
Jesus means that his own witness concerning himself is true
(*alēthes*) even if it contravenes their technical rules of evidence. He can and does tell the truth all by himself concerning himself. *For I know whence I came and whither I go*
(*hoti oida pothen ēlthon kai pou hupagō*). In this terse sentence
with two indirect questions Jesus alludes to his pre-existence
with the Father before his Incarnation as in 17:5 and to the
return to the Father after the death and resurrection as in
13:3; 14:2f. He again puts both ideas together in one crisp
clause in 16:28 for the apostles who profess to understand
him then. But here these Pharisees are blind to the words of
Jesus. "But ye know not whence I come nor whither I go"
(*humeis de ouk oidate pothen erchomai ē pou hupagō*). He had
spoken of his heavenly destiny (7:33). Jesus alone knew his
personal consciousness of his coming from, fellowship with,
and return to the Father. Stier (*Words of the Lord Jesus*)
argues that one might as well say to the sun, if claiming to
be the sun, that it was night, because it bore witness of itself.
The answer is the shining of the sun.

15. *After the flesh* (*kata tēn sarka*). According to the standards of the flesh (II Cor. 5:16). The Baptist had said: "There
stands one among you whom ye know not" (John 1:26).
The Light of the World had come, but they loved darkness
rather than light (3:19), because the god of this age had
blinded their thoughts so that they could not see the illumina-

tion of the gospel of the glory of Christ who is the image of
God (II Cor. 4:4).

16. *Yea and if I judge* (*kai ean krinō de egō*). "And even
if I pass judgment." Condition of third class again. *True*
(*alēthinē*). See 1:9 for *alēthinos*, genuine, soundly based (cf.
dikaia in 5:30), "satisfying our perfect conception" (Westcott), not merely true (*alēthes*) in the particular facts (verse
14). *For I am not alone* (*hoti monos ouk eimi*). Jesus now
takes up the technical criticism in verse 13 after justifying
his right to speak concerning himself. *But I and the Father
that sent me* (*all egō kai ho pempsas me patēr*). See 16:32 for
a like statement about the Father being with Christ. It is
not certain that *patēr* is genuine here (omitted by Aleph D,
but in B L W), but the Father is clearly meant as in 7:18, 33.
Jesus gives the Father as the second witness.

17. *Yea and in your law* (*kai en tōi nomōi de tōi humeterōi*).
Same use of *kai — de* as in verse 16. They claimed possession
of the law (7:49) and so Jesus takes this turn in answer to
the charge of single witness in verse 13. He will use similar
language (your law) in 10:34 in an *argumentum ad hominem*
as here in controversy with the Jews. In 15:24 to the apostles
Jesus even says "in their law" in speaking of the hostile
Jews plotting his death. He does not mean in either case to
separate himself wholly from the Jews and the law, though
in Matthew 5 he does show the superiority of his teaching
to that of the law. For the Mosaic regulation about two
witnesses see Deut. 17:6; 19:15. This combined witness of
two is not true just because they agree, unless true in fact
separately. But if they disagree, the testimony falls to the
ground. In this case the Father confirms the witness of the
Son as Jesus had already shown (5:37).

18. *The Father* (*ho patēr*). Clearly genuine here. So these
are the two witnesses that Jesus presents to the Pharisees
in defence of his claim to be the Light of the World
(verse 12).

19. *Where is thy Father?* (*pou estin ho patēr sou;*). "The testimony of an unseen and unheard witness would not satisfy them" (Vincent). Bernard understands the Pharisees to see that Jesus claims God the Father as his second witness and so ask "where," not "who" he is. Augustine has it: *Patrem Christi carnaliter acceperunt*, Christ's human father, as if the Pharisees were "misled perhaps by the Lord's use of *anthrōpon* (verse 17)" (Dods). Cyril even took it to be a coarse allusion to the birth of Jesus as a bastard according to the Talmud. Perhaps the Pharisees used the question with *double entendre*, even with all three ideas dancing in their hostile minds. *Ye would know my Father also* (*kai ton patera mou an ēideite*). Conclusion of second-class condition determined as unfulfilled with *an* and second perfect active of *oida* used as imperfect in both condition and conclusion. See this same point made to Philip in 14:9. In 14:7 Jesus will use *ginōskō* in the condition and *oida* in the conclusion. The ignorance of the Pharisees about Jesus proves it and is due to their ignorance of the Father. See this point more fully stated in 5:36 to 38 when Jesus had his previous controversy in Jerusalem. In 7:28 Jesus said that they knew his home in Nazareth, but he denied then that they knew the Father who sent him. Jesus will again on this occasion (8:55) deny their knowledge of the Father. Later he will deny their knowledge of the Father and of the Son (16:3). The Pharisees are silenced for the moment.

20. *In the treasury* (*en tōi gazophulakiōi*). See already Mark 12:41 and Luke 21:1 for this word for the treasure-chambers of the temple. "It abutted on the Court of the Women, and against its walls were placed chests, trumpet-like in form, as receptacles for the offerings of the worshippers" (Bernard). The Persian word *gaza* (treasure) occurs only once in the N.T. (Acts 8:27) and the compound (*phu-lakē*, guard) only here in John. Jesus hardly taught within

a treasure-chamber. It probably means "at the treasury in the temple." This court was probably the most public part of the temple (Vincent). *And (kai)* = "and yet" as in 1:10, etc. *Because his hour was not yet come (hoti oupō elēluthei hē hōra autou).* Reason *(hoti)* given why no one seized *(epiasen,* cf. 7:30) him. *Elēluthei* is past perfect active of *erchomai,* "had not yet come." This very use of *hōra* appears in 2:4 and the very clause in 7:30 which see.

21. *Again (palin).* Probably *palin* (again) in verse 12 refers to a day after the feast is over since the last day is mentioned in 7:37. So then here again we probably move on to another day still beyond that in verse 12. *And ye shall seek me (kai zētēsete me).* As in 7:34, "the search of despair" (Bernard), seeking for the Messiah when it is too late, the tragedy of Judaism today (1:11). *And ye shall die in your sin (kai en tēi hamartiāi humōn apothaneisthe).* Future middle indicative of *apothnēskō* which is the emphatic word here (cf. Ezek. 3:18; 18:18; Prov. 24:9). Note singular *hamartiāi* (sin) here, but plural *hamartiais* (sins) when the phrase is repeated in verse 24 (sin in its essence, sin in its acts). *Ye cannot come (humeis ou dunasthe elthein).* Precise language of 7:34 to the Jews and to the apostles in 13:33.

22. *Will he kill himself? (mēti apoktenei heauton;).* Negative answer formally expected, but there is a manifest sneer in the query. "The mockery in these words is alike subtle and bitter" (Vincent). It was a different group of Jews in 7:31 who cynically suggested that he was going to work among the Greeks in the Dispersion. Here they infer that Jesus refers to the next world. They suggest the depths of Gehenna for him as the abode of suicides (Josephus, *War* III. viii. 5). Of course the rabbis could not join Jesus there! Edersheim argues against this view.

23. *Ye are from beneath (humeis ek tōn katō).* This language, peculiar to John, could take up the idea in Josephus

that these rabbis came from Gehenna whence they will go as children of the devil (8:44), but the use of *ek tou kosmou toutou* ("of this world" in origin) as parallel to what we have here seems to prove that the contrast between *katō* and *anō* here is between the earthly (sensual) and the heavenly as in James 3:15–17. See also Col. 3:1. This is the only use of *katō* in John (except 8:6). These proud rabbis had their origin in this world of darkness (1:9) with all its limitations. *I am from above* (*egō ek tōn anō eimi*). The contrast is complete in origin and character, already stated in 3:31, and calculated to intensify their anger.

24. *For except ye believe* (*ean gar mē pisteusēte*). Negative condition of third class with *ean mē* and ingressive aorist active subjunctive of *pisteuō*, "For unless ye come to believe." *That I am he* (*hoti egō eimi*). Indirect discourse, but with no word in the predicate after the copula *eimi*. Jesus can mean either "that I am from above" (verse 23), "that I am the one sent from the Father or the Messiah" (7:18, 28), "that I am the Light of the World" (8:12), "that I am the Deliverer from the bondage of sin" (8:28, 31f., 36), "that I am" without supplying a predicate in the absolute sense as the Jews (Deut. 32:39) used the language of Jehovah (cf. Isa. 43:10 where the very words occur *hina pisteusēte — hoti egō eimi*). The phrase *egō eimi* occurs three times here (8:24, 28, 58) and also in 13:19. Jesus seems to claim absolute divine being as in 8:58.

25. *Who art thou?* (*Su tis ei;*). Proleptic use of *su* before *tis*, "Thou, who art thou?" Cf. 1:19. He had virtually claimed to be the Messiah and on a par with God as in 5:15. They wish to pin him down and to charge him with blasphemy. *Even that which I have also spoken unto you from the beginning* (*tēn archēn hoti kai lalō humin*). A difficult sentence. It is not clear whether it is an affirmation or a question. The Latin and Syriac versions treat it as affirmative. Westcott and Hort follow Meyer and take it as inter-

rogative. The Greek fathers take it as an exclamation. It seems clear that the adverbial accusative *tēn archēn* cannot mean "from the beginning" like *ap' archēs* (15:27) or *ex archēs* (16:4). The LXX has *tēn archēn* for "at the beginning" or "at the first" (Gen. 43:20). There are examples in Greek, chiefly negative, where *tēn archēn* means "at all," "essentially," "primarily." Vincent and Bernard so take it here, "Primarily what I am telling you." Jesus avoids the term Messiah with its political connotations. He stands by his high claims already made.

26. *I have many things to speak and to judge concerning you* (*polla echō peri humōn lalein kai krinein*). Instead of further talk about his own claims (already plain enough) Jesus turns to speak and to judge concerning them and their attitude towards him (cf. verse 16). Whatever they think of Jesus the Father who sent him is true (*alēthēs*). They cannot evade responsibility for the message heard. So Jesus goes on speaking it from the Father.

27. *They perceived not* (*ouk egnōsan*). Second aorist active indicative of *ginōskō*. "Preoccupied as they were with thoughts of an earthly deliverer" (Westcott) and prejudiced against recognizing Jesus as the one sent from God. *That he spake to them of the Father* (*hoti ton patera autois elegen*). Indirect assertion, but with the present indicative (*legei*) changed to the imperfect (*elegen*) as was sometimes done (2:25) after a secondary tense.

28. *When ye have lifted up the Son of man* (*hotan hupsō-sēte ton huion tou anthrōpou*). Indefinite temporal clause with *hotan* (*hote* + *an*) and the first aorist active subjunctive of *hupsoō*, to lift up (*Koiné* verb from *hupsos*, height), used several times in John of the Cross of Christ (3:14; 8:28; 12:32, 34). It is unnecessary to render the aorist subjunctive as if a future perfect, simply "whenever ye lift up" (actually lift up, ingressive aorist). In Acts 2:33 the verb is used of the Ascension. *Shall ye know* (*gnōsesthe*). Future (ingres-

sive aoristic) middle of *ginōskō*. *Cognoscetis ex re quod nunc ex verbo non creditis* (Bengel). But the knowledge from the facts like the fall of Jerusalem will come too late and will not bring a change of heart. The Holy Spirit will convict them concerning judgment (16:8). For *I am* (*egō eimi*) see on verse 24. *As the Father taught me* (*Kathōs edidasken me ho patēr*). This claim Jesus repeats (see verse 26) and clearly makes on his arrival at the feast (7:16f.). This fact marks Jesus off from the rabbis.

29. *Is with me* (*met' emou estin*). The Incarnation brought separation from the Father in one sense, but in essence there is complete harmony and fellowship as he had already said (8:16) and will expand in 17:21-26. *He hath not left me alone* (*ouk aphēken me monon*). First aorist active indicative of *aphiēmi*. "He did not leave me alone." However much the crowds and the disciples misunderstood or left Jesus, the Father always comforted and understood him (Mark 6:46 = Matt. 14:23 = John 6:15). *That are pleasing to him* (*ta aresta autōi*). This old verbal adjective, from *areskō*, to please, in N.T. only here, Acts 6:2; 12:3; I John 3:32. The joy of Jesus was in doing the will of the Father who sent him (4:34).

30. *Many believed on him* (*polloi episteusan eis auton*). Ingressive aorist active indicative, came to believe, nominally at any rate, as in 2:23. But the tension was keen and Jesus proceeded to test the faith of these new believers from among the Pharisees.

31. *Which had believed him* (*tous pepisteukotas autōi*). Articular perfect active participle of *pisteuō* with dative *autōi* (trusted him) rather than *eis auton* (on him) in verse 30. They believed him (cf. 6:30) as to his claims to being the Messiah with their own interpretation (6:15), but they did not commit themselves to him and may represent only one element of those in verse 30, but see 2:23 for *pisteuō eis* there. *If ye abide in my word* (*ean humeis meinēte en tōi*

logōi tōi emōi). Third-class condition with *ean* and first aorist (constative) active subjunctive. *Are ye truly my disciples (alēthōs mathētai mou este)*. Your future loyalty to my teaching will prove the reality of your present profession. So the conclusion of this future condition is put in the present tense. As then, so now. We accept church members on *profession* of trust in Christ. Continuance in the word (teaching) proves the sincerity or insincerity of the profession. It is the acid test of life.

32. *And ye shall know the truth (kai gnōsesthe tēn alētheian)*. Truth is one of the marks of Christ (1:14) and Jesus will claim to Thomas to be the personification of truth (14:6). But it will be for them knowledge to be learned by doing God's will (7:17). The word is from *alēthēs* (*a* privative and *lēthō*, to conceal, unsealed, open). See also verses 40, 44, 45. *And the truth shall make you free (kai hē alētheia eleutherōsei humas)*. Future active indicative of *eleutheroō*, old verb from *eleutheros* (from *erchomai*, to go where one wishes and so free). One of Paul's great words for freedom from the bondage of the law (Rom. 6:18; Gal. 5:1). The freedom of which Jesus here speaks is freedom from the slavery of sin as Paul in Rom. 8:2. See John 8:36. This freedom is won alone by Christ (8:36) and we are sanctified in truth (17:19). In 1:17 truth is mentioned with grace as one of the marks of the gospel through Christ. Freedom (intellectual, moral, spiritual) is only attainable when we are set free from darkness, sin, ignorance, superstition and let the Light of the World shine on us and in us.

33. *We be Abraham's seed (Sperma Abraam esmen)*. "We are Abraham's seed," the proudest boast of the Jews, of Sarah the freewoman and not of Hagar the bondwoman (Gal. 4:22f.). Yes, but the Jews came to rely solely on mere physical descent (Matt. 3:9) and so God made Gentiles the spiritual children of Abraham by faith (3:7; Rom. 9:6f.). *And have never yet been in bondage to any man (kai oudeni*

dedouleukamen pōpote). Perfect active indicative of *douleuō*,
to be slaves. This was a palpable untruth uttered in the
heat of controversy. At that very moment the Jews wore
the Roman yoke as they had worn that of Assyria, Babylon,
Persia, Alexander, the Ptolemies, the Syrian (Seleucid) kings.
They had liberty for a while under the Maccabees. "These
poor believers soon come to the end of their faith" (Stier).
But even so they had completely missed the point in the
words of Jesus about freedom by truth.

34. *Every one that committeth sin is the bondservant of sin*
(*pas ho poiōn tēn hamartian doulos estin* [*tēs hamartias*]).
The Western class omits *tēs hamartias* (sin), but that is the
idea anyhow. Note the use of *poiōn* (present active participle, continuous habit or practice), not *poiēsas* (aorist
active participle for single act), precisely as in I John 3:4–8.
Note also 3:20 for *ho poiōn tēn alētheian* (the one who prac-
tises the truth). Sin, like the worst narcotic, is habit form-
ing. Hence the problem today for criminologists for paroled
or pardoned criminals nearly always go back to crime, sink
again into sin, the slaves of sin. Xenophon has this notion
of the slavery of sin (*Memor.* IV. 5. 3). So Paul clearly in
Rom. 6:17, 20 "slaves of sin" (*douloi tēs hamartias*).

35. *The bondservant* (*ho doulos*) . . . *the son* (*ho huios*).
There is a change in the metaphor by this contrast between
the positions of the son and the slave in the house. The
slave has no footing or tenure and may be cast out at any
moment while the son is the heir and has a permanent place.
Cf. Ishmael and Isaac (Gen. 21:10) and Paul's use of it in
Gal. 4:30. We do not know that there is any reference here
to Hagar and Ishmael. See also Heb. 3:5 (Numb. 12:7)
for a like contrast between Moses as servant (*therapōn*) in
God's house and Christ as Son (*huios*) over God's house.

36. *If therefore the son shall make you free* (*ean oun ho
huios humas eleutherōsēi*). Condition of third class with *ean*
and first aorist (ingressive) active subjunctive. "If there-

fore the Son set you free," as he has the power to do. *Ye shall be free indeed* (*ontōs eleutheroi esesthe*). Old and common adverb from participle *ontōn*, actually, really (cf. Luke 24:34). But this spiritual freedom was beyond the concept or wish of these Jews.

37. *Yet ye seek to kill me* (*alla zēteite me apokteinai*). As at the recent feast (7:20, 25, 30, 32; 8:20). Some of these very professed believers were even now glowering with murderous vengeance. *Hath not free course in you* (*ou chōrei en humin*). Intransitive use of *chōreō*, old verb from *chōros* (space, place), to have space or room for. They would not abide in Christ's word (verse 31). They had no longer room for his word when once they understood the spiritual aspect of his message. Jerusalem was now just like Galilee once before (6:60–66).

38. *With my Father* (*para tōi patri*). Locative case of *patēr* and article used as possessive (common idiom), "by the side of my Father," picture of intimate fellowship like *pros ton theon* (face to face with God) in 1:1. *From your father* (*para tou patros*). Ablative case with *para* (from the side of) and same possessive use of *tou* in each instance, though "the" will really answer both times. But *ho patēr* does not mean the same person. Christ's Father by contrast is not their father.

39. *Our father is Abraham* (*ho patēr hēmōn Abraam estin*). They saw the implication and tried to counter it by repeating their claim in verse 33 which was true so far as physical descent went as Jesus had admitted (verse 37). *If ye were* (*ei este*). Strictly, "if ye are" as ye claim, a condition of the first class assumed to be true. *Ye would do* (*epoieite an*). Read by C L N and a corrector of Aleph while W omits *an*. This makes a mixed condition (protasis of the first class, apodosis of the second. See Robertson, *Grammar*, p. 1022). But B reads *poieite* like the Sin. Syriac which has to be treated as imperative (so Westcott and Hort).

40. *But now* (*nun de*). Clear statement that they are not
doing "the works of Abraham" in seeking to kill him. See
this use of *nun de* after a condition of second class without *an*
in John 16:22, 24. *This did not Abraham* (*touto Abraam ouk
epoiēsen*). Blunt and pointed of their unlikeness to Abraham.
A man that hath told you the truth (*anthrōpon hos tēn alētheian
humin lelalēka*). *Anthrōpon* (here = person, one) is accusative
case in apposition with *me* (*me*) just before. The perfect
active indicative *lelalēka* from *laleō* is in the first person
singular because the relative *hos* has the person of *me*, an
idiom not retained in the English *that hath* (that have or who
have) though it is retained in the English of I Cor. 15:9
"that am" for *hos eimi*. *Which I heard from God* (*hēn ēkousa
para tou theou*). Here we have "I" in the English. "God"
here is equal to "My Father" in verse 38. The only crime of
Jesus is telling the truth directly from God.

41. *Ye do the works of your father* (*humeis poieite ta erga
tou patros humōn*). Who is not Abraham and not God as
Jesus plainly indicates. *We were not born of fornication*
(*hēmeis ek porneias egennēthēmen*). First aorist passive indicative of *gennaō*. This they said as a proud boast. Jesus
had admitted that they were physical (Deut. 23:2) descendants of Abraham (37), but now denies that they are spiritual
children of Abraham (like Paul in Rom. 9:7). *Porneia* is from
pornos (harlot) and that from *pernēmi*, to sell, a woman who
sells her body for sexual uses. It is vaguely possible that in
this stern denial the Pharisees may have an indirect fling at
Jesus as the bastard son of Mary (so Talmud). *We have one
Father, even God* (*hena patera echomen ton theon*). No "even"
in the Greek, "One Father we have, God." This in direct
reply to the implication of Jesus (verse 38) that God was not
their spiritual Father.

42. *Ye would love me* (*ēgapate an eme*). Conclusion of
second-class condition with distinct implication that their
failure to love Jesus is proof that God is not their Father

(protasis). *For I came forth from God* (*egō gar ek tou theou exēlthon*). Second aorist active indicative of *exerchomai*, definite historical event (the Incarnation). See 4:30 for *exēlthon ek*. In 13:3 and 16:30 Jesus is said to have come from (*apo*) God. The distinction is not to be pressed. Note the definite consciousness of pre-existence with God as in 17:5. *And am come* (*kai hēkō*). Present active indicative with perfect sense in the verb stem (state of completion) before rise of the tense and here retained. "I am here," Jesus means. *Of myself* (*ap' emautou*). His coming was not self-initiated nor independent of the Father. "But he (*ekeinos*, emphatic demonstrative pronoun) sent me" and here I am.

43. *My speech* (*tēn lalian tēn emēn*) and *my word* (*ton logon ton emon*). Perhaps *lalia*, old word from *lalos* (talk), means here more manner of speech than just story (4:42), while *logos* refers rather to the subject matter. They will not listen (*ou dunasthe akouein*) to the substance of Christ's teaching and hence they are impatient with the way that he talks. How often that is true.

44. *Ye are of your father the devil* (*humeis ek tou patros tou diabolou*). Certainly they can "understand" (*ginōskete* in 43) this "talk" (*lalian*) though they will be greatly angered. But they had to hear it (*akouein* in 43). It was like a bombshell in spite of the preliminary preparation. *Your will to do* (*thelete poiein*). Present active indicative of *thelō* and present active infinitive, "Ye wish to go on doing." This same idea Jesus presents in Matt. 13:38 (the sons of the evil one, the devil) and 23:15 (twofold more a son of Gehenna than you). See also I John 3:8 for "of the devil" (*ek tou diabolou*) for the one who persists in sinning. In Rev. 12:9 the devil is one who leads all the world astray. The Gnostic view that Jesus means "the father of the devil" is grotesque. Jesus does not, of course, here deny that the Jews, like all men, are children of God the Creator, like Paul's offspring of God for all men in Acts 17:28. What he denies to these

Pharisees is that they are spiritual children of God who do his will. They do the lusts and will of the devil. The Baptist had denied this same spiritual fatherhood to the merely physical descendants of Abraham (Matt. 3:9). He even called them "broods of vipers" as Jesus did later (Matt. 12:34). *A murderer* (*anthrōpoktonos*). Old and rare word (Euripides) from *anthrōpos*, man, and *kteinō*, to kill. In N.T. only here and I John 3:15. The Jews were seeking to kill Jesus and so like their father the devil. *Stood not in the truth* (*en tēi alētheiāi ouk estēken*). Since *ouk*, not *ouch*, is genuine, the form of the verb is *esteken* the imperfect of the late present stem *stēkō* (Mark 11:25) from the perfect active *hestēka* (intransitive) of *histēmi*, to place. *No truth in him* (*ouk estin alētheia en autōi*). Inside him or outside (environment). The devil and truth have no contact. *When he speaketh a lie* (*hotan lalēi to pseudos*). Indefinite temporal clause with *hotan* and the present active subjunctive of *laleō*. But note the article *to:* "Whenever he speaks the lie," as he is sure to do because it is his nature. Hence "he speaks out of his own" (*ek tōn idiōn lalei*) like a fountain bubbling up (cf. Matt. 12:34). *For he is a liar* (*hoti pseustēs estin*). Old word for the agent in a conscious falsehood (*pseudos*). See I John 1:10; Rom. 3:4. Common word in John because of the emphasis on *alētheia* (truth). *And the father thereof* (*kai ho patēr autou*). Either the father of the lie or of the liar, both of which are true as already shown by Jesus. *Autou* in the genitive can be either neuter or masculine. Westcott takes it thus, "because he is a liar and his father (the devil) is a liar," making "one," not the devil, the subject of "whenever he speaks," a very doubtful expression.

45. *Because I speak the truth* (*egō de hoti tēn alētheian legō*). Proleptic emphatic position of *egō*. "Truth is uncongenial to them" (Bernard). See 3:19 for their picture.

46. *Which of you convicteth me of sin?* (*Tis ex humōn elegchei me peri hamaritas;*). See on 3:20 and 16:8 (the work of

the Holy Spirit) for *elegchō* for charge and proof. The use of *hamartia* as in 1:29 means sin in general, not particular sins. The rhetorical question which receives no answer involves sinlessness (Heb. 4:15) without specifically saying so. Bernard suggests that Jesus paused after this pungent question before going on. *Why do ye not believe me?* (*Dia ti humeis ou pisteuete moi;*). This question drives home the irrationality of their hostility to Jesus. It was based on prejudice and predilection.

47. *He that is of God* (*ho ōn ek tou theou*). See this use of *ek* in 3:31f. "Their not listening proved that they were not of God" (Dods). They were of the earth and the devil, not of God.

48. *Thou art a Samaritan and hast a demon* (*Samareitēs ei su kai daimonion echeis*). On the spur of the moment in their rage and fury they can think of no meaner things to say. They know, of course, that Jesus was not a Samaritan, but he had acted like a Samaritan in challenging their peculiar spiritual privileges (4:9, 39). The charge of having a demon was an old one by the Pharisees (Matt. 12:24) and it is repeated later (John 10:20).

49. *I have not a demon* (*egō daimonion ouk echō*). This Jesus says calmly, passing by the reference to the Samaritans as beneath notice. *My Father* (*ton patera mou*). As in 2:16. He is not mad in claiming to honour God (cf. 7:18). They were insulting the Father in insulting him (cf. 5:23). On *atimazō* (*a* privative and *timaō*, to dishonour) see Luke 20:11.

50. *But I seek not mine own glory* (*egō de ou zētō tēn doxan mou*). As they did not seek the glory of God (5:44; 8:4). *And judgeth* (*kai krinōn*). The Father judges between you and me, though the Son is the Judge of mankind (5:22). "It is only the *doxa* (glory) that comes from God that is worth having" (Bernard).

51. *If a man keep my word* (*ean tis ton emon logon tērēsēi*). Condition of third class with *ean* and constative aorist active

subjunctive of *tēreō*. Repeated in verse 52. See verse 43 about hearing the word of Christ. Common phrase in John (8:51, 52, 55; 14:23, 24; 15:20; 17:6; I John 2:5). Probably the same idea as keeping the commands of Christ (14:21). *He shall never see death* (*thanaton ou mē theōrēsēi eis ton aiona*). Spiritual death, of course. Strong double negative *ou mē* with first aorist active subjunctive of *theōreō*. The phrase "see death" is a Hebraism (Psa. 89:48) and occurs with *idein* (see) in Luke 2:26; Heb. 11:5. No essential difference meant between *horaō* and *theōreō*. See John 14:23 for the blessed fellowship the Father and the Son have with the one who keeps Christ's word.

52. *Now we know* (*nun egnōkamen*). Perfect active indicative of *ginōskō*, state of completion, "Now since such talk we have come to certain knowledge that thou hast a demon" (verse 48). *Is dead* (*apethanen*). Second aorist active indicative of *apothnēskō*. "Abraham died." *And thou sayest* (*kai su legeis*). Adversative use of *kai*, "and yet." Emphatic position of *su* (thou). Same condition quoted as in verse 51. *He shall never taste of death* (*ou me geusētai thanatou eis ton aiōna*). Same emphatic negative with subjunctive as in verse 51, but *geusētai* (first aorist middle subjunctive of *geuō* with genitive case *thanatou* (death). Another Hebraism for dying like *theōrēsēi* (see) in verse 51. Used in Heb. 2:9 of the death of Jesus and in Synoptics (Matt. 16:28; Mark 9:1; Luke 9:27). It occurs in the Talmud, but not in the O.T. The Pharisees thus did not misquote Jesus, though they misunderstood him.

53. *Art thou greater than our father Abraham?* (*Mē su meizōn ei tou patros hēmōn Abraam;*). Negative answer expected by *mē* with ablative case of comparison in *patros* after *meizōn*. The question was designed to put Jesus in a difficult position, for Abraham and the prophets all "died." They do not see that Jesus uses death in a different sense. *Whom makest thou thyself?* (*tina seauton poieis;*). *Seauton*

is predicate accusative with *poieis*. They suspect that Jesus is guilty of blasphemy as they charged in 5:18 in making himself equal with God. Later they will make it specifically (10:33; 19:7). They set a trap for Jesus for this purpose.

54. *If I glorify myself* (*ean egō doxasō emauton*). Third-class conditon with *ean* and first aorist active subjunctive (or future active indicative) of *doxazō*. *It is my Father that glorifieth me* (*estin ho patēr mou ho doxazōn me*). The position and accent of *estin* mean: "Actually my Father is the one," etc. *Of whom ye say* (*hon humeis legete*). The accusative of the person (*hon*) with *legete* is regular (cf. 10:36). *Your God* (*theos humōn*). So Aleph B D and apparently correct, though A C L W Δ Θ have *hēmōn* (our God). The *hoti* can be taken as recitative (direct quotation, *hēmōn*, our) or declarative (indirect, that, and so *humōn*). The Jews claimed God as their peculiar national God as they had said in 41. So Jesus turns this confession and claim against them.

55. *And ye have not known him* (*kai ouk egnōkate auton*). Adversative use again of *kai* = "and yet." Perfect active indicative of *ginōskō*, the verb for experiential knowledge. This was true of the *kosmos* (1:10; 17:25) and of the hostile Jews (16:3). Jesus prays that the world may know (17:23) and the handful of disciples had come to know (17:25). *But I know him* (*egō de oida auton*). Equipped by eternal fellowship to reveal the Father (1:1-18). This peculiar intimate knowledge Jesus had already claimed (7:29). Jesus used *oida* (8:19; 15:21) or *ginōskō* (17:23, 25) for the knowledge of the Father. No undue distinction can be drawn here. *And if I should say* (*kán eipō*). Third-class condition (concession), "even if I say," with *kai ean* (*kán*) and second aorist active subjunctive. "Suppose I say." *I shall be like you a liar* (*esomai homoios humin pseustēs*). Apodosis of the condition. *Homoios* (like) is followed by the associative-instrumental case *humin*. The word *pseustēs* (liar), in spite of the statement that they are the children of the devil, the

father of lying (8:44), comes with a sudden jolt because it
is a direct charge. This word liar is not considered polite
today in public speech when hurled at definite individuals.
There is a rather free use of the word in I John 2:4, 22; 4:20;
5:10. It is not hard to imagine the quick anger of these
Pharisees.

56. *Rejoiced* (*ēgalliasato*). First aorist middle indicative
of *agalliaomai*, a word of Hellenistic coinage from *agallomai*,
to rejoice. *To see* (*hina idēi*). Sub-final use of *hina* and
second aorist active subjunctive of *horaō*. This joy of Abraham is referred to in Heb. 11:13 (saluting, *aspasamenoi*,
the promises from afar). There was a Jewish tradition that
Abraham saw the whole history of his descendants in the
vision of Gen. 15:6f., but that is not necessary here. He
did look for and welcome the Messianic time, "my day"
(*tēn hēmeran tēn emēn*). "He saw it, and was glad" (*eiden
kai echarē*). Second aorist active indicative of *horaō* and
second aorist passive indicative of *chairō*. Ye see it and are
angry!

57. *Thou art not yet fifty years old* (*pentēkonta eti oupō
echeis*). Literally, "Thou hast not yet fifty years." Not
meaning that Jesus was near that age at all. It was the crisis
of completed manhood (Numb. 4:3) and a round number.
Jesus was about thirty to thirty-three. *And hast thou seen
Abraham?* (*Kai Abraam heōrakas;*). So A C D and B W θ
have *heōrakes*, both second person singular of the perfect
active indicative of *horaō*. But Aleph, Sin-syr., Coptic
versions (accepted by Bernard) have *kai Abraam heōrake se?*
"Has Abraam seen thee?" Either makes sense here.

58. *Before Abraham was* (*prin Abraam genesthai*). Usual
idiom with *prin* in positive sentence with infinitive (second
aorist middle of *ginomai*) and the accusative of general
reference, "before coming as to Abraham," "before Abraham came into existence or was born." *I am* (*egō eimi*).
Undoubtedly here Jesus claims eternal existence with the

absolute phrase used of God. The contrast between *genesthai* (entrance into existence of Abraham) and *eimi* (timeless being) is complete. See the same contrast between *ēn* in 1:1 and *egeneto* in 1:14. See the contrast also in Psa. 90:2 between God (*ei*, art) and the mountains (*genēthēnai*). See the same use of *eimi* in John 6:20; 9:9; 8:24, 28; 18:6.

59. *They took up stones therefore* (*ēran oun lithous*). First aorist active indicative of *airō*, inferential use of *oun*. The time for argument had past. *To cast at him* (*hina balōsin ep' auton*). Final clause with *hina* and the second aorist active subjunctive of *ballō*. Vivid picture of a mob ready to kill Jesus, already beginning to do so. *Hid himself* (*ekrubē*). Second aorist passive indicative of *kruptō*. He was hidden. No Docetic vanishing, but quietly and boldly Jesus went out of the temple. His hour had not yet come. Once again three months later the Pharisees will try to kill him, but he will pass out of their hands (10:39).

CHAPTER IX

1. *As he passed by* (*paragōn*). Present active participle of *paragō*, old verb to go along, by, or past (Matt. 20:30). Only example in this Gospel, but in I John 2:8, 17. The day was after the stirring scenes in chapter 8, but not at the feast of dedication as Westcott argues. That comes three months later (10:22). *From his birth* (*ek genetēs*). Ablative case with *ek* of old word from *genō, ginomai*. Here alone in N.T., but the phrase *tuphlos ek genetēs* is common in Greek writers. Probably a well-known character with his stand as a beggar (verse 5).

2. *Who did sin?* (*tis hēmarten;*). Second aorist active indicative of *hamartanō*. See Acts 3:2; 14:8 for two examples of lameness from birth. Blindness is common in the Orient and Jesus healed many cases (cf. Mark 8:23; 10:46) and mentions this fact as one of the marks of the Messiah in the message to the Baptist (Matt. 11:5). This is the only example of congenital blindness healed. It is not clear that the disciples expected Jesus to heal this case. They are puzzled by the Jewish notion that sickness was a penalty for sin. The Book of Job had shown that this was not always the case and Jesus shows it also (Luke 13:1–5). If this man was guilty, it was due to prenatal sin on his part, a curious notion surely. The other alternative charged it upon his parents. That is sometimes true (Ex. 20:5, etc.), but by no means always. The rabbinical casuists loved to split hairs on this problem. Ezek. (18:20) says: "The soul that sinneth it shall die" (individual responsibility for sin committed). There is something in heredity, but not everything. *That he should be born blind* (*hina tuphlos gennēthēi*). Probably consecutive (or sub-final) use of *hina* with first aorist passive subjunctive of *gennaō*.

3. *But that the works of God should be made manifest in
him* (*all' hina phanerōthēi ta erga tou theou en autōi*). Jesus
denies both alternatives, and puts God's purpose (*all' hina*
with first aorist subjunctive of *phaneroō*) as the true solution.
It is sometimes true that disease is the result of personal sin
as in the man in 5:14 and parents can hand on the effects
of sin to the third and fourth generations, but there are cases
free from blame like this. There is comfort for many suffer-
ers in the words of Jesus here.

4. *We must work the works of him that sent me* (*hēmas dei
ergazesthai ta erga tou pempsantos me*). This is undoubtedly
the correct text (supported by the Neutral and Western
classes) and not *eme* (I) and *me* (me) of the Syrian class nor
hēmas (we) and *hēmas* (us) of the Alexandrian class. Jesus
associates us with him in the task committed to him by the
Father. Bernard argues vigorously, but vainly, for *eme me*.
We are not able to fathom the depth of the necessity (*dei*)
here involved in each life as in this poor blind man and in
each of us. *While it is day* (*heōs hēmera estin*). This clause
gives the note of urgency upon us all. *The night cometh*
(*erchetai nux*). "Night is coming on," and rapidly. Night
was coming for Jesus (7:33) and for each of us. Cf. 11:9;
12:35. Even electric lights do not turn night into day. *Heōs*
with the present indicative (21:22f.) means "while," not
until as in 13:38.

5. *When I am in the world* (*hotan en tōi kosmōi ō*). Indefinite relative clause with *hotan* and present active subjunctive *ō*, "whenever I am in the world." The Latin Vulgate
renders here *hotan* by *quamdiu* so long as or while as if it
were *heōs*. But clearly Jesus here refers to the historic Incarnation (17:11) and to any previous visitations in the
time of the patriarchs, prophets, etc. Jesus as God's Son is
always the Light of the World (1:4, 10; 8:12), but here the
reference is limited to his manifestation "in the world."
I am the light of the world (*phōs eimi tou kosmou*). The ab-

sence of the definite article (*to phōs* in 8:12) is to be noted (Westcott). Literally, "I am light to the world, whenever I am in the world." "The display of the character varies with the occasion" (Westcott).

6. *He spat on the ground* (*eptusen chamai*). First aorist active indicative of the old verb *ptuō* for which see Mark 7:33. *Chamai* is an old adverb either in the dative or locative (sense suits locative), in N.T. only here and John 18:6. Jesus was not asked to cure this man. The curative effects of saliva are held in many places. The Jews held saliva efficacious for eye-trouble, but it was forbidden on the Sabbath. "That Jesus supposed some virtue lay in the application of the clay is contradicted by the fact that in other cases of blindness He did not use it" (Dods). Cf. Mark 8:23. Why he here accommodated himself to current belief we do not know unless it was to encourage the man to believe. *He made clay* (*epoiēsen pēlon*). Only use of *pēlos*, old word for clay, in N.T. in this chapter and Rom. 9:21. The kneading of the clay and spittle added another offence against the Sabbath rules of the rabbis. *Anointed his eyes with the clay* (*epechrisen autou ton pēlon epi tous ophthalmous*). First aorist active indicative of *epichriō*, old verb, to spread on, anoint, here only and verse 11 in N.T. "He spread the clay upon his eyes." B C read *epethēken* (first aorist active indicative of *epitithēmi*, to put on).

7. *Wash* (*nipsai*). First aorist middle imperative second person singular of *niptō*, later form of *nizō*, to wash, especially parts of the body. Certainly bathing the eyes is good for eye trouble, and yet we are not to infer that the cure was due to the use of the clay or to the washing. *In the pool of Siloam* (*eis tēn kolumbēthran tou Silōam*). The word *kolumbēthra* (from *kolumbaō*, to swim) is a common word for swimming-pool, in N.T. only here and 5:2, 7. The name *Siloam* is Hebrew (Isa. 8:6) and means "sent" (*apestalmenos*, perfect passive participle of *apostellō*). It was situated south

of the temple area and was apparently connected by a sub-
terranean tunnel with the Virgin's Well (5:2) according to
Bernard. The water was conducted artificially to the pool
of Siloam. *Washed* (*enipsato*). First aorist direct middle
(cf. *nipsai*), apparently bathing and not merely washing
his eyes. *Came seeing* (*ēlthen blepōn*). Jesus had healed him.
He was tested by the demand to bathe his eyes.

8. *Neighbours* (*geitones*). From *gē* (land), of the same land,
old word. See Luke 14:2. *Saw him* (*theōrountes*). Present
active participle of *theōreō*, who used to observe him. *Aforetime* (*to proteron*). Adverbial accusative, "the former time,"
formerly. *That he was a beggar* (*hoti prosaitēs ēn*). See 4:19
and 12:19 for declarative *hoti* after *theōreō*. But it is entirely
possible that *hoti* here is "because" (Westcott). *Prosaitēs*
is a late word for beggar, in N.T. only here and Mark 10:46.
It is from *prosaiteō*, to ask in addition (see *prosaitōn* below),
a thing that beggars know how to do. *Is not this he that sat
and begged?* (*Ouch houtos estin ho kathēmenos kai prosaitōn;*).
He had his regular place and was a familiar figure. But now
his eyes are wide open.

9. *Nay but he is like him* (*Ouchi, alla homoios autōi estin*).
Vigorous denial (*ouchi*) and mere similarity suggested. Associative instrumental case *autōi* after *homoios*. The crowd is
divided. *He said* (*ekeinos elegen*). Emphatic demonstrative
(as in 11, 12, 25, 36), "That one spake up." He knew.

10. *How then were thine eyes opened?* (*Pōs oun ēneōich-
thēsan sou hoi ophthalmoi;*). Natural and logical (*oun*)
question. First aorist passive indicative (triple augment)
of *anoigō*. These neighbours admit the fact and want the
manner ("how") of the cure made clear.

11. *The man that is called Jesus* (*ho anthrōpos ho legomenos
Iēsous*). He does not yet know Jesus as the Messiah the
Son of God (9:36). *I received sight* (*aneblepsa*). First aorist
active indicative of *anablepō*, old verb to see again, to recover sight, not strictly true of this man who had never

seen. He got back sight that he had never had. Originally
the verb means to look up (Matt. 14:19).

12. *Where is he?* (*Pou estin ekeinos;*). The very question
of 7:11.

13. *They bring him* (*agousin auton*). Vivid dramatic present active of *agō*. These neighbours bring him. *To the
Pharisees* (*pros tous Pharisaious*). The accepted professional
teachers who posed as knowing everything. The scribes were
usually Pharisees. *Him that aforetime was blind* (*ton pote
tuphlon*). Simply, "the once blind man."

14. *Now it was the sabbath* (*ēn de sabbaton*). Literally,
"Now it was a sabbath" (no article). To the Pharisees this
fact was a far more important matter than whether or how
the thing was done. See Volumes I and II for discussions of
the minute Sabbath regulations of the rabbis.

15. *Again* (*palin*). Besides the questioning of the neighbours (verses 8 and 9). *Therefore* (*oun*). Since he has been
brought to the Pharisees who must make a show of wisdom.
Also asked him (*ērōtōn auton kai*). Inchoative imperfect
active of *erōtaō*, "began also to question him." *How he received his sight* (*pōs aneblepsen*). No denial as yet of the fact,
only interest in the "how." *He put* (*epethēken*). Genuine
here, but see verse 6. *And do see* (*kai blepō*). That is the
overwhelming fact.

16. *Because he keepeth not the sabbath* (*hoti to sabbaton ou
tērei*). This is reason (causal *hoti*) enough. He violates our
rules about the Sabbath and therefore is a Sabbath-breaker
as charged when here before (5:10, 16, 18). Hence he is not
"from God" (*para theou*). So some. *How can a man that is a
sinner do such signs?* (*Pōs dunatai anthrōpos hamartōlos
toiauta sēmeia poiein;*). This was the argument of Nicodemus, himself a Pharisee and one of the Sanhedrin, long ago
(3:2). It was a conundrum for the Pharisees. No wonder
there was "a division" (*schisma*, schism, split, from *schizō*)
as in 7:43; 10:19.

17. *Unto the blind man again* (*tōi tuphlōi palin*). The
doctors disagree and they ask the patient whose story they
had already heard (verse 15). *In that he opened thine eyes*
(*hoti ēneōixen sou tous ophthalmous*). Causal use of *hoti*
and triple augment in the first aorist active indicative of
anoigō. They offer the excuse that the man's experience
particularly qualified him to explain the "how," overlooking
the fact he had already told his story and also trying to
conceal their own hopeless division of. opinion. *He is a
prophet* (*prophētēs estin*). The man will go that far anyhow.

18. *The Jews* (*hoi Ioudaioi*). Probably the incredulous and
hostile section of the Pharisees in verse 16 (cf. 5:10). *Did not
believe* (*ouk episteusan*). The facts told by the man, ";that
he had been blind and had received his sight" (*hoti ēn tuphlos
kai aneblepsen*), conflicted with their theological views of
God and the Sabbath. So they refused belief "until they
called the parents" (*heōs hotou ephōnēsan tous goneis*). Usual
construction of *heōs hotou* (=until which time, like *heōs*
alone) with aorist active indicative of *phōneō*, old verb from
phōnē (voice, sound). They called out loud for his parents
to throw light on this grave problem to cover up their own
stupidity.

19. *Is this your son who ye say was born blind? how doth he
now see?* (*Houtos estin ho huios humōn, hon humeis legete
hoti tuphlos egennēthē; pōs oun blepei arti;*). It was shrewdly
put with three questions in one in order to confuse the
parents if possible and give the hostile Pharisees a handle.

20. *We know that this is our son, and that he was born blind*
(*Oidamen hoti houtos estin ho huios hēmōn kai hoti tuphlos
egennēthē*). These two questions the parents answer clearly
and thus cut the ground from under the disbelief of these
Pharisees as to the fact of the cure (verse 18). So these Pharisees made a failure here.

21. *But how he now seeth we know not* (*pōs de nun blepei
ouk oidamen*). Concerning the third question they profess

ignorance both as to the "how" (*pōs*) and the "who" (*tis*).
Opened (*ēnoixen*). First aorist active indicative with single
augment of *anoigō*, same form as *ēneōixen* (triple augment)
in verse 17. They were not witnesses of the cure and had the
story only from the son as the Pharisees had. *He is of age*
(*hēlikian echei*). "He has maturity of age." He is an adult.
A regular classical phrase in Plato, etc. The parents were
wholly right and within their rights.

22. *Because they feared the Jews* (*hoti ephobounto tous
Ioudaious*). Imperfect middle, a continuing fear and not
without reason. See already the whispers about Jesus because of fear of the Jews (7:13). *Had agreed already* (*ēdē
sunetetheinto*). Past perfect middle of *suntithēmi*, to put
together, to form a compact (7:32, 47–49). *If any man should
confess him to be Christ* (*ean tis auton homologēsēi Christon*).
Condition of third class with *ean* and first aorist active subjunctive of *homologeō* and predicate accusative *Christon*.
Jesus had made confession of himself before men the test
of discipleship and denial the disproof (Matt. 10:32 = Luke
12:8). We know that many of the rulers nominally believed
on Jesus (12:42) and yet "did not confess him because of the
Pharisees" (*alla dia tous Pharisaious ouch hōmologoun*), for
the very reason given here, "that they might not be put out
of the synagogue" (*hina mē aposunagōgoi genōntai*). Small
wonder then that here the parents cowered a bit. *That he
should be put out of the synagogue* (*hina aposunagōgos genētai*).
Sub-final use of *hina* with second aorist middle subjunctive
of *ginomai*. *Aposunagōgos* (*apo* and *sunagōgē*) is found in
N.T. only here and 12:42; 16:2. A purely Jewish word
naturally. There were three kinds of excommunication (for
thirty days, for thirty more, indefinitely).

23. *Therefore* (*dia touto*). "For this reason." Reason
enough for due caution.

24. *A second time* (*ek deuterou*). He had given the Pharisees the facts the first time (9:15). It was really the third

time (see *palin* in 9:17). Now it was like a joke unless the Pharisees meant to imply that his previous story was untrue. *Give glory to God* (*dos doxan tōi theōi*). Second aorist active imperative of *didōmi* (cf. *sches, hes*). This phrase does not mean gratitude to God as in Luke 17:18. It is rather an adjuration to speak the truth (Josh. 7:19; I Sam. 6:5) as if he had not done it before. Augustine says: "*Quid est Da gloriam Deo? Nega quod accepisti.*" *Is a sinner* (*hamartōlos estin*). They can no longer deny the fact of the cure since the testimony of the parents (9:19) and now wish the man to admit that he was lying in saying that Jesus healed him. He must accept their ecclesiastical authority as proving that Jesus had nothing to do with the cure since Jesus is a sinner. They wish to decide the fact by logic and authority like all persecutors through the ages. Recall the Pharisaic distinction between *dikaios* (righteous) and *hamartōlos* (sinner).

25. *One thing I know* (*hen oida*). This man is keen and quick and refuses to fall into the trap set for him. He passes by their quibbling about Jesus being a "sinner" (*hamartōlos*) and clings to the one fact of his own experience. *Whereas I was blind, now I see* (*tuphlos ōn arti blepō*). Literally, "Being blind I now see." The present active participle ōn of *eimi* by implication in contrast with *arti* (just now, at this moment) points to previous and so past time. It must be borne in mind that the man did not at this stage know who Jesus was and so had not yet taken him as Saviour (9:36–38).

26. *What did he do to thee?* (*Ti epoiēsen soi;*). Another cross-examination, now admitting that Jesus opened his eyes and wishing again (9:15, 17) to know "how."

27. *I told you even now* (*eipon humin ēdē*). In verses 15, 17, 25. *Would ye also become his disciples?* (*Mē kai humeis thelete autou mathētai genesthai;*). Negative answer formally expected, but the keenest irony in this gibe. Clearly the healed man knew from the use of "also" (*kai*) that Jesus had some "disciples" (*mathētai*, predicate nominative with

the infinitive *genesthai*) and that the Pharisees knew that fact. "Do ye also (like the Galilean mob) wish, etc." See 7:45–52. It cut to the bone.

28. *They reviled him* (*eloidorēsan auton*). First aorist active indicative of *loidoreō*, old verb from *loidoros* (reviler, I Cor. 5:11), in N.T. only here, Acts 23:4; I Cor. 4:12; I Peter 2:23. *Thou art his disciple* (*su mathētēs ei ekeinou*). Probably a fling in *ekeinou* (of that fellow). He had called him a prophet (9:17) and became a joyful follower later (9:36–38). *But we are disciples of Moses* (*hēmeis de tou Mōuseōs esmen mathētai*). This they said with proud scorn of the healed beggar. All orthodox rabbis so claimed.

29. *We know that God hath spoken unto Moses* (*hēmeis oidamen hoti Mōusei lelalēken ho theos*). Perfect active indicative of *laleō*, so still on record. See Ex. 33:11. For *laleō* used of God speaking see Heb. 1:1. They are proud to be disciples of Moses. *But as for this man, we do not know whence he is* (*touton de ouk oidamen pothen estin*). "This fellow" they mean by "*touton*" in emphatic position, we do not even know whence he is. Some of the people did (7:27), but in the higher sense none of the Jews knew (8:14). These Pharisees neither knew nor cared.

30. *Why, herein is the marvel* (*en toutōi gar to thaumaston estin*). This use of *gar* (*ge + ara*, accordingly indeed) to bring out an affirmation from the previous words is common enough. "Why in this very point is the wonder" (*thaumaston*, old verbal adjective from *thaumazō* as in Matt. 21:42). The man is angry now and quick in his insight and reply. You confess your ignorance of whence he is, ye who know everything, "and yet (adversative use of *kai* again) he opened my eyes" (*kai ēnoixen mou tous ophthalmous*). That stubborn fact stands.

31. *God does not hear sinners* (*ho theos hamartōlōn ouk akouei*). Note genitive case with *akouei*. This was the argument of the Pharisees in 9:16. It is frequent in the O.T.

(Job 27:9; Psa. 66:18; Isa. 1:15; 59:2, etc.). The conclusion is inevitable from this premise. Jesus is not *hamartōlos*. *If any man be a worshipper of God* (*ean tis theosebēs ēi*). Condition of third class with *ean* and present active subjunctive *ēi*. *Theosebēs* (*theos*, God, *sebomai*, to worship) is an old compound adjective, here alone in the N.T. *And do his will* (*kai to thelēma autou poiēi*). Same condition with present active subjunctive of *poieō*, "keep on doing his will."

32. *Since the world began* (*ek tou aiōnos*). Literally, "from the age," "from of old." Elsewhere in the N.T. we have *apo tou aiōnos* or *ap 'aiōnos* (Luke 1:70; Acts 3:31; 15:18) as is common in the LXX. *Of a man born blind* (*tuphlou gegennēmenou*). Perfect passive participle of *gennaō*. This is the chief point and the man will not let it be overlooked, almost rubs it in, in fact. It was congenital blindness.

33. *If this man were not from God* (*ei mē ēn houtos para theou*). Negative condition of second class with imperfect indicative. Assuming that Jesus is not "from God" (*para theou*) as some argued in 9:16, "he could do nothing" (*ouk ēdunato poiein ouden*). Conclusion of the second-class condition with imperfect indicative (double augment in *ēdunato*) without *an* as is usual in conditions of possibility, propriety, obligation (Robertson, *Grammar*, pp. 920, 1014). The man has scored with terrific power in his use of Scripture and logic.

34. *Thou wast altogether born in sin* (*en hamartiais su egennēthēs holos*). First aorist passive indicative of *gennaō*. "In sins thou wast begotten (or born) all of thee." *Holos* is predicate nominative and teaches total depravity in this case beyond controversy, the Pharisees being judges. *And dost thou teach us?* (*kai su didaskeis hēmas;*). The audacity of it all. Note emphasis on *su* (thou). It was insufferable. He had not only taught the rabbis, but had utterly routed them in argument. *And they cast him out* (*kai exebalon auton exō*). Effective second aorist active indicative of *ekballō*

intensified by the addition of *exō*. Probably not yet expulsion from the synagogue (9:22) which required a formal meeting of the Sanhedrin, but certainly forcible driving of the gifted upstart from their presence. See 6:37 for another use of *ekballō exō* besides 9:35.

35. *Finding him* (*heurōn auton*). Second aorist active participle of *heuriskō*, after search because of what he had heard (*ēkousen*). *Dost thou believe on the Son of God?* (*Su pisteueis eis ton huion tou theou;*). So A L Θ and most versions, but Aleph B D W Syr-sin read *tou anthrōpou* (the Son of Man), almost certainly correct. In either case it is a distinct Messianic claim quite beyond the range of this man's limited knowledge, keen as he is.

36. *And who is he, Lord, that I may believe on him?* (*Kai tis estin, kurie;*). The initial *kai* (and) is common (Mark 10:26; Luke 10:29; 18:26). Probably by *kurie* he means only "Sir." It usually comes at the beginning of the sentence, not at the end as here and verse 38. *That I may believe on him* (*hina pisteusō eis auton*). Ellipsis to be supplied before this final clause. He catches up the words of Jesus in the preceding verse, though he does not yet know who the Son of Man (or Son of God) is, but he trusts Jesus.

37. *Thou hast both seen him* (*kai heōrakas auton*). Perfect active indicative (double reduplication) of *horaō*. Since his eyes were opened. *And he it is that speaketh with thee* (*kai ho lalōn meta sou ekeinos estin*). "And the one speaking with thee is that man." See 19:35 for *ekeinos* used of the speaker. In 4:26 Jesus reveals himself in like manner to the Samaritan woman as Messiah while here as the Son of Man (or the Son of God).

38. *Lord, I believe* (*Pisteuō, kurie*). *Kurie* here = Lord (reverence, no longer respect as in 36). A short creed, but to the point. *And he worshipped him* (*kai prosekunēsen autōi*). Ingressive first aorist active indicative of *proskuneō*, old verb to fall down in reverence, to worship. Sometimes of

men (Matt. 18:26). In John (see 4:20) this verb "is always used to express divine worship" (Bernard). It is tragic to hear men today deny that Jesus should be worshipped. He accepted worship from this new convert as he later did from Thomas who called him "God" (John 20:28). Peter (Acts 10:25f.) refused worship from Cornelius as Paul and Barnabas did at Lystra (Acts 14:18), but Jesus made no protest here.

39. *For judgement (eis krima)*. The Father had sent the Son for this purpose (3:17). This world (*kosmos*) is not the home of Jesus. The *krima* (judgement), a word nowhere else in John, is the result of the *krisis* (sifting) from *krinō*, to separate. The Father has turned over this process of sifting (*krisis*) to the Son (5:22). He is engaged in that very work by this miracle. *They which see not (hoi mē blepontes)*. The spiritually blind as well as the physically blind (Luke 4:18; Isa. 42:18). Purpose clause with *hina* and present active subjunctive *blepōsin* (may keep on seeing). This man now sees physically and spiritually. *And that they which see may become blind (kai hoi blepontes tuphloi genōntai)*. Another part of God's purpose, seen in Matt. 11:25 = Luke 10:21, is the curse on those who blaspheme and reject the Son. Note ingressive aorist middle subjunctive of *ginomai* and predicate nominative. *Hoi blepontes* are those who profess to see like these Pharisees, but are really blind. Blind guides they were (Matt. 23:16). Complacent satisfaction with their dim light.

40. *Are we also blind? (Mē kai hēmeis tuphloi esmen;)*. Negative answer expected (*mē*) and yet these Pharisees who overheard the words of Jesus to the new convert vaguely suspected that Jesus was referring to them by the last clause. Up in Galilee Jesus had called the Pharisees blind guides who stumble into the pit (Matt. 15:14).

41. *If ye were blind (ei tuphloi ēte)*. Condition of second class with imperfect indicative in the protasis. The old word

tuphlos is from *tuphō*, to raise a smoke, to blind by smoke (literally and metaphorically). Here, of course, it is moral blindness. If the Pharisees were born morally blind, they would, like idiots, be without responsibility. *Ye would not have sin* (*ouk an eichete hamartian*). Regular form for conclusion of second-class condition, *an* with imperfect. *But now ye say* (*nun de legete*). In contrast to the previous condition. See like contrast in 15:22, 24. They arrogantly asserted superior knowledge. *We see* (*blepomen*). The ignorant mob do not (7:49). It is sin against light and is hopeless (Mark 3:29; Matt. 12:31f.). "Ye are witnesses against yourselves" (*martureite heautois*, Matt. 23:31).

CHAPTER X

1. *Verily, verily* (*Amēn, amēn*). Solemn prelude by repetition as in 1:51. The words do not ever introduce a fresh topic (cf. 8:34, 51, 58). So in 10:7. The Pharisees had previously assumed (Vincent) they alone were the authoritative guides of the people (9:24, 29). So Jesus has a direct word for them. So Jesus begins this allegory in a characteristic way. John does not use the word *parabolē*, but *paroimia* (verse 6), and it really is an allegory of the Good Shepherd and self-explanatory like that of the Prodigal Son in Luke 15. He first tells it in verses 1–5 and then explains and expands it in verses 7–18. *Into the fold of the sheep* (*eis tēn aulēn tōn probatōn*). Originally *aulē* (from *aō*, to blow) in Homer's time was just an uncovered space around the house enclosed by a wall, then a roofless enclosure in the country where flocks were herded as here and verse 16. It later came to mean the house itself or palace (Matt. 26:3, 58, etc.). In the papyri it means the court attached to the house. *Climbeth up* (*anabainōn*). Present active participle of *anabainō*, to go up. One who goes up, not by the door, has to climb up over the wall. *Some other way* (*allachothen*). Rare word for old *allothen*, but in IV Macc. 1:7 and in a papyrus. Only here in N.T. *The same* (*ekeinos*). "That one" just described. *Is a thief and a robber* (*kleptēs estin kai lēistēs*). Both old and common words (from *kleptō*, to steal, *lēizomai*, to plunder). The distinction is preserved in the N.T. as here. Judas was a *kleptēs* (John 12:6), Barabbas a robber (18:40) like the two robbers (Matt. 27:38, 44) crucified with Jesus erroneously termed thieves like "the thief on the cross" by most people. See Mark 11:17. Here the man jumping over the wall comes to steal and to do it by violence like a bandit. He is both thief and robber.

2. *The shepherd of the sheep* (*poimēn estin tōn probatōn*).
No article with *poimēn*, "a shepherd to the sheep." He
comes in by the door with the sheep whom he leads. Old
word is *poimēn*, root meaning to protect. Jesus applies it
to himself in verse 16 and implies it here. It is used of Christ
in I Peter 2:25 and Heb. 13:20. Paul applies it to ministers
in Eph. 4:11. Jesus uses the verb *poimainō*, to shepherd, to
Peter (John 21:16) and Peter uses it to other preachers
(I Peter 5:2) and Paul uses it for bishops (elders) in Acts
20:28. Our word pastor is simply Latin for shepherd. Christ
is drawing a sharp contrast after the conduct of the Pharisees
towards the blind man between himself and them.

3. *To him* (*toutōi*). "To this one," the shepherd, in dative
case. *The porter* (*ho thurōros*). Old word for doorkeeper
(*thura*, door, *ōra*, care, carer for the door). Used for man
(Mark 13:34; John 10:3) or woman (John 18:16ff.), only
N.T. examples. The porter has charge of the sheep in the
fold at night and opens the door in the morning for the
shepherd. It is not certain that Jesus meant this detail to
have a special application. The Holy Spirit, of course,
does open the door of our hearts for Jesus through various
agencies. *Hear his voice* (*tēs phōnēs autou akouei*). Hear and
heed (verse 27). Note genitive case *phōnēs* (accusative in
3:8). *By name* (*kat' onoma*). Several flocks might be herded
in the same fold overnight. But the shepherd knows his
own (*ta idia*) sheep (verse 27) and calls their names. "It
is still common for Eastern shepherds to give particular
names to their sheep" (Bernard). *And leadeth them out*
(*kai exagei auta*). Old and common verb, present active
indicative. The sheep follow readily (verse 27) because
they know their own shepherd's voice and his name for
each of them and because he has led them out before. They
love and trust their shepherd.

4. *When he hath put forth all his own* (*hotan ta idia panta
ekbalēi*). Indefinite temporal clause with *hotan* and the sec-

ond aorist (effective) active subjunctive of *ekballō*. No need
of the *futurum exactum* idea, simply, "when he leads out all
his own sheep." They are all out of the fold. He overlooks
none. *Ekballō* does mean "thrust out" if a reluctant sheep
wishes to linger too long. *He goeth before them* (*emprosthen
autōn poreuetai*). Staff in hand he leads the way in front of
the flock and they follow (*akolouthei*) him. What a lesson
for pastors who seek to drive the church like cattle and fail.
The true pastor leads in love, in words, in deeds.

5. *A stranger* (*allotrioi*). Literally, "One belonging to
another" (from *allos*, opposed to *idios*). A shepherd of
another flock, it may be, not necessarily the thief and robber
of verse 1. Note associative instrumental case after *akol-
outhēsousin* (future active indicative of *akoloutheō*, verse 4).
Note the strong double negative *ou mē* here with the future
indicative, though usually with the aorist subjunctive (Aleph
L W have it here). They simply will not follow such a man
or woman, these well-trained sheep will not. *But will flee
from him* (*alla pheuxontai ap' autou*). Future middle of
pheugō and ablative case with *apo*. They will flee as if from
a wolf or from the plague. Alas and alas, if only our modern
pastors had the sheep (old and young) so trained that they
would run away from and not run after the strange voices
that call them to false philosophy, false psychology, false
ethics, false religion, false life.

6. *This parable* (*tautēn tēn paroimian*). Old word for
proverb from *para* (beside) and *oimos*, way, a wayside saying or saying by the way. As a proverb in N.T. in II Peter
2:22 (quotation from Prov. 26:11), as a symbolic or figurative saying in John 16:25, 29, as an allegory in John 10:6.
Nowhere else in the N.T. Curiously enough in the N.T.
parabolē occurs only in the Synoptics outside of Heb. 9:9;
11:19. Both are in the LXX. *Parabolē* is used as a proverb
(Luke 4:23) just as *paroimia* is in II Peter 2:22. Here clearly
paroimia means an allegory which is one form of the parable.

So there you are. Jesus spoke this *paroimia* to the Pharisees, "but they understood not what things they were which he spake unto them" (*ekeinoi de ouk egnōsan tina ēn ha elalei autois*). Second aorist active indicative of *ginōskō* and note *ēn* in indirect question as in 2:25 and both the interrogative *tina* and the relative *ha*. "Spake" (imperfect *elalei*) should be "was speaking or had been speaking."

7. *Therefore again* (*oun palin*). Jesus repeats the allegory with more detail and with more directness of application. Repeating a story is not usually an exhilarating experience. *I am the door of the sheep* (*egō eimi hē thura tōn probatōn*). The door for the sheep by which they enter. "He is the legitimate door of access to the spiritual *aulē*, the Fold of the House of Israel, the door by which a true shepherd must enter" (Bernard). He repeats it in verse 9. This is a new idea, not in the previous story (1-5). Moffatt follows the Sahidic in accepting *ho poimēn* here instead of *hē thura*, clearly whimsical. Jesus simply changes the metaphor to make it plainer. They were doubtless puzzled by the meaning of the door in verse 1. Once more, this metaphor should help those who insist on the literal meaning of bread as the actual body of Christ in Mark 14:22. Jesus is not a physical "door," but he is the only way of entrance into the Kingdom of God (14:6).

8. *Before me* (*pro emou*). Aleph with the Latin, Syriac, and Sahidic versions omit these words (supported by A B D L W). But with or without *pro emou* Jesus refers to the false Messiahs and self-appointed leaders who made havoc of the flock. These are the thieves and robbers, not the prophets and sincere teachers of old. The reference is to verse 1. There had been numerous such impostors already (Josephus, *Ant.* XVIII. i. 6; *War* II. viii. 1) and Jesus will predict many more (Matt. 24:23f.). They keep on coming, these wolves in sheep's clothing (Matt. 7:15) who grow rich by fooling the credulous sheep. In this case "the sheep did

not hear them" (*ouk ēkousan autōn ta probata*). First aorist active indicative with genitive. Fortunate sheep who knew the Shepherd's voice.

9. *The door* (*hē thura*). Repeated from verse 7. *By me if any man enter in* (*di' emou ean tis eiselthēi*). Condition of third class with *ean* and second aorist active subjunctive of *eiserchomai*. Note proleptic and emphatic position of *di' emou*. One can call this narrow intolerance, if he will, but it is the narrowness of truth. If Jesus is the Son of God sent to earth for our salvation, he is the only way. He had already said it in 5:23. He will say it again more sharply in 14:6. It is unpalatable to the religious dogmatists before him as it is to the liberal dogmatists today. Jesus offers the open door to "any one" (*tis*) who is willing (*thelei*) to do God's will (7:17). *He shall be saved* (*sōthēsetai*). Future passive of *sōzō*, the great word for salvation, from *sōs*, safe and sound. The sheep that comes into the fold through Jesus as the door will be safe from thieves and robbers for one thing. He will have entrance (*eisleusetai*) and outgo (*exeleusetai*), he will be at home in the daily routine (cf. Acts 1:21) of the sheltered flock. *And shall find pasture* (*kai nomēn heurēsei*). Future (linear future) indicative of *heuriskō*, old word from *nemō*, to pasture. In N.T. only here and II Tim. 2:17 (in sense of growth). This same phrase occurs in I Chron. 4:40. The shepherd leads the sheep to pasture, but this phrase pictures the joy of the sheep in the pasture provided by the shepherd.

10. *But that he may steal, and kill, and destroy* (*ei mē hina klepsēi kai thusēi kai apolesēi*). Literally, "except that" (*ei mē*) common without (Matt. 12:4) and with verb (Gal. 1:7), "if not" (literally), followed here by final *hina* and three aorist active subjunctives as sometimes by *hotan* (Mark 9:9) or *hoti* (II Cor. 12:13). Note the order of the verbs. Stealing is the purpose of the thief, but he will kill and destroy if necessary just like the modern bandit or gangster.

I came that they may have life (*egō ēlthon hina zōēn echōsin*). In sharp contrast (*egō*) as the good shepherd with the thieves and robbers of verse 1 came Jesus. Note present active subjunctive (*echōsin*), "that they (people) may keep on having life (eternal, he means)" as he shows in 10:28. He is "the life" (14:6). *And may have it abundantly* (*kai perisson echōsin*). Repetition of *echōsin* (may keep on having) abundance (*perisson*, neuter singular of *perissos*). Xenophon (*Anab*. VII. vi. 31) uses *perisson echein*, "to have a surplus," true to the meaning of overflow from *peri* (around) seen in Paul's picture of the overplus (*hupereperisseusen* in Rom. 5:20) of grace. Abundance of life and all that sustains life, Jesus gives.

11. *I am the good shepherd* (*egō eimi ho poimēn ho kalos*). Note repetition of the article, "the shepherd the good one." Takes up the metaphor of verses 2ff. Vulgate *pastor bonus*. Philo calls his good shepherd *agathos*, but *kalos* calls attention to the beauty in character and service like "good stewards" (I Peter 4:10), "a good minister of Christ Jesus" (I Tim. 4:6). Often both adjectives appear together in the ancient Greek as once in the New Testament (Luke 8:15). "Beauty is as beauty does." That is *kalos*. *Layeth down his life for his sheep* (*tēn psuchēn autou tithēsin huper tōn probatōn*). For illustration see I Sam. 17:35 (David's experience) and Isa. 31:4. Dods quotes Xenophon (*Mem*. ii. 7, 14) who pictures even the sheep dog as saying to the sheep: "For I am the one that saves you also so that you are neither stolen by men nor seized by wolves." Hippocrates has *psuchēn katetheto* (he laid down his life, i.e. died). In Judges 12:3 *ethēka tēn psuchēn* means "I risked my life." The true physician does this for his patient as the shepherd for his sheep. The use of *huper* here (over, in behalf of, instead of), but in the papyri *huper* is the usual preposition for substitution rather than *anti*. This shepherd gives his life for the sin of the world (1:29; I John 2:2).

12. *He that is a hireling* (*ho misthōtos*). Old word from *misthoō*, to hire (Matt. 20:1) from *misthos* (hire, wages, Luke 10:7), in N.T. only in this passage. Literally, "the hireling and not being a shepherd" (*ho misthōtos kai ouk ōn poimēn*). Note *ouk* with the participle *ōn* to emphasize the certainty that he is not a shepherd in contrast with *mē eiserchomenos* in verse 1 (conceived case). See same contrast in I Peter 1:8 between *ouk idontes* and *mē horōntes*. The hireling here is not necessarily the thief and robber of verses 1 and 8. He may conceivably be a nominal shepherd (pastor) of the flock who serves only for the money, a sin against which Peter warned the shepherds of the flock "not for shameful gain" (I Peter 5:2). *Whose own* (*hou idia*). Every true shepherd considers the sheep in his care "his own" (*idia*) even if he does not actually "own" them. The mere "hireling" does not feel so. *Beholdeth* (*theōrei*). Vivid dramatic present, active indicative of *theōreō*, a graphic picture. *The wolf coming* (*ton lukon erchomenon*). Present middle predicate participle of *erchomai*. *Leaveth the sheep, and fleeth* (*aphiēsin ta probata kai pheugei*). Graphic present actives again of *aphiēmi* and *pheugō*. The cowardly hireling cares naught for the sheep, but only for his own skin. The wolf was the chief peril to sheep in Palestine. See Matt. 10:6 where Jesus says: "Behold I send you forth as sheep in the midst of wolves." *And the wolf snatcheth them and scattereth them* (*kai ho lukos harpazei kai skorpizei*). Vivid parenthesis in the midst of the picture of the conduct of the hireling. Bold verbs these. For the old verb *harpazō* see John 6:15 and Matt. 11:12, and for *skorpizō*, late word (Plutarch) for the Attic *skedannumi*, see Matt. 12:30. It occurs in the vision of Ezekiel (34:5) where because of the careless shepherds "the sheep became meat to all the beasts of the field, and were scattered." Jesus uses *harpazō* in 10:29 where no one is able "to snatch" one out of the Father's hand.

13. *Because he is a hireling* (*hoti misthōtos estin*). And only that, without the shepherd heart that loves the sheep. Reason given for the conduct of the hireling after the parenthesis about the wolf. *And careth not for the sheep* (*kai ou melei autōi peri tōn probatōn*). Literally, "and it is no care to him about the sheep." This use of the impersonal *melei* (present active indicative) is quite common, as in Matt. 22:16. But God does care (I Peter 5:7).

14. *I am the good-shepherd* (*egō eimi ho poimēn ho kalos*). Effective repetition. *And mine own know me* (*kai ginōskousin me ta ema*). Jesus as the Good Shepherd knows his sheep by name as he had already said (verse 3) and now repeats. Yes, and they know his voice (verse 4), they have experimental knowledge (*ginōskō*) of Jesus as their own Shepherd. Here (in this mutually reciprocal knowledge) lies the secret of their love and loyalty.

15. *And I know the Father* (*kagō ginōskō ton patera*). Hence he is qualified to reveal the Father (1:18). The comparison of the mutually reciprocal knowledge between the Father and the Son illustrates what he has just said, though it stands above all else (Matt. 11:27 = Luke 10:22; John 17:21–26). We cannot claim such perfect knowledge of the Good Shepherd as exists between the Father and the Son and yet the real sheep do know the Shepherd's voice and do love to follow his leadership here and now in spite of thieves, robbers, wolves, hirelings. *And I lay down my life for the sheep* (*kai tēn psuchēn mou tithēmi huper tōn probatōn*). This he had said in verse 11, but he repeats it now for clearness. This he does, not just as an example for the sheep and for under-shepherds, but primarily to save the sheep from the wolves, the thieves and robbers.

16. *Other sheep* (*alla probata*). Sheep, not goats, but "not of this fold" (*ek tēs aulēs tautēs*). See verse 1 for *aulē*. Clearly "his flock is not confined to those enclosed in the Jewish fold, whether in Palestine or elsewhere" (Westcott). Christ's

horizon takes in all men of all races and times (John 11:52;
12:32). The world mission of Christ for all nations is no
new idea with him (Matt. 8:11 = Luke 13:28). God loved
the world and gave his Son for the race (John 3:16). *Them
also I must bring (kákeina dei me agagein).* Second aorist
active infinitive of *agō* with *dei* expressing the moral urgency
of Christ's passion for God's people in all lands and ages.
Missions in Christ's mind takes in the whole world. This
is according to prophecy (Isa. 42:6; 49:6; 56:8) for the Messiah is to be a Light also to the Gentiles. It was typified by
the brazen serpent (John 3:14). Christ died for every man.
The Pharisees doubtless listened in amazement and even the
disciples with slow comprehension. *And they shall hear my
voice (kai tēs phōnēs mou akousontai).* Future middle indicative of *akouō* with the genitive *phōnēs.* These words read
like a transcript from the Acts and the Epistles of Paul
(Romans 9 to 11 in particular). See especially Paul's words
in Acts 28:28. Present-day Christianity is here foretold.
Only do we really listen to the voice of the Shepherd as we
should? Jesus means that the Gentiles will hearken if the
Jews turn away from him. *And they shall become one flock,
one shepherd (kai genēsontai mia poimnē, heis poimēn).* Future
middle indicative of *ginomai,* plural, not singular *genēsetai*
as some MSS. have it. All (Jews and Gentiles) will form one
flock under one Shepherd. Note the distinction here by
Jesus between *poimnē* (old word, contraction of *poimenē*
from *poimēn,* shepherd), as in Matt. 26:31, and *aulē* (fold)
just before. There may be many folds of the one flock.
Jerome in his Vulgate confused this distinction, but he is
wrong. His use of *ovile* for both *aulē* and *pomnion* has helped
Roman Catholic assumptions. Christ's use of "flock" (*poimnē*) here is just another metaphor for kingdom (*basileia*)
in Matt. 8:11 where the children of the kingdom come from
all climes and nations. See also the various metaphors in
Eph. 2 for this same idea. There is only the one Great

Shepherd of the sheep (Heb. 13:20), Jesus Christ our Lord.

17. *For this reason* (*dia touto*). Points to the following *hoti* clause. The Father's love for the Son is drawn out (John 3:16) by the voluntary offering of the Son for the sin of the world (Rom. 5:8). Hence the greater exaltation (Phil. 2:9). Jesus does for us what any good shepherd does (10:11) as he has already said (10:15). The value of the atoning death of Christ lies in the fact that he is the Son of God, the Son of Man, free of sin, and that he makes the offering voluntarily (Heb. 9:14). *That I may take it again* (*hina palin labō autēn*). Purpose clause with *hina* and second aorist active subjunctive of *lambanō*. He looked beyond his death on the Cross to the resurrection. "The purpose of the Passion was not merely to exhibit his unselfish love; it was in order that He might resume His life, now enriched with quickening power as never before" (Bernard). The Father raised Jesus from the dead (Acts 2:32). There is spontaneity in the surrender to death and in the taking life back again (Dods).

18. *No one taketh it away from me* (*oudeis airei autēn ap' emou*). But Aleph B read *ēren* (first aorist active indicative of *airō*, to take away), probably correct (Westcott and Hort). "John is representing Jesus as speaking *sub specie aeternitatis*" (Bernard). He speaks of his death as already past and the resurrection as already accomplished. Cf. John 3:16. *Of myself* (*ap' emautou*). The voluntariness of the death of Jesus repeated and sharpened. D omits it, probably because of superficial and apparent conflict with 5:19. But there is no inconsistency as is shown by John 3:16 and Rom. 5:8. The Father "gave" the Son who was glad to be given and to give himself. *I have power to lay it down* (*exousian echō theinai autēn*). *Exousia* is not an easy word to translate (right, authority, power, privilege). See 1:12. Restatement of the voluntariness of his death for the sheep.

And I have power to take it again (*kai exousian echō palin labein autēn*). Note second aorist active infinitive in both cases (*theinai* from *tithēmi* and *labein* from *lambanō*), single acts. Recall 2:19 where Jesus said: "And in three days I will raise it up." He did not mean that he will raise himself from the dead independently of the Father as the active agent (Rom. 8:11). *I received from my Father* (*elabon para tou patros mou*). Second aorist active indicative of *lambanō*. He always follows the Father's command (*entolē*) in all things (12:49f.; 14:31). So now he is doing the Father's will about his death and resurrection.

19. *There arose a division again* (*schisma palin egeneto*). As in 7:43 in the crowd (also in 7:12, 31), so now among the hostile Jews (Pharisees) some of whom had previously professed belief in him (8:31). The direct reference of *palin* (again) may be to 9:16 when the Pharisees were divided over the problem of the blind man. Division of opinion about Jesus is a common thing in John's Gospel (6:52, 60, 66; 7:12, 25ff.; 8:22; 9:16f.; 10:19, 24, 41; 11:41ff.; 12:19, 29, 42; 16:18f.).

20. *He has a demon and is mad* (*daimonion echei kai mainetai*). As some had already said (7:20; 8:48 with the addition of "Samaritan"). So long before in Mark 3:21. An easy way of discounting Jesus.

21. *Of one possessed with a demon* (*daimonizomenou*). Genitive of present passive participle of *daimonizō*. They had heard demoniacs talk, but not like this. *Can a demon open the eyes of the blind?* (*mē daimonion dunatai tuphlon ophthalmous anoixai;*). Negative answer expected. Demons would more likely put out eyes, not open them. It was an unanswerable question.

22. *And it was the feast of the dedication at Jerusalem* (*egeneto de ta enkainia en tois Ierosolumois*). But Westcott and Hort read *tote* (then) instead of *de* (and) on the authority of B L W 33 and some versions. This is probably correct:

"At that time came the feast of dedication in Jerusalem." *Tote* does not mean that the preceding events followed immediately after the incidents in 10:1-21. Bernard brings chapter 9 up to this date (possibly also chapter 8) and rearranges chapter 10 in a purely arbitrary way. There is no real reason for this arrangement. Clearly there is a considerable lapse between the events in 10:22-39 and 10:1-21, possibly nearly three months (from just after tabernacles 7:37 to dedication 10:22). The Pharisees greet his return with the same desire to catch him. This feast of dedication, celebrated for eight days about the middle of our December, was instituted by Judas Maccabeus B.C. 164 in commemoration of the cleansing of the temple from the defilements of pagan worship by Antiochus Epiphanes (I Macc. 4:59). The word *enkainia* (*en, kainos*, new) occurs here only in the N.T. It was not one of the great feasts and could be observed elsewhere without coming to Jerusalem. Jesus had apparently spent the time between tabernacles and dedication in Judea (Luke 10:1-13:21). *Winter* (*cheimōn*). Old word from *cheima* (*cheō*, to pour, rain, or from *chiōn*, snow). See Matt. 24:20.

23. *Was walking* (*periepatei*). Imperfect active of *peripateō*, to walk around, picturesque imperfect. *In Solomon's porch* (*en tēi stoāi tou Solomōnos*). A covered colonnade or portico in which people could walk in all weather. See Acts 3:11; 5:12 for this porch. This particular part of Solomon's temple was left uninjured by the Babylonians and survived apparently till the destruction of the temple by Titus A.D. 70 (Josephus, *Ant.* XX. 9, 7). When John wrote, it was, of course, gone.

24. *Came round about him* (*ekuklōsan auton*). Aorist active indicative of *kukloō*, old verb from *kuklos* (cycle, circle). See Acts 14:20 for the circle of disciples around Paul when stoned. Evidently the hostile Jews cherished the memory of the stinging rebuke given them by Jesus when here last, particularly the allegory of the Good Shepherd (10:1-19),

in which he drew so sharply their own picture. *How long dost thou hold us in suspense?* (*heōs pote tēn psuchēn hēmōn aireis;*). Literally, "Until when dost thou lift up our soul?" But what do they mean by this metaphor? *Airō* is common enough to lift up the eyes (John 11:41), the voice (Luke 17:13), and in Psa. 25:1; 86:4 (Josephus, *Ant.* III. ii. 3) we have "to lift up the soul." We are left to the context to judge the precise meaning. Clearly the Jews mean to imply doubt and suspense. The next remark makes it clear. *If thou art the Christ* (*ei su ei ho Christos*). Condition of first class assumed to be true for the sake of argument. *Tell us plainly* (*eipon hēmin parrēsiāi*). Conclusion with *eipon* rather than the usual *eipe* as if first aorist active imperative like *luson*. The point is in "plainly" (*parrēsiāi*), adverb as in 7:13, 26 which see. That is to say "I am the Christ" in so many words. See 11:14; 16:29 for the same use of *parrēsiāi*. The demand seemed fair enough on the surface. They had made it before when here at the feast of tabernacles (8:25). Jesus declined to use the word *Christos* (Messiah) then as now because of the political bearing of the word in their minds. The populace in Galilee had once tried to make him king in opposition to Pilate (John 6:14f.). When Jesus does confess on oath before Caiaphas that he is the Christ the Son of God (Mark 14:61f. = Matt. 26:63f.), the Sanhedrin instantly vote him guilty of blasphemy and then bring him to Pilate with the charge of claiming to be king as a rival to Caesar. Jesus knew their minds too well to be caught now.

25. *I told you, and you believe not* (*eipon humin kai ou pisteuete*). It was useless to say more. In 7:14 to 10:18 Jesus had shown that he was the Son of the Father as he had previously claimed (5:17–47), but it was all to no purpose save to increase their rage towards him. *These bear witness of me* (*tauta marturei peri emou*). His works confirm his words as he had shown before (5:36). They believe neither his words nor his works.

26. *Because ye are not of my sheep* (*hoti ek tōn probatōn mou*). This had been the point in the allegory of the Good Shepherd. In fact, they were the children of the devil in spirit and conduct (8:43), pious ecclesiastics though they seemed, veritable wolves in sheep's clothing (Matt. 7:15).

27. *My sheep* (*ta probata ta ema*). In contrast with you they are not in doubt and suspense. They know my voice and follow me. Repetition of the idea in 10:4, 14.

28. *And I give unto them eternal life* (*kágō didōmi autois zōēn aiōnion*). This is the gift of Jesus now to his sheep as stated in 6:27, 40 (cf. I John 2:25; 5:11). *And they shall never perish* (*kai ou mē apolōntai*). Emphatic double negative with second aorist middle (intransitive) subjunctive of *apollumi*, to destroy. The sheep may feel secure (3:16; 6:39; 17:12; 18:9). *And no one shall snatch them out of my hand* (*kai ouch harpasei tis auta ek tēs cheiros mou*). Jesus had promised this security in Galilee (6:37, 39). No wolf, no thief, no bandit, no hireling, no demon, not even the devil can pluck the sheep out of my hand. Cf. Col. 3:3 (Your life is hid together with Christ in God).

29. *Which* (*hos*). Who. If *ho* (which) is correct, we have to take *ho patēr* as nominative absolute or independent, "As for my Father." *Is greater than all* (*pantōn meizōn estin*). If we read *hos*. But Aleph B L W read *ho* and A B Θ have *meizon*. The neuter seems to be correct (Westcott and Hort). But is it? If so, the meaning is: "As for my Father, that which he hath given me is greater than all." But the context calls for *hos* . . . *meizōn* with *ho patēr* as the subject of *estin*. The greatness of the Father, not of the flock, is the ground of the safety of the flock. Hence the conclusion that "no one is able to snatch them out of the Father's hand."

30. *One* (*hen*). Neuter, not masculine (*heis*). Not one person (cf. *heis* in Gal. 3:28), but one essence or nature. By the plural *sumus* (separate persons) Sabellius is refuted, by *unum* Arius. So Bengel rightly argues, though Jesus is not

THE FOURTH GOSPEL 187

referring, of course, to either Sabellius or Arius. The Pharisees had accused Jesus of making himself equal with God as his own special Father (John 5:18). Jesus then admitted and proved this claim (5:19–30). Now he states it tersely in this great saying repeated later (17:11, 21). Note *hen* used in I Cor. 3:3 of the oneness in work of the planter and the waterer and in 17:11, 23 of the hoped for unity of Christ's disciples. This crisp statement is the climax of Christ's claims concerning the relation between the Father and himself (the Son). They stir the Pharisees to uncontrollable anger.

31. *Took up stones again (ebastasan palin lithous).* First aorist active indicative of *bastazō*, old verb to pick up, to carry (John 12:6), to bear (Gal. 6:5). The *palin* refers to John 8:59 where *ēran* was used. They wanted to kill him also when he made himself equal to God in 5:18. Perhaps here *ebastasan* means "they fetched stones from a distance." *To stone him (hina lithasōsin auton).* Final clause with *hina* and the first aorist active subjunctive of *lithazō*, late verb (Aristotle, Polybius) from *lithos* (stone, small, Matt. 4:6, or large, Matt. 28:2), in John 10:31–33; 11:8; Acts 5:26; 14:19; II Cor. 11:25; Heb. 11:37, but not in the Synoptics. It means to pelt with stones, to overwhelm with stones.

32. *From the Father (ek tou patros).* Proceeding out of the Father as in 6:65 and 16:28 (cf. 7:17; 8:42, 47) rather than *para* as in 1:14; 6:46; 7:29; 17:7. *For which of those works (dia poion autōn ergon).* Literally, "For what kind of work of them" (referring to the "many good works" *polla erga kala).* Noble and beautiful deeds Jesus had done in Jerusalem like healing the impotent man (chapter 5) and the blind man (chapter 9). *Poion* is a qualitative interrogative pronoun pointing to *kala* (good). *Do ye stone me (lithazete).* Conative present active indicative, "are ye trying to stone me." They had the stones in their hands stretched back to fling at him, a threatening attitude.

33. *For a good work we stone thee not* (*peri kalou ergou ou lithazomen*). "Concerning a good deed we are not stoning thee." Flat denial that the healing of the blind man on the Sabbath had led them to this attempt (8:59) in spite of the facts. *But for blasphemy* (*alla peri blasphēmias*). See Acts 26:7 where *peri* with the genitive is also used with *egkaloumai* for the charge against Paul. This is the only example in John of the word *blasphēmia* (cf. Matt. 12:31). *And because that thou, being a man, makest thyself God* (*kai hoti su anthrō-pos ōn poieis seauton theon*). In 5:18 they stated the charge more accurately: "He called God his own Father, making himself equal with God." That is, he made himself the Son of God. This he did beyond a doubt. But was it blasphemy? Only if he was not the Son of God. The penalty for blasphemy was death by stoning (Lev. 24:16; I Kings 21:10, 13).

34. *Is it not written?* (*ouk estin gegrammenon;*). Peri-phrastic perfect passive indicative of *graphō* (as in 2:17) in place of the usual *gegraptai*. "Does it not stand written?" *In your law* (*en tōi nomōi humōn*). From Psa. 82:6. The term *nomos* (law) applying here to the entire O.T. as in 12:34; 15:25. Rom. 3:19; I Cor. 14:21. Aleph D Syr-sin. omit *humōn*, but needlessly. We have it already so from Jesus in 8:17. They posed as the special custodians of the O.T. *I said* (*hoti egō eipa*). Recitative *hoti* before a direct quotation like our quotation marks. *Eipa* is a late second aorist form of indicative with -*a* instead of -*on*. *Ye are gods* (*theoi este*). Another direct quotation after *eipa* but without *hoti*. The judges of Israel abused their office and God is represented in Psa. 82:6 as calling them "gods" (*theoi, elohim*) because they were God's representatives. See the same use of *elohim* in Ex. 21:6; 22:9, 28. Jesus meets the rabbis on their own ground in a thoroughly Jewish way.

35. *If he called them gods* (*ei ekeinous eipen theous*). Condi-tion of first class, assumed as true. The conclusion (verse 36)

is *humeis legete; (Do ye say?).* As Jews (and rabbis) they
are shut out from charging Jesus with blasphemy because
of this usage in the O.T. It is a complete *ad hominem* argument. To be sure, it is in Psa. 82:6 a lower use of the term
theos, but Jesus did not call himself "Son of Jahweh," but
"*huios theou*" which can mean only "Son of *Elohim.*" It
must not be argued, as some modern men do, that Jesus
thus disclaims his own deity. He does nothing of the kind.
He is simply stopping the mouths of the rabbis from the
charge of blasphemy and he does it effectually. The sentence
is quite involved, but can be cleared up. *To whom the word
of God came (pros hous ho logos tou theou egeneto).* The relative points to *ekeinous,* before. These judges had no other
claim to the term *theoi (elohim). And the scripture cannot be
broken (kai ou dunatai luthēnai hē graphē).* A parenthesis
that drives home the pertinency of the appeal, one that the
Pharisees had to accept. *Luthēnai* is first aorist passive
infinitive of *luō,* to loosen, to break.

36. *Of him whom the Father sanctified and sent into the
world (hon ho patēr hēgiasen kai apesteilen eis ton kosmon).*
Another relative clause with the antecedent (*touton,* it would
be, object of *legete*) unexpressed. Every word counts heavily
here in contrast with the mere judges of Psa. 82:6. *Thou
blasphemest (hoti blasphēmeis).* Recitative *hoti* again before
direct quotation. *Because I said (hoti eipon).* Causal use
of *hoti* and regular form *eipon* (cf. *eipa* in verse 34). *I am
the Son of God (huios tou theou eimi).* Direct quotation again
after *eipon.* This Jesus had implied long before as in 2:16
(my Father) and had said in 5:18–30 (the Father, the Son),
in 9:35 in some MSS., and virtually in 10:30. They will
make this charge against Jesus before Pilate (19:7). Jesus
does not use the article here with *huios,* perhaps (Westcott)
fixing attention on the character of Son rather than on the
person as in Heb. 1:2. There is no answer to this question
with its arguments.

37. *If I do not* (*ei ou poiō*). Condition of first class, assumed as true, with negative *ou*, not *ei mē* = unless. *Believe me not* (*mē pisteuete moi*). Prohibition with *mē* and the present active imperative. Either "cease believing me" or "do not have the habit of believing me." Jesus rests his case on his doing the works of "my Father" (*tou patros mou*), repeating his claims to sonship and deity.

38. *But if I do* (*ei de poiō*). Condition again of the first class, assumed as true, but with the opposite results. *Though ye believe not me* (*kãn emoi mē pisteuēte*). Condition now of third class, undetermined (but with prospect), "Even if you keep on (present active subjunctive of *pisteuo*) not believing me." *Believe the works* (*tois ergois pisteuete*). These stand irrefutable. The claims, character, words, and works of Jesus challenge the world today as then. *That ye may know and understand* (*hina gnōte kai ginōskēte*). Purpose clause with *hina* and the same verb *ginōskō* repeated in different tenses (first *gnōte*, the second ingressive aorist active subjunctive, that ye may come to know; then the present active subjunctive, "that ye may keep on knowing"). This is Christ's deepest wish about his enemies who stand with stones in their uplifted hands to fling at him. *That the Father is in me, and I in the Father* (*hoti en emoi ho patēr kágō en tōi patri*). Thus he repeats (verse 30) sharply his real claim to oneness with the Father as his Son, to actual deity. It was a hopeless wish.

39. *They sought again to seize him* (*ezētoun auton palin piazai*). Imperfect active, "They kept on seeking to seize (ingressive aorist active infinitive of *piazō* for which see 7:30) as they had tried repeatedly (7:1, 30, 44; 8:20), but in vain. They gave up the effort to stone him. *Out of their hand* (*ek tēs cheiros autōn*). Overawed, but still angry, the stones fell to the ground, and Jesus walked out.

40. *Again* (*palin*). Referring to 1:28 (Bethany beyond Jordan). *Palin* does not mean that the other visit was a

recent one. *At the first* (*to prōton*). Adverbial accusative (extent of time). Same idiom in 12:16; 19:39. Here tne identical language of 1:28 is used with the mere addition of *to prōton* (*hopou ēn Iōanēs baptizōn*, "where John was baptizing"). *And there he abode* (*kai emenen ekei*). Imperfect (continued) active of *menō*, though some MSS. have the constative aorist active *emeinen*. Probably from here Jesus carried on the first part of the later Perean Ministry (Luke 13:22–16:10) before the visit to Bethany at the raising of Lazarus (John 11:1–44).

41. *Many came to him* (*polloi ēlthon pros auton*). Jesus was busy here and in a more congenial atmosphere than Jerusalem. John wrought no signs the crowds recall, though Jesus did many here (Matt. 19:2). The crowds still bear the impress of John's witness to Christ as "true" (*alēthē*). Here was prepared soil for Christ.

42. *Many believed on him there* (*polloi episteusan eis auton ekei*). See 1:12; 2:11 for same idiom. Striking witness to the picture of the Messiah drawn by John. When Jesus came they recognized the original. See John 1:29–34. What about our sermons about Jesus if he were to walk down the aisle in visible form according to A. J. Gordon's dream?

CHAPTER XI

1. *Was sick (ēn asthenōn).* Periphrastic imperfect active of *astheneō*, old verb (from *asthenēs*, *a* privative, and *sthenos*, strength). *Lazarus (Lazaros).* See on Luke 16:20 for the name of another man in the parable, a shortened form of Eleazer, only other N.T. use, but in Josephus and rabbinical writings. No connexion between this Lazarus and the one in the parable. *Of Bethany (apo Bēthanias).* Use of *apo* as in 1:44 Philip of Bethsaida and 1:45 Joseph of Nazareth. This Bethany is about two miles (11:18) east of Jerusalem on the south-east slope of Olivet and is now called El Azariyeh, from the name Lazarus. Jesus is still apparently at the other Bethany beyond Jordan (10:40). It is doubtful if a distinction is meant here by *apo* and *ek* between Bethany as the residence and some other village (*ek tēs kōmēs*) as the birthplace of Lazarus and the sisters. *Of Mary and Martha (Marias kai Marthas).* Note *Marthas*, not *Marthēs* for the genitive. Elsewhere (John 11:19; Luke 10:38) Martha comes first as the mistress and hostess. The two sisters are named for further identification of Lazarus. Martha was apparently the elder sister (11:5, 19; Luke 10:38f.). "The identification of Mary with Mary Magdalene is a mere conjecture supported by no direct evidence, and opposed to the general tenor of the Gospels" (Westcott).

2. *And it was that Mary which anointed the Lord with ointment, and wiped his feet with her hair (ēn de Mariam hē aleipsasa ton kurion murōi kai ekmaxasa tous podas autou tais thrixin autēs).* This description is added to make plainer who Mary is "whose brother Lazarus was sick" (*hēs ho adelphos Lazaros ēsthenei).* There is an evident proleptic allusion to the incident described by John in 12:1–8 just

192

after chapter 11. As John looks back from the end of the century it was all behind him, though the anointing (*hē aleipsasa*, first aorist active articular participle of *aleiphō*, old verb for which see Mark 6:13) took place after the events in chapter 11. The aorist participle is timeless and merely pictures the punctiliar act. The same remark applies to *ekmaxasa*, old verb *ekmassō*, to wipe off or away (Isa. 12:3; 13:5; Luke 7:38, 44). Note the Aramaic form *Mariam* as usual in John, but *Marias* in verse 1. When John wrote, it was as Jesus had foretold (Matt. 26:13), for the fame of Mary of Bethany rested on the incident of the anointing of Jesus. The effort to link Mary of Bethany with Mary Magdalene and then both names with the sinful woman of Luke 7:36–50 is gratuitous and to my mind grotesque and cruel to the memory of both Mary of Bethany and Mary Magdalene. Bernard may be taken as a specimen: "The conclusion is inevitable that John (or his editor) regarded Mary of Bethany as the same person who is described by Luke as *hamartōlos*." This critical and artistic heresy has already been discussed in Vol. II on Luke's Gospel. Suffice it here to say that Luke introduces Mary Magdalene as an entirely new character in 8:2 and that the details in Luke 7:36–50 and John 12:1–8 have only superficial resemblances and serious disagreements. John is not here alluding to Luke's record, but preparing for his own in chapter 12. What earthly difficulty is there in two different women under wholly different circumstances doing a similar act for utterly different purposes?

3. *Sent saying* (*apesteilan legousai*). First aorist active indicative of *apostellō* and present active participle. The message was delivered by the messenger. *Thou lovest* (*phileis*). *Phileō* means to love as a friend (see *philos* in verse 11) and so warmly, while *agapaō* (akin to *agamai*, to admire, and *agathos*, good) means high regard. Here both terms occur of the love of Jesus for Lazarus (*ēgapa* in verse 5).

Both occur of the Father's love for the Son (*agapāi* in 3:35, *philei* in 5:20). Hence the distinction is not always observed.

4. *Heard it* (*akousas*). The messenger delivered the message of the sisters. The reply of Jesus is for him and for the apostles. *Is not unto death* (*ouk estin pros thanaton*). Death in the final issue, to remain dead. Lazarus did die, but he did not remain dead. See *hamartia pros thanaton* in I John 5:16, "sin unto death" (final death). *But for the glory of God* (*all' huper tēs doxēs tou theou*). In behalf of God's glory, as the sequel shows. Cf. 9:3 about the man born blind. The death of Lazarus will illustrate God's glory. In some humble sense those who suffer the loss of loved ones are entitled to some comfort from this point made by Jesus about Lazarus. In a supreme way it is true of the death of Christ which he himself calls glorification of himself and God (13:31). In 7:39 John had already used *doxazō* of the death of Christ. *That the Son of God may be glorified thereby* (*hina doxasthēi ho huios tou theou di' autēs*). Purpose clause with *hina* and the first aorist passive subjunctive of *doxazō*. Here Jesus calls himself "the Son of God." In 8:54 Jesus had said: "It is my Father that glorifieth me." The raising of Lazarus from the tomb will bring glory to the Son of God. See 17:1 for this idea in Christ's prayer. The raising of Lazarus will also bring to an issue his own death and all this involves the glorification of the Father (7:39; 12:16; 13:31; 14:13). The death of Lazarus brings Jesus face to face with his own death.

5. *Now Jesus loved* (*ēgapa de*). Imperfect active of *agapaō* picturing the continued love of Jesus for this noble family where he had his home so often (Luke 10:38–42; John 12:1–8). The sisters expected him to come at once and to heal Lazarus.

6. *That he was sick* (*hoti asthenei*). Present active indicative retained in indirect discourse after a secondary tense (*ēkousen*). *Two days* (*duo hēmeras*). Accusative of extent

of time. *In the place where he was* (*en hōi ēn topōi*). Incorporation of the antecedent *topōi* into the relative clause, "in which place he was." It was long enough for Lazarus to die and seemed unlike Jesus to the sisters.

7. *Then after this* (*epeita meta touto*). *Epeita* (only here in John) means thereafter (Luke 16:7) and it is made plainer by the addition of *meta touto* (cf. 2:12; 11:11), meaning after the two days had elapsed. *Let us go into Judea again* (*Agōmen eis tēn Ioudaian palin*). Volitive (hortative) subjunctive of *agō* (intransitive use as in verses 11, 16). They had but recently escaped the rage of the Jews in Jerusalem (10:39) to this haven in Bethany beyond Jordan (10:40).

8. *Were but now seeking to stone thee* (*nun ezētoun se lithasai*). Conative imperfect of *zēteō* with reference to the event narrated in 10:39 in these very words. *Goest thou thither again?* (*palin hupageis ekei;*). Present active intransitive use of the compound *hupagō*, to withdraw (6:21; 8:21) from this safe retreat (Vincent). It seemed suicidal madness to go back now.

9. *In the day* (*tēs hēmeras*). Genitive of time, within the day, the twelve-hour day in contrast with night. The words of Jesus here illustrate what he had said in 9:4. It is not blind fatalism that Jesus proclaims, but the opposite of cowardice. He has full confidence in the Father s purpose about his "hour" which has not yet come. Jesus has courage to face his enemies again to do the Father's will about Lazarus. *If a man walk in the day* (*ean tis peripatēi en tēi hēmerāi*). Condition of the third class, a conceived case and it applies to Jesus who walks in the full glare of noonday. See 8:12 for the contrast between walking in the light and in the dark. *He stumbleth not* (*ou proskoptei*). He does not cut (or bump) against this or that obstacle, for he can see. *Koptō* is to cut and *pros*, against.

10. *But if a man walk in the night* (*ean de tis peripatēi en tēi nukti*). Third condition again. It is spiritual darkness

that Jesus here pictures, but the result is the same. See the same figure in 12:35 (I John 2:11). The ancients had poor illumination at night as indeed we did before Edison gave us electric lights. Pedestrians actually used to have little lamps fastened on the feet to light the path. *In him* (*en autōi*). Spiritual darkness, the worst of all (cf. Matt. 6:23; John 8:12). Man has the capacity for light, but is not the source of light. "By the application of this principle Christianity is distinguished from Neo-Platonism" (Westcott).

11. *Is fallen asleep* (*kekoimētai*). Perfect passive indicative of *koimaō*, old verb to put to sleep. Common as a metaphor for death like our cemetery. *I go* (*poreuomai*). Futuristic use of the present tense as in 14:2. *That I may awake him out of sleep* (*hina exupnisō auton*). Purpose clause with *hina* and the first aorist active subjunctive of *exupnizō*, a late compound (*ex, hupnos*, sleep) for the older *aphupnizō*, here only in the N.T. See Job 14:12 where also it occurs along with *koimaomai*.

12. *He will recover* (*sōthēsetai*). Future passive indicative of *sōzō* used in its original sense of being or getting well (safe and sound). Conclusion of the condition of the first class (*ei kekoimētai*).

13. *Had spoken* (*eirēkei*). Past perfect of *eipon* (*erō*). The disciples had misunderstood Christ's metaphor for death. *That he spake* (*hoti legei*). Present active indicative retained in indirect discourse after the secondary tense (*edoxan*). *Of taking rest in sleep* (*peri tēs koimēseōs tou hupou*). Only use of *koimēsis* (from *koimaō*) in the N.T., but it also was used of death (*Sirach* 46:19). *Hupnou* (in sleep) is objective genitive of *hupnos* (sleep, Matt. 1:24).

14. *Plainly* (*parrēsiāi*). Adverb (see on 7:4), without metaphor as in 16:29. *Is dead* (*apethanen*). First aorist active indicative, "died."

15. *For your sakes* (*di' humas*). That they may witness his raising from the grave. *That I was not there* (*hoti ouk*

ēmēn ekei). Imperfect middle *ēmēn* of the later Greek instead of the common active *ēn* in indirect discourse in place of the usual present retained as in verse 13. *To the intent ye may believe (hina pisteusēte).* Purpose clause with *hina* and the ingressive aorist active subjunctive, "that ye may come to believe" (more than you do). See the same use of the ingressive aorist in *episteusan* (2:11) where the disciples gained in belief. *Nevertheless let us go to him (alla agōmen pros auton).* Volitive subjunctive, repeating the proposal of verse 7. He is dead, but no matter, yea all the more let us go on to him.

16. *Didymus (Didumos).* The word means twin. Clearly Thomas had a twin brother or sister. Applied two other times to him (20:24; 21:2). The Aramaic word for Thomas means Twin and Didymus is just the Greek equivalent of Thomas. He may even in Greek circles have been called Didymus. *His fellow disciples (tois sunmathētais).* Dative case and article use like "his." Only use of *sunmathētes* in the N.T., rare word (in Plato). *Us also (kai hēmeis).* As well as Jesus, since he is bent on going. *That we may die with him (hina apothanōmen met' autou).* Purpose clause with *hina* and the second aorist active subjunctive of *apothnēskō.* Die with Jesus, Thomas means. Lazarus is already dead and they will kill Jesus (verse 8). Pessimistic courage surely.

17. *Found (heuren).* Second aorist active indicative of *heuriskō.* *That he had been in the tomb four days already (auton tessaras ēdē hēmeras echonta).* Literally, "him [accusative object of *heuren*] having already four days in the tomb." See 5:5 for the same idiom (*etē echōn*) for expression of time (having 38 years). In Jewish custom burial took place on the day of death (Acts 6:6, 10).

18. *About fifteen furlongs off (hōs apo stadiōn dekapente).* The idiom of *apo* with the ablative for distance is like the Latin *a millibus passum duobus* (Caesar, *Bell. Gall.* ii. 7), but it (*pro* also, John 12:1) occurs already in the Doric and in

the *Koiné* often (Moulton, *Proleg.*, p. 101; Robertson, *Grammar*, p. 110). See it again in 21:8; Rev. 14:20.

19. *Had come (elēlutheisan).* Past perfect of *erchomai.* These Jews were probably not hostile to Jesus. There were seven days of solemn mourning (I Sam. 31:13). The presence of so many indicates the prominence of the family. *To Martha and Mary (pros tēn Marthan kai Mariam).* Correct text, not the Textus Receptus *pros tas peri Marthan kai Mariam* (to the women about Martha and Mary). *To console them (hina paramuthēsōntai).* Purpose clause with *hina* and first aorist middle subjunctive of *paramutheomai*, old verb (*para*, beside, *muthos*, word), to put in a word beside, to offer consolation. Again in verse 31. See I Thess. 2:11; 5:14. See Job 2:13 for these visits of consolation, often deplorable enough, though kindly meant.

20. *That Jesus was coming (hoti Iēsous erchetai).* Present middle indicative retained in indirect discourse after the secondary tense *ēkousen* (first aorist active). *Went and met him (hupēntēsen autōi).* First aorist (ingressive) active indicative of *hupantaō*, old compound verb, to go to meet (Matt. 8:28) with the associative instrumental case *autōi.* *But Mary still sat in the house (Mariam de en tōi oikōi ekathezeto).* Imperfect middle of *kathezomai*, old verb to sit down, graphic picture of Mary, "while Mary was sitting in the house." Both Martha and Mary act true to form here as in Luke 10:38-42.

21. *Lord, if thou hadst been here, my brother had not died (Kurie, ei ēs hōde ouk an apethanen ho adelphos mou).* Condition of the second class with *ei* and the imperfect *ēs* (no aorist of *eimi*, to be) in the condition and *an* with the second aorist active indicative of *apothnēskō.* Mary (verse 32) uses these identical words to Jesus. Clearly they had said so to each other with wistful longing if not with a bit of reproach for his delay. But they used *ēs*, not *ēlthes* or *egenou.* But busy, practical Martha comes to the point.

22. *And even now I know* (*kai nun oida*). Rather just, "Even now I know." *Alla* (but) of the Textus Receptus is not genuine. *Whatsoever thou shalt ask of God* (*hosa an aitēsēi ton theon*). Indefinite relative (*hosa*, as many things as) with *an* and the first aorist middle (indirect middle, thou thyself asking) subjunctive of *aiteō*. Martha uses *aiteō* (usual word of prayer of men to God) rather than *erōtaō* (usual word of Jesus praying to the Father), but in 16:23 we have *erōtaō* used of prayer to Jesus and *aiteō* of prayer to God. But the distinction is not to be pressed. "As many things as thou dost ask of God." *God will give* (*dōsei soi ho theos*). Repetition of *ho theos* for emphasis. Martha still has courageous faith in the power of God through Jesus and Jesus in verse 41 says practically what she has said here.

23. *Thy brother will rise again* (*anastēsetai ho adelphos sou*). Future middle (intransitive) of *anistēmi*. The words promise Martha what she has asked for, if Jesus means that.

24. *In the resurrection at the last day* (*en tēi anastasei en tēi eschatēi hēmerāi*). Did Jesus mean only that? She believed it, of course, and such comfort is often offered in case of death, but that idea did not console Martha and is not what she hinted at in verse 22.

25. *I am the resurrection and the life* (*Egō eimi hē anastasis kai hē zōē*). This reply is startling enough. They are not mere doctrines about future events, but present realities in Jesus himself. "The Resurrection is one manifestation of the Life: it is involved in the Life" (Westcott). Note the article with both *anastasis* and *zōē*. Jesus had taught the future resurrection often (6:39), but here he means more, even that Lazarus is now alive. *Though he die* (*kàn apothanēi*). "Even if he die," condition (concession) of third class with *kai ean* (*kàn*) and the second aorist active subjunctive of *apothnēskō* (physical death, he means). *Yet shall he live* (*zēsetai*). Future middle of *zaō* (spiritual life, of course).

26. *Shall never die* (*ou mē apothanēi eis ton aiōna*). Strong double negative *ou mē* with second aorist active subjunctive of *apothnēskō* again (but spiritual death, this time), "shall not die for ever" (eternal death). *Believest thou this?* (*pisteueis touto;*) Sudden test of Martha's insight and faith with all the subtle turns of thought involved.

27. *Yea, Lord* (*Nai, kurie*). Martha probably did not understand all that Jesus said and meant, but she did believe in the future resurrection, in eternal life for believers in Christ, in the power of Christ to raise even the dead here and now. She had heroic faith and makes now her own confession of faith in words that outrank those of Peter in Matt. 16:16 because she makes hers with her brother dead now four days and with the hope that Jesus will raise him up now. *I have believed* (*pepisteuka*). Perfect active indicative of *pisteuō*. It is my settled and firm faith. Peter uses this same tense in 6:69. *That thou art the Son of God* (*hoti su ei ho Christos ho huios tou theou*). The Messiah or the Christ (1:41) was to be also "the Son of God" as the Baptist said he had found Jesus to be (1:34), as Peter confessed on Hermon for the apostles (Matt. 16:16), as Jesus claimed to be (John 11:41) and confessed on oath before Caiaphas that he was (Matt. 26:63f.), and as John stated that it was his purpose to prove in his Gospel (20:31). But no one said it under more trying circumstances than Martha. *Even he that cometh into the world* (*ho eis ton kosmon erchomenos*). No "even" in the Greek. This was a popular way of putting the people's expectation (6:14; Matt. 11:3). Jesus himself spoke of his coming into the world (9:39; 16:28; 18:37).

28. *Called Mary* (*ephōnēsen Mariam*). First aorist active indicative of *phōneō*. Out of the house and away from the crowd. *Secretly* (*lathrāi*). Old adverb from *lathros* (*lanthanō*). To tell her the glad news. *The Master* (*ho didaskalos*). "The Teacher." So they loved to call him as he was (13:13).

Is here (*parestin*). "Is present." *Calleth thee* (*phōnei se*). This rouses Mary.

29. *And she* (*kai ekeinē*). Emphatic use of the demonstrative *ekeinos* as often in John, "And that one." *Arose quickly* (*ēgerthē*). First aorist (ingressive) passive of *egeirō* and intransitive. Naturally so on the sudden impulse of joy. *And went unto him* (*kai ērcheto pros auton*). Imperfect middle, possibly inchoative, started towards him, certainly picturing her as she was going.

30. *Now Jesus was not yet come into the town* (*oupō de elēluthei ho Iēsous eis tēn kōmēn*). Explanatory parenthesis with past perfect as in verse 19. Martha had her interview while he was still coming (verse 20) and left him (went off, *apēlthen*, verse 28) to hurry to Mary with the news. Why Jesus tarried still where he had met Martha we do not know. Westcott says, "as though He would meet the sisters away from the crowd of mourners."

31. *Followed her* (*ēkolouthēsan autēi*). First aorist active indicative of *akoloutheō* with associative instrumental case (*autēi*). This crowd of consolers (*paramuthoumenoi*) meant kindly enough, but did the one wrong thing for Mary wished to see Jesus alone. People with kind notions often so act. The secrecy of Martha (verse 28) was of no avail. *Supposing that she was going unto the tomb* (*doxantes hoti hupagei eis to mnēmeion*). First aorist active participle of *dokeō*, justifying their conduct by a wrong inference. Note retention of present tense *hupagei* in indirect discourse after the secondary tense *ēkolouthēsan*. *To weep there* (*hina klausēi ekei*). Purpose clause with *hina* and the first aorist active subjunctive of *klaiō*, old verb to weep. Sometimes to wail or howl in oriental style of grief, but surely not that here. At any rate this supposed purpose of Mary was a real reason for this crowd *not* to go with her.

32. *Fell down at his feet* (*epesen autou pros tous podas*). Second aorist active of *piptō*, to fall. Note unusual position

of *autou*. This impulsive act like Mary. She said precisely what Martha had said to Jesus (verse 21). But she said no more, only wept (verse 33).

33. *When Jesus therefore saw her weeping* (*Iēsous oun hōs eiden autēn klaiousan*). Proleptic position of "Jesus," "Jesus therefore when he saw." She was weeping at the feet of Jesus, not at the tomb. *And the Jews also weeping* (*kai tous Ioudaious klaiontas*). Mary's weeping was genuine, that of the Jews was partly perfunctory and professional and probably actual "wailing" as the verb *klaiō* can mean. *Klaiō* is joined with *alalazō* in Mark 5:38, with *ololuzō* in James 5:1, with *thorubeō* in Mark 5:39, with *pentheō* in Mark 16:10. It was an incongruous combination. *He groaned in the spirit* (*enebrimēsato tōi pneumati*). First aorist middle indicative of *embrimaomai*, old verb (from *en*, and *brimē*, strength) to snort with anger like a horse. It occurs in the LXX (Dan. 11:30) for violent displeasure. The notion of indignation is present in the other examples of the word in the N.T. (Mark 1:43; 14:5; Matt. 9:30). So it seems best to see that sense here and in verse 38. The presence of these Jews, the grief of Mary, Christ's own concern, the problem of the raising of Lazarus — all greatly agitated the spirit of Jesus (locative case *tōi pneumati*). He struggled for self-control. *Was troubled* (*etaraxen heauton*). First aorist active indicative of *tarassō*, old verb to disturb, to agitate, with the reflexive pronoun, "he agitated himself" (not passive voice, not middle). "His sympathy with the weeping sister and the wailing crowd caused this deep emotion" (Dods). Some indignation at the loud wailing would only add to the agitation of Jesus.

34. *Where have ye laid him?* (*Pou tetheikate auton;*). Perfect active indicative of *tithēmi*. A simple question for information. The only other like it in John is in 6:6 where it is expressly stated that Jesus knew what he was going to do. So it was here, only he politely asked for direction to the

tomb of Lazarus. The people invite him to come and see, the very language used by Philip to Nathanael (1:46). It was a natural and polite reply as they would show Jesus the way, but they had no idea of his purpose.

35. *Jesus wept* (*edakrusen ho Iēsous*). Ingressive first aorist active indicative of *dakruō*, old verb from *dakru* or *dakruon*, a tear (Acts 20:19), only here in N.T. It never means to wail, as *klaiō* sometimes does. "Jesus burst into tears." *Klaiō* is used of Jesus in Luke 19:41. See Heb. 5:7 "with strong crying and tears" (*meta kraugēs kai dakruōn*). Apparently this was as Jesus started towards (see verse 38) the tomb. In a sense it was a reaction from the severe strain in verse 33, but chiefly it was the sheer human sympathy of his heart with Martha and Mary touched with the feeling of our common weakness (Heb. 4:15). Often all that we can do is to shed tears in grief too deep for words. Jesus understood and understands. This is the shortest verse in the Bible, but no verse carries more meaning in it.

36. *Loved* (*ephilei*). As in verse 3 which see. Imperfect active. Even the Jews saw that Jesus loved Lazarus.

37. *Could not this man* (*ouk edunato houtos*). Imperfect middle of *dunamai*. They do not say *dunatai* (can, present middle indicative). But clearly the opening of the blind man's eyes (chapter 9) had made a lasting impression on some of these Jews, for it was done three months ago. *Have caused that this man also should not die* (*poiēsai hina kai houtos mē apothanēi*). First aorist active infinitive of *poieō* with *hina*, like the Latin *facere ut* (sub-final use, Robertson, *Grammar*, p. 985), with the second aorist active subjunctive *apothanēi* and negative *mē*. These Jews share the view expressed by Martha (verse 21) and Mary (verse 32) that Jesus could have *prevented* the death of Lazarus.

38. *Again groaning in himself* (*palin embrimōmenos en heautōi*). Direct reference to the use of this same word (present middle participle here) in verse 33, only with *en*

heautōi (in himself) rather than *tōi pneumati* (in his spirit), practically the same idea. The speculation concerning his power stirred the depths of his nature again. *Cometh to the tomb* (*erchetai eis to mnēmeion*). Vivid historical present. *A cave* (*spēlaion*). Old word (from *speos*, cavern). Cf. Matt. 21:13. *Lay against it* (*epekeito ep' autōi*). Imperfect middle of *epikeimai*, old verb to lie upon as in 21:9 and figuratively (I Cor. 9:16). Note repetition of *epi* with locative case. The use of a cave for burial was common (Gen. 23:19). Either the body was let down through a horizontal opening (hardly so here) or put in a tomb cut in the face of the rock (if so, *epi* can mean "against"). The stones were used to keep away wild animals from the bodies.

39. *Take ye away the stone* (*arate ton lithon*). First aorist active imperative of *airō*. They could do this much without the exercise of Christ's divine power. It was a startling command to them. *By this time he stinketh* (*ēdē ozei*). Present active indicative of old verb, here only in N.T. (cf. Ex. 8:14). It means to give out an odour, either good or bad. *For he hath been dead four days* (*tetartaios gar estin*). The Greek simply says, "For he is a fourth-day man." It is an old ordinal numeral from *tetartos* (fourth). Herodotus (ii. 89) has *tetartaios genesthai* of one four days dead as here. The word is only here in the N.T. The same idiom occurs in Acts 28:13 with *deuteraioi* (second-day men). Lightfoot (*Hor. Hebr.*) quotes a Jewish tradition (*Beresh: Rabba*) to the effect that the soul hovers around the tomb for three days hoping to return to the body, but on the fourth day leaves it. But there is no suggestion here that Martha held that notion. Her protest is a natural one in spite of her strong faith in verses 22 to 27.

40. *Said I not unto thee?* (*Ouk eipon soi;*). Jesus pointedly reminds Martha of his promise to raise Lazarus (verses 25f.). *That if thou believedst* (*hoti ean pisteusēis*). Indirect discourse with *ean* and the first aorist active subjunctive (condition

of third class) retained after the secondary tense *eipon*. He had not said this very phrase, *ean pisteusēis*, to Martha, but he did say to her: *Pisteueis touto;* (Believest thou this?). He meant to test Martha as to her faith already hinted at (verse 22) on this very point. Jesus had also spoken of increase of faith on the part of the disciples (verse 15). *Thou shouldest see the glory of God* (*opsei tēn doxan tou theou*). Future middle indicative of the old defective verb *horaō* retained in the conclusion of this condition in indirect discourse. Jesus means the glory of God as shown in the resurrection of Lazarus as he had already said to the disciples (verse 4) and as he meant Martha to understand (verse 25) and may in fact have said to her (the report of the conversation is clearly abridged). Hence Bernard's difficulty in seeing how Martha could understand the words of Jesus about the resurrection of Lazarus here and now seems fanciful and far-fetched.

41. *So they took away the stone* (*ēran oun ton lithon*). First aorist active indicative of *airō*, but without the explanatory gloss of the Textus Receptus "from the place where the dead was laid" (not genuine). *I thank thee that thou heardest me* (*eucharistō soi hoti ēkousas mou*). See 6:11 for *eucharisteō*. Clearly Jesus had prayed to the Father concerning the raising of Lazarus. He has the answer before he acts. "No pomp of incantation, no wrestling in prayer even; but simple words of thanksgiving, as if already Lazarus was restored" (Dods). Jesus well knew the issues involved on this occasion. If he failed, his own claims to be the Son of God (the Messiah), would be hopelessly discredited with all. If he succeeded, the rulers would be so embittered as to compass his own death.

42. *And I knew* (*egō de ēidein*). Past perfect of *oida* used as imperfect. This confident knowledge is no new experience with Jesus. It has "always" (*pantote*) been so. *Which standeth around* (*ton periestōta*). Second perfect active (in-

transitive) articular participle of *periistēmi*. It was a picturesque and perilous scene. *That they may believe* (*hina pisteusōsin*). Purpose clause with *hina* and first ingressive aorist active subjunctive of *pisteuō*, "that they may come to believe." *That thou didst send me* (*hoti su me apesteilas*). First aorist active indicative of *apostellō* and note position of *su me* side by side. This claim Jesus had long ago made (5:36) and had repeatedly urged (10:25, 38). Here was a supreme opportunity and Jesus opens his heart about it.

43. *He cried with a loud voice* (*phōnēi megalēi ekraugasen*). First aorist active indicative of *kraugazō*, old and rare word from *kraugē* (Matt. 25:6). See Matt. 12:19. Occurs again in John 18:40; 19:6, 12. Only once in the LXX (Ezra 3:13) and with *phōnēi megalēi* (either locative or instrumental case makes sense) as here. For this "elevated (great) voice" see also Matt. 24:31; Mark 15:34, 37; Rev. 1:10; 21:3. The loud voice was not for the benefit of Lazarus, but for the sake of the crowd standing around that they might see that Lazarus came forth simultaneously with the command of Jesus. *Lazarus, come forth* (*Lazare, deuro exō*). "Hither out." No verb, only the two adverbs, *deuro* here alone in John. Lazarus heard and obeyed the summons.

44. *He that was dead came forth* (*exēlthen ho tethnēkōs*). Literally, "Came out the dead man," (effective aorist active indicative and perfect active articular participle of *thnēskō*). Just as he was and at once. *Bound hand and foot* (*dedemenos tous podas kai tas cheiras*). Perfect passive participle of *deō* with the accusative loosely retained according to the common Greek idiom (Robertson, *Grammar*, p. 486), but literally "as to the feet and hands" (opposite order from the English). Probably the legs were bound separately. *With grave-clothes* (*keiriais*). Or "with bands." Instrumental case of this late and rare word (in Plutarch, medical papyrus in the form *kēria*, and Prov. 7:16). Only here in N.T. *His face* (*hē opsis autou*). Old word, but *prosōpon* is usual in

N.T. See Rev. 1:16 for another instance. *Was bound about* (*periededeto*). .Past perfect passive of *perideō*, old verb to bind around, only here in N.T. *With a napkin* (*soudariōi*). Instrumental case of *soudarion* (Latin word *sudarium* from *sudor*, sweat). In N.T. here, 20:7; Luke 19:20; Acts 19:12. Our handkerchief. *Loose· him* (*lusate auton*). First aorist active imperative of *luō*. From the various bands. *Let him go* (*aphete auton hupagein*). Second aorist active imperative of *aphiēmi* and present active infinitive.

45. *Beheld that which he did* (*theasamenoi ho epoiēsen*). First aorist middle participle of *theaomai* and first aorist active indicative of *poieō* in the relative (*ho*) clause. They were eye-witnesses of all the details and did not depend on hearsay. *Believed on him* (*episteusan eis auton*). Such a result had happened before (7:31), and all the more in the presence of this tremendous miracle which held many to Jesus (12:11, 17).

46. *Went away to the Pharisees* (*apēlthon pros tous Pharisaious*). Second aorist active indicative of *aperchomai*. This "some" (*tines*) did who were deeply impressed and yet who did not have the courage to break away from the rabbis without consulting them. It was a crisis for the Sanhedrin.

47. *Gathered a council* (*sunēgagon sunedrion*). Second aorist active indicative of *sunagō* and *sunedrion*, the regular word for the Sanhedrin (Matt. 5:22, etc.), only here in John. Here a sitting or session of the Sanhedrin. Both chief priests (Sadducees) and Pharisees (mentioned no more in John after 7:57 save 12:19, 42) combine in the call (cf. 7:32). From now on the chief priests (Sadducees) take the lead in the attacks on Jesus, though loyally supported by their opponents (the Pharisees). *And said* (*kai elegon*). Imperfect active of *legō*, perhaps inchoative, "began to say." *What do we?* (*Ti poioumen;*). Present active (linear) indicative of *poieō*. Literally, "What are we doing?" *Doeth* (*poiei*). Better, "is doing" (present, linear action). He is active and we are idle.

There is no mention of the raising of Lazarus as a fact, but it is evidently included in the "many signs."

48. *If we let him thus alone* (*ean aphōmen auton houtōs*). Condition of third class with *ean* and second aorist active subjunctive of *apiēmi.* "Suppose we leave him thus alone." Suppose also that he keeps on raising the dead right here next door to Jerusalem! *All will believe on him* (*pantes pisteusousin eis auton*). Future active of *pisteuō.* The inevitable conclusion, "all" (*pantes*), not just "some" (*tines*) as now. *And the Romans will come* (*kai eleusontai hoi Rōmaioi*). Another inevitable result with the future middle of *erchomai.* Only if the people take Jesus as their political Messiah (6:15) as they had once started to do. This is a curious muddle for the rulers knew that Jesus did not claim to be a political Messiah and would not be a rival to Caesar. And yet they use this fear (their own belief about the Messiah) to stir themselves to frenzy as they will use it with Pilate later. *And take away both our place and our nation* (*kai arousin hēmōn kai ton topon kai to ethnos*). Future active of *airō,* another certain result of their inaction. Note the order here when "place" (job) is put before nation (patriotism), for all the world like modern politicians who make the fate of the country turn on their getting the jobs which they are seeking. In the course of time the Romans will come, not because of the leniency of the Sanhedrin toward Jesus, but because of the uprising against Rome led by the Zealots and they will destroy both temple and city and the Sanhedrin will lose their jobs and the nation will be scattered. Future historians will say that this fate came as punishment on the Jews for their conduct toward Jesus.

49. *Caiaphas* (*Kaiaphas*). Son-in-law of Annas and successor and high priest for 18 years (A.D. 18 to 36). *That year* (*tou eniautou ekeinou*). Genitive of time; his high-priesthood included that year (A.D. 29 or 30). So he took the lead at this meeting. *Ye know nothing at all* (*humeis ouk*

oidate ouden). In this he is correct, for no solution of their problem had been offered.

50. *That it is expedient for you* (*hoti sumpherei humin*). Indirect discourse with present active indicative of *sumpherō* used with the *hina* clause as subject. It means to bear together, to be profitable, with the dative case as here (*humin*, for you). It is to your interest and that is what they cared most for. *That one man die* (*hina heis anthrōpos apothanēi*). Sub-final use of *hina* with second aorist active subjunctive of *apothnēskō* as subject clause with *sumpherei*. See 16:7 and 18:7 for the same construction. *For the people* (*huper tou laou*). *Huper* simply means *over*, but can be in behalf of as often, and in proper context the resultant idea is "instead of" as the succeeding clause shows and as is clearly so in Gal. 3:13 of the death of Christ and naturally so in II Cor. 5:14f.; Rom. 5:6. In the papyri *huper* is the usual preposition used of one who writes a letter for one unable to write. *And that the whole nation perish not* (*kai mē holon to ethnos apolētai*). Continuation of the *hina* construction with *mē* and the second aorist subjunctive of *apollumi*. What Caiaphas has in mind is the giving of Jesus to death to keep the nation from perishing at the hands of the Romans. Politicians are often willing to make a sacrifice of the other fellow.

51. *Not of himself* (*aph' heautou ouk*). Not wholly of himself, John means. There was more in what Caiaphas said than he understood. His language is repeated in 18:14. *Prophesied* (*eprophēteusen*). Aorist active indicative of *prophēteuō*. But certainly unconscious prophecy on his part and purely accidental. Caiaphas meant only what was mean and selfish. *That Jesus should die* (*hoti emellen Iēsous apothnēskein*). Imperfect active of *mellō* in indirect discourse instead of the usual present retained after a secondary tense (*eprophēteusen*) as sometimes occurs (see 2:25).

52. *But that he might also gather together into one* (*all' hina sunagagēi eis hen*). Purpose clause with *hina* and the second

aorist active subjunctive of *sunagō*. Caiaphas was thinking only of the Jewish people (*laou*, *ethnos*, verse 50). The explanation and interpretation of John here follow the lead of the words of Jesus about the other sheep and the one flock in 10:16. *That are scattered abroad* (*ta dieskorpismena*). Perfect passive articular participle of *diaskorpizō*, late verb (Polybius, LXX) to scatter apart, to winnow grain from chaff, only here in John. The meaning here is not the Diaspora (Jews scattered over the world), but the potential children of God in all lands and all ages that the death of Christ will gather "into one" (*eis hen*). A glorious idea, but far beyond Caiaphas.

53. *So from that day* (*ap' ekeinēs oun tēs hēmeras*). The raising of Lazarus brought matters to a head so to speak. It was now apparently not more than a month before the end. *They took counsel* (*ebouleusanto*). First aorist middle indicative of *bouleuō*, old verb to take counsel, in the middle voice for themselves, among themselves. The Sanhedrin took the advice of Caiaphas seriously and plotted the death of Jesus. *That they might put him to death* (*hina apokteinōsin auton*). Purpose clause with *hina* and first aorist active subjunctive of *apokteinō*. It is an old purpose (5:18; 7:19; 8:44, 59; 10:39; 11:8) now revived with fresh energy due to the raising of Lazarus.

54. *Therefore walked no more openly* (*oun ouketi parrēsiāi periepatei*). Imperfect active of *peripateō*, to walk around. Jesus saw clearly that to do so would bring on the end now instead of his "hour" which was to be at the passover a month ahead. *Into the country near to the wilderness* (*eis tēn chōran eggus tēs erēmou*). It was now in Jerusalem as it had become once in Galilee (7:1) because of the plots of the hostile Jews. The hill country northeast of Jerusalem was thinly populated. *Into a city called Ephraim* (*eis Ephraim legomenēn polin*). *Polis* here means no more than town or village (*kōmē*). The place is not certainly known, not men-

tioned elsewhere in the N.T. Josephus mentions (*War*, IV.
ix. 9) a small fort near Bethel in the hill country and in
II Chron. 13:19 Ephron is named in connexion with Bethel.
Up here Jesus would at least be free for the moment from the
machinations of the Sanhedrin while he faced the coming
catastrophe at the passover. He is not far from the mount
of temptation where the devil showed and offered him the
kingdoms of the world for the bending of the knee before
him. Is it mere fancy to imagine that the devil came to see
Jesus again here at this juncture with a reminder of his
previous offer and of the present plight of the Son of God with
the religious leaders conspiring his death? At any rate Jesus
has the fellowship of his disciples this time (*meta tōn mathētōn*). But what were they thinking?

55. *Was near* (*ēn eggus*). See 2:13 for the same phrase.
This last passover was the time of destiny for Jesus. *Before
the passover to purify themselves* (*pro tou pascha hina hagnisō-
sin heautous*). Purpose clause with *hina* and the first aorist
active subjunctive of *hagnizō*, old verb from *hagnos* (pure),
ceremonial purification here, of course. All this took time.
These came "from the country" (*ek tēs chōras*), from all
over Palestine, from all parts of the world, in fact. John
shifts the scene to Jerusalem just before the passover with
no record of the way that Jesus came to Jerusalem from
Ephraim. The Synoptic Gospels tell this last journey up
through Samaria into Galilee to join the great caravan that
crossed over into Perea and came down on the eastern side
of the Jordan opposite Jericho and then marched up the
mountain road to Bethany and Bethphage just beside
Jerusalem. This story is found in Luke 17:11 to 19:28;
Mark 10:1–52; Matt. 19:1–20:34. John simply assumes the
Synoptic narrative and gives the picture of things in and
around Jerusalem just before the passover (11:56 and 57).

56. *They sought therefore for Jesus* (*ezētoun oun ton Iēsoun*).
Imperfect active of *zēteō* and common *oun* of which John is

so fond. They were seeking Jesus six months before at the feast of tabernacles (7:11), but now they really mean to kill him. *As they stood in the temple* (en tōi hierōi hestēkotes). Perfect active participle (intransitive) of *histēmi*, a graphic picture of the various groups of leaders in Jerusalem and from other lands, "the knots of people in the Temple precincts" (Bernard). They had done this at the tabernacles (7:11-13), but now there is new excitement due to the recent raising of Lazarus and to the public order for the arrest of Jesus. *That he will not come to the feast?* (hoti ou mē elthēi eis tēn heortēn;). The form of the question (indirect discourse after *dokeite*) assumes strongly that Jesus will not (ou mē, double negative with second aorist active *elthēi* from *erchomai*) dare to come this time for the reason given in verse 57.

57. *The chief priests and the Pharisees* (hoi archiereis kai hoi Pharisaioi). The Sanhedrin. *Had given commandment* (dedōkeisan entolas). Past perfect active of *didōmi*. *That he should shew it* (hina mēnusēi). Sub-final *hina* with first aorist active subjunctive of *mēnuō*, old verb to disclose, to report formally (Acts 23:30). *If any man knew* (ean tis gnōi). Third-class condition with *ean* and second aorist active subjunctive of *ginōskō*. *Where he was* (pou estin). Indirect question with interrogative adverb and present indicative *estin* retained like *gnōi* and *mēnusēi* after the secondary tense *dedōkeisan*. *That they might take him* (hopōs piasōsin auton). Purpose clause with *hopōs* instead of *hina* and first aorist active subjunctive of *piazō* so often used before (7:44, etc.).

CHAPTER XII

1. *Jesus therefore (Iēsous oun).* Here *oun* is not causal, but simply copulative and transitional, "and so" (Bernard), as often in John (1:22, etc.). *Six days before the passover (pro hex hēmerōn tou pascha).* This idiom, transposition of *pro*, is like the Latin use of *ante*, but it occurs in the old Doric, in the inscriptions and the papyri. See Amos 1:1 for it also (cf. Moulton, *Proleg.*, pp. 100ff.; Robertson, *Grammar*, pp. 621f.). If the crucifixion was on Friday, as seems certain from both John and the Synoptics, then six days before would be the Jewish Sabbath preceding or more probably the Friday afternoon before, since Jesus would most likely arrive before the Sabbath. Probably we are to put together in one scene for the atmosphere John 11:55–57; John 12:1, 9–11. *Came to Bethany, where Lazarus was, whom Jesus raised from the dead (ētlhen eis Bēthanian, hopou ēn Lazaros, hon ēgeiren ek nekrōn Iēsous).* Each phrase explains the preceding. There is no reason for thinking this a gloss as Bernard does. It was a place of danger now after that great miracle and the consequent rage of the Sanhedrin (12:9–11). The crowd of eager spectators to see both Lazarus and Jesus would only intensify this rage.

2. *So they made him a supper there (epoiēsan oun autōi deipnon ekei).* Here again *oun* is not inferential, but merely transitional. This supper is given by Mark (14:3–9) and Matthew (26:6–13) just two days (Mark 14:1) before the passover, that is on our Tuesday evening (beginning of Jewish Wednesday), while John mentions (12:2–9) it immediately after the arrival of Jesus in Bethany (12:1). One must decide which date to follow. Mark and Matthew and Luke follow it with the visit of Judas to the Sanhedrin with an

offer to betray Jesus as if exasperated by the rebuke by
Jesus at the feast. Bernard considers that John "is here
more probably accurate." It all turns on John's purpose in
putting it here. This is the last mention of Jesus in Bethany
and he may have mentioned it proleptically for that reason
as seems to me quite reasonable. Westcott notes that in
chapter 12 John closes his record of the public ministry
of the Lord relative to the disciples at this feast (1–11), to
the multitude in the triumphal entry (12–19), to the world
outside in the visit of the Greeks (20–36a), and with two
summary judgements (36b–50). There is no further reason to
refer to the feast in the house of another Simon when a sinful
woman anointed Jesus (Luke 7:36–50). It is no credit to
Luke or to John with Mark and Matthew to have them all
making a jumble like that. There were two anointings by
two absolutely different women for wholly different purposes. See the discussion on Luke for further details. *And
Martha served* (*kai hē Martha diēkonei*). Imperfect active
of *diakoneō*, picturing Martha true to the account of her in
Luke 10:40 (*pollēn diakonian, diakonein* as here). But this
fact does not show that Martha was the wife of this Simon
at all. They were friends and neighbours and Martha was following her bent. It is Mark (14:3) and Matthew (26:6) who
mention the name of the host. It is not Simon the Pharisee
(Luke 7:36), but Simon the leper (Mark 14:3 = Matt. 26:6)
in whose house they meet. The name is common enough.
The Simon in Luke was sharply critical of Jesus; this one is
full of gratitude for what Jesus has done for him. *That sat
at meat* (*tōn anakeimenōn*). "That lay back," reclined as
they did, articular participle (ablative case after *ek*) of the
common verb *anakeimai*. Perhaps Simon gave the feast
partly in honour of Lazarus as well as of Jesus since all were
now talking of both (John 12:9). It was a gracious occasion.
The guests were Jesus, the twelve apostles, and Martha,
Mary, and Lazarus.

3. *A pound* (*litran*). Latin *libra*, late *Koiné* (Polybius, Plutarch) word with weight of 12 ounces, in N.T. only here and 19:39. Mark (14:3) and Matthew (26:7) have alabaster cruse. *Of ointment of spikenard* (*murou nardou pistikēs*). "Of oil of nard." See already 11:2 for *murou* (also Matt. 26:7). Nard is the head or spike of an East Indian plant, very fragrant. Occurs also in Mark 14:3. *Pistikēs* here and in Mark 14:3 probably means genuine (*pistikos*, from *pistos*, reliable). Only two instances in the N.T. *Very precious* (*polutimou*). Old compound adjective (*polus*, much, *timē*), in N.T. only here, Matt. 13:46; I Peter 1:7. Mark has *polutelous* (very costly). Matthew (26:7) has here *barutimou* of weighty value (only N.T. instance). *Anointed* (*ēleipsen*). First aorist active indicative of *aleiphō*, old word (Mark 16:1). *The feet* (*tous podas*). Mark (14:3) and Matthew (26:7) have "his head." Why not both, though neither Gospel mentions both? The Latin MS. *fuldensis* and the Syriac Sinatic do give both head and feet here. *Wiped* (*exemaxen*). First aorist active indicative of *ekmassō*, old verb to wipe off already in 11:2; Luke 7:38, 44. *With her hair* (*tais thrixin autēs*). Instrumental plural. It is this item that is relied on largely by those who identify Mary of Bethany with the sinful woman in Luke 7 and with Mary Magdalene. It is no doubt true that it was usually considered immodest for a woman to wear her hair loose. But it is not impossible that Mary of Bethany in her carefully planned love-offering for Jesus on this occasion was only glad to throw such a punctilio to the winds. Such an act on this occasion does not brand her a woman of loose character. *Was filled with the odour of the ointment* (*eplērōthē ek tēs osmēs tou murou*). Effective first aorist passive of *pleroō* and a natural result.

4. *Judas Iscariot* (*Ioudas ho Iskariōtēs*). See *ho Iskariōtēs* in 14:22. See 6:71 and 13:1 for like description of Judas save that in 6:71 the father's name is given in the genitive, *Simōnos* and *Iskariōtou* (agreeing with the father), but in

13:1 *Iskariotēs* agrees with *Ioudas*, not with *Simōnos*. Clearly then both father and son were called "Iscariot" or man of Kerioth in the tribe of Judah (Josh. 15:25). Judas is the only one of the twelve not a Galilean. *One of his disciples* (*heis tōn mathētōn autou*). Likewise in 6:71, only there *ek* is used after *heis* as some MSS. have here. This is the shameful fact that clung to the name of Judas. *Which should betray him* (*ho mellōn auton paradidonai*). John does not say in 6:71 (*emellen paradidonai auton*) or here that Judas "was predestined to betray Jesus" as Bernard suggests. He had his own responsibility for his guilt as Jesus said (Matt. 26:24). *Mellō* here simply points to the act as future, not as necessary. Note the contrast between Mary and Judas. "Mary in her devotion unconsciously provides for the honour of the dead. Judas in his selfishness unconsciously brings about the death itself" (Westcott).

5. *Sold* (*eprathē*). First aorist passive indicative of *pipraskō*, old verb to sell (Matt. 13:46). *For three hundred pence* (*triakosiōn dēnariōn*). Genitive of price. Same item in Mark 14:5, while in Matt. 26:9 it is simply "for much" (*pollou*). But all three have "given to the poor" (*edothē ptōchois*). First aorist passive indicative of *didōmi* with dative case *ptōchois* (note absence of the article, poor people), real beggars, mendicants (Matt. 19:21; Luke 14:13). But only John singles out Judas as the one who made the protest against this waste of money while Mark says that "some" had indignation and Matthew has it that "the disciples" had indignation. Clearly Judas was the spokesman for the group who chimed in and agreed with his protest. The amount here spent by Mary (ten guineas) would equal a day labourer's wages for a year (Dods).

6. *Not because he cared for the poor* (*ouch hoti peri tōn ptōchōn emelen autōi*). Literally, "not because it was a care to him concerning the poor" (impersonal imperfect of *melei*, it was a care). John often makes explanatory com-

ments of this kind as in 2:21f.; 7:22, 39. *But because he was a thief (alle hoti kleptēs ēn)*. Clearly the disciples did not know then that Judas was a petty thief. That knowledge came later after he took the bribe of thirty pieces of silver for betraying Jesus (Matt. 26:15), for the disciples did not suspect Judas of treachery (13:28f.), let alone small peculations. There is no reason for thinking that John is unfair to Judas. "Temptation commonly comes through that for which we are naturally fitted" (Westcott). In this case Judas himself was "the poor beggar" who wanted this money. *And having the bag took away what was put therein (kai to glōssokomon echōn ta ballomena ebastazen)*. This is the correct text. This compound for the earlier *glōssokomeion* (from *glōssa*, tongue, and *komeō*, to tend) was originally a receptacle for the tongues or mouth-pieces of wind instruments. The shorter form is already in the Doric inscriptions and is common in the papyri for "money-box" as here. It occurs also in Josephus, Plutarch, etc. In N.T. only here and 13:29 in same sense about Judas. *Ballomena* is present passive participle (repeatedly put in) of *ballō*, to cast or fling. The imperfect active (custom) of *bastazō*, old verb to pick up (John 10:31), to carry (19:17), but here and 20:15 with the sense to bear away as in Polybius, Josephus, Diogenes Laertes, and often so in the papyri.

7. *Suffer her to keep it against the day of my burying (Aphes autēn, hina eis tēn hēmeran tou entaphiasmou mou tērēsēi auto)*. This reading (*hina tērēsēi*, purpose clause with *hina* and first aorist active subjunctive of *tēreō*) rather than that of the Textus Receptus (just *tetēreken*, perfect active indicative) is correct. It is supported by Aleph B D L W θ. The *hina* can be rendered as above after *aphes* according to Koiné idiom or more probably: "Let her alone: it was that," etc. (supplying "it was"). Either makes good sense. The word *entaphiasmos* is a later and rare, substantive from the late verb *entaphiazō*, to prepare for burial (Matt. 26:12;

John 19:40), and means preparation for burial. In N.T. only here and Mark 14:8. "Preparation for my burial" is the idea here and in Mark. The idea of Jesus is that Mary had saved this money to use in preparing his body for burial. She is giving him the flowers before the funeral. We can hardly take it that Mary did not use all of the ointment for Mark (14:3) says that she broke it and yet he adds (14:8) what John has here. It is a paradox, but Jesus is fond of paradoxes. Mary has kept this precious gift by giving it now beforehand as a preparation for my burial. We really keep what we give to Christ. This is Mary's glory that she had some glimmering comprehension of Christ's death which none of the disciples possessed.

8. *Ye have always* (*pantote echete*). Jesus does not discredit gifts to the poor at all. But there is relativity in one's duties. *But me ye have not always* (*eme de ou pantote echete*). This is what Mary perceived with her delicate woman's intuition and what the apostles failed to understand though repeatedly and plainly told by Jesus. John does not mention the precious promise of praise for Mary preserved in Mark 14:9 and Matt. 26:13, but he does show her keen sympathetic insight and Christ's genuine appreciation of her noble deed. It is curiously *mal-a-propos* surely to put alongside this incident the other incident told long before by Luke (7:35ff.) of the sinful woman. Let Mary alone in her glorious act of love.

9. *The common people* (*ho ochlos polus*). This is the right reading with the article *ho*, literally, "the people much or in large numbers." One is reminded of the French idiom. Gildersleeve (*Syntax*, p. 284) gives a few rare examples of the idiom *ho anēr agathos*. Westcott suggests that *ochlos polus* came to be regarded as a compound noun. This is the usual order in the N.T. rather than *polus ochlos* (Robertson, *Grammar*, p. 774). Mark (12:37) has *ho polus ochlos*. Moulton (*Proleg.*, p. 84) terms *ho ochlos polus* here

and in verse 12 "a curious misplacement of the article."
John's use of *ochlos* is usually the common crowd as "riff-
raff." *That he was* (*hoti estin*). Present active indicative
retained in indirect discourse after the secondary tense
(*egnō*, second aorist active indicative of *ginōskō*). These
"Jews" are not all hostile to Jesus as in 5:10; 6:41, etc.,
but included some who were friendly (verse 11). *But that*
they might see Lazarus also (*all' hina kai ton Lazaron idōsin*).
Purpose clause with *hina* and second aorist active subjunctive of *horaō*. Motive enough to gather a great crowd, to
see one raised from the dead (cf. verse 1 for the same
phrase, "whom he had raised from the dead"). Some of the
very witnesses of the raising of Lazarus will bear witness
later (verse 17). It was a tense situation.

   10. *The chief priests took counsel* (*ebouleusanto hoi arch-*
iereis). First aorist middle indicative of *bouleuō*, old verb,
seen already in 11:53 which see. The whole Sanhedrin
(7:32) had decided to put Jesus to death and had asked for
information concerning him (11:57) that might lead to his
arrest, but the Sadducees were specially active now to
accomplish the death of Lazarus also (*hina* with first aorist
active subjunctive of *apokteinō* as in 11:53). Perhaps they
argued that, if they should kill both Jesus and Lazarus, then
Lazarus would remain dead. The raising of Lazarus has
brought matters to a crisis. Incidentally, it may be observed that here we may see the reason why the Synoptics
do not tell the story of the raising of Lazarus, if he was still
living (cf. the case of Malchus's name in John 18:10).

   11. *Because that* (*hoti*). Causal use of *hoti*. *By reason of*
him (*di' auton*). "Because of him," regular idiom, accusative
case with *dia*. *Went away* (*hupēgon*). Cf. 6:67 for this verb.
Inchoative imperfect active of *hupagō*, "began to withdraw"
as happened at the time of the raising of Lazarus (11:45f.)
and the secession was still going on. *And believed on Jesus*
(*kai episteuon eis ton Iēsoun*). Imperfect active of *pisteuō*

(note aorist in 11:45). There was danger of a mass movement of the people to Jesus.

12. *On the morrow* (*tēi epaurion*). Locative case. Supply *hēmerāi* (day) after the adverb *epaurion* ("on the tomorrow day"). That is on our Sunday, Palm Sunday. *A great multitude* (*ho ochlos polus*). Same idiom rendered "the common people" in verse 9 and should be so translated here. *That had come* (*ho elthōn*). Second aorist active participle, masculine singular of *erchomai* agreeing with *ochlos*, "that came." *When they heard* (*akousantes*). First aorist active masculine plural participle of *akouō*, construction according to sense (plural, though *ochlos* singular). *Was coming* (*erchetai*). Present middle indicative of *erchomai* retained in indirect discourse after a secondary tense. It is a vivid picture. What they heard was: "Jesus is coming into Jerusalem." He is defying the Sanhedrin with all their public advertisement for him.

13. *Took* (*elabon*). Second aorist active indicative of *lambanō*. *The branches of the palm-trees* (*ta baia tōn phoinikōn*). *Phoinix* is an old word for palm-tree (Rev. 7:9 for the branches) and in Acts 27:12 the name of a city. *Baion* is apparently a word of Egyptian origin, palm branches, here only in N.T., but in the papyri and I Macc. 13:51. Here we have "the palm branches of the palm-trees." The use in I Macc. 13:51 (cf. II Macc. 10:7) is in the account of Simon's triumphal entry into Jerusalem. Bernard notes that to carry palms was a mark of triumphant homage to a victor or a king (Rev. 7:9). Palm-trees grew on the Mount of Olives (Mark 11:8) on the road from Bethany to Jerusalem. The crowds (one in front and one behind, Mark 11:9; Matt. 21:9; John 2:18) cut the branches as they came (Matt. 21:8). *To meet him* (*eis hupantēsin autōi*). Literally, "for a meeting (*hupantēsis*, late word from the verb *hupantaō*, Matt. 8:28; John 11:20, 30; 12:18, in the papyri, but only here in the N.T.) with him" (*autōi*, associative instrumental

case after *hupantēsin* as after the verb in verse 18). It was a scene of growing excitement. *And cried out* (*kai ekraugazon*). Imperfect active of *kraugazō*, old and rare verb (from *kraugē*) as in Matt. 12:19; John 19:15. *Hosannah* (*Hōsannah*). Transliteration of the Hebrew word meaning "Save now." The LXX renders it by *Sōson dē* (Save now). *Blessed is he that cometh in the name of the Lord* (*eulogēmenos ho erchomenos en onomati kuriou*). Perfect passive participle of *eulogeō*. Quotation from Psa. 118:25f., written, some think, for the dedication of the second temple, or, as others think, for the feast of tabernacles after the return (Ezra 3:1f.). It was sung in the processional recitation then as a welcome to the worshippers. Here the words are addressed to the Messiah as is made plain by the addition of the words, "even the king of Israel" (*kai ho basileus tou Israēl*) as Nathanael called him (1:49). Jesus is here hailed by the multitudes as the long-looked for Messiah of Jewish hope and he allows them so to greet him (Luke 19:38–40), a thing that he prevented a year before in Galilee (John 6:14f.). It is probable that "in the name of the Lord" should be taken with "blessed" as in Deut. 21:5; II Sam. 6:18; I Kings 22:16; II Kings 2:24. The Messiah was recognized by Martha as the Coming One (John 11:27) and is so described by the Baptist (Matt. 11:3). Mark (11:10) adds "the kingdom that cometh" while Luke (19:38) has "the king that cometh." "It was this public acclamation of Jesus as King of Israel or King of the Jews which was the foundation of the charge made against him before Pilate (18:33)" (Bernard).

14. *Found* (*heurōn*). Second aorist active participle of *heuriskō*. Through the disciples, of course, as in Mark 11:2–6 (=Matt. 21:2–3, 6=Luke 19:30f.). *A young ass* (*onarion*). Late diminutive of *onos*, in Epictetus and the papyri (even the double diminitive, *onaridion*), only here in the N.T. See discussion of Matt. 21:5 where *kai* has been

wrongly rendered "and" instead of "even." Rightly understood Matthew has Jesus riding only the colt like the rest.

15. *Daughter of Zion* (*thugatēr Siōn*). Nominative form
(instead of *thugater*) but vocative case. The quotation is
from Zech. 9:9 shortened. *Thy King cometh* (*ho basileus
erchetai*). Prophetic futuristic present. The ass was the
animal ridden in peace as the horse was in war (Judges
10:4; 12:14; II Sam. 17:23; 19:26). Zechariah pictures one
coming in peace. So the people here regarded Jesus as the
Prince of Peace in the triumphal entry. *Sitting on an ass's
colt* (*kathēmenos epi pōlon onou*). Matthew (21:6f.) does
speak of both the ass and the colt having garments put on
them, but he does not say that Jesus "sat upon" both
animals at once, for *epanō autōn* (upon them) probably
refers to the garments, not to the colts. When John wrote
(end of the century), Jerusalem had fallen. Jesus will
lament over Jerusalem (Luke 19:41ff.). So "Fear not"
(*mē phobou*).

16. *Understood not* (*ouk egnōsan*). Second aorist active
indicative of *ginōskō*. Another comment by John concerning
the failure of the disciples to know what was happening
(cf. 2:22; 7:39). *At the first* (*to prōton*). Adverbial accusative,
as in 10:40; 19:39. *Was glorified* (*edoxasthē*). First aorist
passive indicative of *doxazō*, to glorify, used of his death
already in 7:39 and by Jesus himself of his death, resurrection, and ascension in 12:23; 13:31. *Then remembered
they* (*tote emnēsthēsan*). First aorist passive indicative of
mimnēskō. It was easier to understand then and they had
the Holy Spirit to help them (16:13–15). *Were written of him*
(*ēn ep' autōi gegrammena*). Periphrastic past perfect passive
of *graphō* with neuter plural participle agreeing with *tauta*
(these things) and singular verb, though the plural *ēsan*
could have been used. Note the threefold repetition of *tauta*
in this verse, "clumsy" Bernard calls it, but making for
clarity. The use of *ep' autōi* for "of him" rather than *peri*

autou is unusual, but occurs in Rev. 10:11; 22:16. *They had done* (*epoiēsan*). First aorist active indicative of *poieō*, simply, "they did."

17. *Bare witness* (*emarturei*). Imperfect active of *martureō*. This crowning triumph of Jesus gave an added sense of importance to the crowds that were actually with Jesus when he called Lazarus out of the tomb and raised him from the dead. For this description of this portion of the crowd see 11:45f.; 12:1, 9–11.

18. *The multitude* (*ho ochlos*). The multitude of verse 13, not the crowd just mentioned that had been with Jesus at the raising of Lazarus. There were two crowds (one following Jesus, one meeting Jesus as here). *Went and met him* (*hupēntēsen autōi*). First aorist active indicative of *hupantaō*, old compound verb (*hupo, antaō*) to go to meet, with associative instrumental case *autōi*. Cf. John 4:51. *That he had done this sign* (*touto auton pepoiēkenai to sēmeion*). Perfect active infinitive in indirect discourse after *ēkousan* (first aorist active indicative of *akouō*, to hear) (instead of a *hoti* clause) with the accusative of general reference *auton* (as to him) and another accusative (*sēmeion*, sign) the object of the infinitive. Clearly there was much talk about the raising of Lazarus as the final proof that Jesus in truth is the Messiah of Jewish hope.

19. *The Pharisees therefore said among themselves* (*hoi oun Pharisaioi eipan pros heautous*). Graphic picture of the predicament of the Pharisees standing off and watching the enthusiastic crowds sweep by. As people usually do, they blame each other for the defeat of their plots against Jesus and for his final victory, as it seemed. *Behold how ye prevail nothing* (*theōreite hoti ouk ōpheleite ouden*). It was a pathetic confession of failure because the rest of the plotters had bungled the whole thing. "Ye help nothing at all" by your plots and plans. *Lo, the world is gone after him* (*ide ho kosmos opisō autou apēlthen*). Exclamatory use of *ide* and

timeless aorist active indicative of *aperchomai*. The "world" is a bunch of fools, they feel, but see for yourselves. And the Sanhedrin had advertised to "find" Jesus! They can find him now!

20. *Certain Greeks* (*Hellēnes tines*). Real Greeks, not Greek-speaking Jews (Hellenists, Acts 6:1), but Greeks like those in Antioch (Acts 11:20, correct text *pros tous Hellēnas*) to whom Barnabas was sent. These were probably proselytes of the gate or God-fearers like those worshipping Greeks in Thessalonica whom Paul won to Christ (Acts 17:4). *To worship at the feast* (*hina proskunēsōsin en tēi heortēi*). Purpose clause with *hina* and the first aorist active subjunctive of *proskuneō*, old and common verb to kiss the hand in reverence, to bow the knee in reverence and worship. We do not know whence they came, whether from Decapolis, Galilee, or further away. They found the pilgrims and the city ringing with talk about Jesus. They may even have witnessed the triumphal entry.

21. *To Philip which was of Bethsaida of Galilee* (*Philippōi tōi apo Bēthsaida tēs Galilaias*). He had a Greek name and the Greeks may have seen Philip in Galilee where there were many Greeks, probably (Mark 6:45) the Western Bethsaida in Galilee, not Bethsaida Julias on the Eastern side (Luke 9:10). *Asked* (*ērōtōn*). Imperfect active, probably inchoative, "began to ask," in contrast with the aorist tense just before (*prosēlthan*, came to). *Sir* (*Kurie*). Most respectfully and courteously. *We would see Jesus* (*thelomen ton Iēsoun idein*). "We desire to see Jesus." This is not abrupt like our "we wish" or "we want," but perfectly polite. However, they could easily "see" Jesus, had already done so, no doubt. They wish an interview with Jesus.

22. *Andrew* (*tōi Andreāi*). Another apostle with a Greek name and associated with Philip again (John 6:7f.), the man who first brought his brother Simon to Jesus (1:41). Andrew was clearly a man of wisdom for a crisis. Note the vivid

dramatic presents here, *cometh* (*erchetai*), *telleth* (*legei*). What was the crisis? These Greeks wish an interview with Jesus. True Jesus had said something about "other sheep" than Jews (10:16), but he had not explained. Philip and Andrew wrestle with the problem that will puzzle Peter on the housetop in Joppa (Acts 10:9–18), that middle wall of partition between Jew and Gentile that was only broken down by the Cross of Christ (Eph. 2:11–22) and that many Christians and Jews still set up between each other. Andrew has no solution for Philip and they bring the problem, but not the Greeks, to Jesus.

23. *The hour is come* (*elēluthen hē hōra*). The predestined hour, seen from the start (2:4), mentioned by John (7:30; 8:20) as not yet come and later as known by Jesus as come (13:1), twice again used by Jesus as already come (in the prayer of Jesus, 17:1; Mark 14:41, just before the betrayal in the Garden). The request from the Greeks for this interview stirs the heart of Jesus to its depths. *That the Son of man should be glorified* (*hina doxasthēi ho huios tou anthrōpou*). Purpose clause with *hina* (not in the sense of *hote*, when) and the first aorist passive subjunctive of *doxazō*, same sense as in 12:16 and 13:31. The Cross must come before Greeks can really come to Jesus with understanding. But this request shows that interest in Jesus now extends beyond the Jewish circles.

24. *Except* (*ean mē*). Negative condition of third class (undetermined, supposable case) with second aorist active participle *pesōn* (from *piptō*, to fall) and the second aorist active subjunctive of *apothnēskō*, to die. *A grain of wheat* (*ho kokkos tou sitou*). Rather, "the grain of wheat." *By itself alone* (*autos monos*). Both predicate nominatives after *menei*. It is not necessary to think (nor likely) that Jesus has in mind the Eleusinian mysteries which became a symbol of the mystery of spring. Paul in I Cor. 15:36 uses the same illustration of the resurrection that Jesus does here. Jesus

shows here the paradox that life comes through death. Whether the Greeks heard him or not we do not know. If so, they heard something not in Greek philosophy, the Christian ideal of sacrifice, "and this was foreign to the philosophy of Greece" (Bernard). Jesus had already spoken of himself as the bread of life (6:35-65). *But if it die* (*ean de apothanēi*). Parallel condition of the third class. Grains of wheat have been found in Egyptian tombs three or four thousand years old, but they are now dead. They bore no fruit.

25. *Loseth it* (*apolluei autēn*). The second paradox. Present active indicative of *apolluō*. This great saying was spoken at various times as in Mark 8:35 (=Matt. 16:25 = Luke 9:24) and Mark 10:39 (=Luke 17:33). See those passages for discussion of *psuchē* (life or soul). For "he that hateth his life" (*ho misōn tēn psuchēn autou*) see the sharp contrasts in Luke 14:26-35 where *miseō* is used of father, mother, wife, children, brothers, sisters, as well as one's own life. Clearly *miseō* means "hate" when the issue is between Christ and the dearest things of life as happens when the choice is between martyrdom and apostasy. In that case one keeps his soul for eternal life by losing his life (*psuchē*, each time) here. That is the way to "guard" (*phulaxei*) life by being true to Christ. This is the second paradox to show Christ's philosophy of life.

26. *If any man serve me* (*ean emoi tis diakonēi*). Condition of third class again (*ean* with present active subjunctive of *diakoneō*, keep on serving with dative *emoi*). *Let him follow me* (*emoi akoloutheitō*). "Me (associative instrumental case) let him keep on following" (present active imperative of *akoloutheō*). *Where . . . there* (*hopou . . . ekei*). In presence and spiritual companionship here and hereafter. Cf. 14:3; 17:24; Matt. 28:20. *Shall honour* (*timēsei*). Future active of *timaō*, but it may be the kind of honour that Jesus will get (verse 23).

27. *My soul* (*hē psuchē mou*). The soul (*psuchē*) here is synonymous with spirit (*pneuma*) in 13:21. *Is troubled* (*tetaraktai*). Perfect passive indicative of *tarassō*, used also in 11:33 and 13:21 of Jesus. While John proves the deity of Jesus in his Gospel, he assumes throughout his real humanity as here (cf. 4:6). The language is an echo of that in Psa. 6:4 and 42:7. John does not give the agony in Gethsemane which the Synoptics have (Mark 14:35f. =Matt. 26:39 = Luke 22:42), but it is quite beside the mark to suggest, as Bernard does, that the account here is John's version of the Gethsemane experience. Why do some critics feel called upon to level down to a dead plane every variety of experience in Christ's life? *And what shall I say?* (*kai ti eipō;*). Deliberative subjunctive which expresses vividly "a genuine, if momentary indecision" (Bernard). The request of the Greeks called up graphically to Jesus the nearness of the Cross. *Father, save me from this hour* (*pater, sōson me ek tēs hōras tautēs*). Jesus began his prayers with "Father" (11:41). Dods thinks that this should be a question also. Westcott draws a distinction between *ek* (out of) and *apo* (from) to show that Jesus does not pray to draw back from the hour, but only to come safely out of it all and so interprets *ek* in Heb. 5:7, but that distinction will not stand, for in John 1:44 *ek* and *apo* are used in the same sense and in the Synoptics (Mark 14:35f. =Matt. 26:39 = Luke 52:42) we have *apo*. If it holds here, we lose the point there. Here as in Gethsemane the soul of Jesus instinctively and naturally shrinks from the Cross, but he instantly surrenders to the will of God in both experiences. *But for this cause came I unto this hour* (*alla dia touto ēlthon eis tēn hōran tautēn*). It was only a moment of human weakness as in Gethsemane that quickly passed. Thus understood the language has its natural meaning.

28. *Father, glorify thy name* (*pater, doxason sou to onoma*). First aorist (note of urgency) active imperative of *doxazō* and

in the sense of his death already in verses 16 and 23 and again in 13:31 and 17:5. This is the prayer of the *pneuma* (or *psuchē*) as opposed to that of the *sarx* (flesh) in verse 27. The "name" (*onoma*) of God expresses the character of God (1:12; 5:43; 17:11). Cf. Matt. 6:9. *A voice out of heaven* (*phōnē ek tou ouranou*). This was the Father's answer to the prayer of Jesus for help. See already the Father's voice at the baptism of Jesus (Mark 1:11) and at the transfiguration (Mark 9:7). The rabbis called the audible voice of God *bath-qol* (the daughter of a voice). *I have both glorified it and will glorify it again* (*kai edoxasa kai palin doxasō*). This definite assurance from the Father will nerve the soul of Jesus for the coming ordeal. Cf. 11:40 for *edoxasa* and 13:31 and 17:5 for *doxasō*.

29. *That it had thundered* (*brontēn gegonenai*). Perfect active infinitive of *ginomai* in indirect discourse after *elegen* and the accusative of general reference (*brontēn*, thunder, as in Mark 3:17), "that thunder came to pass." So the crowd "standing by" (*hestōs*, second perfect active participle of *histēmi*), but Jesus understood his Father's voice. *An angel hath spoken to him* (*Aggelos autōi lelalēken*). Perfect active indicative of *laleō*. So, when Jesus spoke to Saul on the way to Damascus, those with Saul heard the voice, but did not understand (Acts 9:7; 22:9).

30. *Not for my sake, but for your sakes* (*ou di' eme, alla di' humas*). These words seem to contradict verses 28 and 29. Bernard suggests an interpolation into the words of Jesus. But why not take it to be the figure of exaggerated contrast, "not merely for my sake, but also for yours"?

31. *The judgement* (*krisis*). No article, "A judgement." The next few days will test this world. *The prince of this world* (*ho archōn tou kosmou toutou*). This phrase here, descriptive of Satan as in possession of the evil world, occurs again in 14:30 and 16:11. In the temptations Satan claims power over the world and offers to share it with

Jesus (Matt. 4:8-10=Luke 4:5-8). Jesus did not deny
Satan's power then, but here proclaims final victory over
him. *Shall be cast out* (*ekblēthēsetai exō.*) Future passive of
ekballō. Note *exō*, clean out. The Book of Revelation also
proclaims final victory over Satan.

32. *And I, if I be lifted from the earth* (*kágō an hupsōthō
ek tēs gēs*). Note proleptic position of *egō* (I). Condition of
third class (undetermined with prospect) with *an* (=*ean*
here) with first aorist passive subjunctive of *hupsoō*, the verb
used in 3:14 of the brazen serpent and of the Cross of Christ
as here and also in 8:28. Westcott again presses *ek* instead
of *apo* to make it refer to the ascension rather than to the
Cross, a wrong interpretation surely. *Will draw all men unto
myself* (*pantas helkusō pros emauton*). Future active of
helkuō, late form of *helkō*, to draw, to attract. Jesus had
already used this verb of the Father's drawing power (6:44).
The magnetism of the Cross is now known of all men, however little they understand the mystery of the Cross. By
"all men" (*pantas*) Jesus does not mean every individual
man, for some, as Simeon said (Luke 2:34) are repelled by
Christ, but this is the way that Greeks (verse 22) can and
will come to Christ, by the way of the Cross, the only way
to the Father (14:6).

33. *Signifying* (*sēmainōn*). Present active participle of
semainō, old verb to give a sign (*sēmeion*) as in Acts 25:27,
and the whole phrase repeated in 18:32 and nearly so in
21:19. The indirect question here and in 18:32 has the imperfect *emellen* with present infinitive rather than the usual
present *mellei* retained while in 21:19 the future indicative
doxasei occurs according to rule. The point in *poiōi* (qualitative relative in the instrumental case with *thanatōi*) is the
Cross (lifted up) as the kind of death before Christ.

34. *Out of the law* (*ek tou nomou*). That is, "out of the
Scriptures" (10:34; 15:25). *The Christ abideth forever* (*ho
Christos menei eis ton aiōna*). Timeless present active indica-

tive of *menō*, to abide, remain. Perhaps from Psa. 89:4;
110:4; Isa. 9:7; Ezek. 37:25; Dan. 7:14. *How sayest thou?*
(*pōs legeis su;*). In opposition to the law (Scripture). *The
Son of man* (*ton huion tou anthrōpou*). Accusative case of
general reference with the infinitive *hupsōthēnai* (first aorist
passive of *hupsoō* and taken in the sense of death by the
cross as Jesus used it in verse 32). Clearly the crowd understand Jesus to be "the Son of man" and take the phrase to
be equivalent to "the Christ." This is the obvious way
to understand the two terms in their reply, and not, as
Bernard suggests, that they saw no connexion between "the
Christ" (the Messiah) and "the Son of man." The use of
"this" (*houtos*) in the question that follows is in contrast
to verse 32. The Messiah (the Son of man) abides forever
and is not to be crucified as you say he "must" (*dei*) be.

35. *Yet a little while is the light among you* (*eti mikron
chronon to phōs en humin estin*). *Chronon* is the accusative of
extent of time. Jesus does not argue the point of theology
with the crowd who would not understand. He turns to the
metaphor used before when he claimed to be the light of the
world (8:12) and urges that they take advantage of their
privilege "while ye have the light" (*hōs to phōs echete*). *That
darkness overtake you not* (*hina mē skotia humas katalabēi*).
Purpose (negative) with *hina mē* and second aorist active
subjunctive of *katalambanō*. See this verb in 1:5. In I
Thess. 5:4 this verb occurs with *hēmera* (day) overtaking one
like a thief. *Knoweth not whither he goeth* (*ouk oiden pou
hupagei*). See 11:10 for this idea and the same language in
I John 2:11. The ancients did not have our electric street
lights. The dark streets were a terror to travellers.

36. *Believe in the light* (*pisteuete eis to phōs*). That is,
"believe in me as the Messiah" (8:12; 9:5). *That ye may
become sons of light* (*hina huioi phōtos genēsthe*). Purpose
clause with *hina* and second aorist subject of *ginomai*, to
become. They were not "sons of light," a Hebrew idiom

(cf. 17:12; Luke 16:8 with the contrast), an idiom used by Paul in I Thess. 5:5; Eph. 5:8. It is equivalent to "enlightened men" (Bernard) and Jesus called his disciples the light of the world (Matt. 5:14). *Hid himself from them (ekrubē ap' autōn).* Second aorist passive indicative of *kruptō*, late form (in LXX) for old *ekruphē*, "was hidden from them," as in 8:59. This part of verse 36 begins a new paragraph.

37. *Though he had done so many signs before them (tosauta autou sēmeia pepoiēkotos emprosthen autōn).* Genitive absolute with perfect active participle in concessive sense of *poieō*. *Yet they believed not on him (ouk episteuon eis auton).* No "yet" in the Greek. Negative imperfect active of *pisteuō*, "they kept on not believing on him," stubborn refusal in face of the light (verse 35).

38. *That might be fulfilled (hina plērōthēi).* It is usually assumed that *hina* here with the first aorist passive subjunctive of *pleroō* has its full telic force. That is probable as God's design, but it is by no means certain since *hina* is used in the N.T. with the idea of result, just as *ut* in Latin is either purpose or result, as in John 6:7; 9:2; I Thess. 5:4; Gal. 5:17; Rom. 11:11 (Robertson, *Grammar*, p. 998). Paul in Rom. 10:16 quotes Isa. 53:1 as John does here but without *hina*. See Rom. 10:16 for discussion of the quotation. The next verse adds strength to the idea of design.

39. *For this cause they could not believe (dia touto ouk edunanto pisteuein).* *Touto* (this) seems to have a double reference (to what precedes and to what follows) as in 8:47. The negative imperfect (double augment, *edunanto*) of *dunamai*. John is not absolving these Jews from moral responsibility, but only showing that the words of Isaiah "had to be fulfilled, for they were the expression of Divine foreknowledge" (Bernard).

40. *He hath blinded (tetuphlōken).* Perfect active indicative of *tuphloō*, old causative verb to make blind (from *tuphlos*, blind), in N.T. only here, II Cor. 4:4; I John 2:11.

He hardened (*epōrōsen*).   First aorist active indicative of *pōroō*, a late causative verb (from *pōros*, hard skin), seen already in Mark 6:52, etc.   This quotation is from Isa. 6:10 and differs from the LXX.   *Lest they should see* (*hina mē idōsin*).   Negative purpose clause with *hina mē* instead of *mēpote* (never used by John) of the LXX.   Matthew (13:15) has *mēpote* and quotes Jesus as using the passage as do Mark (4:12) and Luke (8:10).   Paul quotes it again (Acts 28:26) to the Jews in Rome.   In each instance the words of Isaiah are interpreted as forecasting the doom of the Jews for rejecting the Messiah.   Matthew (13:15) has *sunōsin* where John has *noēsōsin* (perceive), and both change from the subjunctive to the future (*kai iasomai*), "And I should heal them."   John has here *straphōsin* (second aorist passive subjunctive of *strephō*) while Matthew reads *epistrepsōsin* (first aorist active of *epistrephō*).

41. *Because he saw his glory* (*hoti eiden tēn doxan autou*). Correct reading here *hoti* (because), not *hote* (when).   Isaiah with spiritual vision saw the glory of the Messiah and spoke (*elalēsen*) of him, John says, whatever modern critics may think or say.   So Jesus said that Abraham saw his day (8:56).   Cf. Heb. 11:13.

42. *Nevertheless even* (*homōs mentoi kai*).   For the old *homōs* see I Cor. 14:7; Gal. 3:15 (only other examples in N.T.), here only with *mentoi*, "but yet," and *kai*, "even." In spite of what has just been said "many (*polloi*) even of the rulers" (recall the lonely shyness of Nicodemus in 3:1ff.).   These actually "believed on him" (*episteusan eis auton*) in their convictions, a remarkable statement as to the effect that Christ had in Jerusalem as the Sanhedrin plotted his death.   Cf. Nicodemus and Joseph of Arimathea.   *But because of the Pharisees* (*alla dia tous Pharisaious*).   Like the whispered talk in 7:13 "because of the fear of the Jews." Once the Pharisees sneeringly asked the officers (7:48): "Hath any one of the rulers believed on him?"   And now

"many of the rulers have believed on him." *They did not confess* (*ouch hōmologoun*). Negative imperfect in contrast to the punctiliar aorist *episteusan*. "They kept on not confessing." How like the cowardly excuses made today by those under conviction who refuse to step out for Christ. *Lest they should be put out of the synagogue* (*hina mē aposunagōgoi genōntai*). Cf. 9:22 where this very word occurs in a purpose clause like this. Only once more in the N.T. (16:2), a Jewish word not in profane authors. This ostracism from the synagogue was dreaded by the Jews and made cowards of these "believing elders." *More than* (*mallon ēper*). They preferred the glory and praise of men more than the glory and praise of God. How *apropos* these words are to some suave cowards today.

44. *Cried and said* (*ekraxen kai eipen*). First aorist active indicative of *krazō*, to cry aloud, and second aorist active of defective verb *erō*, to say. This is probably a summary of what Jesus had already said as in verse 36 John closes the public ministry of Jesus without the Synoptic account of the last day in the temple on our Tuesday (Mark 11:27–12:44 = Matt. 21:23–23:39 = Luke 20:1–21:4). *Not on me, but on him* (*ou eis eme, alla eis ton*). "Not on me only, but also on," another example of exaggerated contrast like that in verse 30. The idea of Jesus here is a frequent one (believing on Jesus whom the Father has sent) as in 3:17f.; 5:23f., 30, 43; 7:16; 8:42; 13:20; 14:1; Matt. 10:40; Luke 9:48.

46. *I am come a light* (*Egō phōs elēlutha*). As in 3:19; 9:5; 8:12; 12:35. Final clause (negative) also here (*hina mē meinēi*, first aorist active subjunctive) as in 12:35. Light dispels darkness.

47. *If any one* (*ean tis*). Third-class condition with *ean* and first aorist active subjunctive (*akousēi*) of *akouō* and same form (*phulaxēi*) of *phulassō* with negative *mē*. *But to save the world* (*all' hina sōsō ton kosmon*). Purpose clause again (cf. *hina krinō*, just before) with *hina* and first aorist

active of *sōzō*. Exaggerated contrast again, "not so much to judge, but also to save." See 3:17 for same contrast. And yet Jesus does judge the world inevitably (8:15f.; 9:39), but his primary purpose is to save the world (3:16). See close of the Sermon on the Mount for the same insistence on hearing and keeping (obeying) the words of Jesus (Matt. 7:24, 26) and also Luke 11:28.

48. *Rejecteth* (*athetōn*). Present active participle of *atheteō*, late *Koiné* verb (from *athetos*, *a* privative, and *tithēmi*), to render null and void, only here in John, but see Mark 6:26; 7:9. *One that judgeth him* (*ton krinonta auton*). Articular present active participle of *krinō*. See same idea in 5:45; 9:50. *The same* (*ekeinos*). "That" very word of Christ which one rejects will confront him and accuse him to the Father "at the last day" (*en tēi eschatēi hēmerāi*, this phrase peculiar to John). There is no escaping it. And yet Jesus himself will bear witness for or against the one whose conduct has already revealed his attitude towards the message of God (Matt. 10:32; Luke 12:8f.).

49. *He hath given* (*dedōken*). Perfect active indicative. Christ has permanent commission. *What I should say and what I should speak* (*ti eipō kai ti lalēsō*). Indirect question retaining the deliberative subjunctive (second aorist active *eipō*, first aorist active *lalēsō*). Meyer and Westcott take *eipō* to refer to the content and *lalēsō* more to the varying manner of delivery. Possibly so.

50. *Life eternal* (*zōē aiōnios*). See 3:15 and Matt. 25:46 for this great phrase. In 6:68 Peter says to Jesus, "Thou hast the words of eternal life." Jesus had just said (6:63) that his words were spirit and life. The secret lies in the source, "as the Father hath said to me" (*eirēken*).

CHAPTER XIII

1. *Now before the feast of the passover (pro de tēs heortēs tou pascha).* Just before, John means, not twenty-four hours before, that is our Thursday evening (beginning of 15th of Nisan, sunset to sunset Jewish day), since Jesus was crucified on Friday 15th of Nisan. Hence Jesus ate the regular passover meal at the usual time. The whole feast, including the feast of unleavened bread, lasted eight days. For a discussion of the objections to this interpretation of John in connexion with the Synoptic Gospels one may consult my *Harmony of the Gospels*, pp. 279–84, and David Smith's *In the Days of His Flesh*, Appendix VIII. The passover feast began on the 15th Nisan at sunset, the passover lamb being slain the afternoon of 14th Nisan. There seems no real doubt that this meal in John 13:1–30 is the real passover meal described by the Synoptics also (Mark 14:18–21 = Matt. 26:21–25 = Luke 22:21–23), followed by the institution of the Lord's Supper. Thus understood verse 1 here serves as an introduction to the great esoteric teaching of Christ to the apostles (John 13:2 to 17:26), called by Barnas Sears *The Heart of Christ*. This phrase goes with the principal verb *ēgapēsen* (loved). *Knowing (eidōs).* Second perfect active participle, emphasizing the full consciousness of Christ. He was not stumbling into the dark as he faced "his hour" (*autou hē hōra*). See 18:4; 19:28 for other examples of the insight and foresight (Bernard) of Jesus concerning his death. See on 12:23 for use before by Jesus. *That he should depart (hina metabēi).* Sub-final use of *hina* with second aorist active subjunctive of *metabainō*, old word, to go from one place to another, here (5:24; I John 3:14) to go from this world (8:23) back to the Father from whom he had come

(14:12, 28; 16:10, 28; 17:5). *His own which were in the world* (*tous idious tous en tōi kosmōi*). His own disciples (17:6, 9, 11), those left in the world when he goes to the Father, not the Jews as in 1:11. See Acts 4:23; I Tim. 5:8 for the idiom. John pictures here the outgoing of Christ's very heart's love (chs. 13 to 17) towards these men whom he had chosen and whom he loved "unto the end" (*eis telos*) as in Matt. 10:22 and Luke 18:15, but here as in I Thess. 2:16 rather "to the uttermost." The culmination of the crisis ("his hour") naturally drew out the fulness of Christ's love for them as is shown in these great chapters (13 to 17).

2. *During supper* (*deipnou ginomenou*). Correct text, present middle participle of *ginomai* (not *genomenou*, second aorist middle participle, "being ended") genitive absolute. Verse 4 shows plainly that the meal was still going on. *The devil having already put* (*tou diabolou ēdē beblēkotos*). Another genitive absolute without a connective (asyndeton), perfect active participle of *ballō*, to cast, to put. Luke (22:3) says that Satan entered Judas when he offered to betray Jesus. Hence John's "already" (*ēdē*) is pertinent. John repeats his statement in verse 27. In John 6:70 Jesus a year ago had seen that Judas was a devil. *To betray him* (*hina paradoi auton*). Cf. Acts 5:3. Purpose clause with *hina* and second aorist active subjunctive of *paradidōmi* (form in -*oi* as in Mark 14:10 rather than the usual -*ōi* in Luke 22:4). Satan had an open door by now into the heart of Judas.

3. *Knowing* (*eidōs*). Repeated from verse 1, accenting the full consciousness of Jesus. *Had given* (*edōken*). So Aleph B L W, aorist active instead of *dedōken* (perfect active) of *didōmi*. Cf. 3:31 for a similar statement with *en* instead of *eis*. See Matt. 11:27 (=Luke 10:22) and 28:18 for like claim by Jesus to complete power. *And that he came forth from God, and goeth unto God* (*kai hoti apo theou exēlthen kai pros ton theon hupagei*). See plain statement by Jesus on this point in 16:28. The use of *pros ton theon* recalls the same

words in 1:1. Jesus is fully conscious of his deity and Messianic dignity when he performs this humble act.

4. *Riseth from supper* (*egeiretai ek tou deipnou*). Vivid dramatic present middle indicative of *egeirō*. From the couch on which he was reclining. *Layeth aside* (*tithēsin*). Same dramatic present active of *tithēmi*. *His garments* (*ta himatia*). The outer robe *tallith* (*himation*) and with only the tunic (*chitōn*) on "as one that serveth" (Luke 22:27). Jesus had already rebuked the apostles for their strife for precedence at the beginning of the meal (Luke 22:24–30). *A towel* (*lention*). Latin word *linteum*, linen cloth, only in this passage in the N.T. *Girded himself* (*diezōsen heauton*). First aorist active indicative of *diazōnnuō* (*-umi*), old and rare compound (in Plutarch, LXX, inscriptions, and papyri), to gird all around. In N.T. only in John (13:4, 5; 21:7). Did Peter not recall this incident when in I Peter 5:5 he exhorts all to "gird yourselves with humility" (*tēn tapeinophrosunēn egkombōsasthe*)?

5. *Poureth* (*ballei*). Vivid present again. Literally, "putteth" (as in verse 2, *ballō*). *Into the basin* (*eis ton niptēra*). From verb *niptō* (later form of *nizō* in this same verse and below) to wash, found only here and in quotations of this passage. Note the article, "the basin" in the room. *Began to wash* (*ērxato niptein*). Back to the aorist again as with *diezōsen* (verse 4). *Niptō* was common for washing parts of the body like the hands or the feet. *To wipe* (*ekmassein*). "To wipe off" as in 12:3. *With the towel* (*tōi lentiōi*). Instrumental case and the article (pointing to *lention* in verse 4). *Wherewith* (*hōi*). Instrumental case of the relative *ho*. *He was girded* (*ēn diezōsmenos*). Periphrastic past perfect of *diazōnnuō* for which verb see verse 4.

6. *So he cometh* (*erchetai oun*). Transitional use of *oun* and dramatic present again (*erchetai*). *Lord, dost thou wash my feet?* (*Kurie, su mou nipteis tous podas;*). Emphatic contrast in position of *su mou* (away from *podas*), "Dost thou

my feet wash?" "Peter, we may suppose, drew his feet up, as he spoke, in his impulsive humility" (Bernard).

7. *I . . . thou* (*egō . . . su*). Jesus repeats the pronouns used by Peter in similar contrast. *Not now* (*ouk arti*). Just now *arti* means (9:19, 25). Used again by Jesus (verse 33) and Peter (verse 37). *But thou shalt understand hereafter* (*gnōsēi de meta tauta*). Future middle of *ginōskō* (instead of the verb *oida*) to know by experience. "Thou shalt learn after these things," even if slowly.

8. *Thou shalt never wash my feet* (*ou mē nipsēis mou tous podas eis ton aiōna*). Strong double negative *ou mē* with first aorist active subjunctive of *niptō* with *eis ton aiōna* (for ever) added and *mou* (my) made emphatic by position. Peter's sudden humility should settle the issue, he felt. *If I wash thee not* (*ean mē nipsō se*). Third-class condition with *ean mē* (negative). Jesus picks up the challenge of Peter whose act amounted to irreverence and want of confidence. "The first condition of discipleship is self-surrender" (Westcott). So "Jesus, waiting with the basin" (Dods), concludes. *Thou hast no part with me* (*ouk echeis meros met' emou*). Not simply here at the supper with its fellowship, but in the deeper sense of mystic fellowship as Peter was quick to see. Jesus does not make foot-washing essential to spiritual fellowship, but simply tests Peter's real pride and mock-humility by this symbol of fellowship.

9. *Not my feet only, but also my hands and my head* (*mē tous podas mou monon alla kai tas cheiras kai tēn kephalēn*). Nouns in the accusative case object of *nipson* understood. Peter's characteristic impulsiveness that does not really understand the Master's act. "A moment ago he told his Master He was doing too much: now he tells Him He is doing too little" (Dods).

10. *He that is bathed* (*ho leloumenos*). Perfect passive articular participle of *louō*, to bathe the whole body (Acts 9:37). *Save to wash his feet* (*ei mē tous podas nipsasthai*).

Aleph and some old Latin MSS. have only *nipsasthai*, but the other words are genuine and are really involved by the use of *nipsasthai* (first aorist middle infinitive of *niptō*, to wash parts of the body) instead of *lousasthai*, to bathe the whole body (just used before). The guest was supposed to bathe (*louō*) before coming to a feast and so only the feet had to be washed (*niptō*) on removing the sandals. *Clean* (*katharos*). Because of the bath. For *katharos* meaning external cleanliness see Matt. 23:26; 27:59; but in John 15:3 it is used for spiritual purity as here in "ye are clean" (*katharoi*). *Every whit* (*holos*). All of the body because of the bath. For this same predicate use of *holos* see 9:34. *But not all* (*all' ouchi pantes*). Strongly put exception (*ouchi*). Plain hint of the treachery of Judas who is reclining at the table after having made the bargain with the Sanhedrin (Mark 14:11). A year ago Jesus knew that Judas was a devil and said to the apostles: "One of you is a devil" (6:64, 70). But it did not hurt them then nor did they suspect each other then or now. It is far-fetched to make Jesus here refer to the cleansing power of his blood or to baptism as some do.

11. *For he knew him that should betray him* (*eidei gar ton paradidonta auton*). Past perfect *eidei* used as imperfect. Jesus had known for a year at least (6:64, 70) and yet he treated Judas with his usual courtesy. The articular present participle of *paradidōmi*, "the betraying one," for Judas was already engaged in the process. Did Judas wince at this thrust from Jesus?

12. *Sat down again* (*anepesen palin*). Second aorist active indicative of *anapiptō*, old compound verb to fall back, to lie down, to recline. *Palin* (again) can be taken either with *anepesen*, as here, or with *eipen* (he said again). *Know ye what I have done to you?* (*ginōskete ti pepoiēka humin;*). "Do ye understand the meaning of my act?" Perfect active indicative of *poieō* with dative case (*humin*). It was a searching question, particularly to Simon Peter and Judas.

13. *Ye* (*humeis*). Emphatic. *Call me* (*phōneite me*). "Address me." *Phōneō* regular for addressing one with his title (1:48). *Master* (*Ho didaskalos*). Nominative form (not in apposition with *me* accusative after *phōneite*), but really vocative in address with the article (called titular nominative sometimes) like *Ho Kurios kai ho theos mou* in 20:28. "Teacher." See 11:28 for Martha's title for Jesus to Mary. *Lord* (*Ho Kurios*). Another and separate title. In 1:38 we have *Didaskale* (vocative form) for the Jewish *Rabbei* and in 9:36, 38 *Kurie* for the Jewish *Mari*. It is significant that Jesus approves (*kalōs*, well) the application of both titles to himself as he accepts from Thomas the terms *kurios* and *theos*. *For I am* (*eimi gar*). Jesus distinctly claims here to be both Teacher and Lord in the full sense, at the very moment when he has rendered this menial, but symbolic, service to them. Here is a hint for those who talk lightly about "the peril of worshipping Jesus!"

14. *If I then* (*ei oun egō*). Argumentative sense of *oun* (therefore). Condition of first class, assumed to be true, with first aorist active indicative of *niptō*, "If I, being what I am, washed your feet" (as I did). *Ye also ought* (*kai humeis opheilete*). The obligation rests on you *a fortiori*. Present active indicative of the old verb *opheilō*, to owe a debt (Matt. 18:30). The mutual obligation is to do this or any other needed service. The widows who washed the saints' feet in I Tim. 5:10 did it "as an incident of their hospitable ministrations" (Bernard). Up to 1731 the Lord High Almoner in England washed the feet of poor saints (*pedilavium*) on Thursday before Easter, a custom that arose in the fourth century, and one still practised by the Pope of Rome.

15. *An example* (*hupodeigma*). For the old *paradeigma* (not in N.T.), from *hupodeiknumi*, to show under the eyes as an illustration or warning (Matt. 3:7), common in the papyri for illustration, example, warning, here only in John, but in James 5:10; II Peter 2:6; Heb. 4:11; 8:5; 9:26. Peter

uses *tupoi* (I Peter 5:3) with this incident in mind. In Jude 7 *deigma* (without *hupo*) occurs in the sense of example. *That ye also should do* (*hina kai humeis poiēte*). Purpose clause with *hina* and the present active subjunctive of *poieō* (keep on doing). Doing what? Does Jesus here institute a new church ordinance as some good people today hold? If so, it is curious that there is no record of it in the N.T. Jesus has given the disciples an object lesson in humility to rebuke their jealousy, pride, and strife exhibited at this very meal. The lesson of the "example" applies to all the relations of believers with each other. It is one that is continually needed.

16. *Is not greater* (*ouk estin meizōn*). Comparative adjective of *megas* (greater) followed by the ablative case *kuriou* (contrast between slave, lord) and *tou pempsantos* [articular participle of *pempō*, to send, with contrast with apostle, "one sent" (*apostolos*) from *apostellō*]. Jesus here enforces the dignity of service. In Luke 22:27 Jesus argues this point a bit. In Luke 6:40 the contrast is between the pupil and the teacher, though some pupils consider themselves superior to the teacher. In Matt. 10:24 Jesus uses both forms of the saying (pupil and slave). He clearly repeated this *logion* often.

17. *If ye know* (*ei oidate*). Condition of first class assumed as true, *ei* and present (*oidate* used as present) active indicative. *If ye do* (*ean poiēte*). Third-class condition, *ean* and present active subjunctive, assumed as possible, "if ye keep on doing." Both conditions with the one conclusion coming in between, "happy are ye." Just knowing does not bring happiness nor just occasional doing.

18. *Not of you all* (*ou peri pantōn*). As in verse 11, he here refers to Judas whose treachery is no surprise to Jesus (6:64, 70). *Whom I have chosen* (*tinas exelexamēn*). Indirect question, unless *tinas* is here used as a relative like *hous*. The first aorist middle indicative of *eklegō* is the same form

used in 6-70. Jesus refers to the choice (Luke 6:13 *eklexa-menos*, this very word again) of the twelve from among the large group of disciples. *That the scripture might be fulfilled* (*all' hina hē graphē plērōthēi*). See the same clause in 17:12. Purpose clause with *hina* and first aorist passive subjunctive of *pleroō*. This treachery of Judas was according to the eternal counsels of God (12:4), but none the less Judas is responsible for his guilt. For a like elliptical clause see 9:3; 15:25. The quotation is from the Hebrew of Psa. 41:9. *He that eateth* (*ho trōgōn*). Present active participle of old verb to gnaw, to chew, to eat, in N.T. only in John (6:54, 56, 57, 58; 13:18) and Matt. 26:38. LXX has here *ho esthiōn*. *Lifted up his heel against me* (*epēren ep' eme tēn pternan autou*). First aorist active indicative of *epairō*. *Pterna*, old word for heel, only here in N.T. The metaphor is that of kicking with the heel or tripping with the heel like a wrestler. It was a gross breach of hospitality to eat bread with any one and then turn against him so. The Arabs hold to it yet.

19. *From henceforth* (*ap' arti*). "From now on," as in 14:7; Matt. 23:39; Rev. 14:13. *Before it come to pass* (*pro tou genesthai*). *Pro* with ablative of the articular second aorist middle infinitive *ginomai* (before the coming to pass). *When it is come to pass* (*hotan genētai*). Indefinite relative clause with *hotan* and the second aorist middle subjunctive of *ginomai*, "whenever it does come to pass." *That ye may believe* (*hina pisteuēte*). Purpose clause with *hina* and present active subjunctive of *pisteuō*, "that ye may keep on believing." Cf. Isa. 48:5. *That I am he* (*hoti egō eimi*). As Jesus has repeatedly claimed to be the Messiah (8:24, 58, etc.). Cf. also 14:29 (*pisteusēte* here); 16:4.

20. *Whomsoever I send* (*an tina pempsō*). More precisely, "If I send any one" (third-class condition, *an=ean* and *tina*, indefinite pronoun accusative case, object of *pempsō*, first aorist active subjunctive of *pempō*, to send). This use of *ei tis* or *ean tis* (if any one) is very much like the indefinite

relative *hostis* and *hos an* (or *ean*), but the idiom is different. In Mark 8:34f. we have both *ei tis thelei* and *hos ean* while in John 14:13f. we find *hoti an* and *ean ti* (Robertson, *Grammar*, p. 956).

21. *He was troubled in the spirit* (*etarachthē tōi pneumati*). First aorist passive indicative of *tarassō* and the locative case of *pneuma*. See already 11:33 and 12:27 for this use of *tarassō* for the agitation of Christ's spirit. In 14:1, 27 it is used of the disciples. Jesus was one with God (5:19) and yet he had our real humanity (1:14). *Testified* (*emarturēsen*). First aorist active indicative of *martureō*, definite witness as in 4:44; 18:37. *One of you shall betray me* (*heis ex humōn paradōsei me*). Future active of *paradidōmi*, to betray, the word so often used of Judas. This very language occurs in Mark 14:18 and Matt. 26:21 and the idea in Luke 22:21. Jesus had said a year ago that "one of you is a devil" (John 6:70), but it made no such stir then. Now it was a bolt from the blue sky as Jesus swept his eyes around and looked at the disciples.

22. *Looked one on another* (*eblepon eis allēlous*). Inchoative imperfect of *blepō*, "began to glance at one another in bewilderment (doubting, *aporoumenoi*, present passive participle of *aporeō*, to be at a loss, to lose one's way, *a* privative and *poros*, way). They recalled their strife about precedence and Judas betrayed nothing. *Concerning whom he spake* (*peri tinos legei*). Indirect question retaining present active indicative *legei*. See same note in Mark 14:19=Matt. 26:22=Luke 22:23.

23. *Was at the table reclining in Jesus' bosom* (*ēn anakeimenos en tōi kolpōi tou Iēsou*). No word for "table" in the text. Periphrastic imperfect of *anakeimai*, to lie back, to recline. *Kolpos* usual word for bosom (1:18). *Whom Jesus loved* (*hon ēgapa Iēsous*). Imperfect active of *agapaō*, John's description of himself of which he was proud (19:26; 20:2; 21:7, 20), identified in 21:24 as the author of the book and

necessarily one of the twelve because of the "explicit" (Bernard) language of Mark (14:17=Luke 22:14). John son of Zebedee and brother of James. At the table John was on the right of Jesus lying obliquely so that his head lay on the bosom of Jesus. The centre, the place of honour, Jesus occupied. The next place in rank was to the left of Jesus, held by Peter (Westcott) or by Judas (Bernard) which one doubts.

24. *Beckoneth* (*neuei*). Old verb to nod, in N.T. only here and Acts 24:10. They were all looking in surprise at each other. *Tell us who it is of whom he speaketh* (*eipe tis estin peri hou legei*). Second aorist active imperative with indirect question (*tis*) and relative clause (*peri hou*). Peter was cautious, but could not contain his curiosity. John in front of Jesus was in a favourable position to have a whispered word with him. *Breast* (*stēthos*). As in 21:20; Luke 18:13 in place of *kolpon* (verse 23). This is the moment represented in Leonardo da Vinci's "Last Supper," only he shows the figures like the monks for whom he painted it.

25. *He* (*ekeinos*). "That one" (John). *Leaning back* (*anapesōn*). Second aorist active participle of *anapiptō*, to fall back. *As he was* (*houtōs*). "Thus." It was easily done.

26. *He* (*ekeinos*). Emphatic pronoun again. *For whom I shall dip the sop* (*hōi egō bapsō to psōmion*). Dative case of the relative (*hōi*) and future active of *baptō*, to dip (Luke 16:24). *Psōmion* is a diminutive of *psōmos*, a morsel, a common *Koiné* word (in the papyri often), in N.T. only in this passage. It was and is in the orient a token of intimacy to allow a guest to dip his bread in the common dish (cf. Ruth 2:14). So Mark 14:20. Even Judas had asked: "Is it I?" (Mark 14:19=Matt. 26:22). *Giveth it to Judas* (*didōsin Ioudāi*). Unobserved by the others in spite of Christ's express language, because "it was so usual a courtesy" (Bernard), "the last appeal to Judas' better feeling" (Dods). Judas now knew that Jesus knew his plot.

27. *Then entered Satan into him* (*tote eiselthen eis ekeinon ho Satanas*). The only time the word Satan occurs in the Gospel. As he had done before (13:2; Luke 22:3) until Christ considered him a devil (6:70). This is the natural outcome of one who plays with the devil. *That thou doest, do quickly* (*Ho poieis poieson tacheion*). Aorist active imperative of *poieo*. "Do more quickly what thou art doing." *Tacheion* is comparative of *tacheos* (John 11:31) and in N.T. only here, 20:4; Heb. 13:19, 23. See the eagerness of Jesus for the passion in Luke 12:50.

28. *No one knew* (*oudeis egno*). Second aorist active indicative of *ginosko*. The disciples had not yet perceived the treacherous heart of Judas.

29. *Some thought* (*tines edokoun*). Imperfect active of *dokeo*. Mere inference in their ignorance. *The bag* (*to glossokomon*). See on 12:6 for this word. *What things we have need of* (*hon chreian echomen*). Antecedent (*tauta*) of the relative (*hon*) not expressed. *For the feast* (*eis ten heorten*). The feast of unleavened bread beginning after the passover meal and lasting eight days. If this was twenty-four hours ahead of the passover meal, there was no hurry for next day would be in ample time. *Or that he should give something to the poor* (*e tois ptochois hina ti doi*). Another alternative in their speculation on the point. Note prolepsis of *tois ptochois* (dative case) before *hina doi* (final clause with *hina* and second aorist active subjunctive of *didomi*).

30. *Having received the sop* (*labon to psomion*). Second aorist active participle of *lambano*. Judas knew what Jesus meant, however ignorant the disciples. So he acted "straightway" (*euthus*). *And it was night* (*en de nux*). Darkness falls suddenly in the orient. Out into the terror and the mystery of this dreadful night (symbol of his devilish work) Judas went.

31. *Now* (*nun*). Now at last, the crisis has come with a sense of deliverance from the presence of Judas and of

surrender to the Father's will (Westcott). *Is glorified*
(*edoxasthē*). First aorist passive of *doxazō*, consummation of
glory in death both for the Son and the Father. For this
verb in this sense see already 7:39; 12:16 and later 17:3.
Four times here in verses 31f.

32. *In himself* (*en hautōi*). Reflexive pronoun. God is the
source of the glory (17:5) and is the glory succeeding the
Cross (the glory with the Father in heaven). *And straightway*
(*kai euthus*). No postponement now. First and quickly the
Cross, then the Ascension.

33. *Little children* (*teknia*). Diminutive of *tekna* and affectionate address as Jesus turns to the effect of his going on
these disciples. Only here in this Gospel, but common in
I John (2:1, etc.), and nowhere else in N.T. *Yet a little while*
(*eti mikron*). Accusative of extent of time. See also 7:33;
8:21 (to which Jesus here refers); 16:16–19. *So now I say
unto you* (*kai humin legō arti*). This juncture point (*arti*) of
time relatively to the past and the future (9:25; 16;12, 31).

34. *New* (*kainēn*). First, in contrast with the old (*archaios,
palaios*), the very adjective used in I John 2:7) of the "commandment" (*entolēn*) at once called old (*palaia*). They had
had it a long time, but the practice of it was new. Jesus
does not hesitate, like the Father, to give commandments
(15:10, 12). *That ye love one another* (*hina agapāte allēlous*).
Non-final use of *hina* with present active subjunctive of
agapaō, the object clause being in the accusative case in
apposition with *entolēn*. Note the present tense (linear
action), "keep on loving." *Even as* (*kathōs*). The measure of
our love for another is set by Christ's love for us.

35. *By this* (*en toutōi*). Locative case with *en*, "In this
way," viz., "if ye have love" (*ean agapēn echēte*), condition
of third class (in apposition with *en toutōi*) with *ean* and
present active subjunctive of *echō* ("keep on having love").
See 17:23 where Jesus prays for mutual love among the
disciples "that the world may know" that the Father sent

him. Jerome (*ad Galat*. vi. 10) says that in his extreme old age John repeated often this command of Jesus and justified it: "Because it is the Lord's commandment; and if it be fulfilled it is enough." See also 14:31. Tertullian (*Apol*. 39) urges it also as proof of being disciples. Hatred of one another *per contra*, is an argument that we are *not* disciples (learners) of Jesus.

36. *Whither goest thou?* (*pou hupageis;*). Peter is puzzled just as the Pharisees were twice (7:35; 8:21f.).

37. "*Why can I not follow thee even now?*" (*dia ti ou dunamai soi akolouthein arti;*). The use of *arti* (right now, this minute) instead of *nun* (at this time, verse 36) illustrates the impatience of Peter. *I will lay down my life for thee* (*tēn psuchēn mou huper sou thēsō*). Future active indicative of *tithēmi*. Peter, like the rest, had not yet grasped the idea of the death of Christ, but, like Thomas (11:16), he is not afraid of danger. He had heard Christ's words about the good shepherd (10:11) and knew that such loyalty was the mark of a good disciple.

38. *Wilt thou lay down?* (*thēseis;*). Jesus picks up Peter's very words and challenges his boasted loyalty. See such repetition in 16:16f., 31; 21:17. *Shall not crow* (*phōnēsēi*). Aorist active subjunctive of *phōneō*, to use the voice, used of animals and men. Note strong double negative *ou mē*. Mark adds *dis* (twice). John's report is almost identical with that in Luke 22:34. The other disciples joined in Peter's boast (Mark 14:31 = Matt. 26:35). *Till thou hast denied* (*heōs hou arnēsēi*). Future middle indicative or aorist middle subjunctive second person singular (form identical) with compound conjunction *heōs hou* (until which time), "till thou deny or deniest" (*futurum exactum* needless). Peter is silenced for the present. They all "sat astounded and perplexed" (Dods).

CHAPTER XIV

1. *Let not your heart be troubled* (*mē tarassesthō humōn hē kardia*). Not here the physical organ of life (Luke 21:34), but the seat of spiritual life (*pneuma, psuchē*), the centre of feeling and faith (Rom. 10:10), "the focus of the religious life" (Vincent) as in Matt. 22:37. See these words repeated in 14:27. Jesus knew what it was to have a "troubled" heart (11:33; 13:31) where *tarassō* is used of him. Plainly the hearts of the disciples were tossed like waves in the wind by the words of Jesus in 13:38. *Ye believe . . . believe also* (*pisteuete . . . kai pisteuete*). So translated as present active indicative plural second person and present active imperative of *pisteuō*. The form is the same. Both may be indicative (ye believe . . . and ye believe), both may be imperative (believe . . . and believe or believe also), the first may be indicative (ye believe) and the second imperative (believe also), the first may be imperative (keep on believing) and the second indicative (and ye do believe, this less likely). Probably both are imperatives (Mark 11:22), "keep on believing in God and in me."

2. *Mansions* (*monai*). Old word from *menō*, to abide, abiding places, in N.T. only here and verse 23. There are many resting-places in the Father's house (*oikia*). Christ's picture of heaven here is the most precious one that we possess. It is our heavenly home with the Father and with Jesus. *If it were not so* (*ei de mē*). Ellipsis of the verb (Mark 2:21; Rev. 2:5, 16; John 14:11). Here a suppressed condition of the second class (determined as unfulfilled) as the conclusion shows. *I would have told you* (*eipon an humin*). Regular construction for this apodosis (*an* and aorist — second active — indicative). *For I go* (*hoti poreuomai*).

248

Reason for the consolation given, futuristic present middle indicative, and explanation of his words in 13:33 that puzzled Peter so (13:36f.). *To prepare a place for you* (*hetoimasai topon humin*). First aorist active infinitive of purpose of *hetoimazō*, to make ready, old verb from *hetoimos*. Here only in John, but in Mark 10:40 (=Matt. 20:23). It was customary to send one forward for such a purpose (Numb. 10:33). So Jesus had sent Peter and John to make ready (this very verb) for the passover meal (Mark 14:12 =Matt. 26:17). Jesus is thus our Forerunner (*prodromos*) in heaven (Heb. 6:20).

3. *If I go* (*ean poreuthō*). Third-class condition (*ean* and first aorist passive subjunctive of *poreuomai*). *And prepare* (*kai hetoimasō*). Same condition and first aorist active subjunctive of the same verb *hetoimazō*. *I come again* (*palin erchomai*). Futuristic present middle, definite promise of the second coming of Christ. *And will receive you unto myself* (*kai paralēmpsomai humas pros emauton*). Future middle of *paralambanō*. Literally, "And I shall take you along (*para-*) to my own home" (cf. 13:36). This blessed promise is fulfilled in death for all believers who die before the Second Coming. Jesus comes for us then also. *That where I am there ye may be also* (*hina hopou eimi egō kai humeis ēte*). Purpose clause with *hina* and present active subjunctive of *eimi*. This the purpose of the departure and the return of Christ. And this is heaven for the believer to be where Jesus is and with him forever.

4. *Ye know the way* (*oidate tēn hodon*). Definite allusion to the puzzle of Peter in 13:36f. The path to the Father's house is now plain.

5. *Whither* (*pou*) — *how* (*pōs*). It is Thomas, not Peter (13:36f.) who renews the doubt about the destination of Jesus including the path or way thither (*tēn hodon*). Thomas is the spokesman for the materialistic conception then and now.

6. *I am the way, and the truth, and the life* (*Egō eimi hē
hodos kai hē alētheia kai hē zōē*). Either of these statements is
profound enough to stagger any one, but here all three
together overwhelm Thomas. Jesus had called himself "the
life" to Martha (11:25) and "the door" to the Pharisees
(10:7) and "the light of the world" (8:12). He spoke "the
way of God in truth" (Mark 12:14). He is the way to God
and the only way (verse 6), the personification of truth, the
centre of life. *Except by me* (*ei mē di' emou*). There is no
use for the Christian to wince at these words of Jesus. If
he is really the Incarnate Son of God (1:1, 14, 18, they are
necessarily true.

7. *If ye had known me* (*ei egnōkeite me*). Past perfect indicative of *ginōskō*, to know by personal experience, in condition of second class as is made plain by the conclusion (*an
ēidete*) where *oida*, not *ginōskō* is used. Thomas and the rest
had not really come to know Jesus, much as they loved him.
From henceforth ye know him (*ap' arti ginōskete auton*).
Probably inchoative present active indicative, "ye are beginning to know the Father from now on." *And have seen
him* (*kai heōrakate*). Perfect active indicative of *horaō*.
Because they had seen Jesus who is the Son of God, the
Image of God, and like God (1:18). Hence God is like Jesus
Christ. It is a bold and daring claim to deity. The only
intelligible conception of God is precisely what Jesus here
says. God is like Christ.

8. *Show us* (*deixon hēmin*). Philip now speaks up, possibly
hoping for a theophany (Ex. 33:18f.), certainly not grasping
the idea of Jesus just expressed.

9. *So long time* (*tosouton chronon*). Accusative of extent
of time. *And dost thou not know me?* (*kai ouk egnōkas me;*).
Perfect active indicative of *ginōskō*. Jesus patiently repeats
his language to Philip with the crisp statement: "he that
hath seen me hath seen the Father" (*ho heōrakōs eme eōraken
ton patera*). Perfect active participle and perfect active

indicative of *horaō*, state of completion. *Thou (su)*. Emphatic — After these years together.

10. *Believest thou not? (ou pisteueis;)*. Jesus had a right to expect greater faith from these men than from the blind man (9:35) or Martha (11:27). His words in 14:1 are clearly needed. This oneness with the Father Jesus had already stated (10:38) as shown by his "words" (*rēmata*) and his "works" (*erga*). Cf. 3:34; 5:19; 6:62.

11. *Believe me (pisteuete moi)*. Repeated appeal (present active imperative of *pisteuō*) as in 14:1 to his disciples and as he had done with the hostile Jews to be influenced by his "works" at any rate (10:38).

12. *Shall he do also (kåkeinos poiēsei)*. Emphatic pronoun *ekeinos*, "that one also." *Greater works than these (meizona toutōn)*. Comparative adjective neuter plural from *megas* with ablative case *toutōn*. Not necessarily greater miracles and not greater spiritual works in quality, but greater in quantity. Cf. Peter at Pentecost and Paul's mission tours. "Because I go" (*hoti egō poreuomai*). Reason for this expansion made possible by the Holy Spirit as Paraclete (16:7).

13. *Whatsoever ye shall ask (hoti an aitēsēte)*. Indefinite relative clause with *hoti* (neuter accusative singular of *hostis*), *an* and the aorist active subjunctive of *aiteō*. This is an advance thought over verse 12. *In my name (en tōi onomati mou)*. First mention of his "name" ·as the open sesame to the Father's will. See also 14:26; 15:16; 16:23, 24, 26. *That will I do (touto poiēsō)*. The Father answers prayers (15:16; 16:23), but so does the Son (here and verse 14). The purpose (*hina* clause with first aorist passive subjunctive of *doxazō*) is "that the Father may be glorified in the Son." Plead Christ's name in prayer to the Father.

14. *If ye shall ask me anything in my name .(ean ti aitēsēte me en tōi onomati mou)*. Condition of third class with *ean* and first aorist active subjunctive of *aiteō*. The use of *me*

(me) here is supported by Aleph B 33 Vulgate Syriac Peshitta. Just this phrase does not occur elsewhere in John and seems awkward, but see 16:23. If it is genuine, as seems likely, here is direct prayer to Jesus taught as we see it practiced by Stephen in Acts 7:59 and in Rev. 22:20.

15. *If ye love me* (*ean agapāte me*). Third-class condition "if ye keep on loving (present active subjunctive, same contract form as indicative) me." Cf. verse 23. *Ye will keep* (*tērēsete*). Future active of *tēreō*, not aorist imperative *tērēsate* (keep) as some MSS. have. For this phrase see also 8:51; 14:23, 24, 14:20; I John 2:5. Continued love prevents disobedience.

16. *And I will pray the Father* (*kágō erōtēsō ton patera*). *Erōtaō* for prayer, not question (the old use), also in 16:23 (prayer to Jesus in same sense as *aiteō*), 26 (by Jesus as here); 17:9 (by Jesus), "make request of." *Another Comforter* (*allon paraklēton*). Another of like kind (*allon*, not *heteron*), besides Jesus who becomes our Paraclete, Helper, Advocate, with the Father (I John 2:1, cf. Rom. 8:26f.). This old word (Demosthenes), from *parakaleō*, was used for legal assistant, pleader, advocate, one who pleads another's cause (Josephus, Philo, in illiterate papyrus), in N.T. only in John's writings, though the idea of it is in Rom. 8:26–34. Cf. Deissmann, *Light, etc.*, p. 336. So the Christian has Christ as his Paraclete with the Father, the Holy Spirit as the Father's Paraclete with us (John 14:16, 26; 15:26; 16:7; I John 2:1). *For ever* (*eis ton aiōna*). This the purpose (*hina*) in view and thus Jesus is to be with his people here forever (Matt. 28:20). See 4:14 for the idiom.

17. *The Spirit of truth* (*to pneuma tēs alētheias*). Same phrase in 15:27 and 16:13; I John 4:6, "a most exquisite title" (Bengel). The Holy Spirit is marked by it (genitive case), gives it, defends it (cf. 1:17), in contrast to the spirit of error (I John 4:6). *Whom* (*ho*). Grammatical neuter gender (*ho*) agreeing with *pneuma* (grammatical), but rightly rendered in English by "whom" and note masculine *ekeinos*

(verse 26). He is a person, not a mere influence. *Cannot receive* (*ou dunatai labein*). Left to itself the sinful world is helpless (I Cor. 2:14; Rom. 8:7f.), almost Paul's very language on this point. The world lacks spiritual insight (*ou theōrei*) and spiritual knowledge (*oude ginōskei*). It failed to recognize Jesus (1:10) and likewise the Holy Spirit. *Ye know him* (*humeis ginōskete auto*). Emphatic position of *humeis* (ye) in contrast with the world (15:19), because they have seen Jesus the Revealer of the Father (verse 9). *Abides* (*menei*). Timeless present tense. *With you* (*par' humin*). "By your side," "at home with you," not merely "with you" (*meth' humōn*) "in the midst of you." *In you* (*en humin*). In your hearts. So note *meta* (16), *para*, *en*.

18. *I will not leave* (*ouk aphēsō*). Future active of *aphiēmi*, to send away, to leave behind. *Desolate* (*orphanous*). Old word (*orphos*, Latin *orbus*), bereft of parents, and of parents bereft of children. Common in papyri of orphan children. In 13:33 Jesus called the disciples *teknia* (little children), and so naturally the word means "orphans" here, but the meaning may be "helpless" (without the other Paraclete, the Holy Spirit). The only other N.T. example is in James 1:27 where it means "fatherless." *I come* (*erchomai*). Futuristic present as in verse 3.

19. *But ye behold me* (*humeis de theōreite me*). Emphatic position of *humeis* (ye) in contrast to the blind, unseeing world. Cf. 13:33 and 16:10, 16. *Because I live, ye shall live also* (*hoti egō zō kai humeis zēsete*). This is our blessed guarantee of immortal, eternal life, the continued living of Jesus. He is the surety of a better covenant (Heb. 7:22), the Risen Christ Jesus. He had said it before (6:57).

20. *In that day* (*en ekeinēi tēi hēmerāi*). The New Dispensation of the Holy Spirit, beginning with Christ's Resurrection and the Coming of the Holy Spirit at pentecost. *Shall know* (*gnōsesthe*). Future middle of *ginōskō*. Chapters 1 to 3 of Acts bear eloquent witness to these words.

21. *He it is that loveth me (ekeinos estin ho agapōn me).* Emphatic demonstrative pronoun *ekeinos:* "that is the one who loves me." *And will manifest myself unto him (kai emphanisō autōi emauton).* Future active of *emphanizō*, old verb from *emphanēs* (Acts 10:40; Rom. 10:20). The Unseen and Risen Christ will be a real and spiritual Presence to the obedient and loving believer.

22. *Not Iscariot (ouch ho Iskariōtēs).* Judas Iscariot had gone (13:30), but John is anxious to make it clear that this Judas (common name, two apostles also named James) was not the infamous traitor. He is also called Thaddaeus or Lebbaeus (Mark 3:17 = Matt. 10:3) and the brother (or son) of James (6:15; Acts 1:13). This is the fourth interruption of the talk of Jesus (by Peter, 13:36; by Thomas, 14:5; by Philip, 14:8; by Judas, 14:22). *And not to the world (kai ouchi tōi kosmōi).* Judas caught at the word *emphanizō* in verse 21 as perhaps a Messianic theophany visible to all the world as at the judgment (5:27f.). He seems to suspect a change of plan on the part of Jesus *(ti gegonen hoti =* how has it happened that).

23. *If a man love me (ean tis agapāi me).* Condition of third class with *ean* and present active subjunctive, "if one keep on loving me." That is key to the spiritual manifestation *(emphanizō). We will come (eleusometha).* Future middle of *erchomai* and first person plural (the Father and I), not at the judgment, but here and now. *And make our abode with him (kai monēn par' autōi poiēsometha).* See verse 2 for the word *monē* (dwelling, abiding place). If the Holy Spirit "abides" *(menei,* verse 17) in you, that heart becomes a temple *(naos)* of the Holy Spirit (I Cor. 3:16f.), and so a fit dwelling place for the Father and the Son, a glorious and uplifting reality.

24. *He that loveth me not (ho mē agapōn me).* Present active articular participle of *agapaō* with negative *mē*, "the one who keeps on not loving me." *Is not mine, but the Father's*

(*ouk estin emos, alla tou patros*). Predicative possessive pronoun *emos* and the predicate genitive of possession *patros*.

25. *Have I spoken* (*lelalēka*). Perfect active indicative of *laleō*, for permanent keeping (*tēreō* verse 23). *While yet abiding with you* (*par' humin menōn*). Present active participle, no "yet" (*eti*) in the Greek, "while remaining beside (*par'*) you" before departing for the coming of the other Paraclete.

26. *Whom* (*ho*). Grammatical neuter, but "whom" is correct translation. The Father will send the Holy Spirit (14:16; Luke 24:49; Acts 2:33), but so will the Son (John 15:26; 16:7) as Jesus breathes the Holy Spirit upon the disciples (20:22). There is no contradiction in this relation of the Persons in the Trinity (the Procession of the Holy Spirit). Here the Holy Spirit (full title as in Mark 3:29; Matt. 12:32; Luke 12:10) is identified with the Paraclete. *He* (*ekeinos*). Emphatic demonstrative pronoun and masculine like *paraklētos*. *Shall teach you all things* (*humas didaxei panta*). The Holy Spirit knows "the deep things of God" (I Cor. 2:10) and he is our Teacher in the Dispensation of the Holy Spirit of both new truth (verse 25) and old. *Bring to your remembrance* (*hupomnēsei humas*). Future active indicative of *hupomimnēskō*, old verb to remind, to recall, here only in this Gospel (cf. III John 10; II Tim. 2:14) and with two accusatives (person and thing). After pentecost the disciples will be able better to recall and to understand what Jesus had said (how dull they had been at times) and to be open to new revelations from God (cf. Peter at Joppa and Caesarea).

27. *My peace* (*eirēnēn tēn emēn*). This is Christ's bequest to the disciples before he goes, the *shalom* of the orient for greeting and parting, used by Jesus in his appearances after the resurrection (20:19, 21, 26) as in II John 3 and III John 14, but here and in 16:33 in the sense of spiritual peace such as only Christ can give and which his Incarnation offers to

men (Luke 2:14). *Neither let it be fearful (medē deiliatō).*
Added to the prohibition in verse 1, only N.T. example of
deiliaō (rare word in Aristotle, in a papyrus of one condemned
to death), common in LXX, like palpitating of the heart
(from *deilos*).

28. *I go away, and I come (hupagō kai erchomai)*, both
futuristic presents (7:33; 14:3, 18). *If ye loved me (ei ēgapāte
me).* Second-class condition with the imperfect active of
agapaō referring to present time, implying that the disciples
are not loving Jesus as they should. *Ye would have rejoiced
(echarēte an).* Second aorist passive indicative of *chairō* with
an, conclusion of second-class condition referring to past
time, "Ye would already have rejoiced before this" at
Christ's going to the Father (verse 12). *Greater than I
(meizōn mou).* Ablative case *mou* after the comparative
meizōn (from positive *megas*). The filial relation makes this
necessary. Not a distinction in nature or essence (cf. 10:30),
but in rank in the Trinity. No Arianism or Unitarianism
here. The very explanation here is proof of the deity of the
Son (Dods).

30. *The prince of the world (ho tou kosmou archōn).* Satan
as in 12:31 which see.

31. *But that the world may know (all' hina gnōi ho kosmos).*
Purpose clause with *hina* and the second aorist active subjunctive of *ginōskō*. Elliptical construction (cf. 9:3; 13:18;
15:25). "But I surrendered myself to death," etc., before
hina. *Arise, let us go hence (egeiresthe, agōmen enteuthen).*
Imperative present middle of *egeirō* and the volitive (horta-
tory) subjunctive *agōmen* (the word used in 11:7, 16) of going
to meet death. Apparently the group arose and walked out
into the night and the rest of the talk (chs. 15 and 16) and
prayer (ch. 17) was in the shadows on the way to Gethsemane.

CHAPTER XV

1. *The true vine (hē ampelos hē alēthinē)*. "The vine the
genuine." Assuming that the Lord's Supper had just been
instituted by Jesus the metaphor of the vine is naturally suggested by "the fruit of the vine" (Mark 14:25; Matt. 26:29).
Ampelos in the papyri (Moulton and Milligan's *Vocabulary*)
is sometimes used in the sense of *ampelōn* (vineyard), but not
so here. Jesus uses various metaphors to illustrate himself
and his work (the light, 8:12; the door, 10:7; the shepherd,
10:11; the vine, 15:1). The vine was common in Palestine.
See Psa. 80:8f. "On the Maccabean coinage Israel was represented by a vine" (Dods). Jesus is the genuine Messianic
vine. *The husbandman (ho geōrgos)* as in Mark 12:1; James
5:7; II Tim. 2:6. cf. I Cor. 3:9, *theou geōrgion* (God's field).

2. *Branch (klēma)*. Old word from *klaō*, to break, common
in LXX for offshoots of the vine, in N.T. only here (verses
2–6), elsewhere in N.T. *klados* (Mark 4:32, etc.), also from
klaō, both words meaning tender and easily broken parts.
In me (en emoi). Two kinds of connexion with Christ as the
vine (the merely cosmic which bears no fruit, the spiritual
and vital which bears fruit). The fruitless (not bearing
fruit, *mē pheron karpon*) the vine-dresser "takes away"
(*airei*) or prunes away. Probably (Bernard) Jesus here refers to Judas. Cleanseth (*kathairei*). Present active indicative of old verb *kathairō* (clean) as in verse 3, only use in
N.T., common in the inscriptions for ceremonial cleansing,
though *katharizō* is more frequent (Heb. 10:2). *That it may
bear more fruit (hina karpon pleiona pherēi)*. Purpose clause
with hina and present active subjunctive of *pherō*, "that it
may keep on bearing more fruit" (more and more). A good
test for modern Christians and church members.

3. *Already ye are clean* (*ēdē humeis katharoi este*).   Potentially cleansed (Westcott) as in 13:10 which see and 17:19.

4. *Abide in me* (*meinate en emoi*).   Constative aorist active imperative of *menō*. The only way to continue "clean" (pruned) and to bear fruit is to maintain vital spiritual connexion with Christ (the vine). Judas is gone and Satan will sift the rest of them like wheat (Luke 22:31f.). Blind complacency is a peril to the preacher. *Of itself* (*aph' heautou*). As source (from itself) and apart from the vine (cf. 17:17). *Except it abide* (*ean mē menēi*). Condition of third class with *ean*, negative *mē*, and present active (keep on abiding) subjunctive of *menō*. Same condition and tense in the application, "except ye abide in me."

5. *Ye the branches* (*humeis ta klēmata*). Jesus repeats and applies the metaphor of verse 1. *Apart from me* (*chōris emou*). See Eph. 2:12 for *chōris Christou*. There is nothing for a broken off branch to do but wither and die. For the cosmic relation of Christ see John 1:3 (*chōris autou*).

6. *He is cast forth* (*eblēthē exō*). Timeless or gnomic use of the first aorist passive indicative of *ballō* as the conclusion of a third-class condition (see also verses 4 and 7 for the same condition, only constative aorist subjunctive *meinēte* and *meinēi* in verse 7). The apostles are thus vividly warned against presumption. Jesus as the vine will fulfil his part of the relation as long as the branches keep in vital union with him. *As a branch* (*hōs to klēma*). *And is withered* (*exēranthē*). Another timeless first aorist passive indicative, this time of *xērainō*, same timeless use in James 1:11 of grass, old and common verb. *They gather* (*sunagousin*). Plural though subject not expressed, the servants of the vine-dresser gather up the broken off branches. *Are burned* (*kaietai*). Present passive singular of *kaiō*, to burn, because *klēmata* (branches) is neuter plural. See this vivid picture also in Matt. 13:41f., 49f.

7. *Ask whatsoever ye will* (*ho ean thelēte aitēsasthe*). Indefinite relative with *ean* and present active subjunctive of *thelō*, to wish, to will, and aorist middle imperative of *aiteō*, to ask. This astounding command and promise (*genēsetai*, future middle of *ginomai*, it will come to pass) is not without conditions and limitations. It involves such intimate union and harmony with Christ that nothing will be asked out of accord with the mind of Christ and so of the Father. Christ's name is mentioned in 15:16; cf. 14:13; 16:23.

8. *Herein* (*en toutōi*). That is in the vital union and the much fruit bearing. It points here backwards and forwards. *Is glorified* (*edoxasthē*). Another gnomic or timeless first aorist passive indicative. *Bear* (*pherete*). Present active subjunctive, "keep on bearing" much fruit. *And so shall ye be* (*kai genēsesthe*). Rather "become." Future middle indicative of *ginomai*, though B D L read *genēsthe* (after *hina* like *pherēte*). "Become" my disciples (learners) in the fullest sense of rich fruit-bearing according to the text in 8:31.

9. *Abide* (*meinate*). Constative first aorist active imperative of *menō*, summing up the whole. *In my love* (*en tēi agapēi tēi emēi*). Subjunctive possessive pronoun, "in the love that I have for you." Our love for Christ is the result of Christ's love for us and is grounded at bottom in the Father's love for the world (3:16). John has *emos* 37 times and always in the words of Jesus (Bernard). But he uses *mou* also (verse 10).

10. *Ye will abide* (*meneite*). Future tense of *menō*, conclusion of the third-class condition (*ean* and first aorist active subjunctive *tērēsēte*). The correlative of 14:15. Each involves the other (love and keeping the commandments of Jesus). *And abide* (*kai menō*). The high example of Jesus (the Son) in relation to the Father is set before us as the goal.

11. *That my joy may be in you* (*hina hē chara hē emē en humin ēi*). Purpose clause with *hina* and the present sub-

junctive *ēi* (some MSS. have *meinēi*, may remain), Christ's permanent absolute joy in the disciples. *And that your joy be fulfilled* (*Kai hē chara humōn plērōthēi*). Same construction with first aorist (effective) passive subjunctive of *plēroō*, consummation of the process preceding.

12. *That ye love one another* (*hina agapāte allēlous*). Nonfinal use of *hina*, introducing a subject clause in apposition with *entolē* (commandment) and the present active subjunctive of *agapaō*, "that ye keep on loving one another." See 13:34.

13. *Than this* (*tautēs*). Ablative case after the comparative adjective *meizona* and feminine agreeing with *tēs agapēs* (love) understood. *That a man lay down his life* (*hina tis tēn psuchēn autou thēi*). Object clause (non-final use of *hina* in apposition with the ablative pronoun *tautēs* and the second aorist active subjunctive of *tithēmi*. For the phrase see 10:11 of the good shepherd. Cf. I John 3:16; Rom. 5:7f. *For his friends* (*huper tōn philōn autou*). "In behalf of his friends" and so "in place of his friends." "Self-sacrifice is the high-water mark of love" (Dods). For this use of *huper* see John 11:50; Gal. 3:13; II Cor. 5:14f.; Rom. 5:7f.

14. *If ye do* (*ean poiēte*). Condition of third class with *ean* and the present active subjunctive, "if ye keep on doing," not just spasmodic obedience. Just a different way of saying what is in verse 10. Obedience to Christ's commands is a prerequisite to discipleship and fellowship (spiritual friendship with Christ). He repeats it in the Great Commission (Matt. 28:20, *eneteilamēn*, I commanded) with the very word used here (*entellomai*, I command).

15. *No longer* (*ouketi*). As he had done in 13:16. He was their Rabbi (1:38; 13:13) and Lord (13:13). Paul gloried in calling himself Christ's *doulos* (bond-slave). *Servants* (*doulous*). Bond-servants, slaves. *I have called you friends* (*humas eirēka philous*). Perfect active indicative, permanent state of new dignity. They will prove worthy of it by con-

tinued obedience to Christ as Lord, by being good *douloi*.
Abraham was called the Friend of God (James 2:23). Are
we friends of Christ?

16. *But I chose you* (*all' egō exelexamēn humas*). First
aorist middle indicative of *eklegō*. See this same verb and
tense used for the choice of the disciples by Christ (6:70;
13:18; 15:19). Jesus recognizes his own responsibility in the
choice after a night of prayer (Luke 6:13). So Paul was
"a vessel of choice" (*skeuos eklogēs*, Acts 9:15). Appointed
(*ethēka*). First aorist active indicative (*k* aorist) of *tithēmi*.
Note three present active subjunctives with *hina* (purpose
clause) to emphasize continuance (*hupagēte*, keep on going,
pherēte, keep on bearing fruit, *menēi*, keep on abiding), not
a mere spurt, but permanent growth and fruit-bearing. *He
may give* (*dōi*). Second aorist active subjunctive of *didōmi*
with *hina* (purpose clause). Cf. 14:13 for the same purpose
and promise, but with *poiēsō* (I shall do). See also 16:23f., 26.

17. *That ye may love one another* (*hina agapāte allēlous*).
Repetition of 13:34 and 15:12. This very night the disciples
had been guilty of jealousy and wrangling (Luke 22:24;
John 13:5, 15).

18. *If the world hateth you* (*ei ho kosmos humas misei*).
Condition of the first class. As it certainly does. *Ye know*
(*ginōskete*). Present active second person plural indicative
of *ginōskō* or present active imperative (know), same form.
Hath hated (*memisēken*). Perfect active indicative, "has
hated and still hates." *Before it hateth you* (*prōton humōn*).
Ablative case *humōn* after the superlative *prōton* as with
prōtos mou in 1:15.

19. *The world would love its own* (*ho kosmos an to idion
ephilei*). Conclusion of second-class condition (determined
as unfulfilled), regular idiom with *an* and imperfect indicative in present time. *But because ye are not of the world* (*hoti
de ek tou kosmou ouk este*). Definite and specific reason for
the world's hatred of real Christians whose very existence is

a reproach to the sinful world. Cf. 7:7; 17:14; I John 3:13. Does the world hate us? If not, why not? Has the world become more Christian or Christians more worldly?

20. *Remember* (*mnēmoneuete*). Present active imperative of *mnēmoneuō*, old verb from *mnēmōn*, in John again in 16:4, 21. See 13:16 for this word. *If they persecuted me* (*ei eme ediōxan*). Condition of first class. They certainly did persecute (first aorist active of *diōkō*, to chase like a wild beast like the Latin *persequor*, our "persecute") Jesus (5:16). They will persecute those like Jesus. Cf. 16:33; Mark 10:30; Luke 21:12; I Cor. 4:12; II Cor. 4:9; Gal. 4:29; II Tim. 3:12 for proof that this prophecy came true. But the alternative is true and is stated by Jesus with a like condition of the first class, "if they kept my word" (*ei ton logon mou etērēsan*). The world does praise the word of Jesus, but dreads to follow it.

21. *Unto you* (*eis humas*). Like the dative *humin* (Textus Receptus) as in the papyri and modern Greek (Robertson, *Grammar*, p. 594). *For my name's sake* (*dia to onoma mou*). See verse 20. See this same warning and language in Matt. 10:22; Mark 13:13 = Matt. 24:9 = Luke 21:17). There is little difference in meaning from *heneken mou* (Mark 13:9 = Luke 21:12). Loyalty to the name of Christ will bring persecution as they will soon know (Acts 5:41; Phil. 1:29; I Peter 4:14). About the world's ignorance of God see Luke 23:34; Acts 3:17; John 16:3.

22. *They had not had sin* (*hamartian ouk eichosan*). Conclusion of condition of second class without *an* because context makes it clear (*nun de*) without it (Robertson, *Grammar*, p. 1013). The imperfect active indicative with -*osan* instead of -*on* (also in verse 24) as common in the LXX, and occurs in the papyri and the inscriptions and the Boeotian dialect. *Excuse* (*prophasin*). Old word (I Thess. 2:5) either from *prophainō*, to show forth, or *prophēmi*, to speak forth. Mere pretence, in John only here and verse 24.

23. *My Father also* (*kai ton patera mou*). Because Christ reveals God (14:9) and to dishonour Christ is to dishonour God (5:23). The coming of Christ has revealed the weight of sin on those who reject him.

24. *They have both seen and hated* (*kai heōrakasin kai memisēkasin*). Perfect active indicative of *horaō* and *miseō*, permanent attitude and responsibility. The "world" and the ecclesiastics (Sanhedrin) had united in this attitude of hostility to Christ and in reality to God.

25. *But this cometh to pass* (*all'*). Ellipsis in the Greek (no verb), as in 9:3; 13:18. *In their law* (*en tōi nomōi autōn*). Cf. 8:17 and 10:34 for this standpoint. "Law" (*nomos*) here is for the whole of Scripture as in 12:34. The allusion is to Psa. 69:4 (or Psa. 35:19). The hatred of the Jews toward Jesus the promised Messiah (1:11) is "part of the mysterious purpose of God" (Bernard) as shown by *hina plērōthēi* (first aorist passive subjunctive of *pleroō*, to fulfil). *Without a cause* (*dōrean*). Adverbial accusative of *dōrea* from *didōmi*, gratuitously, then unnecessarily or *gratis* (in two *Koiné* tablets, Nägeli) as here and Gal. 2:21.

26. *When the Comforter is come* (*hotan elthēi ho paraklētos*). Indefinite temporal clause with *hotan* and the second aorist active subjunctive of *erchomai*, "whenever the Comforter comes." *Whom I will send unto you from the Father* (*hon egō pempsō humin para tou patros*). As in 16:7, but in 14:16, 26 the Father sends at the request of or in the name of Jesus. Cf. Luke 24:49; Acts 2:33. This is the Procession of the Holy Spirit from the Father and from the Son. *Which* (*ho*). Grammatical neuter to agree with *pneuma*, and should be rendered "who" like *ho* in 14:26. *Proceedeth from the Father* (*para tou patros ekporeuetai*). "From beside the Father" as in the preceding clause. *He* (*ekeinos*). Emphatic masculine pronoun, not neuter (*ekeino*) though following *ho*. *Shall bear witness of me* (*marturēsei peri emou*). Future active of *martureō*. This is the mission of the Paraclete (16:14) as it should be ours.

27. *And ye also bear witness* (*kai humeis de martureite*).
Present active indicative or imperative (do ye bear witness),
same form of *martureō*. "Ye also" as well as the Holy
Spirit, ye also when filled with and taught by the Holy Spirit
the things concerning Jesus. It is here that Christians fail
most. *Have been* (*este*). Progressive present of *eimi*, "are
with me from the beginning of my ministry as in 14:9. They
were chosen to be with Christ (Mark 3:14).

CHAPTER XVI

1. *That ye should not be made to stumble* (*hina mē skandalis-thēte*). Purpose clause with negative *mē* and first aorist passive of *skandalizō*, common verb in the Synoptics (Matt. 13:21) "the *skandala* of faith, the stumblingblocks which trip up a disciple" (Bernard), in John only 6:61 and here (cf. I John 2:10).

2. *They shall put you out of the synagogues* (*aposunagōgous poiēsousin humas*). "They will make you outcasts from the synagogues." Predicate accusative of the compound adjective *aposunagōgos* for which see 9:22 and 12:42. *Yea* (*all'*). Use of *alla* as co-ordinating conjunction, not adversative. *That* (*hina*) not in the sense of "when" (*hote*), but as in 12:23 for God's purpose (Luke 2:34, *hopōs*). *Shall think* (*doxēi*). First aorist active subjunctive of *dokeō*. "So blind will he be" (Bernard). *That he offereth service unto God* (*latreian prospherein tōi theōi*). Infinitive (present active) indirect discourse after *doxēi*. For the phrase see Heb. 6:1ff.; 8:3ff.; 9:7ff. The rabbis so felt when they crucified Jesus and when they persecuted the disciples (Acts 6:13; 7:57f.). No persecution is more bitter than when done by religious enthusiasts and bigots like the Spanish Inquisition.

3. *Because* (*hoti*). Definite reason for the religious hatred is ignorance of God and Christ as in 15:21.

4. *Have I spoken* (*lelalēka*). Perfect active indicative as in 15:11 and 16:1. Solemn repetition. *When their hour is come* (*hotan elthēi hē hōra autōn*). Indefinite temporal clause, *hotan* with the second aorist active subjunctive of *erchomai*, "whenever their hour comes." The time appointed for these things. *Now that* (*hoti*). Simply "that" (declarative conjunction in indirect discourse. Forewarned is to be fore-

armed. Cf. 13:19. *From the beginning* (*ex archēs*). As in 6:64 but practically like *ap' archēs* in 15:27. While Christ was with them, he was the object of attack (15:18).

5. *And none of you asketh me* (*kai oudeis ex humōn erōtāi me*). Adversative use of *kai* ="and yet" as in 1:10. Now that they realize that Jesus is going, the thoughts of the disciples turn on themselves and they cease asking the query of Peter (13:36).

6. *Sorrow hath filled* (*hē lupē peplērōken*). This word is not used of Jesus in the Gospels, in John only in this chapter. Perfect active indicative of *pleroō*. They do not see their way to go on without Jesus.

7. *It is expedient for you* (*sumpherei humin*). Present active indicative of *sumpherō*, old verb to bear together. See 11:50 where the phrase is used by Caiaphas "for us," here "for you" (*humin* ethical dative). *That I go away* (*hina egō apelthō*). Subject clause the subject of *sumpherei*, hina and second aorist active subjunctive of *aperchomai*. The reason (*gar*) for this startling statement follows. *If I go not away* (*ean mē apelthō*). Third-class condition with *ean* and the negative *mē* with *apelthō* as before. *Will not come* (*ou mē elthēi*). Strong double negative with second aorist active subjunctive of *erchomai*. The Holy Spirit was, of course, already at work in the hearts of men, but not in the sense of witnessing as Paraclete which could only take place after Jesus had gone back to the Father. *But if I go* (*ean de poreuthō*). Third-class condition again (*ean* and the first aorist passive subjunctive of *poreuomai*). *I will send* (*pempsō*). First person future as in 15.

8. *And he* (*kai ekeinos*). Emphatic demonstrative masculine pronoun. *When he is come* (*elthōn*). Second aorist active participle of *erchomai*, "having come" or "coming." *Will convict the world* (*elegxei ton kosmon*). Future active of *elegchō*, old word for confuting, convicting by proof already in 3:29; 8:46. Jesus had been doing this (7:7), but this is

pre-eminently the work of the Holy Spirit and the most
needed task today for our complacent age. *In respect of sin*
(*peri hamartias*). Concerning the reality of sin as missing
the mark and as wronging God and man, and not a mere slip
or animal instinct or devoid of moral responsibility or evil.
Some scientists and psychologists (Freudians and behaviour-
ists) seem bent on destroying man's sense of sin. Hence
crime waves even in youth. *And of righteousness* (*kai peri
dikaiosunēs*). The opposite of "sin" and to be yearned for
after conviction. Cf. Rom. 1:19–3:21 about the necessity of
the God-kind of righteousness and the Sermon on the Mount
for Christ's idea of righteousness. *And of judgment* (*kai peri
kriseōs*). As certain to come as condemnation because of sin
and the lack of righteousness. These are not played out
motives in human life, but basal. For this ministry we have
the help of the Paraclete. The Paraclete is here spoken of
"not as man's advocate with God (I John 2:1), but as
Christ's advocate with the world" (Bernard).

9. *Because they believe not on me* (*hoti ou pisteuousin eis
eme*). Without this conviction by the Paraclete such men
actually have a pride of intellectual superiority in refusing
to believe on Jesus.

10. *And ye behold me no more* (*kai ouketi theōreite me*).
With the bodily eyes and without the Holy Spirit they are
unable to behold Jesus with the spiritual vision (14:19).
Without Christ they lose the sense of righteousness as is seen
in the "new morals" (immorality, loose views of marriage,
etc.).

11. *Because the prince of this world hath been judged* (*hoti
ho archōn tou kosmou toutou kekritai*). Cf. 12:31; 14:31 for
the title. Perfect passive indicative of *krinō*. He stands
condemned. The sinful world is in his grip, but he will be
cast out (12:31).

12. *But ye cannot bear them now* (*all' ou dunasthe bastazein
arti*). The literal sense of *bastazō*, to bear, occurs in 12:6.

For the figurative as here see Acts 15:10. The untaught cannot get the full benefit of teaching (I Cor. 3:1; Heb. 5:11–14). The progressive nature of revelation is a necessity.

13. *Howbeit* (*de*). One of the most delicate and difficult particles to translate, varying from "and" to "but." *When he, the Spirit of truth, is come* (*hotan elthēi ekeinos, to pneuma tēs alētheias*). Indefinite relative clause (*hotan* and the second aorist active subjunctive of *erchomai*, no *futurum exactum*), "whenever he comes." Note *ekeinos* (masculine demonstrative pronoun, though followed by neuter *pneuma* in apposition. See 15:26 for this phrase about the Holy Spirit. *He shall guide you* (*hodēgēsei humas*). Future active of old verb *hodēgeō* (from *hodēgos*, from *hodos*, way, *hēgeomai*, to lead). See Psa. 24:5 for "lead me into thy truth" (*hodēgēson me eis tēn alētheian sou*). Christ is both the Way and the Truth (14:6) and the Holy Spirit is the Guide who shows the way to the Truth (verse 14). This he does gradually. We are still learning the truth in Christ. *From himself* (*aph' heautou*). In this he is like Christ (1:26; 12:49; 14:10). *He shall declare* (*anaggelei*). Future active of *anaggellō*, as in 4:25. See it also repeated in verse 14. *The things that are yet to come* (*ta erchomena*). Neuter plural articular participle of *erchomai*, "the coming things." This phrase only here in the N.T. The things already begun concerning the work of the Kingdom (Luke 7:19ff.; 18:30) not a chart of future history. See Luke 7:20; John 6:14; 11:27 for *ho erchomenos* (the coming one) used of the Messiah.

14. *He shall glorify me* (*ekeinos eme doxasei*). This is the glory of the Holy Spirit, to glorify Jesus Christ. *For he shall take of mine* (*hoti ek tou emou lēmpsetai*). Future middle of *lambanō* and a definite promise of the Spirit's guidance in interpreting Christ. One need only refer to Peter's sermon at pentecost after the coming of the Holy Spirit, to Peter's Epistles, to Paul's Epistles, to Hebrews, to John's Epistles,

to see how under the tutelage of the Holy Spirit the disciples grew into the fulness of the knowledge of God in the face of Christ (II Cor. 6:4).

15. *Therefore said I* (*dia touto eipon*). Jesus explains how and why the Holy Spirit can and will reveal to the disciples what they need to know further concerning him. They had failed so far to understand Christ's words about his death and resurrection. The Holy Spirit as Guide and Teacher will teach them what they can only receive and understand after the resurrection and ascension of Jesus.

16. *A little while* (*mikron*). The brief period now till Christ's death as in 7:33; 13:33; 14:19. *Again a little while* (*palin mikron*). The period between the death and the resurrection of Jesus (from Friday afternoon till Sunday morning). *Ye shall see me* (*opsesthe me*). Future middle of *optomai*, the verb used in 1:51 and 16:22 as here of spiritual realities (Bernard), though *theōreō* is so used in 20:14.

17. *Some of the disciples* (*ek tōn mathētōn autou*). Ellipsis of time (some) before *ek* as in 7:40. Jesus seemed to contradict himself, for the disciples took both verbs in the same sense and were still puzzled over the going to the Father of 14:3. But they talk to one another, not to Jesus.

18. *We know not what he saith* (*ouk oidamen ti lalei*). The questions to Jesus cease and the disciples frankly confess to each other their own ignorance.

19. *Jesus perceived* (*egnō Iēsous*). Second aorist active indicative of *ginōskō*. *That they were desirous to ask him* (*hoti ēthelon auton erōtāin*). Imperfect active tense of *thelō* in indirect discourse instead of the retention of the present *thelousin* (the usual idiom), just like our English. Their embarrassment was manifest after four inquiries already (Peter, Thomas, Philip, Judas). So Jesus takes the initiative.

20. *Ye shall weep and lament* (*klausete kai thrēnēsete*). Future active of *klaiō* and *thrēneō*, both old words (for

klaiō see John 11:31, for *thrēneō* see Matt. 11:17), both words used of the loud lamentations so common in the east. *Shall rejoice (charēsetai).* Second future passive of *chairō* in violent contrast. Picture the women on the way to the Cross (Luke 23:27, *ekoptonto kai ethrēnoun*, two descriptive imperfects) and Mary Magdalene by the tomb (John 20:11, *klaiousa*). *Ye shall be sorrowful (lupēthēsesthe).* First future passive of *lupeō*, word for inward grief. See the change from sorrow to joy in 20:14–16 when "they disbelieved for joy" (Luke 24:41). So violent was the reaction on the sudden appearance of Jesus.

21. *A woman (hē gunē).* "The woman," any woman. *When she is in travail (hotan tiktēi).* Indefinite temporal clause, "whenever she is about to bear (or give birth)," *hotan* and present active subjunctive of *tiktō*, common O.T. image for pain. *Her hour is come (ēlthen hē hōra autēs).* Second aorist active indicative, timeless aorist, "her hour" for giving birth which she knows is like a living death. *But when she is delivered of the child (hotan de gennēsēi to paidion).* Indefinite temporal clause with *hotan* and first aorist active subjunctive of *gennaō.* "But whenever she bears the child." *The anguish (tēs thlipseōs).* Genitive case after *mnēmoneuei* of *thlipsis*, usual word for tribulation (Matt. 13:21). *Is born (egennēthē).* First aorist (effective) passive indicative of *gennaō.*

22. *And ye therefore now (kai humeis oun nun).* See 8:38 for like emphasis on *ye (humeis).* The "sorrow" *(lupēn)* is like that of the mother in childbirth (real, but fleeting, with permanent joy following). The metaphor points, of course, to the resurrection of Jesus which did change the grief of the disciples to gladness, once they are convinced that Jesus has risen from the dead. *But I will see you again (palin de opsomai humas).* Future middle of *horaō*, to see. In verses 16 and 19 Jesus had said "ye shall see me" *(opsesthe me),* but here we have one more blessed promise, "I shall see

you," showing "that we are the objects of God's regard" (Westcott). *Shall rejoice* (*charēsetai*). Second future passive of *chairō*. *Taketh away* (*airei*). Present active indicative, futuristic present, but B D have *arei* the future active (shall take away). This joy is a permanent possession.

23. *Ye shall ask me nothing* (*eme ouk erōtēsete*). Either in the sense of question (original meaning of *erōtaō*) as in verses 19 and 30 since he will be gone or in the sense of request or favours (like *aiteō* in this verse) as in 14:16; Acts 3:2. In verse 26 both *aiteō* and *erōtaō* occur in this sense. Either view makes sense here. *If ye shall ask* (*an ti aitēsēte*). Third-class condition, *an* like *ean* with first aorist active subjunctive of *aiteō*. Note 14:26 for "in my name."

24. *Hitherto* (*heōs arti*). Up till now the disciples had not used Christ's name in prayer to the Father, but after the resurrection of Jesus they are to do so, a distinct plea for parity with the Father and for worship like the Father. *May be fulfilled* (*ēi peplērōmenē*). Periphrastic perfect passive subjunctive of *pleroō* in a purpose clause with *hina*. See 15:11 for some verb (first aorist passive subjunctive with *hina*) and I John 1:4 for same form as here, emphasizing the abiding permanence of the joy.

25. *In proverbs* (*en paroimiais*). See on 10:6 for this word. *Shall tell* (*apaggelō*). Future active of *apaggellō*, to report, correct text and not *anaggelō* (verses 13, 14, 15), as in I John 1:2f. *Plainly* (*parrēsiāi*). See on 7:13 for this word.

26. *I say not* (*ou legō*). "I speak not." Christ did pray for the disciples before his death (John 14:16; 17:9, 15, 24) and he prays also for sinners (Luke 23:34; I John 2:1). Here it is the special love of God for disciples of Jesus (John 14:21, 23; 17:23; I John 4:19). Note *aiteō* and *erōtaō* used in practically the same sense as in verse 23.

27. *Loveth* (*philei*). Present active indicative of *phileō*, the word for warm and friendly love, here used of God's love for the disciples, while in 3:16 *agapaō* occurs of God's

love for the world. *Ye have loved me (pephilēkate).* Perfect active indicative of *phileō*, "loved and still love me warmly." *And have believed (pepisteukate).* Perfect active indicative again. Recall the exhortation in 14:1.

28. *I came out from the Father (exēlthon ek tou patros).* Definite act (aorist), the Incarnation, with repetition of *ek* (out of), while in verse 27 we have *para tou patros exēlthon)* with no practical distinction between *ek* and *para* in resultant idea. *Am come (elēlutha).* Perfect active indicative of *erchomai*, as in 18:37. The Incarnation is now a permanent fact, once only a blessed hope (11:27). His leaving the world and going to the Father does not set aside the fact of the Incarnation. Both *aphiēmi* (I leave) and *poreuomai* (I go) are futuristic present indicatives.

29. *No proverb (paroimian oudemian).* No wayside saying, no dark saying. See 10:6; 16:25.

30. *Now know we (nun oidamen).* They had failed to understand the plain words of Jesus about going to the Father heretofore (16:5), but Jesus read their very thoughts (16:19f.) and this fact seemed to open their minds to grasp his idea. *Should ask (erōtāi).* Present active subjunctive with *hina* in original sense of asking a question. *By this (en toutōi).* In Christ's supernatural insight into their very hearts. *From God (apo theou).* Compare *para tou patros* (verse 27) and *ek tou patros* (verse 28), *apo, ek, para* all with the ablative of source or origin.

31. *Do ye now believe? (arti pisteuete;).* For *arti* (just now) see 9:19; 13:33, 37. Their belief in Christ was genuine *as far as it went,* but perils await them of which they are ignorant. They are too self-confident as their despair at Christ's death shows.

32. *Cometh (erchetai).* Futuristic present middle indicative of *erchomai*. *Yea, is come (kai elēluthen).* Explanatory use of *kai* and the perfect active indicative as in 12:23. The long-looked-for hour (*hōra*) is so close that it has virtually

begun. The time for the arrest of Jesus is near. See also 17:1. *That* (*hina*). See verse 2 for this same use of *hina* (not *hote*) with *erchomai hōra*. *Ye shall be scattered* (*skorpis-thēte*). First aorist passive subjunctive of *skorpizō*, used in 10:12 of sheep scampering from the wolf. Cf. Matt. 12:30 = Luke 11:33. *To his own* (*eis ta idia*). "To his own home" as in 1:11; 19:27. So Appian VI. 23. *Shall leave* (*aphēte*). Second aorist subjunctive of *aphiēmi* with *hina*. *And yet* (*kai*). Clear case of *kai* in adversative sense, not just "and."

33. *That in me ye may have peace* (*hina en emoi eirēnēn echēte*). Present active subjunctive of *echō*, "that ye may keep on having peace in me," even when I am put to death, peace to be found nowhere save in me (14:27). *Be of good cheer* (*tharseite*). Imperative active from *tharsos*, courage (Acts 28:15). A word for courage in the face of danger, only here in John, but see Matt. 9:2, 22; Mark 10:49. *I have overcome the world* (*egō, nenikēka ton kosmon*). Perfect active indicative of *nikaō*, to be victorious, to conquer. Always of spiritual victory in the N.T. See I John 5:4f. This majestic proclamation of victory over death may be compared with *tetelestai* (*It is finished*) in John 19:30 as Christ died and with Paul's *hupernikōmen* (we are more than conquerors) in Rom. 8:37.

CHAPTER XVII

1. *Lifting up (eparas).* First aorist active participle of *epairō*, old and common verb with *ophthalmous* (eyes) as in 4:35; 6:5; 11:41. *Father (Pater).* Vocative form as in verses 5, 11, and 11:41, Christ's usual way of beginning his prayers. It is inconceivable that this real *Lord's Prayer* is the free composition of a disciple put into the mouth of Jesus. It is rather "the tenacious memory of an old man recalling the greatest days of his life" (Bernard), aided by the Holy Spirit promised for this very purpose (John 14:26; 16:13f.). Jesus had the habit of prayer (Mark 1:35; 6:46; Matt. 11:25f.; Luke 3:21; 5:16; 6:12; 9:18, 28; 11:22, 42; 23:34, 46; John 11:41; 12:27). He prayed here for himself (1–5), for the disciples (6–19), for all believers (20–26). The prayer is similar in spirit to the Model Prayer for us in Matt. 6:9–13. The hour for his glorification has come as he had already told the disciples (13:31f.; 12:23). *Glorify thy Son (doxason sou ton huion).* First aorist active imperative of *doxazō*, the only personal petition in this prayer. Jesus had already used this word *doxazō* for his death (13:31f.). Here it carries us into the very depths of Christ's own consciousness. It is not merely for strength to meet the Cross, but for the power to glorify the Father by his death and resurrection and ascension, "that the Son may glorify thee" (*hina ho huios doxasēi se*). Purpose clause with *hina* and the first aorist active subjunctive.

2. *Authority over all flesh (exousian pasēs sarkos).* *Sarkos* is objective genitive. Stupendous claim impossible for a mere man to make. Made already in Matt. 11:27 and Luke 10:22 (Q, the Logia of Jesus, our earliest known document about Jesus) and repeated in Matt. 28:18 after his resurrec-

tion. *That (hina).* Secondary purpose with *hina dōsei* (future active indicative) carrying on the idea of *hina doxasēi.* See 13:34 and 17:21 for *hina, kathōs, hina. Whatsoever (pān ho).* A peculiar classical Greek idiom, the collective use of the singular *pān ho* as in 6:37, 39 and *ho* in 17:24 and the nominative absolute (*nom. pendens*) with *autois* (to them), the dative plural explaining the construction. See Robertson, *Grammar,* p. 653.

3. *Should know (ginōskōsin).* Present active subjunctive with *hina* (subject clause), "should keep on knowing." *Even Jesus Christ (Iēsoun Christon).* See 1:17 for the only other place in John's Gospel where the words occur together. Coming here in the Lord's own prayer about himself they create difficulty, unless, as Westcott suggests, *Christon* be regarded as a predicate accusative, "Jesus as the Christ" (Messiah). Otherwise the words would seem to be John's parenthetical interpretation of the idea of Jesus. Lücke thinks that the solemnity of this occasion explains Jesus referring to himself in the third person. The knowledge of "the only true God" is through Jesus Christ (14:6–9).

4. *I glorified thee on the earth (egō se edoxasa epi tēs gēs).* Verse 3 is parenthetical and so verse 4 goes on after verse 2. He had prayed for further glorification. *Having accomplished (teleiōsas).* First aorist active participle of *teleioō,* old verb from *teleios* (perfect). Used in 4:34 by Jesus with *to ergon* as here. That was Christ's "food" (*brōma*) and joy. Now as he faces death he has no sense of failure as some modern critics say, but rather fulness of attainment as in 19:30 (*tetelestai*). Christ does not die as a disappointed man, but as the successful messenger, apostle (*apesteilas,* verse 3) of the Father to men. *Thou hast given (dedōkas).* Perfect active indicative of *didōmi,* regarded as a permanent task.

5. *With thine own self (para seautōi).* "By the side of thyself." Jesus prays for full restoration to the pre-incarnate glory and fellowship (cf. 1:1) enjoyed before the Incarnation

(John 1:14). This is not just ideal pre-existence, but actual and conscious existence at the Father's side (*para soi*, with thee) "which I had" (*hēi eichon*, imperfect active of *echō*, I used to have, with attraction of case of *hēn* to *hēi* because of *doxēi*), "before the world was" (*pro tou ton kosmon einai*), "before the being as to the world" (cf. verse 24). It is small wonder that those who deny or reject the deity of Jesus Christ have trouble with the Johannine authorship of this book and with the genuineness of these words. But even Harnack admits that the words here and in verse 24 are "undoubtedly the reflection of the certainty with which Jesus himself spoke" (*What Is Christianity*, Engl. Tr., p. 132). But Paul, as clearly as John, believes in the actual pre-existence and deity of Jesus Christ (Phil. 2:5–11).

6. *I manifested* (*ephanerōsa*). First aorist active indicative of *phaneroō* (from *phaneros*, manifest). Another word for claiming successful accomplishment of his task as in verse 4 with *edoxasa* and in verse 26 with *egnōrisa*. *Whom* (*hous*). Accusative case after *edōkas*, not attracted to case of antecedent (*anthrōpois*). Jesus regards the apostles as the Father's gift to him. Recall the night of prayer before he chose them. *They have kept* (*tetērēkan*). Perfect active indicative, late *Koiné* form for the third plural instead of the usual *tetērēkasin*. Jesus claims loyalty and fidelity in these men with the one exception of Judas (verse 12). He does not claim perfection for them, but they have at least held on to the message of the Father in spite of doubt and wavering (6:67–71; Matt. 16:15–20).

7. *Now they know* (*nun egnōkan*). Perfect active indicative third plural like *tetērēkan* above. They have come to know, not as fully as they felt (16:30), and yet in a real sense.

8. *The words* (*ta rēmata*). Plural, each word of God, as in 3:34, and of Christ (5:47; 6:63, 68), while the singular (*ton logon sou*) in verses 6 and 14 views God's message as a whole. *Knew* (*egnōsan*). Second aorist active indicative of

ginōskō like *elabon* in contrast with *egnōkan* (perfect) in verse 7. They definitely "received and recognized truly" (*alēthōs*). There was comfort to Christ in this fact. *They believed* (*episteusan*). Another aorist parallel with *elabon* and *egnōsan*. The disciples believed in Christ's mission from the Father (John 6:69; Matt. 16:16). Note *apesteilas* here as in verse 3. Christ is God's *Apostle* to man (Heb. 3:1). This statement, like a solemn refrain (Thou didst send me), occurs five times in this prayer (verses 8, 18, 21, 23, 25).

9. *I pray* (*egō erōtō*). Request, not question, as in 16:23. *Not for the world* (*ou peri tou kosmou*). Now at this point in the prayer Christ means. In verse 19 Jesus does pray for the world (for future believers) that it may believe (verse 21). God loves the whole world (3:16). Christ died for sinners (Rom. 5:8) and prayed for sinners (Luke 23:34) and intercedes for sinners (I John 2:1f.; Rom. 8:34; Heb. 7:25). *For those whom* (*peri hōn*). A condensed and common Greek idiom for *peri toutōn hous* with *toutōn* (the demonstrative antecedent) omitted and the relative *hous* attracted from the accusative *hous* (object of *dedōkas*) to the case (genitive) of the omitted antecedent.

10. *Are* (*estin*). Singular number in the Greek (is), not the plural *eisin* (are), emphasizing the unity of the whole as in 16:15. "This no creature can say in reference to God" (Luther). *I am glorified in them* (*dedoxasmai en autois*). "I stand glorified (perfect passive indicative of *doxazō*) in the disciples" (*en autois*), in spite of all their shortcomings and failings. There is comfort for us in this.

11. *And these* (*kai houtoi* or *autoi*, they). Note adversative use of *kai* (= but these). *I come* (*erchomai*). Futuristic present, "I am coming." Cf. 13:3; 14:12; 17:13. Christ will no longer be visibly present to the world, but he will be with the believers through the Holy Spirit (Matt. 28:20). *Holy Father* (*pater hagie*). Only here in the N.T., but see I John 2:20 and Luke 1:49 for the holiness of God, a thor-

oughly Jewish conception. See John 6:69 where Peter calls Jesus *ho hagios tou theou*. For the word applied to saints see Acts 9:13. See verse 25 for *patēr dikaie* (Righteous Father). *Keep them (tērēson autous)*. First aorist (constative) active imperative of *tēreō*, as now specially needing the Father's care with Jesus gone (urgency of the aorist tense in prayer). *Which (hōi)*. Locative case of the neuter relative singular, attracted from the accusative *ho* to the case of the antecedent *onomati* (name). *That they may be one (hina ōsin hen)*. Purpose clause with *hina* and the present active subjunctive of *eimi* (that they may keep on being). Oneness of will and spirit (*hen*, neuter singular), not one person (*heis*, masculine singular) for which Christ does not pray. Each time Jesus uses *hen* (verses 11, 21, 22) and once, *eis hen*, "into one" (verse 23). This is Christ's prayer for all believers, for unity, not for organic union of which we hear so much. The disciples had union, but lacked unity or oneness of spirit as was shown this very evening at the supper (Luke 22:24; John 13:4–15). Jesus offers the unity in the Trinity (three persons, but one God) as the model for believers. The witness of the disciples will fail without harmony (17:21).

12. *I kept (etēroun)*. Imperfect active of *tēreō*, "I continued to keep." *I guarded (ephulaxa)*. First aorist (constative) active of *phulassō*. Christ was the sentinel (*phulax*, Acts 5:23) for them. Is he our sentinel now? *But the son of perdition (ei mē ho huios tēs apōleias)*. The very phrase for antichrist (II Thess. 2:3). Note play on *apōleto*, perished (second aorist middle indicative of *apollumi*). It means the son marked by final loss, not annihilation, but meeting one's destiny (Acts 2:25). A sad and terrible exception (Mark 14:21). *The scripture (hē graphē)*. It is not clear whether this is John's own comment or the word of Jesus. Not in 18:9. The Scripture referred to is probably Psa. 41:9 quoted in 13:18 with the same formula *hina plērōthēi* which see there.

13. *That they may have my joy fulfilled in themselves* (*hina echōsin tēn charan tēn emēn peplērōmenēn en heautois*). Purpose clause with present active subjunctive of *echō*, "that they may keep on having Christ's joy in their faithfulness realized in themselves." *Peplērōmenēn* is the perfect passive participle of *pleroō* in the predicate position. For the use of *pleroō* with *chara* (joy) see 15:11; 16:24; Phil. 2:2.

14. *Not of the world* (*ouk ek tou kosmou*). They are "in the world" (*en tōi kosmōi*, verse 13) still and Christ sends them "into the world" (*eis ton kosmon*, verse 18), but they must not be like the world nor get their spirit, standards, and message "out of the world," else they can do the world no good. These verses (14 to 19) picture the Master's ideal for believers and go far towards explaining the failure of Christians in winning the world to Christ. Too often the world fails to see the difference or the gain by the change.

15. *Shouldest take* (*arēis*). First aorist active subjunctive of *airō* (liquid verb). *From the evil one* (*ek tou ponērou*). Ablative case with *ek*, but can mean the evil man, Satan, or the evil deed. See same ambiguity in Matt. 6:13. But in I John 5:18 *ho ponēros* is masculine (the evil one). Cf. Rev. 3:10.

16. Repetition of verse 14 for emphasis.

17. *Sanctify* (*hagiason*). First aorist active imperative of *hagiazō*. To consecrate or set apart persons or things to God. See Ex. 28:41; 29:1, 36; 40:13. See Paul's prayer for the Thessalonians (I Thess. 5:23). This is done in the sphere (*en*) of truth (God's truth), God's Word (not human speculation, but God's message to us).

18. *Sent I them* (*apesteila autous*). The very verb (*apostellō*) used of the original commission of these men (Mark 3:14) and the special commission (Luke 9:2) and the renewal of the commission after the resurrection (John 20:21f., both *apostellō* and *pempō* here).

19. *I sanctify myself* (*egō hagiazō emauton*). To his holy ministry to which the Father "sanctified" (*hēgiasen*) him (John 10:36). *That they themselves also may be sanctified in truth* (*hina ōsin kai autoi hēgiasmenoi en alētheiāi*). Purpose clause with *hina* and the periphrastic perfect passive subjunctive of *hagiazō* (that they may remain sanctified). The act of Christ helps us, but by no means takes the place of personal consecration on the part of the believer. This high and holy prayer and act of Christ should shame any one who uses the livery of heaven to serve the devil in as does, alas, sometimes happen (II Cor. 11:13–15).

20. *Through their word* (*dia tou logou autōn*). Through the agency of conversation and preaching, blessed privilege open to all believers thus to win men to Christ, but an agency sadly limited by the lives of those who speak in Christ's name.

21. *That they also may be in us* (*hina kai autoi en hēmin ōsin*). Another purpose clause with *hina* and the present active subjunctive of *eimi*. The only possible way to have unity among believers is for all of them to find unity first with God in Christ. *That the world may believe* (*hina ho kosmos pisteuēi*). Another purpose clause with *hina* and the present active subjunctive of *pisteuō*, "may keep on believing." Beyond a doubt, strife, wrangling, division are a stumblingblock to the outside world.

22. *And the glory* (*kágō tēn doxan*). Literally, "And I the glory," with emphasis on "I." It is the glory of the Incarnate Word (Bernard), cf.1:14 and 2:11, not the glory of the Eternal Word mentioned in 17:24. Bengel says: *Quanta majestas Christianorum!* Then verse 22 repeats the unity prayed for in verse 21.

23. *That they may be perfected into one* (*hina ōsin teteleiōmenoi eis hen*). Purpose clause again with *hina* (nineteen times in this prayer, this the fifteenth) with the periphrastic perfect passive subjunctive of *teleioō* (verse 4), permanent

state, with *eis hen* (into one) as the goal and final result. *That the world may know* (*hina ginōskēi*). Present active subjunctive of *ginōskō* with *hina* like the present tense of *pisteuō* in verse 21, "that the world may keep on knowing" with the same pregnant phrase "that thou me didst send" (*hoti su me apesteilas*) as in 8 and 25. *And lovedst them* (*kai ēgapēsas autous*). Timeless aorist, but love shown by sending Christ (John 3:16) and illustrated and proven by the way Christians love one another.

24. *I will* (*thelō*). Perfect identity of his will with that of the Father in "this moment of spiritual exaltation" (Bernard), though in Gethsemane Jesus distinguishes between his human will and that of the Father (Mark 14:36). *Where I am* (*hopou eimi egō*). That is heaven, to be with Jesus (12:26; 13:36; 14:3; Rom. 8:17; II Tim. 2:11f.). *That they may behold* (*hina theōrōsin*). Another purpose clause with *hina* and the present active subjunctive of *theōreō*, "that they may keep on beholding," the endless joy of seeing Jesus "as he is" (I John 3:2) in heaven. *Before the foundation of the world* (*pro katabolēs kosmou*). This same phrase in Eph. 1:4 and I Peter 1:20 and six other times we have *katabolē kosmou* (Matt. 25:34; Luke 11:50; Heb. 4:3; 9:26; Rev. 13:8; 17:8). Here we find the same pre-incarnate consciousness of Christ seen in 17:5.

25. *O righteous Father* (*Patēr dikaie*). Nominative form with *patēr* used as vocative (cf. John 20:28), but vocative form *dikaie*. Then the righteousness of God is appealed to like God's holiness in verse 11. *The world* (*kai ho kosmos*). The translations usually slur over the *kai* as untranslatable in English. Westcott suggests "while" as a sort of correlative. It is quite possible that here *kai* is almost concessive like "though" and *de*=yet: "though the world did not know thee, yet I knew thee, and these knew thee." See Robertson, *Grammar*, p. 1182 for *kai — de — kai* and various other uses of *kai* in John's Gospel.

26. *And will make it known* (*kai gnōrisō*).   Future active
of *gnōrizō*, the perpetual mission of Christ through the Spirit
(16:12, 25; Matt. 28:20) as he himself has done heretofore
(17:6). *Wherewith* (*hen*).   Cognate accusative relative with
ēgapēsas which has also the accusative of the person *me*
(me).

CHAPTER XVIII

1. *With* (*sun*). See 12:2 for another example of *sun* in John (common in Paul). The usual *meta* reappears in verse 2. *Over* (*peran*). "Beyond," preposition with the ablative as in 6:22, 25. *Brook* (*cheimarrou*). Old word, flowing (*roos, reō*) in winter (*cheima*), only here in N.T. *Kidron* (*tōn Kedrōn*). Literally, "of the Cedars," "Brook of the Cedars." Only here in N.T. So II Sam. 15:23. Textus Receptus like Josephus (*Ant.* VIII, 1, 5) has the singular *tou Kedrōn* (indeclinable). As a matter of fact it was always dry save after a heavy rain. *A garden* (*kēpos*). Old word, in N.T. only here, verse 26; 19:41 (Joseph's); Luke 13:19. John, like Luke, does not give the name Gethsemane (only in Mark 14:32=Matt. 26:36). The brook of the cedars had many unhallowed associations (I Kings 2:37; 15:13; II Kings 23:4ff.; II Chron. 29:16; Jer. 31:40).

2. *Resorted thither* (*sunēchthē ekei*). First aorist passive indicative of *sunagō*, old verb to gather together. A bit awkward here till you add "with his disciples." Judas knew the place, and the habit of Jesus to come here at night for prayer (Luke 22:39). Hence his offer to catch Jesus while the feast was going on, catch him at night and alone in his usual place of prayer (the very spirit of the devil).

3. *The band of soldiers* (*tēn speiran*). No word for "of soldiers" in the Greek, but the Latin *spira* (roll or ball) was used for a military cohort (Polybius 11, 23, 1) as in Matt. 27:27; Acts 10:1, etc., here for a small band secured from the Tower of Antonia. The Synoptics do not mention the soldiers, but only the "officers" as here (*hupēretas* for which see Matt. 26:58=Mark 14:54, 65) or temple police from the Sanhedrin. *Cometh* (*erchetai*). Dramatic historical present

middle indicative. *With lanterns and torches (meta phanōn kai lampadōn).* Both old words, *phanos* only here in N.T., *lampas*, an oil lamp (Matt. 25:1). It was full moon, but Judas took no chances for it may have been cloudy and there were dark places by the walls and under the olive trees. *Meta* is accompanied with *and weapons (kai hoplōn).* Mark (14:43) mentions "swords and staves." Probably the temple guard had weapons as well as the soldiers.

4. *Knowing all the things that were coming upon him (eidōs panta ta erchomena ep' auton).* Mentioned already in John 13:1. He was not taken by surprise. The surrender and death of Jesus were voluntary acts, though the guilt of Judas and the rest remains.

5. *Was standing (histēkei).* Second past perfect active of *histēmi* used as imperfect, a vivid picture of Judas in the very act of betraying Jesus. John does not mention the kiss by Judas as a sign to the soldiers and police. Tatian suggests that it came before verse 4. Then Jesus stepped forth and affirmed that he was the one whom they were seeking.

6. *Fell to the ground (epesan chamai).* Second aorist active indicative of *piptō* with first aorist ending (*-an*). This recoil made them stumble. But why did they step back? Was it the former claim of Jesus (*I am, egō eimi*) to be on an equality with God (8:58; 13:19) or mere embarrassment and confusion or supernatural power exerted by Jesus? B adds *Iēsous* which must mean simply: "I am Jesus."

7. *Again (palin).* The repeated question receives the same answer. The soldiers and officers know who it is, but are still overawed.

8. *Let these go their way (aphete toutous hupagein).* Second aorist active imperative of *aphiēmi*. The verb *hupagein* means to withdraw (11:44). Jesus shows solicitude for the eleven as he had warned them and prayed for them (Luke 22:31f.). He is trying to help them.

THE FOURTH GOSPEL 285

9. *That might be fulfilled* (*hina plērōthēi*). The regular
formula (17:12) for Scripture, here applied to the prophecy
of Jesus (17:12) as in verse 32. John treats the saying of
Jesus as on a par with the O.T.

10. *Having a sword* (*echōn machairan*). It was unlawful
to carry a weapon on a feast-day, but Peter had become
alarmed at Christ's words about his peril. They had two
swords or knives in the possession of the eleven according
to Luke (22:38). After the treacherous kiss of Judas (on the
hand or the cheek?) the disciples asked: "Lord, shall we smite
with the sword?" (Luke 22:49). Apparently before Jesus
could answer Peter with his usual impulsiveness jerked out
(*heilkusen*, first aorist active indicative of *helkuō* for which
see 6:44) his sword and cut off the right ear of Malchus
(John 18:10), a servant of the high priest. Peter missed the
man's head as he swerved to his left. Luke also (22:50)
mentions the detail of the right ear, but John alone mentions
the man's name and Peter's. There was peril to Peter in his
rash act as comes out later (John 18:26), but he was dead
long before John wrote his Gospel as was Lazarus of whom
John could also safely write (12:9–11). For *ōtarion*, diminutive
of *ous*, see Mark 14:47 (only other N.T. example), another diminutive *ōtion* in Matt. 26:51 (=Mark 14:47=Luke 22:51).

11. *Into the sheath* (*eis tēn thēkēn*). Old word from *tithēmi*,
to put for box or sheath, only here in N.T. In Matt. 26:52
Christ's warning is given. *The cup* (*to potērion*). Metaphor
for Christ's death, used already in reply to request of James
and John (Mark 10:39=Matt. 20:22) and in the agony in
Gethsemane before Judas came (Mark 14:36=Matt. 26:39
=Luke 22:42), which is not given by John. The case of
to potērion is the suspended nominative for note *auto* (it)
referring to it. *Shall I not drink?* (*ou mē piō;*). Second aorist
active subjunctive of *pinō* with the double negative *ou mē*
in a question expecting the affirmative answer. Abbott takes
it as an exclamation and compares 6:37 and Mark 14:25.

12. *The chief captain* (*ho chiliarchos*). They actually had the Roman commander of the cohort along (cf. Acts 21:31), not mentioned before. *Seized* (*sunelabon*). Second aorist active of *sullambanō*, old verb to grasp together, to arrest (technical word) in the Synoptics in this context (Mark 14:48 = Matt. 26:55), here alone in John. *Bound* (*edēsan*). First aorist active indicative of *deō*, to bind. As a matter of course, with the hands behind his back, but with no warrant in law and with no charge against him. *To Annas first* (*pros Annan prōton*). Ex-high priest and father-in-law (*pentheros*, old word, only here in N.T.) of Caiaphas the actual high priest. Then Jesus was subjected to a preliminary and superfluous inquiry by Annas (given only by John) while the Sanhedrin were gathering before Caiaphas. Bernard curiously thinks that the night trial actually took place here before Annas and only the early morning ratification was before Caiaphas. So he calmly says that "Matthew inserts the name *Caiaphas* at this point (the night trial) in which he seems to have been mistaken." But why "mistaken"? *That year* (*tou eniautou ekeinou*). Genitive of time.

14. *He which gave command* (*ho sumbouleusas*). First aorist active articular participle of *sumbouleuō*, old verb (Matt. 26:4). The reference is to John 11:50. *It was expedient* (*sumpherei*). Present active indicative retained in indirect assertion after secondary tense (*ēn*, was). Here we have the second aorist active infinitive *apothanein* as the subject of *sumpherei*, both good idioms in the *Koinē*.

15. *Followed* (*ēkolouthei*). Imperfect active of *akoloutheō*, "was following," picturesque and vivid tense, with associative instrumental case *tōi Iēsou*. *Another disciple* (*allos mathētēs*). Correct text without article *ho* (genuine in verse 16). Peter's companion was the Beloved Disciple, the author of the book (John 21:24). *Was known unto the high priest* (*ēn gnōstos tōi archierei*). Verbal adjective from *ginōskō*, to know (Acts 1:19) with dative case. How well known the

word does not say, not necessarily a personal friend, well enough known for the portress to admit John. "The account of what happened to Peter might well seem to be told from the point of view of the servants' hall" (Sanday, *Criticism of the Fourth Gospel*, p. 101). *Entered in with Jesus (suneisēlthen tōi Iēsou).* Second aorist active indicative of the double compound *suneiserchomai*, old verb, in N.T. here and 6:22. With associative instrumental case. *Into the court (eis tēn aulēn).* It is not clear that this word ever means the palace itself instead of the courtyard (uncovered enclosure) as always in the papyri (very common). Clearly courtyard in Mark 14:66 (=Matt. 26:69=Luke 22:55). Apparently Annas had rooms in the official residence of Caiaphas.

16. *Was standing (histēkei).* Same form in verse 5 which see. So also *histēkeisan* in 18. Picture of Peter standing outside by the door. *Unto the high priest (tou archiereōs).* Objective genitive here, but dative in verse 15. *Unto her that kept the door (tēi thurōrōi).* Old word (*thura*, door, *ōra*, care), masculine in 10:3, feminine here, door-keeper (male or female).

17. *The maid (hē paidiskē).* Feminine form of *paidiskos*, diminutive of *pais*. See Matt. 26:69. When "the maid the portress" (apposition). *Art thou also? (mē kai su ei;).* Expecting the negative answer, though she really believed he was. *This man's (tou anthrōpou toutou).* Contemptuous use of *houtos* with a gesture toward Jesus. She made it easy for Peter to say no.

18. *A fire of coals (anthrakian).* Old word, in LXX, only here and 21:9 in N.T. A heap of burning coals (*anthrax*, coal). Cf. our "anthracite." *It was cold (psuchos ēn).* "There was coldness." The soldiers had apparently returned to their barracks. *Were warming themselves (ethermainonto).* Direct middle imperfect indicative of *thermainō* (from *thermos*). So as to *thermainomenos* about Peter. "Peter, unabashed by his lie, joined himself to the group and stood in the light of the fire (Dods).

19. *Asked* (*erōtēsen*). First aorist active indicative of *erōtaō*, to question, usual meaning. This was Annas making a preliminary examination of Jesus probably to see on what terms Jesus made disciples whether as a mere rabbi or as Messiah.

20. *Openly* (*parrēsiāi*). As already shown (7:4; 8:26; 10:24, 39; 16:25, 29. See 7:4 for same contrast between *en parrēsiāi* and *en kruptōi*. *I ever taught* (*egō pantote edidaxa*). Constative aorist active indicative. For the temple teaching see John 2:19; 7:14, 28; 8:20; 19:23; Mark 14:49 and John 6:59 for the synagogue teaching (often in the Synoptics). Examples of private teaching are Nicodemus (ch. 3) and the woman of Samaria (ch. 4). Jesus ignores the sneer at his disciples, but challenges the inquiry about his teaching as needless.

21. *Ask them that have heard me* (*erōtēson tous akēkootas*). First aorist (tense of urgent and instant action) active imperative of *erōtaō* and the articular perfect active participle accusative masculine plural of *akouō*, to hear. There were abundant witnesses to be had. Multitudes had heard Jesus in the great debate in the temple on Tuesday of this very week when the Sanhedrin were routed to the joy of the common people who heard Jesus gladly (Mark 12:37). They still know.

22. *When he had said this* (*tauta autou eipontos*). Genitive absolute of second aorist active participle of *eipon*, to say. *Standing by* (*parestēkōs*). Perfect active (intransitive) participle of *paristēmi* (transitive), to place beside. One of the temple police who felt his importance as protector of Annas. *Struck Jesus with his hand* (*edōken rapisma tōi Iēsou*). Late word *rapisma* is from *rapizō*, to smite with a rod or with the palm of the hand (Matt. 26:67). It occurs only three times in the N.T. (Mark 14:65; John 18:22; 19:3), in each of which it is uncertain whether the blow is with a rod or with the palm of the hand (probably this, a most insulting act). The

papyri throw no real light on it. "He gave Jesus a slap in the face." Cf. II Cor. 11:20. *So* (*houtōs*). As Jesus had done in verse 21, a dignified protest in fact by Jesus.

23. *If I have spoken evil* (*ei kakōs elalēsa*). Condition of first class (assumed to be true), with *ei* and aorist active indicative. Jesus had not spoken evilly towards Annas, though he did not here turn the other cheek, one may note. For the sake of argument, Jesus puts it as if he did speak evilly. Then prove it, that is all. *Bear witness of the evil* (*marturēson peri tou kakou*). First aorist active imperative of *martureō*, to testify. This is the conclusion (apodosis). Jesus is clearly entitled to proof of such a charge if there is any. *But if well* (*ei de kalōs*). Supply the same verb *elalēsa*. The same condition, but with a challenging question as the apodosis. *Smitest* (*dereis*). Old verb *derō*, to flay, to skin, to beat, as in Matt. 21:35; Luke 22:63; II Cor. 11:20 (of an insulting blow in the face as here).

24. *Therefore sent him* (*apesteilen oun auton*). First aorist active of *apostellō*, not past perfect (had sent). The preliminary examination by Annas was over. *Bound* (*dedemenon*). Perfect passive participle of *deō*, to bind. Jesus was bound on his arrest (verse 12) and apparently unbound during the preliminary examination by Annas.

25. *Was standing and warming himself* (*ēn hestōs kai thermainomenos*). Two periphrastic imperfects precisely as in verse 18, vivid renewal of the picture drawn there. John alone gives the examination of Jesus by Annas (18:19–24) which he places between the first and the second denials by Peter. Each of the Four Gospels gives three denials, but it is not possible to make a clear parallel as probably several people joined in each time. This time there was an hour's interval (Luke 22:59). The question and answer are almost identical with verse 17 and "put in a form which almost *suggested* that Peter should say 'No'" (Bernard), a favourite device of the devil in making temptation attractive.

26. *Did not I see thee in the garden with him?* (*ouk egō se eidon en tōi kēpōi met' autou;*). This staggering and sudden thrust expects an affirmative answer by the use of *ouk*, not *mē* as in verses 17 and 25, but Peter's previous denials with the knowledge that he was observed by a kinsman of Malchus whom he had tried to kill (verse 10) drove him to the third flat denial that he knew Jesus, this time with cursing and swearing (Mark 14:71 = Matt. 26:73). Peter was in dire peril now of arrest himself for attempt to kill. *Straightway* (*eutheōs*). As in Matt. 26:74 while Luke has *parachrēma* (22:60). Mark (14:68, 72) speaks of two crowings as often happens when one cock crows. See Matt. 26:34 for *alektōr* (cock). That was usually the close of the third watch of the night (Mark 13:35), about 3 A.M. Luke (22:61) notes that Jesus turned and looked on Peter probably as he passed from the rooms of Annas to the trial before Caiaphas and the Sanhedrin (the ecclesiastical court). See Mrs. Browning's beautiful sonnets on "The Look".

28. *They lead* (*agousin*). Dramatic historical present of *agō*, plural "they" for the Sanhedrists (Luke 23:1). John gives no details of the trial before the Sanhedrin (only the fact, John 18:24, 28) when Caiaphas presided, either the informal meeting at night (Mark 14:53, 55–65=Matt. 26:57, 59–68=Luke 22:54, 63–65) or the formal ratification meeting after dawn (Mark 15:1 =Matt. 27:1 =Luke 22:66–71), but he gives much new material of the trial before Pilate (18:28–38). *Into the palace* (*eis to praitōrion*). For the history and meaning of this interesting Latin word, *praetorium*, see on Matt. 27:27; Acts 23:35; Phil. 1:13. Here it is probably the magnificent palace in Jerusalem built by Herod the Great for himself and occupied by the Roman Procurator (governor) when in the city. There was also one in Caesarea (Acts 23:35). Herod's palace in Jerusalem was on the Hill of Zion in the western part of the upper city. There is something to be said for the Castle of Antonia, north of the temple

area, as the location of Pilate's residence in Jerusalem. *Early* (*prōï*). Technically the fourth watch (3 A.M. to 6 A.M.). There were two violations of Jewish legal procedure (holding the trial for a capital case at night, passing condemnation on the same day of the trial). Besides, the Sanhedrin no longer had the power of death. A Roman court could meet any time after sunrise. John (19:14) says it was "about the sixth hour" when Pilate condemned Jesus. *That they might not be defiled* (*hina mē mianthōsin*). Purpose clause with *hina mē* and first aorist passive subjunctive of *miainō*, to stain, to defile. For Jewish scruples about entering the house of a Gentile see Acts 10:28; 11:3. *But might eat the passover* (*alla phagōsin to pascha*). Second aorist active subjunctive of the defective verb *esthiō*, to eat. This phrase may mean to eat the passover meal as in Matt. 27:17 (=Mark 14:12, 14=Luke 22:11, 15), but it does not have to mean that. In II Chron. 30:22 we read: "And they did eat the festival seven days" when the paschal festival is meant, not the paschal lamb or the paschal supper. There are eight other examples of *pascha* in John's Gospel and in all of them the feast is meant, not the supper. If we follow John's use of the word, it is the feast here, not the meal of John 13:2 which was the regular passover meal. This interpretation keeps John in harmony with the Synoptics.

29. *Went out* (*exēlthen exō*). Note both *ex* and *exō* (went out outside), since the Sanhedrin would not come into Pilate's palace. Apparently on a gallery over the pavement in front of the palace (John 19:13). *Accusation* (*katēgorian*). Old word for formal charge, in N.T. only here, I Tim. 5:19; Titus 1:6. *Against this man* (*tou anthrōpou toutou*). Objective genitive after *katēgorian*. A proper legal inquiry.

30. *If this man were not an evil-doer* (*ei mē ēn houtos kakon poiōn*). Condition (negative) of second class (periphrastic imperfect indicative), assumed to be untrue, with the usual apodosis (*an* and aorist indicative, first aorist plural with *k*).

This is a pious pose of infallibility not in the Synoptics. They then proceeded to make the charges (Luke 23:2) as indeed John implies (18:31, 33). Some MSS. here read *kakopoios* (malefactor) as in I Peter 2:12, 14, with which compare Luke's *kakourgos* (23:32f.; so also II Tim. 2:9), both meaning evil-doer. Here the periphrastic present participle *poiōn* with *kakon* emphasizes the idea that Jesus was a habitual evil-doer (Abbott). It was an insolent reply to Pilate (Bernard).

31. *Yourselves* (*humeis*). Emphatic. Pilate shrewdly turns the case over to the Sanhedrin in reply to their insolence, who have said nothing whatever about their previous trial and condemnation of Jesus. He drew out at once the admission that they wanted the death of Jesus, not a fair trial for him, but Pilate's approval of their purpose to kill him (John 7:1, 25).

32. By what manner of death (*poiōi thanatōi*). Instrumental case of the qualitative interrogative *poios* in an indirect question, the very idiom used in John 12:32 concerning the Cross and here treated as prophecy (Scripture) with *hina plērōthēi* like the saying of Jesus in verse 9 which see.

33. *Again* (*palin*). Back into the palace where Pilate was before. *Called* (*ephōnēsen*). First aorist active indicative of *phōneō*. Jesus was already inside the court (verse 28). Pilate now summoned him to his presence since he saw that he had to handle the case. The charge that Jesus claimed to be a king compelled him to do so (Luke 23:2). *Art thou the King of the Jews?* (*su ei ho basileus tōn Ioudaiōn;*). This was the vital problem and each of the Gospels has the question (Mark 15:2 = Matt. 27:1 = Luke 23:3 = John 18:33), though Luke alone (23:2) gives the specific accusation. *Thou* (*su*). Emphatic. Jesus did claim to be the spiritual king of Israel as Nathanael said (John 1:49) and as the ecstatic crowd hailed him on the Triumphal Entry (John 12:13), but the Sanhedrin wish Pilate to understand this in a civil sense

as a rival of Caesar as some of the Jews wanted Jesus
to be (John 6:15) and as the Pharisees expected the
Messiah to be.

34. *Of thyself* (*apo seautou*). Whether a sincere inquiry
on Pilate's part or a trap from the Sanhedrin.

35. *Am I a Jew?* (*mēti egō Ioudaios eimi;*). Proud and
fine scorn on Pilate's part at the idea that he had a personal
interest in the question. Vehement negation implied.
Cf. 4:29 for *mēti* in a question. The gulf between Jew and
Gentile yawns wide here. *Nation* (*ethnos* as in 11:48-52,
rather than *laos*, while both in 11:50). For *paredōkan*
see verse 30. *What hast thou done?* (*ti epoiēsas;*). First aorist
active indicative of *poieō*. Blunt and curt question. "What
didst thou do?" "What is thy real crime?" John's picture
of this private interview between Pilate and Jesus is told
with graphic power.

36. *My kingdom* (*hē basileia hē emē*). Christ claims to be
king to Pilate, but of a peculiar kingdom. For "world"
(*kosmou*) see 17:13-18. *My servants* (*hoi hupēretai hoi emoi*).
For the word see verse 3 where it means the temple police or
guards (literally, under-rowers). In the LXX always (Prov.
14:35; Isa. 32:5; Dan. 3:46) officers of a king as here. Christ
then had only a small band of despised followers who could
not fight against Caesar. Was he alluding also to legions of
angels on his side? (Matt. 26:56). *Would fight* (*ēgōnizonto an*).
Imperfect middle of *agōnizomai* common verb (only here in
John, but see I Cor. 9:25) from *agōn* (contest) with *an*, a conclusion of the second-class condition (assumed as untrue).
Christians should never forget the profound truth stated
here by Jesus. *That I should not be delivered* (*hina mē
paradothō*). Negative final clause with *hina mē* and first aorist
passive subjunctive of *paradidōmi* (see verses 28,36). Jesus
expects Pilate to surrender to the Jews. *But now* (*nun de*).
In contrast to the condition already stated as in 8:40; 9:41;
15:22, 24.

37. *Art thou a king then?* (*oukoun basileus ei su;*). Compound of *ouk* and *oun* and is clearly ironical expecting an affirmative answer, only here in the N.T., and in LXX only in A text in II Kings 5:23. *Thou sayest that* (*su legeis hoti*). In Matt. 27:11; Mark 15:2; Luke 23:3, *su legeis* clearly means "yes," as *su eipas* (thou saidst) does in Matt. 26:64 (="I am," *egō eimi*, in Mark 41:62). Hence here *hoti* had best be taken to mean "because": "Yes, because I am a king." *Have I been born* (*egō gegennēmai*). Perfect passive indicative of *gennaō*. The Incarnation was for this purpose. Note repetition of *eis touto* (for this purpose), explained by *hina marturēsō tēi alētheiāi* (that I may bear witness to the truth), *hina* with first aorist active subjunctive of *martureō*. Paul (I Tim. 6:13) alludes to this good confession when Christ bore witness (*marturēsantos*) before Pilate. Jesus bore such witness always (John 3:11, 32; 7:7; 8:14; Rev. 1:5).

38. *What is truth?* (*ti estin alētheia;*). This famous sneer of Pilate reveals his own ignorance of truth, as he stood before Incarnate Truth (John 14:6). *Quid est veritas?* The answer in Latin is *Vir est qui adest* as has been succinctly said by the use of the same letters. Pilate turned with indifference from his own great question and rendered his verdict: "I find no crime in him" (*egō oudemian heuriskō en autōi aitian*). For this use of *aitia* see Matt. 27:37; Mark 15:26. Pilate therefore should have set Jesus free at once.

39. *A custom* (*sunētheia*). Old word for intimacy, intercourse, from *sunēthēs* (*sun, ēthos*), in N.T. only here, I Cor. 8:7; 11:16. This custom, alluded to in Mark 15:6; Matt. 27:15, is termed necessity (*anagkē*) in Luke 23:17 (late MSS., not in older MSS.). All the Gospels use the verb *apoluō* (release, set free). Then *hina apolusō* is a subject clause (*hina* and first aorist active subjunctive) in apposition with *sunētheia*. *Will ye therefore that I release?* (*boulesthe oun apolusō;*). Without the usual *hina* before *apolusō*, asyndeton, as in Mark 10:36, to be explained either as parataxis or two

questions (Robertson, *Grammar*, p. 430) or as mere omission of *hina* (*ibid.*, p. 994). There is contempt and irony in Pilate's use of the phrase "the king of the Jews."

40. *Cried out* (*ekraugasan*). First aorist active of *kraugazō*, old and rare verb from *kraugē*, outcry (Matt. 25:6), as in Matt. 12:19. *Not this man* (*mē touton*). Contemptuous use of *houtos*. The priests put the crowd up to this choice (Mark 15:11) and Pilate offered the alternative (Matt. 27:17, one MS. actually gives Jesus as the name of Barabbas also). The name *Barabbas* in Aramaic simply means son of a father. *A robber* (*lēistēs*). Old word from *lēizomai*, to plunder, and so a brigand and possibly the leader of the band to which the two robbers belonged who were crucified with Jesus. Luke terms him an insurgent and murderer (23:19, 25). They chose Barabbas in preference to Jesus and apparently Jesus died on the very cross planned for Barabbas.

CHAPTER XIX

1. *Took and scourged (elaben kai emastigōsen).* First aorist active indicative of *lambanō* and *mastigoō* (from *mastix*, whip). For this redundant use of *lambanō* see also verse 6. It is the causative use of *mastigoō*, for Pilate did not actually scourge Jesus. He simply ordered it done, perhaps to see if the mob would be satisfied with this penalty on the alleged pretender to royalty (Luke 23:22) whom Pilate had pronounced innocent (John 18:38), an illegal act therefore. It was a preliminary to crucifixion, but Jesus was not yet condemned. The Sanhedrin had previously mocked Jesus (Mark 14:65 = Matt. 26:67f. = Luke 22:63ff.) as the soldiers will do later (Mark 15:16-19 = Matt. 27:27-30). This later mock coronation (Mark and Matthew) was after the condemnation. *Plaited a crown of thorns (plexantes stephanon ex akanthōn).* Old verb *plekō*, to weave, in the N.T. only here, Mark 15:17; Matt. 27:19. Not impossible for the mock coronation to be repeated. *Arrayed him (periebalon auton).* "Placed around him" (second aorist active indicative of *periballō).* *In a purple garment (himation porphuroun).* Old adjective *porphureos* from *porphura*, purple cloth (Mark 15:17, 20), dyed in purple, in the N.T. only here and Rev. 18:16. Jesus had been stripped of his outer garment *himation* (Matt. 27:28) and the scarlet cloak of one of the soldiers may have been put on him (Matt. 27:28).

3. *They came (ērchonto).* Imperfect middle of repeated action, "they kept coming and saying" (*elegon*) in derision and mock reverence with *Ave (chaire, Hail!) as if to Caesar. Note *ho basileus* (the king) in address. *They struck him with their hands (edidosan autōi rapismata).* Imperfect of *didōmi*, repetition, "they kept on giving him slaps with their hands." See on 18:22 for this use of *rapisma*.

4. *I bring him out to you* (*agō humin auton exō*). Vividly pictures Pilate leading Jesus out of the palace before the mob in front. *That ye may know* (*hina gnōte*). Final clause with *hina* and the second aorist active subjunctive of *ginōskō*, "that ye may come to know," by this mockery the sincerity of Pilate's decision that Jesus is innocent (18:38). It is a travesty on justice and dignity, but Pilate is trying by a bit of humour to turn the mob from the grip of the Sanhedrin.

5. *Wearing* (*phorōn*). Present active participle of *phoreō*, an early frequentative of *pherō*, denoting a continual wearing, though not true here (only temporary). Jesus bore the mockery with kingly dignity as part of the shame of the Cross (Heb. 12:2). *Behold, the man* (*Idou ho anthrōpos*). *Ecce Homo!* by Pilate. This exclamatory introduction of Jesus in mock coronation robes to the mob was clearly intended to excite pity and to show how absurd the charge of the Sanhedrin was that such a pitiable figure should be guilty of treason. Pilate failed utterly in this effort and did not dream that he was calling attention to the greatest figure of history, the Man of the ages.

6. *Crucify him, crucify him* (*staurōson, staurōson*). First aorist active imperative of *stauroō* for which verb see Matt. 29:19, etc. Here the note of urgency (aorist imperative) with no word for "him," as they were led by the chief priests and the temple police till the whole mob takes it up (Matt. 27:22). *For I find no crime in him* (*egō gar ouch heuriskō*). This is the third time Pilate has rendered his opinion of Christ's innocence (18:38; 19:4). And here he surrenders in a fret to the mob and gives as his reason (*gar*, for) for his surrender the innocence of Jesus (the strangest judicial decision ever rendered). Perhaps Pilate was only franker than some judges!

7. *Because he made himself the Son of God* (*hoti huion theou heauton epoiēsen*). Here at last the Sanhedrin give

the real ground for their hostility to Jesus, one of long standing for probably three years (John 5:18) and the one on which the Sanhedrin voted the condemnation of Jesus (Mark 14:61–64 = Matt. 27:23–66), but even now they do not mention their own decision to Pilate, for they had no legal right to vote Christ's death before Pilate's consent which they now have secured.

8. *He was the more afraid* (*mallon ephobēthē*). First aorist passive indicative of *phobeomai*. He was already afraid because of his wife's message (Matt. 27:19). The claim of Jesus to deity excited Pilate's superstitious fears.

9. *Whence art thou?* (*pothen ei su;*). Pilate knew that Jesus was from Galilee (Luke 23:6f.). He is really alarmed. See a like question by the Jews in 8:25. *Gave him no answer* (*apokrisin ouk edōken autōi*). See same idiom in 1:22. *Apokrisis* (old word from *apokrinomai*) occurs also in Luke 2:47; 20:26. The silence of Jesus, like that before Caiaphas (Mark 14:61 = Matt. 26:63) and Herod (Luke 23:9), irritates the dignity of Pilate in spite of his fears.

10. *Unto me* (*emoi*). Emphatic position for this dative. It amounted to contempt of court with all of Pilate's real "authority" (*exousia*), better here than "power."

11. *Thou wouldest have* (*ouk eiches*). Imperfect active indicative without *an*, but apodosis of second-class condition as in 15:22, 24. *Except it were given thee* (*ei mē ēn dedomenon*). Periphrastic past perfect indicative of *didōmi* (a permanent possession). *From above* (*anōthen*). From God (cf. 3:3), the same doctrine of government stated by Paul in Rom. 13:1f. Pilate did not get his "authority" from the Sanhedrin, but from Caesar. Jesus makes God the source of all real "authority." *Hath greater sin* (*meizona hamartian echei*). The same idiom in 9:41. Caiaphas has his authority from God also and has used Pilate for his own base end.

12. *Sought* (*ezētei*). Imperfect active, "kept on seeking," "made renewed efforts to release him." He was afraid to act

boldly against the will of the Jews. *If thou release this man* (*ean touton apoluseis*). Condition of third class, a direct threat to Pilate. He knew all the time that the Sanhedrin might tell Caesar on him. *Thou art not Caesar's friend* (*ouk ei philos tou kaisaros*). Later to Vespasian this was an official title, here simply a daring threat to Pilate. *Speaketh against Caesar* (*antilegei tōi kaisari*). Caesar brooks no rival. Jesus had allowed himself to be acclaimed king of Israel in the Triumphal Entry (John 12:13; Mark 11:10; Luke 19:38). The Sanhedrin have caught Pilate in their toils.

13. *Sat down on the judgement seat* (*ekathisen epi bēmatos*). "Took his seat upon the *bēma*" (the raised platform for the judge outside the palace as in Acts 7:5). The examination is over and Pilate is now ready for the final stage. *The Pavement* (*Lithostrōton*). Late compound from *lithos*, stone, and the verbal adjective *strōtos* form *strōnnumi*, to speak, a mosaic or tesselated pavement, spread with stones, in II Chron. 7:3, Josephus, Epictetus, papyri. The Chaldean name *Gabbathā*, an elevation, was apparently given because of the shape.

14. *The Preparation of the passover* (*paraskeuē tou pascha*). That is, Friday of passover week, the preparation day before the Sabbath of passover week (or feast). See also verses 31, 42; Mark 15:42; Matt. 27:62; Luke 23:54 for this same use of *paraskeuē* for Friday. It is the name for Friday today in Greece. *About the sixth hour* (*hōs hektē*). Roman time, about 6 A.M. (a little after 6 no doubt) when Pilate rendered his final decision. Mark (15:25) notes that it was the third hour (Jewish time), which is 9 A.M. Roman time, when the crucifixion began. Why should John give Jewish time writing at the close of the first century when Jerusalem and the Jewish state passed away in A.D. 70? He is writing for Greek and Roman readers. *Behold your king* (*Ide ho basileus humōn*). *Ide* is here an exclamation with no effect on the case of *basileus* just as in 1:29. The sarcasm of Pilate is aimed at the Jews, not at Jesus.

15. *Away with him, away with him* (*āron, āron*). First aorist active imperative of *airō*. See *aire* in Luke 23:18. This thing has gotten on the nerves of the crowd. Note the repetition. In a second-century papyrus letter (Moulton and Milligan's *Vocabulary*) a nervous mother cries "He upsets me; away with him" (*arron auton*). Pilate weakly repeats his sarcasm: ".Your king shall I crucify? (Ton basilea humōn staurōsō;). But Caesar (ei mē kaisara). The chief priests (hoi archiereis)* were Sadducees, who had no Messianic hope like that of the Pharisees. So to carry their point against Jesus they renounce the principle of the theocracy that God was their King (I Sam. 12:12).

16. *He delivered* (*paredōken*). Kappa aorist active of *paradidōmi*, the very verb used of the Sanhedrin when they handed Jesus over to Pilate (18:30, 35). Now Pilate hands Jesus back to the Sanhedrin with full consent for his death (Luke 23:25). *To be crucified* (*hina staurōthēi*). Purpose clause with *hina* and the first aorist passive subjunctive of *stauroō*. John does not give the dramatic episode in Matt. 27:24f. when Pilate washed his hands and the Jews took Christ's blood on themselves and their children. But it is on Pilate also.

17. *They took* (*parelabon*). Second aorist active indicative of *paralambanō*, they took Jesus from Pilate. Cf. 1:11; 14:3. This is after the shameful scourging between 6 A.M. and 9 A.M. when the soldiers insult Jesus *ad libitum* (Mark 15:16–19=Matt. 27:27–30).

Bearing the cross for himself (*bastazōn hautōi ton stauron*). Cf. Luke 14:27 for this very picture in the words of Jesus. The dative case of the reflexive pronoun *hautōi* "for himself" is in strict accord with Roman custom. "A criminal condemned to be crucified was required to carry his own cross" (Bernard). But apparently Jesus under the strain of the night before and the anguish of heart within him gave out so that Simon of Cyrene was impressed to carry

it for Jesus (Mark 15:21f.=Matt. 27:32f.=Luke 23:26). See
Mark 15:22f.=Matt. 27:33f.=Luke 23:33 for the meaning
of "place of a skull" or Calvary and Golgotha in Hebrew
(Aramaic). Luke has simply *Kranion* (Skull), a skull-looking
place.

18. *They crucified* (*estaurōsan*). The soldiers just as in
Acts 22:24f.; the scourging of Paul was to be done by the
soldiers. *And Jesus in the midst* (*meson de ton Iēsoun*).
Predicate adjective *meson*. A robber (*lēistēs*, not a thief,
kleptēs) was on each side of Jesus (Mark 15:27=Matt.
27:38) like Barabbas (John 18:40) and probably members
of his band, malefactors (*kakourgoi*) Luke terms them
(23:32).

19. *Pilate wrote a title also* (*egrapsen kai titlon ho Peilatos*).
Only John tells us that Pilate himself wrote it and John alone
uses the technical Latin word *titlon* (several times in inscriptions), for the board with the name of the criminal and
the crime in which he is condemned; Mark (15:26) and Luke
(23:28) use *epigraphē* (superscription). Matthew (27:37)
has simply *aitian* (accusation). The inscription in John is
the fullest of the four and has all in any of them save the
words "this is" (*houtos estin*) in Matt. 27:37.

20. *Read* (*anegnōsan*). Second aorist active indicative of
anaginōskō. It was meant to be read. Latin was the legal
and official language; Aramaic (Hebrew) was for the benefit
of the people of Jerusalem; Greek was for everybody who
passed by who did not know Aramaic. Many of the Jews
mocked as they read the accusation. This item alone in
John.

21. *But that he said* (*all' hoti ekeinos eipen*). The chief
priests were uneasy for fear that the joke in the mock title
was on them instead of on Jesus. They were right in their
fear.

22. *What I have written I have written* (*ho gegrapha gegrapha*). With emphasis on the permanence of the accusation on

the board. Pilate has a sudden spirit of stubbornness in this detail to the surprise of the chief priests. Technically he was correct, for he had condemned Jesus on this charge made by the chief priests.

23. *Four parts* (*tessera merē*). There were four soldiers, the usual quaternion (*tetradion*, Acts 12:9) besides the centurion (Mark 15:39=Matt. 27:54=Luke 23:47). The clothes (*himatia*, outer clothes) of the criminal were removed before the crucifixion and belonged to the soldiers. Luke (23:34) mentions the division of the garments, but not the number four. The four pieces would be the head gear, the sandals, the girdle, the *tallith* (outer garment with fringes). *The coat was without seam* (*ho chitōn araphos*). For *chitōn* (the inner garment) see Matt. 5:40. *Araphos* is compound of *a* privative and *raptō*, to sew together, and so seamless (unsewed together), only here in N.T. It occurs elsewhere in Josephus, *Ant.* III. 6, 4. *Woven* (*huphantos*). Verbal (old word) from *huphainō* (some MSS. in Luke 12:27), only here in N.T.

24. *Let us not rend it* (*mē schisōmen auton*). *Mē* with first aorist active volitive subjunctive of *schizō*, to split. It was too valuable to ruin. *Cast lots* (*lachōmen*). Second aorist active volitive subjunctive of *lagchanō*. The usual meaning is to obtain by lot (Luke 1:9; Acts 1:17). Field (*Ot. Norv.* 72) holds that no example has been found where it means "cast lots" as here, but Thayer cites *Isocrates*, p. 144b and *Diod.* 4, 63. John here quotes with the usual formula Psa. 22:18 (LXX verbatim) and finds a fulfilment here. The enemies of the Lord's Anointed treated him as already dead (Westcott) and so cast lots (*elabon klēron*, the common phrase as in Matt. 27:35).

25. *Were standing by the cross of Jesus* (*histēkeisan para tōi staurōi tou Iēsou*). Perfect of *histēmi*, to place, used as imperfect (intransitive) with *para* (beside) and the locative case. Vivid contrast this to the rude gambling of the soldiers. This group of four (or three) women interests us more.

Matt. (27:55f.) spoke of women beholding from afar and names three (Mary Magdalene, Mary the mother of James the less and of Joses, and the mother of the sons of Zebedee). Mark also (15:40) names three (Mary Magdalene, Mary the mother of James the less and of Joses, and Salome). They have clearly drawn near the Cross by now. John alone mentions the mother of Jesus in the group. It is not clear whether the sister of the mother of Jesus is Salome the mother of the sons of Zebedee or the wife of Clopas. If so, two sisters have the name Mary and James and John are cousins of Jesus. The point cannot be settled with our present knowledge.

26. *His mother* (*tēn mētera*). Common Greek idiom, the article as possessive. *Standing by* (*parestōta*). Perfect active (intransitive) participle of *paristēmi*, vivid and picturesque scene. The dying Saviour thinks of the comfort of his mother. *Whom he loved* (*hon ēgapa*). Imperfect active. Surely John is justified in inserting this phrase here. If John were his cousin, that helps explain why Jesus turns the care of his mother over to him. But the brothers of Jesus are not present and disbelieved his claims. John is the only one of the apostles with courage enough to take his stand with the women by the Cross. There is no disrespect in the use of "Woman" (*Gunai*) here as there was not in 2:4. This trust is to John, though Salome, John's own mother, was standing there.

27. *Unto his own home* (*eis ta idia*). See this same idiom and sense in 1:11; 16:32; Acts 21:6. John had a lodging in Jerusalem, whether a house or not, and the mother of Jesus lived with him there.

28. *Are now finished* (*ēdē tetelestai*). Perfect passive indicative of *teleō*. See same form in verse 30. As in 13·1, where Jesus is fully conscious (knowing, *eidōs*) of the meaning of his atoning death. *Might be accomplished* (*teleiōthēi*). First aorist passive subjunctive of *teleioō* rather than the usual

plērōthei (verse 24) with *hina*. John sees the thirst of Jesus in Psa. 69:21f. Jesus, of course, did not make the outcry in any mechanical way. Thirst is one of the severest agonies of crucifixion. For the "perfecting" of the Messiah by physical suffering see Heb. 2:10; 5:7ff.

29. *Was set* (*ekeito*). Imperfect middle. John, as eyewitness, had noticed it there. *Of vinegar* (*oxous*). Not vinegar drugged with myrrh (Mark 15:23) and gall (Matt. 27:34) which Jesus had refused just before the crucifixion. *Sponge* (*spoggon*). Old word, in N.T. only here, Mark 15:36; Matt. 27:48, our "sponge." *They put* (*perithentes*). Second aorist active participle of *peritithēmi*, to place around. *Upon hyssop* (*hussōpōi*). *A reed* (*kalamōi*) as Mark and Matthew have it. The reed of the hyssop bush was only three or four feet long.

30. *Had received* (*elaben*). Second aorist active indicative of *lambanō*. Jesus took the vinegar (a stimulant), though he had refused the drugged vinegar. It is finished (*tetelestai*). Same for as in verse 28. A cry of victory in the hour of defeat like *nenikēka* in 16:33. Jesus knew the relation of his death to redemption for us (Mark 10:45; Matt. 20:28; 26:28). *Bowed his head* (*klinas tēn kephalēn*). First aorist active participle of *klinō*. This vivid detail only in John. *Gave up his spirit* (*paredōken to pneuma*). With the quotation of Psa. 31:5 according to Luke 23:46, "Father, into thy hands I commend my spirit" (the last of the seven sayings of Jesus on the Cross that are preserved for us). Jesus died with the words of this Psalm upon his lips. The apostle John had come back to the Cross.

31. *The Preparation* (*paraskeuē*). Friday. See verse 14. *Might not remain* (*mē meinei*). Negative final clause with *hina mē* and first aorist active (constative) subjunctive of *menō*. *A high day* (*megalē*). A "great" day, since "the sabbath day following synchronized with the first day of unleavened bread which was a 'great' day" (Bernard). A

double reason therefore for wanting the bodies removed before sunset when the Sabbath began. *That their legs might be broken* (*hina kateagōsin autōn ta skelē*). Purpose clause with *hina* and the second aorist passive subjunctive of *katagnumi* with the augment retained in the subjunctive, a "false augment" common in later Greek as in the future in Matt. 12:20 with this verb (Robertson, *Grammar*, p. 365). This *crurifragium* was done with a heavy mallet and ended the sufferings of the victim. *Legs* (*skelē*). Old word, here only in N.T. *Might be taken away* (*arthōsin*). First· aorist passive subjunctive of *airō* with *hina* also.

32. *Which was crucified with him* (*tou sunstaurōthentos autōi*). First aorist passive articular participle of *sunstauroō* with associative instrumental case. Cf. Paul's *Christōi sunestaurōmai* (Gal. 2:19).

33. *Already dead* (*ēdē tethnēkota*). Perfect active participle of *thnēskō*. So then Jesus died before the robbers, died of a broken heart. *They brake not* (*ou kateaxan*). The augment is proper here (see 32).

34. *With a spear* (*logchēi*). Instrumental case of this old word, here only in the N.T. *Pierced his side* (*autou tēn pleuran enuxen*). First aorist active indicative of *nussō*, old word to pierce, here only in N.T., and *pleuran* (side), another old word, occurs in N.T. only here and John 20:20, 25, 27. *Blood and water* (*haima kai hudōr*). Dr. W. Stroud (*Physical Cause of the Death of Christ*) argues that this fact proves that the spear pierced the left side of Jesus near the heart and that Jesus had died literally of a broken heart since blood was mixed with water.

35. *He that hath seen* (*ho heōrakōs*). Perfect active articular participle of *horaō*. John the Apostle was there and saw this fact (still sees it, in fact). This personal witness disproves the theory of the Docetic Gnostics that Jesus did not have a real human body. *He knoweth* (*ekeinos oiden*). That is John does like 9:37. It is possible that *ekeinos* may be a

solemn appeal to God as in 1:33 or Christ as in I John 3:5. Bernard argues that the final editor is distinguishing the Beloved Disciple from himself and is endorsing him. But the example of Josephus (*War*. III. 7, 16) is against this use of *ekeinos*. John is rather referring to himself as still alive.

36. *Be broken* (*suntribēsetai*). Second future passive of *suntribō*, to crush together. A free quotation of Ex. 12:46 about the paschal lamb.

37. *They pierced* (*exekentēsan*). First aorist active of *ekkenteō*, late verb, correct translation of the Hebrew of Zech. 12:10, but not like the LXX, in N.T. only here and Rev. 1:7.

38. *But secretly for fear of the Jews* (*kekrummenos de dia ton phobon tōn Ioudaiōn*). Perfect passive participle of *kruptō*. An example of the rulers described in 12:41–43 who through cowardice feared to own their faith in Jesus as the Messiah. But it must be put down to the credit of Joseph that he showed courage in this darkest hour when the majority had lost heart. *That he might take away* (*hina arēi*). Final clause with *hina* and the first aorist active subjunctive of *airō*. Else the body of Jesus might have gone to the potter's field. Pilate gladly consented.

39. *Nicodemus also* (*kai Nikodēmos*). The Synoptics tell about Joseph of Arimathea, but only John adds the help that Nicodemus gave him in the burial of Jesus, these two timid disciples, Nicodemus now at last taking an open stand. *At the first* (*to prōton*). Adverbial accusative and reference to 3:1ff. *Mixture* (*migma*). Late word from *mignumi*, to mix, only here in the N.T. Many old MSS. have here *heligma* (roll), from *helissō* (Heb. 1:12), another late word here only in N.T. It was common to use sweet-smelling spices in the burial (II Chron. 16:14). *Pound* (*litras*). Late word for twelve ounces, in N.T. only here and 12:3. Nicodemus was a rich man and probably covered the entire body with the spices.

40. *In linen cloths* (*othoniois*). Late diminutive for the old *othonē*, used for ships' sails, in N.T. here and Luke 24:12. Case here either locative or instrumental. *With the spices* (*meta tōn arōmatōn*). Late word *arōma* for spices, from fumes. *To bury* (*entaphiazein*). Late verb, from *entaphia* (*en, taphos*) the burial preparations of all sorts (flowers, perfumes, etc.), in N.T. only here and Matt. 26:12.

41. *A garden* (*kēpos*). See 18:1, 26. *New* (*kainon*). Fresh, unused. *Was never yet laid* (*oudepō ēn tetheimenos*). Periphrastic past perfect passive of *tithēmi*. It was Joseph's mausoleum, a rock tomb hewn out of the mountain side (Mark 15:56 = Matt. 27:60 = Luke 23:53), a custom common with the rich then and now. For royal tombs in gardens see II Kings 21:18, 26; Neh. 3:16.

42. *Was nigh at hand* (*eggus ēn*). This tomb was outside of the city, near a road as the Cross was, and in a garden. The hill looked like a skull and was probably Gordon's Calvary seen from the Mount of Olives today.

CHAPTER XX

1. *Now on the first day of the week (tēi de miāi tōn sabbatōn).*
Locative case of time when. Both Mark (16:2) and Luke
(24:1) have this very idiom of the cardinal *tēi miāi*, instead
of the usual ordinal *tēi prōtēi* (first), an idiom common in the
papyri and in the modern Greek (Robertson, *Grammar*,
p. 671). In all three instances also we have the genitive
plural *tōn sabbatōn* for "the week" as in Acts 20:7. The
singular *sabbaton* also occurs for "the week" as in Luke
18:12; Mark 16:9. *Cometh Mary Magdalene (Maria hē
Magdalēnē erchetai).* Vivid historical present. Mary Magdalene is not to be confounded with Mary of Bethany. *While
it was yet dark (skotias eti ousēs).* Genitive absolute. For
skotia see John 6:17; Matt. 10:27. Mark (16:2) says the sun
was risen on their actual arrival. She started from the house
while still dark. *Taken away (ērmenon).* Perfect passive
participle of *airō*, predicate accusative in apposition with
ton lithon.

2. *Runneth (trechei).* Vivid dramatic present indicative
of *trechō*. John deals only with Mary Magdalene. She left
the tomb at once before the rest and without seeing the
angels as told in the Synoptics (Mark 16:2-8 = Matt.
28:5-8 = Luke 24:1-8). Luke (24:9-12) does not distinguish
between the separate report of Mary Magdalene and that of
the other women. *To Simon Peter (pros Simōna Petron).*
Full name as usual in John and back with John and the other
disciples. The association of Peter and the other disciple in
John 18 to 21 is like that between Peter and John in Acts 1
to 5. *Loved (ephilei).* Imperfect of *phileō* for which see
5:20; 11:3 and for distinction from *agapaō* see 11:5; 13:23;
21:7, 15, 17. *They have taken away (ēran).* First aorist active

indicative of *airō*, indefinite plural. *We know not (ouk oid-amen)*. Mary associates the other women with her in her ignorance. For *ethēkan* (have laid) see 19:42. Mary fears a grave robbery. She has no idea of the resurrection of Jesus.

3. *They went (ērchonto)*. Imperfect middle picturing the scene, "they were going." The two started instantly (*exēlthen*, aorist active indicative).

4. *They both (hoi duo)*. "The two" (Peter and the other disciple whom Jesus loved). *Ran together (etrechon homou)*. Imperfect active of *trechō*. It was a race in eagerness to reach the tomb of Jesus. *Outran Peter (proedramen tacheion tou Petrou)*. Second aorist active indicative of *protrechō*, old verb, in N.T. only here and Luke 19:4, to run on before (ahead). "He ran ahead more swiftly (see John 13:27) than Peter" (ablative case after comparative adverb *tacheion*, Koiné for older *thāsson*). *First (prōtos)*. Predicative nominative (not adverb *prōton*) and superlative used where only two involved. John won the race.

5. *Stooping and looking in (parakupsas)*. Originally to stoop and look, but in the LXX (Gen. 26:8; Judges 5:28; I Kings 6:4, etc.) and the papyri rather just to peep in and so Field (*Ot. Norv.*) urges here. See also verse 11 and Luke 24:12 (the verse bracketed by Westcott and Hort). For *othonia* (linen cloth) see John 19:40. *Lying (keimena)*. Present middle participle of *keimai*, predicative accusative. John notices this fact at once. If the body had been removed, these clothes would have gone also. John's timid nature made him pause (yet, *mentoi*, however).

6. *Entered and beholdeth (eisēlthen kai theōrei)*. Aorist active and present active indicative. Peter impulsively went on in and beholds (*theōrei*, vivid term again, but of careful notice, *theōreō*, not a mere glance *blepō* such as John gave in verse 5).

7. *The napkin (to soudarion)*. Already in 11:44 which see. This napkin for the head was in a separate place.

Rolled up (entetuligmenon). Perfect passive participle, predicate accusative like *keimenon*, from *entulissō*, late verb, to wrap in, to roll up, already in Matt. 27:59 and Luke 23:53. It was arranged in an orderly fashion. There was no haste. *By itself (chōris)*. Old adverb, "apart," "separately."

8. *Then therefore (tote oun)*. After Peter in time and influenced by the boldness of Peter. *And he saw and believed (kai eiden kai episteusen)*. Both aorist active indicative (second and first). Peter saw more after he entered than John did in his first glance, but John saw into the meaning of it all better than Peter. Peter had more sight, John more insight. John was the first to believe that Jesus was risen from the tomb even before he saw him. According to Luke 24:12 Peter went away "wondering" still. The Sinaitic Syriac and 69 and 124 wrongly read here "they believed." John was evidently proud to be able to record this great moment when he believed without seeing in contrast to Thomas (20:29). Peter and John did not see the angels.

9. *For (gar)*. Explanatory use of *gar*. *The Scripture (tēn graphēn)*. Probably Psa. 16:10. Jesus had repeatedly foretold his resurrection, but that was all forgotten in the great sorrow on their hearts. Only the chief priests and Pharisees recalled the words of Jesus (Matt. 27:62ff.). *Must (dei)*. For this use of *dei* concerning Christ's death and resurrection see Mark 8:31; Matt. 26:54; Luke 9:22; 17:25; 22:37; 24:7, 26, 44; John 3:14; 12:34; Acts 1:16. Jesus had put emphasis on both the fact and the necessity of his resurrection which the disciples slowly perceived.

10. *Unto their own home (pros hautous)*. "To themselves." Luke (24:12) has *pros hauton* about Peter ("to his home"). This use of the reflective pronoun for home (literally, "to themselves"), like the French *chez eux*, occurs in Josephus (*Ant.* VII. 4, 6). John had taken the mother of Jesus to his home (19:27) and so he now hurried home to tell her the glorious news as he believed.

11. *Was standing* (*histēkei*). Past perfect of *histēmi* as imperfect as in 19:25. *At the tomb* (*pros tōi mnēmeiōi*). *Pros* (in front of) with locative while *para* (by the side of) with locative in 19:25. Pathetic and common picture of a woman weeping by the tomb. See 11:31. *As she wept* (*hōs eklaien*). Imperfect, "as she was weeping." *She stooped and looked* (*parekupsen*). Aorist active indicative of *parakuptō* for which see verse 5. Mary "peeped into" the tomb, but did not enter.

12. *Beholdeth* (*theōrei*). Vivid historical present again as in verses 6 and 14. Peter and John had not seen the two angels. Westcott suggests an "economy" in such manifestations as the explanations. Better our own ignorance as to the reason why only the women saw them. Angels were commonly believed to be clad in white. See Mark 16:5 (a young man in a white robe), Matt. 28:5 (the angel), Luke 24:4 (two men in dazzling apparel). For other angels in John's Gospel see 1:41; 12:29; 20:12. *Had lain* (*ekeito*). Imperfect in progressive sense, "had been lying," though not there now.

13. *I do not know* (*ouk oida*). Singular here, not plural as in verse 2, because clearly Mary is alone here. But the problem is the same. She did not see Peter and John at the tomb.

14. *She turned herself back* (*estraphē eis ta opisō*). Second aorist passive indicative of *strephō* in an intransitive and almost reflective sense. In the disappearance of the aorist middle before the aorist passive see Robertson, *Grammar*, p. 817. See also *strapheisa* (second aorist passive participle) in verse 16. On *eis ta opisō* see 6:66; 18:6. *Standing* (*hestōta*). Second perfect active (intransitive) of *histēmi*. Instinctively Mary felt the presence of some one behind her. *Was* (*estin*). Present active indicative retained in indirect discourse after *ēidei* (knew).

15. *Sir* (*Kurie*). Clearly not "Lord" here, for she thought him to be "the gardener" (*ho kēpouros*), old word (*kēpos*,

ouros), keeper of the garden, only here in the N.T. *If thou hast borne him hence (ei su ebastasos auton)*. Condition of the first class. Note emphasis on *su* (thou). A new idea struck Mary as mistaken as the other one. Jesus had repeated the question of the angels, but she did not recognize him. *And I (kágō)*. Emphasis and crasis.

16. *Mary (Mariam)*. Aramaic form in Aleph B W, though *Maria* in 19:25. Clearly the old familiar tone of Jesus was in the pronunciation of her name. *Rabboni (Rabbounei)*. Aramaic again for *Didaskale* (Teacher), "my Teacher." In N.T. only here and Mark 10:51 though practically the same as *Rabbi*. See 11:28 for "the Teacher" (Rabbi). These two simple words tell the great fact that Christ is risen and Mary has seen him. One says little in really great moments.

17. *Touch me not (mē mou haptou)*. Present middle imperative in prohibition with genitive case, meaning "cease clinging to me" rather than "Do not touch me." Jesus allowed the women to take hold of his feet *(ekratēsan)* and worship *(prosekunēsan)* as we read in Matt. 28:9. The prohibition here reminds Mary that the previous personal fellowship by sight, sound, and touch no longer exists and that the final state of glory was not yet begun. Jesus checks Mary's impulsive eagerness. *For I am not yet ascended (oupō gar anabebēka)*. Perfect active indicative. Jesus is here at all only because he has not yet gone home. He had said (16:7) that it was good for them that he should go to the Father when the Holy Spirit will come through whom they will have fellowship with the Father and Christ. *My God (theou mou)*. Jesus had said "My God" on the Cross (Mark 15:34). Note it also in Rev. 3:2. So Paul in Rom. 15:6, etc., has "the God and Father of our Lord Jesus Christ."

18. *And telleth (aggellousa)*. Present active participle, "announcing." *I have seen the Lord (Heōraka ton kurion)*. Perfect active indicative of *horaō*. She will always carry in her heart that vision (picture) of the Risen Christ. She tells

this fact before she delivers Christ's message to the brethren of Christ. *How that.* No word in the Greek, but a conjunction like *hōs* is implied. *Hoti* here is recitative. The disciples (brethren) did not believe Mary's story nor that of the other women (Luke 24:11; Mark 16:11). Paul does not mention the vision to Mary or the women in I Cor. 15:5–7. But Mary Magdalene was the first one to see the Risen Lord.

19. *When therefore it was evening on that day (ousēs oun opsias tēi hēmerāi ekeinei).* Genitive absolute with *opsia* (*opsios*, late), old word with *hōra* (hour) understood and here for the time from six to nine (6:16) and the locative case of time with *hēmerāi* (day). John often uses this note of time (1:39; 5:9; 11:53; 14:20; 16:23, 26). The addition of *tēi miāi sabbatōn* (see 20:1 for this use of *miāi* like *prōtēi*) proves that John is using Roman time, not Jewish, for here evening follows day instead of preceding it. *When the doors were shut (tōn thurōn kekleismenōn).* Genitive absolute again with perfect passive participle of *kleiō*, shut to keep the Jews out. News of the empty tomb had already spread (Matt. 28:11). See John 7:13 for the phrase "for fear of the Jews"; cf. 12:42. *Stood in the midst (estē eis to meson).* Second aorist (ingressive) active (intransitive) of *histēmi*, "stepped into the midst." *Peace be unto you (Eirēnē humin).* The usual oriental salutation as in verses 21, 26 and Luke 24:36, here with probable reference to John 14:27 (Christ's legacy of peace).

20. *Showed (edeixen).* First aorist active indicative of *deiknumi.* This body, not yet glorified, retained the marks of the nails and of the soldier's spear, ample proof of the bodily resurrection against the modern view that only Christ's "spirit" arose and against the Docetic notion that Jesus had no actual human body. Luke (24:39f.) adds feet to hands and side. *Were glad (echarēsan).* Second aorist passive indicative of *chairō.* Jesus had said (16:22) that it

would be so. Luke adds (24:41) that they "disbelieved for joy." It was too good to be true, though terror had first seized them when Jesus appeared (Luke 24:37) because of the suddenness of Christ's appearance and their highly wrought state.

21. *Even so send I you* (*kágō pempō humas*). Jesus has often spoken of the Father's sending him using both *apostellō* and *pempō*. Here he employs both words in practically the same sense. Jesus still bears the Commission of the Father (perfect active indicative). For this balanced contention (as . . . so) see 6:57; 10:15. This is the first of the three commissions given by the Risen Christ (another on the mountain in Galilee (Matt. 28:16-20; I Cor. 15:6), another on the Mount of Olives (Luke 24:44-51; Acts 1:3-11).

22. *He breathed on them* (*enephusēsen*). First aorist active indicative of *emphusaō*, late verb, here only in N.T. though eleven times in the LXX and in the papyri. It was a symbolic art with the same word used in the LXX when God breathed the breath of life upon Adam (Gen. 2:7). It occurs also in Ezek. 37:9. See Christ's promise in John 16:23. Jesus gives the disciples a foretaste of the great pentecost. *Receive ye the Holy Ghost* (*labete pneuma hagion*). Second aorist (ingressive) active imperative of *lambanō*. Note absence of article here (*pneuma hagion*) though *to pneuma to hagion* in 14:26. No real distinction is to be observed, for Holy Spirit is treated as a proper name with or without the article.

23. *Whosesoever sins ye forgive* (*an tinōn aphēte tas hamartias*). "If the sins of any ye forgive" (*aphēte*, second aorist active subjunctive with *an* in the sense of *ean*), a condition of the third class. Precisely so with "retain" (*kratēte*, present active subjunctive of *krateō*). *They are forgiven* (*apheōntai*). Perfect passive indicative of *aphiēmi*, Doric perfect for *apheintai*. *Are retained* (*kekratēntai*). Perfect passive indicative of *krateō*. The power to forgive sin belongs only

to God, but Jesus claimed to have this power and right
(Mark 2:5–7). What he commits to the disciples and to us
is the power and privilege of giving assurance of the forgiveness of sins by God by correctly announcing the terms
of forgiveness. There is no proof that he actually transferred
to the apostles or their successors the power in and of themselves to forgive sins. In Matt. 16:19 and 18:18 we have a
similar use of the rabbinical metaphor of binding and loos-
ing by proclaiming and teaching. Jesus put into the hands
of Peter and of all believers the keys of the Kingdom which
we should use to open the door for those who wish to enter.
This glorious promise applies to all believers who will tell
the story of Christ's love for men.

24. *Didymus* (*Didumos*). The same expression applied
to Thomas in 11:16 and in 21:2, but nowhere else in N.T.
Old word for twin (double), "the pessimist of the apostolic
band" (Bernard). The term twelve is still applied to the
group, though Judas, the traitor, is dead.

25. *We have seen the Lord* (*heōrakamen ton kurion*). The
very language in the plural that Mary Magdalene had used
(20:18) when no one believed her. *Except I shall see* (*ean mē
idō*). Negative condition of third class with *ean* and second
aorist active subjunctive and so as to *balō* (from *ballō*) "and
put." *The print* (*ton tupon*). The mark or stamp made by
the nails, here the original idea. Various terms as in Acts
7:44; I Tim. 4:12. Finally our "type" as in Rom. 5:14.
Clearly the disciples had told Thomas that they had seen
the *tupon* of the nails in his hands and the spear in his side.
I will not believe (*ou mē pisteusō*). Strong refusal with *ou mē*
(doubtful negative) and first aorist active subjunctive (or
future indicative).

26. *After eight days* (*meth' hēmeras oktō*). That is the
next Sunday evening, on the eighth day in reality just like
"after three days" and "on the third day." *Within* (*esō*).
Apparently in the same room as before. *Cometh* (*erchetai*).

Vivid dramatic present. The other items precisely as in verse 19 save Thomas was with them.

27. *Then saith he to Thomas* (*eita legei tōi Thomāi*). Jesus turns directly to Thomas as if he had come expressly for his sake. He reveals his knowledge of the doubt in the mind of Thomas and mentions the very tests that he had named (25). *Be not faithless* (*mē ginou apistos*). Present middle imperative of *ginomai* in prohibition, "stop becoming disbelieving." The doubt of Thomas in the face of the witness of the others was not a proof of his superior intelligence. Sceptics usually pose as persons of unusual mentality. The medium who won Sir Arthur Conan Doyle to spiritualism has confessed that it was all humbug, but he deceived the gullible novelist. But Thomas had carried his incredulity too far. Note play on *apistos* (disbelieving) and *pistos* (believing).

28. *My Lord and my God* (*Ho kurios mou kai ho theos mou*). Not exclamation, but address, the vocative case though the form of the nominative, a very common thing in the *Koiné*. Thomas was wholly convinced and did not hesitate to address the Risen Christ as Lord and God. And Jesus accepts the words and praises Thomas for so doing.

29. *Thou hast believed* (*pepisteukas*). Perfect active indicative. Probably interrogative, but "it was *sight*, not *touch* that convinced Thomas" (Bernard). *And yet* (*kai*). Clear use of *kai* in the adversative sense. Thomas made a noble confession, but he missed the highest form of faith without the evidence of the senses. Peter (I Peter 1:8) uses language that seems like a reminiscence of the words of Jesus to Thomas which Peter heard.

30. *Many other signs* (*polla alla sēmeia*). Not only those described in the Synoptic Gospels or referred to in general statements, but many alluded to in John's Gospel (2:23; 4:45; 12:37). *Are not written* (*ouk estin gegrammena*). Periphrastic perfect passive indicative of *graphō*, do not stand written, are not described "in this book." John has made a

selection of the vast number wrought by Jesus "in the presence of the disciples" (*enōpion tōn mathētōn*), common idiom in Luke, not in Mark and Matthew, and by John elsewhere only in I John 3:22. John's book is written with a purpose which he states.

31. *Are written* (*gegraptai*). Perfect passive indicative of *graphō*, "have been written" by John. *That ye may believe* (*hina pisteuēte*). Purpose with *hina* and the present active subjunctive of *pisteuō*, "that you may keep on believing." The book has had precisely this effect of continuous and successive confirmation of faith in Jesus Christ through the ages. *Jesus is the Christ, the Son of God* (*Iēsous estin ho Christos ho huios tou theou*). The man named Jesus is identical with the Messiah (the Anointed One) as opposed to the Cerinthian separation of the Jesus of history and the Christ (*aeon*) of theology. And the Docetic notion of a phantom body for Jesus with no actual human body is also false. Jesus is the Son of God with all that this high term implies, the Logos of John 1:1–18 (the Prologue). "Very God of very God," Incarnate Revealer of God. But there is a further purpose. *And that believing ye may have life in his name* (*kai hina pisteuontes zōēn echēte en tōi onomati autou*). Note present participle *pisteuontes* (continuing to believe) and the present active subjunctive *echēte* (keep on having). "Life" (*zōēn*) is eternal life so often mentioned in this Gospel, life to be found only in the name (and power) of Jesus Christ the Son of God. This verse constitutes a fitting close for this wonderful book and John may at first have intended to stop here. But before he published the work he added the Epilogue (Chapter XXI) which is written in the same style and gives a beautiful picture of the Risen Christ with a sidelight on John and Peter (restored to fellowship).

CHAPTER XXI

1. *Manifested himself (ephanerosen heauton)*. First aorist active indicative of *phaneroō* with the reflexive pronoun (cf. 7:4; 13:4). For the passive. see 1:31 and 21:14. Jesus was only seen during the forty days now and then (Acts 1:3), ten instances being recorded. The word *phaneroō* is often used of Christ on earth (John 1:31; 2:11; I Peter 1:20; I John 1:2), of his works (John 3:5), of the second coming (I John 2:28), of Christ in glory (Col. 3:4; I John 3:2). *At (epi)*. By or upon. *Of Tiberias (tēs Tiberiados)*. As in 6:1 instead of the usual "Sea of Galilee." Tiberias, the capital city of Galilee, gave this epithet to the Sea of Galilee. This is not the appearance in Galilee prearranged by Jesus (Mark 16:7; Matt. 28:7, 16).

2. *There were together (ēsan homou)*. These seven (Peter, Thomas, Nathanael, the sons of Zebedee, and two others). We know that the sons of Zebedee were James and John (Matt. 4:21), mentioned by name nowhere in John's Gospel, apparently because John is the author. We do not know who the "two others of his disciples" were, possibly Andrew and Philip. It seems to me to be crass criticism in spite of Harnack and Bernard to identify the incident here with that in Luke 5:1-11. There are a few points of similarity, but the differences are too great for such identification even with a hypothetical common source.

3. *I go a fishing (hupagō halieuein)*. The present active infinitive *halieuein* expresses purpose as often. It is a late verb from *halieus* (fisherman) and occurs in Jer. 16:16, in Philo, Plutarch, and one papyrus. Peter's proposal was a natural one. He had been a fisherman by practice and they were probably waiting in Galilee for the appointed meeting

with Christ on the mountain. Andrew and Peter, James and John were fishermen also. Peter's proposition met a ready response from all. *They took* (*epiasan*). First aorist active indicative of *piazō*, Doric form for *piezō*, to catch.

4. *When day was now breaking* (*prōias ēdē ginomenēs*). Genitive absolute and note present middle participιe (dawn coming on and still dark). In Matt. 27:1 the aorist participle (*genomenēs*) means that dawn had come. For "beach" (*aigialon*) see Matt. 13:2. *Was* (*estin*). Present indicative retained in indirect assertion.

5. *Children* (*Paidia*). Diminutive of *pais* and used here alone by Jesus in addressing his disciples. It is a colloquial expression like "my boys." The aged Apostle John uses it in I John 2:13, 18. *Have ye aught to eat?* (*mē ti prosphagion echete;*). The negative answer is expected by this polite inquiry as in 4:29. The rare and late word *prosphagion* from the root *phag* (*esthiō*, to eat) and *pros* (in addition) was used for a relish with bread and then for fish as here. So in the papyri. Nowhere else in the N.T.

6. *The right side* (*eis ta dexia merē*). Jesus knew where the fish were. For "net" (*diktuon*) see Matt. 4:20, here alone in John. *Were now not able to draw it* (*ouketi auto helkusai ischuon*). Imperfect active picturing the disciples tugging at the net.

7. *It is the Lord* (*ho kurios estin*). John's quick insight appears again. *Girt his coat about him* (*ton ependutēn diezōsato*). First aorist middle (indirect) indicative with which note *diezōsen heauton* in 13:4. Apparently Peter threw on the upper garment or linen blouse (*ependutēn*) worn by fishers over his waistcloth and tucked it under his girdle.

8. *In the little boat* (*tōi ploiariōi*). Locative case of *ploiarion* (diminutive) for the larger boat (*ploion*, verses 3 and 6) could come no closer to shore. But the words seem interchangeable in 6:17, 19, 21, 22, 24. *About two hundred cubits off* (*hōs apo pēchōn diakosiōn*). For *pēchus*, cubit, see Matt.

6:27 and for *hōs apo* see 11:18. *Dragging (surontes)*. Present active participle of *surō* for which see Acts 8:3.

9. *Got out (apebēsan)*. As in Luke 5:2. *They see (blepousin)*. Vivid historical present. *A fire of coals (anthrakian)*. See 18:18 for this word. Cf. our "anthracite." *There (keimenēn)*. Lying as placed, present middle participle of *keimai*. *Fish (opsarion)*. As in 6:9, 11, like *prosphagion* above. *Laid thereon (epikeimenon)*. So broiling with bread ready (toast).

10. *Which (hōn)*. Ablative case by attraction from *ha* to agree with *opsariōn*. They had caught the fish by Christ's direction.

11. *Went up (anebē)*. Into the little boat or dinghy. *Drew (heilkusen)*. Same verb as *helkusai* in verse 6. Peter now did what they had failed to do. *Three (triōn)*. The addition "three" to the "hundred and fifty" looks as if they were actually counted these "large" (*megalōn*) fish. It was a great fish story that John recalls vividly. *Was not rent (ouk eschisthē)*. First aorist passive indicative of *schizō*, to split (our word "schism").

12. *Break your fast (aristēsate)*. First aorist active imperative of *aristaō* from *ariston*, first to breakfast, as here and then later to dine as in Luke 11:37. What a delightful breakfast of fresh broiled fish just caught (verse 10) with the hush of joyful surprise in the presence of the Risen Lord. *Durst (etolma)*. Imperfect active of *tolmaō*. The restraint of silence continued.

13. *Taketh the bread, and giveth them (lambanei ton arton kai didōsin autois)*. Vivid presents again. Jesus acts as host at this early breakfast, his last meal with these seven faithful followers.

14. *Now the third time (to ēdē triton)*. "To the disciples" (apostles) John says, the two others being told by him (20:19, 26) on the two Sunday evenings. There were four other appearances already (to Mary Magdalene, to the group of women, to the two on the way to Emmaus, to Peter).

15. *Lovest thou me more than these?* (*agapāis me pleon toutōn;*). Ablative case of comparison *toutōn* (disciples) after *pleon*. Peter had even boasted that he would stand by Christ though all men forsook him (Mark 14:29). We do not know what passed between Jesus and Peter when Jesus first appeared to him (Luke 24:34). But here Christ probes the inmost recesses of Peter's heart to secure the humility necessary for service. *I love thee* (*philō su*). Peter makes no claim here to superior love and passes by the "more than these" and does not even use Christ's word *agapāō* for high and devoted love, but the humbler word *phileō* for love as a friend. He insists that Christ knows this in spite of his conduct. *Feed my lambs* (*Boske ta arnia mou*). For the old word *boskō* (to feed as a herdsman) see Matt. 8:33. Present active imperative here. *Arnia* is a diminutive of *arnos* (lamb).

16. *Lovest thou me?* (*agapāis me;*). This time Jesus drops the *pleon toutōn* and challenges Peter's own statement. Peter repeats the same words in reply. *Tend my sheep* (*poimaine ta probatia*). Present active imperative of *poimainō*, old verb from *poimēn* (shepherd), "shepherd my lambs" (*probatia*, diminutive of *probaton*, sheep).

17. *Lovest thou me?* (*phileis me;*). This time Jesus picks up the word *phileō* used by Peter and challenges that. These two words are often interchanged in the N.T., but here the distinction is preserved. Peter was cut to the heart (*elupēthē*, first aorist passive of *lupeō*, to grieve) because Jesus challenges this very verb, and no doubt the third question vividly reminds him of the three denials in the early morning by the fire. He repeats his love for Jesus with the plea: "Thou knowest all things." *Feed my sheep* (*boske ta probatia*). Many MSS. both here and in verse 16 read *probata* (sheep) instead of *probatia* (little sheep or lambs).

18. *Thou girdest thyself* (*ezōnnues seauton*). Imperfect active of customary action of *zōnnuō*, old verb, in N.T. only

here and Acts 12:8. So as to *periepateis* (walkedst) and *ētheles* (wouldest), two other imperfects of customary action. *When thou shalt be old* (*hotan gēraseis*). Indefinite temporal clause with *hotan* and the first aorist active subjunctive of *gē-raskō*, old verb to grow old, in N.T. only here and Heb. 8:13, "whenever thou growest old."

19. *By what manner of death* (*poiōi thanatōi*). Undoubtedly John, who is writing long after Peter's death, seems to mean that Peter was to die (and did die) a martyr's death. "Whither thou wouldest not." There is a ·tradition that Peter met death by crucifixion and asked to be crucified head downwards, but that is not made plain here.

20. *Turning about* (*epistrapheis*). Second aorist passive participle of *epistrephō*, old verb, here a sudden turning round (ingressive aorist). For the simplex verb *strephō* see 20:14, 16. *Following* (*akolouthounta*). Following both Jesus and Peter, perhaps having heard the graphic dialogue above.

21. *And what shall this man do?* (*houtos de ti;*). Literally, "But this one . . . what?" The abrupt ellipsis is intelligible.

22. *If I will* (*ean thelō*). Condition of the third class with *ean* and the present active subjunctive of *thelō*. *Till I come* (*heōs erchomai*). Literally, "while I am coming" (*heōs* and the present indicative, not *heōs elthō* (second aorist active subjunctive). *What is that to thee?* (*ti pros se;*). A sharp rebuke to Peter's keen curiosity. *Follow thou me* (*su moi akolouthei*). "Do thou me keep on following." That lesson Peter needed.

23. *That that disciple should not die* (*hoti ho mathētēs ekeinos ouk apothnēskei*) (present active indicative), because Peter or others misunderstood what Jesus meant as John now carefully explains. He was rebuking Peter's curiosity, not affirming that John would live on till the Master returned. John is anxious to set this matter right.

24. *That is* (*houtos estin*). The one just mentioned in verse 20, "the disciple whom Jesus loved." *And wrote these things* (*kai ho grapsas tauta*). Here there is a definite statement that the Beloved Disciple wrote this book. *We know* (*oidamen*). The plural here seems intentional as the identification and endorsement of a group of disciples who know the author and wish to vouch for his identity and for the truthfulness of his witness. Probably we see here a verse added by a group of elders in Ephesus where John had long laboured.

25. *If they should be written every one* (*ean graphētai kath' hen*). Condition of the third class with *ean* and present passive subjunctive of *graphō*, "If they should be written one by one" (in full detail). *I suppose* (*oimai*). Note change back to the first person singular by the author. *Would not contain* (*oud' auton ton kosmon chōrēsein*). Future active infinitive in indirect discourse after *oimai*. This is, of course, natural hyperbole, but graphically pictures for us the vastness of the work and words of Jesus from which the author has made a small selection (20:30f.) and by which he has produced what is, all things considered, the greatest of all the books produced by man, the eternal gospel from the eagle who soars to the very heavens and gives us a glimpse of the glory of God in the face of Jesus Christ.

THE EPISTLE TO THE HEBREWS

ABOUT 69 A.D.

BY WAY OF INTRODUCTION

Unsettled Problems

Probably no book in the New Testament presents more unsettled problems than does the Epistle to the Hebrews. On that score it ranks with the Fourth Gospel, the Apocalypse of John, and Second Peter. But, in spite of these unsolved matters, the book takes high rank for its intellectual grasp, spiritual power, and its masterful portrayal of Christ as High Priest. It is much briefer than the Fourth Gospel, but in a sense it carries on further the exalted picture of the Risen Christ as the King-Priest who reigns and pleads for us now.

The Picture of Christ

At once we are challenged by the bold stand taken by the author concerning the Person of Christ as superior to the prophets of the Old Testament because he is the Son of God through whom God has spoken in the new dispensation (1:1–3), this Son who is God's Agent in the work of creation and of grace as we see it stated in Phil. 2:5–11; Col. 1:13–20; John 1:1–18. This high doctrine of Jesus as God's Son with the glory and stamp of God's nature is never lowered, for as God's Son he is superior to angels (1:4–2:4), though the humanity of Jesus is recognized as one proof of the glory of Jesus (2:5–18). Jesus is shown to be superior to Moses as God's Son over God's house (3:1–4:13). But the chief portion of the Epistle is devoted to the superiority of Jesus Christ as priest to the work of Aaron and the whole Levitical line (4:14–12:3). Here the author with consummate skill, though with rabbinical refinements at times, shows that Jesus is like Melchizedek and so superior to Aaron (4:14–

327

7:28), works under a better covenant of grace (8:1–13), works in a better sanctuary which is in heaven (9:1–12), offers a better sacrifice which is his own blood (9:13–10:18), and gives us better promises for the fulfilment of his task (10:19–12:3). Hence this Epistle deserves to be called the Epistle of the Priesthood of Christ. So W. P. Du Bose calls his exposition of the book, *High Priesthood and Sacrifice* (1908). This conception of Christ as our Priest who offered himself on the Cross and as our Advocate with the Father runs all through the New Testament (Mark 10:46; Matt. 20:28; John 10:17; Matt. 26:28; Rom. 8:32; I Peter 1:18f.; I John 2:1f.; Rev. 5:9, etc.). But it is in Hebrews that we have the full-length portrait of Jesus Christ as our Priest and Redeemer. The Glory of Jesus runs through the whole book.

The Style

It is called an epistle and so it is, but of a peculiar kind. In fact, as has been said, it begins like a treatise, proceeds like a sermon, and concludes like a letter. It is, in fact, more like a literary composition than any other New Testament book as Deissmann shows: "It points to the fact that the Epistle to the Hebrews, with its more definitely artistic, more literary language (corresponding to its more theological subject matter), constituted an epoch in the history of the new religion. Christianity is beginning to lay hands on the instruments of culture; the literary and theological period has begun" (*Light from the Ancient East*, pp. 70f.). But Blass (*Die Rhythmen der asianischen und römischen Kunstprosa*, 1905) argues that the author of Hebrews certainly and Paul probably were students of Greek oratory and rhetoric. He is clearly wrong about Paul and probably so about the author of Hebrews. There is in Hebrews more of "a studied rhetorical periodicity" (Thayer), but with many "parenthetical involutions" (Westcott) and with less of "the impetuous eloquence of Paul." The eleventh chapter reveals a studied style and as a whole the Epistle belongs to the literary *Koiné* rather than to the vernacular. Moulton (*Cambridge Biblical Essays*, p. 483) thinks that the author did not know Hebrew but follows the Septuagint throughout in his abundant use of the Old Testament.

THE AUTHOR

Origen bluntly wrote: "Who wrote the Epistle God only knows certainly" as quoted by Eusebius. Origen held that the thoughts were Paul's while Clement of Rome or Luke may have written the book. Clement of Alexandria (Eusebius says) thought that Paul wrote it in Hebrew and that Luke translated it into Greek. No early writer apparently attributed the Greek text to Paul. Eusebius thought it was originally written in Hebrew whether by Paul or not and translated by Clement of Rome. But there is no certainty anywhere in the early centuries. It was accepted first in the east and later in the west which first rejected it. But Jerome and Augustine accepted it. When the Renaissance came Erasmus had doubts, Luther attributed it to Apollos, Calvin denied the Pauline authorship. In North Africa it was attributed to Barnabas. In modern times Harnack has suggested Priscilla, but the masculine participle in 11:32 (*me diēgoumenon*) disposes of that theory. The oldest Greek MSS. (Aleph A B) have simply *Pros Hebraious* as the title, but they place it before the Pastoral Epistles, while the Textus Receptus puts it after the Pastoral Epistles and Philemon. In the light of all the facts one can only make a guess without a sense of certainty. For myself I should with Luther guess Apollos as the most likely author of this book which is full of the Spirit of God.

THE RECIPIENTS

If the title is allowed to be genuine or a fair interpretation of the Epistle, then it is addressed to Jewish (Hebrew)

Christians in a local church somewhere. Dr. James Moffatt in his *Commentary* (pp. xv to xvii) challenges the title and insists that the book is written for Gentile Christians as truly as First Peter. He argues this largely from the author's use of the LXX. For myself Dr. Moffatt's reasons are not convincing. The traditional view that the author is addressing Jewish Christians in a definite locality, whether a large church or a small household church, is true, I believe. The author seems clearly to refer to a definite church in the experiences alluded to in 10:32–34. The church in Jerusalem had undergone sufferings like these, but we really do not know where the church was. Apparently the author is in Italy when he writes (13:24), though "they of Italy" (*hoi apo tēs Italias*) can mean those who have come from Italy. These Jewish Christians may even have lived in Rome itself.

THE DATE

Here again modern scholars differ widely. Westcott places it between A.D. 64 and 67. Harnack and Holtzmann prefer a date between 81 and 96. Marcus Dods argues strongly that the Epistle was written while the temple was still standing. If it was already destroyed, it is hard to understand how the author could have written 10:1f.: "Else would they not have ceased to be offered?" And in 8:13 "nigh to vanishing away" (*eggus aphanismou*) is only intelligible with the temple service still going on. The author makes use of the tabernacle instead of the temple because the temple was patterned after the tabernacle. On the other hand, the mention of Timothy in 13:23 as being "set free" (*apolelumenon*) raises an inquiry concerning Paul's last plea to Timothy to come to him in Rome (II Tim. 4:11–13). Apparently Timothy came and was put in prison. If so, since Paul was put to death before Nero's own death (June 8, A.D. 68), there is left only the years 67 to 69 A.D. as probable or even possible. It is thus the last of the New Testament books before the Johannine Writings all of which come towards the close of the century and after the destruction of Jerusalem.

THE PURPOSE

The author states it repeatedly. He urges the Jewish Christians to hold fast the confession which they have made in Jesus as Messiah and Saviour. Their Jewish neighbours have urged them to give up Christ and Christianity and to come back to Judaism. The Judaizers tried to make Jews out of Gentile Christians and to fasten Judaism upon Christianity with a purely sacramental type of religion as the result. Paul won freedom for evangelical and spiritual Christianity against the Judaizers as shown in the Corinthian Epistles, Galatians, and Romans. The Gnostics in subtle fashion tried to dilute Christianity with their philosophy and esoteric mysteries and here again Paul won his fight for the supremacy of Christ over all these imaginary *aeons* (Colossians and Ephesians). But in Hebrews the author is battling to stop a stampede from Christ back to Judaism, a revolt (apostasy) in truth from the living God. These Jews argued that the prophets were superior to Jesus, the law came by the ministry of angels, Moses was greater than Jesus, and Aaron than Jesus. The author turns the argument on the Jews and boldly champions the Glory of Jesus as superior at every point to all that Judaism had, as God's Son and man's Saviour, the crown and glory of the Old Testament prophecy, the hope of mankind. It is the first great apologetic for Christianity and has never been surpassed. Moffatt terms it "a profound homily."

SOME BOOKS ON HEBREWS

ANDEL, *De Brief aan de Hebräer* (1906).

ANDERSON, R., *The Hebrews Epistle in the Light of the Types* (1911).

AYLES, *Destination, Date and Authorship of the Epistle to the Hebrews* (1899).

BAILEY, *Leading Ideas of the Epistle to the Hebrews* (1907).

BLASS, F., *Brief an die Hebräer, Text, Angabe der Rhythmen* (1903).

BLEEK, F., *Der Hebräerbrief Erklärt* (1840).

BRUCE, A. B., *The Epistle to the Hebrews* (1899).

DALE, R. W., *The Jewish Temple in the Christian Church* (1865).

DAVIDSON, A. B., *The Epistle to the Hebrews* (1882).

DELITZSCH, F., *Commentary on the Hebrews* (1857).

DIBELIUS, M., *Der Verfasser des Hebräerbriefes* (1910).

DODS, M., *Expositor's Greek Testament* (1910).

DU BOSE, W. P., *High Priesthood and Sacrifice* (1908).

EDWARDS, T. C., *Expositor's Bible* (1888).

FARRAR, F. W., *Cambridge Greek Testament* (1893).

GOODSPEED, E. J., *Bible for Home and School* (1908).

GRIFFTH-THOMAS, W. H., *Let Us Go On* (1923).

HEIGL, *Verfasser und Addresse des Briefes an die Hebräer* (1905).

HOLLMANN, *Schriften d. N.T.* 2 Aufl. (1907).

KENDRICK, A. C., *American Commentary* (1890).

LIDGETT, J. S., *Sonship and Salvation* (1921).

LOWRIE, *An Explanation of Hebrews* (1921).

LUNEMANN, G., *Meyer Komm.* (1882).

MACFADYEN, J. F., *Through the Eternal Spirit* (1925).

MACNEILL, *The Christology of the Epistle to the Hebrews* (1914).

MÉNÉGOZ, E., *La Théologie de l'épitre aux Hébreaux* (1894).

MILLIGAN, G., *The Theology of the Epistle to the Hebrews* (1899).

MOFFATT JAMES, *Int. and Cosit. Comm.* (1924)

MOULE, H. C., *Messages from the Epistle to the Hebrews* (1909).

MURRAY, ANDREW, *Devotional Commentary.*

NAIRNE, A., *The Epistle of Priesthood* (1913).

NAIRNE, A., *The Alexandrian Gospel* (1917).

PEAKE, A. S., *New Century Bible* (1904).

PORTER, S. J., *The Twelve-Gemmed Crown* (1913).

RENDALL, F., *The Theology of the Hebrew Christians* (1886).

RIGGENBACH, M., *Zoeckler Komm.* 2 Aüfl. (1913).

ROTHERHAM, *The Epistle to the Hebrews* (1906).

SAPHIR, A., *Exposition of Hebrews.*

SCOTT, E. F., *The Epistle to the Hebrews* (1922).

SEEBERG, A., *Der Brief an die Hebräer* (1912).

SLOT, *De Letterkundige Vorm van den Brief aan de Hebräer* (1912).

SODEN, VON, *Hand-Comm.* (1899).

THOLUCK, A., *Komm. zum Briefe an die Hebräer.*

VAUGHAN, C. J., *Epistle to the Hebrews* (1899).

WADE, *The Epistle to the Hebrews* (1923).

WEISS, B., *Meyer-Komm.* 6 Aufl. (1902).

WEISS, B., *Der Hebräerbrief in Zeitgeschichtlicher Beleuchtung* (1910).

WELCH, *Authorship of the Epistle to the Hebrews* (1899).

WESTCOTT, B. F., *Epistle to the Hebrews* (3rd ed. 1906).

WICKHAM, E. C., *Westminster Comm.* (1910).

WINDISCH, H., *Handbuch zum N.T.* (1913).

WREDE, W., *Das literarisches Rätsel des Hebräerbriefs* (1906).

CHAPTER I

1. *God* (*ho theos*). This Epistle begins like Genesis and the Fourth Gospel with God, who is the Author of the old revelation in the prophets and of the new in his Son. Verses 1 to 3 are a *proemium* (Delitzsch) or introduction to the whole Epistle. The periodic structure of the sentence (1–4) reminds one of Luke 1:1–4, Rom. 1:1–7, I John 1:1–4. The sentence could have concluded with *en huiōi* in verse 2, but by means of three relatives (*hon, di' hou, hos*) the author presents the Son as "the exact counterpart of God" (Moffatt). *Of old time* (*palai*). "Long ago" as in Matt. 11:21. *Having spoken* (*lalēsas*). First aorist active participle of *laleō*, originally chattering of birds, then used of the highest form of speech as here. *Unto the fathers* (*tois patrasin*). Dative case. The Old Testament worthies in general without "our" or "your" as in John 6:58; 7:22; Rom. 9:5. *In the prophets* (*en tois prophētais*). As the quickening power of their life (Westcott). So 4:7. *By divers portions* (*polumerōs*). "In many portions." Adverb from late adjective *polumerēs* (in papyri), both in *Vettius Valens*, here only in N.T., but in Wisdom 7:22 and Josephus (*Ant.* VIII, 3, 9). The Old Testament revelation came at different times and in various stages, a progressive revelation of God to men. *In divers manners* (*polutropōs*). "In many ways." Adverb from old adjective *polutropos*, in Philo, only here in N.T. The two adverbs together are "a sonorous hendiadys for 'variously'" (Moffatt) as Chrysostom (*diaphorōs*). God spoke by dream, by direct voice, by signs, in different ways to different men (Abraham, Jacob, Moses, Elijah, Isaiah, etc.).

2. *At the end of these days* (*ep' eschatou tōn hēmerōn toutōn*). In contrast with *palai* above. *Hath spoken* (*ela-*

lēsen). First aorist indicative of *laleō*, the same verb as above, "did speak" in a final and full revelation. *In his Son (en huiōi*). In sharp contrast to *en tois prophētais.* "The Old Testament slopes upward to Christ" (J. R. Sampey). No article or pronoun here with the preposition *en*, giving the absolute sense of "Son." Here the idea is not merely what Jesus said, but what he is (Dods), God's Son who reveals the Father (John 1:18). "The revelation was a *son-revelation*" (Vincent). *Hath appointed (ethēken*). First aorist (kappa aorist) active of *tithēmi*, a timeless aorist. *Heir of all things (klēronomon pantōn*). See Mark 12:6 for *ho klēronomos* in Christ's parable, perhaps an allusion here to this parable (Moffatt). The idea of sonship easily passes into that of heirship (Gal. 4:7; Rom. 8:17). See the claim of Christ in Matt. 11:27; 28:18 even before the Ascension. *Through whom (di' hou*). The Son as Heir is also the Intermediate Agent (*dia*) in the work of creation as we have it in Col. 1:16f. and John. 1:3. *The worlds (tous aiōnas*). "The ages" (*secula*, Vulgate). See 11:3 also where *tous aiōnas = ton kosmon* (the world) or the universe like *ta panta* (the all things) in 1:3 and Rom. 11:36; Col. 1:16. The original sense of *aiōn* (from *aei*, always) occurs in Heb. 5:20, but here "by metonomy of the container for the contained" (Thayer) for "the worlds" (the universe) as in LXX, Philo, Josephus.

3. *Being (ōn*). Absolute and timeless existence (present active participle of *eimi*) in contrast with *genomenos* in verse 4 like *ēn* in John 1:1 (in contrast with *egeneto* in 1:14) and like *huparchōn* and *genomenos* in Phil. 2:6f. *The effulgence of his glory (apaugasma tēs doxēs*). The word *apaugasma*, late substantive from *apaugazō*, to emit brightness (*augē, augazō* in II Cor. 4:4), here only in the N.T., but in Wisdom 7:26 and in Philo. It can mean either reflected brightness, refulgence (Calvin, Thayer) or effulgence (ray from an original light body) as the Greek fathers hold. Both senses are true of Christ in his relation to God as Jesus shows

in plain language in John 12:45; 14:9. "The writer is using metaphors which had already been applied to Wisdom and the Logos" (Moffatt). The meaning "effulgence" suits the context better, though it gives the idea of eternal generation of the Son (John 1:1), the term Father applied to God necessarily involving Son. See this same metaphor in II Cor. 4:6. *The very image of his substance* (*charaktēr tēs hupostaseōs*). *Charaktēr* is an old word from *charassō*, to cut, to scratch, to mark. It first was the agent (note ending =*tēr*) or tool that did the marking, then the mark or impress made, the exact reproduction, a meaning clearly expressed by *charagma* (Acts 17:29; Rev. 13:16f.). Menander had already used (Moffatt) *charaktēr* in the sense of our "character." The word occurs in the inscriptions for "person" as well as for "exact reproduction" of a person. The word *hupostasis* for the being or essence of God "is a philosophical rather than a religious term" (Moffatt). Etymologically it is the sediment or foundation under a building (for instance). In 11:1 *hypostasis* is like the "title-deed" idea found in the papyri. Athanasius rightly used Heb. 1:1-4 in his controversy with Arius. Paul in Phil. 2:5-11 pictures the real and eternal deity of Christ free from the philosophical language here employed. But even Paul's simpler phrase *morphē theou* (the form of God) has difficulties of its own. The use of *Logos* in John 1:1-18 is parallel to Heb. 1:1-4. *And upholding* (*pherōn te*). Present active participle of *pherō* closely connected with *ōn* (being) by *te* and like Col. 1:17 in idea. The newer science as expounded by Eddington and Jeans is in harmony with the spiritual and personal conception of creation here presented. *By the word of his power* (*tōi rēmati tēs dunameōs autou*). Instrumental case of *rēma* (word). See 11:3 for *rēmati theou* (by the word of God) as the explanation of creation like Genesis, but here *autou* refers to God's Son as in 1:2. *Purification of sins* (*katharismon tōn hamartiōn*). *Katharismos* is from *katharizō*, to cleanse (Matt. 8:3; Heb.

9:14), here only in Hebrews, but in same sense of cleansing from sins, II Peter 1:9 and in Job 7:21. Note middle participle *poiēsamenos* like *heuramenos* in 9:12. This is the first mention of the priestly work of Christ, the keynote of this Epistle. *Sat down* (*ekathisen*). First aorist active of *kathizō*, "took his seat," a formal and dignified act. *Of the Majesty on high* (*tēs megalosunēs en hupsēlois*). Late word from *megas*, only in LXX (Deut. 32:3; II Sam. 7:23, etc.), Aristeas, Heb. 1:3; 8:1; Jude 25. Christ resumed his original dignity and glory (John 17:5). The phrase *en hupsēlois* occurs in the Psalms (93:4), here only in N.T., elsewhere *en hupsistois* in the highest (Matt. 21:9; Luke 2:14) or *en tois epouraniois* in the heavenlies (Eph. 1:3, 20). Jesus is here pictured as King (Prophet and Priest also) Messiah seated at the right hand of God.

4. *Having become* (*genomenos*). Second aorist middle participle of *ginomai*. In contrast with on in verse 3. *By so much* (*tosoutōi*). Instrumental case of *tosoutos* correlative with *hosōi* (as) with comparative in both clauses (*kreittōn*, better, comparative of *kratus*, *diaphorōteron*, more excellent, comparative of *diaphoros*). *Than the angels* (*tōn aggelōn*). Ablative of comparison after *kreittōn*, as often. *Than they* (*par' autous*). Instead of the ablative *autōn* here the preposition *para* (along, by the side of) with the accusative occurs, another common idiom as in 3:3; 9:23. *Diaphoros* only in Hebrews in N.T. except Rom. 12:6. *Hath inherited* (*keklēronomēken*). Perfect active indicative of *klēronomeō* (from *klēronomos*, heir, verse 2), and still inherits it, the name (*onoma*, oriental sense of rank) of "Son" which is superior to prophets as already shown (1:2) and also to angels (1:4-2:18) as he now proceeds to prove. Jesus is superior to angels as God's Son, his deity (1:4-2:4). The author proves it from Scripture (1:4-14).

5. *Unto which* (*Tini*). "To which individual angel." As a class angels are called sons of God (Elohim) (Psa. 29:1),

but no single angel is called God's Son like the Messiah in Psa. 2:7. Dods takes "have I begotten thee" (*gegennēka se*, perfect active indicative of *gennaō*) to refer to the resurrection and ascension while others refer it to the incarnation. *And again* (*kai palin*). This quotation is from II Sam. 7:14. Note the use of *eis* in the predicate with the sense of "as" like the Hebrew (LXX idiom), not preserved in the English. See Matt. 19:5; Luke 2:34. Like Old English "to" or "for." See II Cor. 6:18 and Rev. 21:7 for the same passage applied to relation between God and Christians while here it is treated as Messianic.

6. *And when he again bringeth in* (*hotan de palin eisagagēi*). Indefinite temporal clause with *hotan* and second aorist active subjunctive of *eisagō*. If *palin* is taken with *eisagagēi*, the reference is to the Second Coming as in 9:28. If *palin* merely introduces another quotation (Psa. 97:7) parallel to *kai palin* in verse 5, the reference is to the incarnation when the angels did worship the Child Jesus (Luke 2:13f.). There is no way to decide certainly about it. *The first-born* (*ton prōtotokon*). See Psa. 89:28. For this compound adjective applied to Christ in relation to the universe see Col. 1:15, to other men, Rom. 8:29; Col. 1:18, to the other children of Mary, Luke 2:7; here it is used absolutely. *The world* (*tēn oikoumenēn*). "The inhabited earth." See Acts 17:6. *Let worship* (*proskunēsatōsan*). Imperative first aorist active third plural of *proskuneō*, here in the full sense of worship, not mere reverence or courtesy. This quotation is from the LXX of Deut. 32:43, but is not in the Hebrew, though most of the LXX MSS. (except F) have *huioi theou*, but the substance does occur also in Psa. 97:7 with *hoi aggeloi autou*.

7. *Of the angels* (*pros tous aggelous*). "With reference to" (*pros*) as in Luke 20:9. So "of the Son" in verse 8. Note *men* here and *de* in verse 8 in carefully balanced contrast. The quotation is from Psa. 104:4. *Winds* (*pneumata*).

"Spirits" the word also means. The meaning (note article with *aggelous*, not with *pneumata*) apparently is one that can reduce angels to the elemental forces of wind and fire (Moffatt). *A flame of fire (puros phloga)*. Predicate accusative of *phlox*, old word, in N.T. only here and Luke 16:24. Lünemann holds that the Hebrew here is wrongly rendered and means that God makes the wind his messengers (not angels) and flaming fire his servants. That is all true, but that is not the point of this passage. Preachers also are sometimes like a wind-storm or a fire.

8. *O God (ho theos)*. This quotation (the fifth) is from Psa. 45:7f. A Hebrew nuptial ode (*epithalamium*) for a king treated here as Messianic. It is not certain whether *ho theos* is here the vocative (address with the nominative form as in John 20:28 with the Messiah termed *theos* as is possible, John 1:18) or *ho theos* is nominative (subject or predicate) with *estin* (is) understood: "God is thy throne" or "Thy throne is God." Either makes good sense. *Sceptre (rabdos)*. Old word for walking-stick, staff (Heb. 11:21).

9. *Hath anointed thee (echrisen se)*. First aorist active indicative of *chriō*, to anoint, from which verb the verbal *Christos* (Anointed One) comes. See Christ's use of *echrisen* in Luke 4:18 from Isa. 66:1. *With the oil of gladness (elaion agalliaseōs)*. Accusative case with *echrisen* (second accusative besides *se*). Perhaps the festive anointing on occasions of joy (12:2). See Luke 1:44. *Fellows (metochous)*. Old word from *metechō*, partners, sharers, in N.T. only in Hebrews save Luke 5:7. Note *para* with accusative here, beside, beyond, above (by comparison, extending beyond).

10. *Lord (Kurie)*. In the LXX, not in the Hebrew. Quotation (the sixth) from Psa. 102:26–28 through verses 10 to 12. Note emphatic position of *su* here at the beginning as in verses 11 and 12 (*su de*). This Messianic Psalm pictures the Son in his Creative work and in his final triumph. *Hast laid the foundation (ethemeliōsas)*. First aorist active

of *themelioō*, old verb from *themelios* (foundation) for which see Col. 1:23.

11. *They* (*autoi*). The heavens (*ouranoi*). *Shall perish* (*apolountai*). Future middle of *apollumi*. Modern scientists no longer postulate the eternal existence of the heavenly bodies. *But thou continuest* (*su de diameneis*). This is what matters most, the eternal existence of God's Son as Creator and Preserver of the universe (John 1:1–3; Col. 1:14ff.). *Shall wax old* (*palaiōthēsontai*). First future passive indicative of *palaioō*, from *palaios*, for which see Luke 12:33 and Heb. 8:13.

12. *A mantle* (*peribolaion*). Old word for covering from *pariballō*, to fling around, as a veil in I Cor. 11:15, nowhere else in N.T. *Shalt thou roll up* (*helixeis*). Future active of *helissō*, late form for *heilissō*, in N.T. only here and Rev. 6:14, to fold together. *As a garment* (*hōs himation*). LXX repeats from 11. *They shall be changed* (*allagēsontai*). Second future passive of *allassō*, old verb, to change. *Shall not fail* (*ouk ekleipsousin*). Future active of *ekleipō*, to leave out, to fail, used of the sun in Luke 23:45. "Nature is at his mercy, not he at nature's" (Moffatt).

13. *Hath he said* (*eirēken*). Perfect active common use of the perfect for permanent record. This seventh quotation is proof of the Son's superiority as the Son of God (his deity) to angels and is from Psa. 110:1, a Messianic Psalm frequently quoted in Hebrews. *Sit thou* (*kathou*). Second person singular imperative middle of *kathēmai*, to sit, for the longer form *kathēso*, as in Matt. 22:44; James 2:3. *On my right hand* (*ek dexiōn mou*). "From my right." See 1:3 for *en dexiāi* "at the right hand." *Till I make* (*heōs an thō*). Indefinite temporal clause about the future with *heōs* and the second aorist active subjunctive of *tithēmi* with *an* (often not used), a regular and common idiom. Quoted also in Luke 20:43. For the pleonasm in *hupodion* and *tōn podōn* (objective genitive) see Matt. 5:35.

14. *Ministering spirits (leitourgika pneumata)*. Thayer says that *leitourgikos* was not found in profane authors, but it occurs in the papyri for "work tax" (money in place of service) and for religious service also. The word is made from *leitourgia* (Luke 1:23; Heb. 8:6; 9:21). *Sent forth (apostellomena)*. Present passive participle of *apostellō*, sent forth repeatedly, from time to time as occasion requires. *For the sake of (dia)*. With the accusative, the usual causal meaning of *dia*. *That shall inherit (tous mellontas klēronomein)*. "That are going to inherit," common idiom of *mellō* (present active participle) with the infinitive (present active here), "destined to inherit" (Matt. 11:14). *Salvation (sōtērian)*. Here used of the final salvation in its consummation. Only here in the N.T. do we have "inherent salvation," but see 6:12; 12:17. We do not have here the doctrine of special guardian angels for each of us, but simply the fact that angels are used for our good. "And if so, may we not be aided, inspired, guided by a cloud of witnesses — not witnesses only, but helpers, agents like ourselves of the immanent God?" (Sir Oliver Lodge, *The Hibbert Journal*, Jan., 1903, p. 223).

CHAPTER II

1. *Therefore* (*dia touto*). Because Jesus is superior to prophets and angels and because the new revelation is superior to the old. The author often pauses in his argument, as here, to drive home a pungent exhortation. *Ought* (*dei*). It is necessity, necessity rather than obligation (*chrē*). *To give heed* (*prosechein*). Present active infinitive with *noun* (accusative singular of *nous*) understood as in Acts 8:6. *More earnest* (*perissoterōs*). Comparative adverb, "more earnestly," "more abundantly" as in I Thess. 2:7. *To the things that were heard* (*tois akoustheisin*). Dative plural neuter of the articular participle first aorist passive of *akouō*. *Lest haply we drift away* (*mē pote pararuōmen*). Negative clause of purpose with *mē pote* and the second aorist passive subjunctive of *pararreō*, old verb to flow by or past, to glide by, only here in N.T. (cf. Prov. 3:21). Xenophon (*Cyrop.* IV. 52) uses it of the river flowing by. Here the metaphor is that "of being swept along past the sure anchorage which is within reach" (Westcott), a vivid picture of peril for all ("we," *hēmas*).

2. *For if . . . proved steadfast* (*ei gar . . . egeneto bebaios*). Condition of first class, assumed as true. *Through angels* (*di' aggelōn*). Allusion to the use of angels by God at Sinai as in Acts 7:38, 53; Gal. 3:19, though not in the O.T., but in Josephus (*Ant.* XV. 156). *Transgression and disobedience* (*parabasis kai parakoē*). Both words use *para* as in *pararuōmen*, refused to obey (stepping aside, *para-basis* as in Rom. 2:23), neglect to obey (*par-akoē* as in Rom. 5:19), more than a mere hendiadys. *Recompense of reward* (*misthapodosian*). Late double compound, like *misthapodotēs* (Heb. 11:6), from *misthos* (reward) and *apodidōmi*, to give back. The old Greeks used *misthodosia*. *Just* (*endikon*). Old compound adjective, in N.T. only here and Rom. 3:8.

3. *How shall we escape?* (*pōs hēmeis ekpheuxometha;*). Rhetorical question with future middle indicative of *ekpheugō* and conclusion of the condition. *If we neglect* (*amelēsantes*). First aorist active participle of *ameleō*, "having neglected." *So great salvation* (*tēlikautēs sōtērias*). Ablative case after *amelēsantes*. Correlative pronoun of age, but used of size in the N.T. (James 3:4; II Cor. 1:10). *Which* (*hētis*). "Which very salvation," before described, now summarized. *Having at the first been spoken* (*archēn labousa laleisthai*). Literally, "having received a beginning to be spoken," "having begun to be spoken," a common literary *Koinē* idiom (Polybius, etc.). *Through the Lord* (*dia tou kuriou*). The Lord Jesus who is superior to angels. Jesus was God's full revelation and he is the source of this new and superior revelation. *Was confirmed* (*ebebaiōthē*). First aorist passive indicative of *bebaioō*, from *bebaios* (stable), old verb as in I Cor. 1:6. *By them that heard* (*hupo tōn akousantōn*). Ablative case with *hupo* of the articular first aorist active participle of *akouō*. Those who heard the Lord Jesus. Only one generation between Jesus and the writer. Paul (Gal. 1:11) got his message directly from Christ.

4. *God also bearing witness with them* (*sunepimarturountos tou theou*). Genitive absolute with the present active participle of the late double compound verb *sunepimartureō*, to join (*sun*) in giving additional (*epi*) testimony (*martureō*). Here only in N.T., but in Aristotle, Polybius, Plutarch. *Both by signs* (*sēmeiois te kai*) *and wonders* (*kai terasin*) *and by manifold powers* (*kai poikilais dunamesin*) *and by gifts of the Holy Ghost* (*kai pneumatos hagiou merismois*). Instrumental case used with all four items. See Acts 2:22 for the three words for miracles in inverse order (powers, wonders, signs). Each word adds an idea about the *erga* (works) of Christ. *Teras* (wonder) attracts attention, *dunamis* (power) shows God's power, *sēmeion* reveals the purpose of God in the miracles. For *poikilais* (manifold, many-coloured) see

Matt. 4:24; James 1:2. For *merismos* for distribution (old word, in N.T. only here and Heb. 4:12) see I Cor. 12:4–30. *According to his own will* (*kata tēn autou thelēsin*). The word *thelēsis* is called a vulgarism by Pollux. The writer is fond of words in -*is*.

5. *For not unto angels* (*ou gar aggelois*). The author now proceeds to show (2:5–18) that the very humanity of Jesus, the Son of Man, likewise proves his superiority to angels. *The world to come* (*tēn oikoumenēn tēn mellousan*). The new order, the salvation just described. See a like use of *mellō* (as participle) with *sōtēria* (1:14), *aiōn* (6:4f.), *agatha* (9:11; 10:1), *polis* (13:14). *Whereof we speak* (*peri hēs laloumen*). The author is discussing this new order introduced by Christ which makes obsolete the old dispensation of rites and symbols. God did not put this new order in charge of angels.

6. *But one somewhere* (*de pou tis*). See 4:4 for a like indefinite quotation. Philo uses this "literary mannerism" (Moffatt). He quotes Psa. 8:5–7 and extends here to 8a. *Hath testified* (*diemarturato*). First aorist middle indicative of *diamarturomai*, old verb to testify vigorously (Acts 2:40). *What* (*Ti*). Neuter, not masculine *tis* (who). The insignificance of man is implied. *The son of man* (*huios anthrōpou*). Not *ho huios tou anthrōpou* which Jesus used so often about himself, but literally here "son of man" like the same words so often in Ezekiel, without Messianic meaning here. *Visited* (*episkeptēi*). Second person singular present indicative middle of *episkeptomai*, old verb to look upon, to look after, to go to see (Matt. 25:36), from which verb *episcopos*, overseer, bishop, comes.

7. *Thou madest him a little lower* (*elattōsas auton brachu ti*). First aorist active of old verb *elattoō* from *elattōn* (less), causative verb to lessen, to decrease, to make less, only here, and verse 9 and John 3:30 in N.T. *Brachu ti* is accusative neuter of degree like II Sam. 16:1, "some little," but of time in Isa. 57:17 (for a little while). *Than the angels*

(*par' aggelous*). "Beside angels" like *para* with the accusative of comparison in 1:4, 9. The Hebrew here has *Elohim*
which word is applied to judges in Psa. 82:1, 6 (John 10:34f.).
Here it is certainly not "God" in our sense. In Psa. 29:1 the
LXX translates *Elohim* by *huoi theou* (sons of God). *Thou
crownedst* (*estephanōsas*). First aorist active indicative of
old verb, *stephanoō*, to crown, in N.T. only here and II Tim.
2:5. The Psalmist refers to God's purpose in creating man
with such a destiny as mastery over nature. The rest of
verse 7 is absent in B.

8. *In that he subjected* (*en tōi hupotaxai*). First aorist active articular infinitive of *hupatassō* in the locative case,
"in the subjecting." *He left* (*aphēken*). First aorist active
indicative (kappa aorist) of *aphiēmi*. *Nothing that is not
subject to him* (*ouden autōi anupotakton*). Later verbal of
hupotassō with *a* privative. Here in passive sense, active
sense in I Tim. 1:9. Man's sovereignty was meant to be all-
inclusive including the administration of "the world to
come." "He is crowned king of nature, invested with a
divine authority over creation" (Moffatt). But how far
short of this destiny has man come! *But now we see not
yet* (*nun de oupō horōmen*). Not even today in the wonderful
twentieth century with man's triumphs over nature has he
reached that goal, wonderful as are the researches by the
help of telescope and microscope, the mechanism of the
airplane, the submarine, steam, electricity, radio.

9. *Even Jesus* (*Iēsoun*). We do not see man triumphant,
but we do see Jesus, for the author is not ashamed of his
human name, realizing man's destiny, "the very one who
has been made a little lower than the angels" (*ton brachu ti
par' aggelous elattōmenon*), quoting and applying the language of the Psalm in verse 7 to Jesus (with article *ton* and
the perfect passive participle of *elattaō*). But this is not
all. Death has defeated man, but Jesus has conquered death.
Because of the suffering of death (*dia to pathēma tou thanatou*).

The causal sense of *dia* with the accusative as in 1:14. Jesus
in his humanity was put lower than the angels "for a little
while" (*brachu ti*). Because of the suffering of death we
see (*blepomen*) Jesus crowned (*estephanōmenon*, perfect passive participle of *stephanoō* from verse 7), crowned already
"with glory and honour" as Paul shows in Phil. 2:9–11
(more highly exalted, *huperupsōsen*) "that at the name of
Jesus every knee should bow." There is more glory to come
to Jesus surely, but he is already at God's right hand (1:3).
That by the grace of God he should taste death for every man
(*hopōs chariti theou huper pantos geusētai thanatou*). This
purpose clause (*hopōs* instead of the more usual *hina*) is
pregnant with meaning. The author interprets and applies
the language of the Psalm to Jesus and here puts Christ's
death in behalf of (*huper*), and so instead of, every man as
the motive for his incarnation and death on the Cross. The
phrase to taste death (*geuomai thanatou*) occurs in the Gospels (Matt. 16:28; Mark 9:1; Luke 9:27; John 8:52), though
not in the ancient Greek. It means to see death (Heb. 11:5),
"a bitter experience, not a rapid sip" (Moffatt). His death
was in behalf of every one (not everything as the early
Greek theologians took it). The death of Christ (Andrew
Fuller) was sufficient for all, efficient for some. It is all "by
the grace (*chariti*, instrumental case) of God," a thoroughly
Pauline idea. Curiously enough some MSS. read *chōris
theou* (apart from God) in place of *chariti theou*, Nestorian
doctrine whatever the origin.

10. *It became him* (*eprepen autōi*). Imperfect active of
prepō, old verb to stand out, to be becoming or seemly. Here
it is impersonal with *teleiōsai* as subject, though personal in
Heb. 7:26. *Autōi* (him) is in the dative case and refers to
God, not to Christ as is made plain by *ton archēgon* (author).
One has only to recall John 3:16 to get the idea here. The
voluntary humiliation or incarnation of Christ the Son a
little lower than the angels was a seemly thing to God the

Father as the writer now shows in a great passage (2:10-18) worthy to go beside Phil. 2:5–11. *For whom (di' hon)*. Referring to *autōi* (God) as the reason (cause) for the universe (*ta panta*). *Through whom (di' hou)*. With the genitive *dia* expresses the agent by whom the universe came into existence, a direct repudiation of the Gnostic view of intermediate agencies (*aeons*) between God and the creation of the universe. Paul puts it succinctly in Rom. 11:36 by his *ex autou kai di' autou kai eis auton ta panta*. The universe comes out of God, by means of God, for God. This writer has already said that God used his Son as the Agent (*di' hou*) in creation (1:2), a doctrine in harmony with Col. 1:15f. (*en autōi, di' autou eis auton*) and John 1:3. *In bringing (agagonta)*. Second aorist active participle of *agō* in the accusative case in spite of the dative *autōi* just before to which it refers. *The author (ton archēgon)*. Old compound word (*archē* and *agō*) one leading off, leader or prince as in Acts 5:31, one blazing the way, a pioneer (Dods) in faith (Heb. 12:2), author (Acts 3:15). Either sense suits here, though author best (verse 9). Jesus is the author of salvation, the leader of the sons of God, the Elder Brother of us all (Rom. 8:29). *To make perfect (teleiōsai)*. First aorist active infinitive of *teleioō* (from *teleios*). If one recoils at the idea of God making Christ perfect, he should bear in mind that it is the humanity of Jesus that is under discussion. The writer does not say that Jesus was sinful (see the opposite in 4:15), but simply that "by means of sufferings" God perfected his Son in his human life and death for his task as Redeemer and Saviour. One cannot know human life without living it. There was no moral imperfection in Jesus, but he lived his human life in order to be able to be a sympathizing and effective leader in the work of salvation.

11. *He that sanctifieth (ho hagiazōn)*. Present active articular participle of *hagiazō*. Jesus is the sanctifier (9:13f.; 13: 12). *They that are sanctified (hoi hagiazomenoi)*. Present

passive articular participle of *hagiazō*. It is a process here as in 10:14, not a single act, though in 10:10 the perfect passive indicative presents a completed state. *Of one (ex henos)*. Referring to God as the Father of Jesus and of the "many sons" above (verse 10) and in harmony with verse 14 below. Even before the incarnation Jesus had a kinship with men though we are not sons in the full sense that he is. *He is not ashamed (ouk epaischunetai)*. Present passive indicative of *epaischunomai*, old compound (Rom. 1:16). Because of the common Father Jesus is not ashamed to own us as "brothers" (*adelphous*), unworthy sons though we be.

12. *Unto my brethren (tois adelphois mou)*. To prove his point the writer quotes Psa. 22:22 when the Messiah is presented as speaking "unto my brethren." *Congregation (ekklēsias)*. The word came to mean the local church and also the general church or kingdom (Matt. 16:18; Heb. 12:23). Here we have the picture of public worship and the Messiah sharing it with others as we know Jesus often did.

13. *I will put my trust in him (Egō esomai pepoithōs ep' autōi)*. A rare periphrastic (intransitive) future perfect of *peithō*, a quotation from Isa. 8:17. The author represents the Messiah as putting his trust in God as other men do (cf. Heb. 12:2). Certainly Jesus did this constantly. The third quotation (*kai palin*, And again) is from Isa. 8:18 (the next verse), but the Messiah shows himself closely linked with the children (*paidia*) of God, the sons. (*huioi*) of verse 10.

14. *Are sharers in flesh and blood (kekoinōnēken haimatos kai sarkos)*. The best MSS. read "blood and flesh." The verb is perfect active indicative of *koinōneō*, old verb with the regular genitive, elsewhere in the N.T. with the locative (Rom. 12:13) or with *en* or *eis*. "The children have become partners (*koinōnoi*) in blood and flesh." *Partook (metesche)*. Second aorist active indicative of *metechō*, to have with, a practical synonym for *koinōneō* and with the genitive also

(*tōn autōn*). *That he might bring to nought* (*hina katargēsēi*).
Purpose of the incarnation clearly stated with *hina* and the
first aorist active subjunctive of *katargeō*, old word to render
idle or ineffective (from *kata, argos*), causative verb (25
times in Paul), once in Luke (13:7), once in Hebrews (here).
"By means of death" (his own death) Christ broke the
power (*kratos*) of the devil over death (paradoxical as it
seems), certainly in men's fear of death and in some unex-
plained way Satan had sway over the realm of death (Zech.
3:5f.). Note the explanatory *tout' estin* (that is) with the
accusative after it as before it. In Rev. 12:7 Satan is identified with the serpent in Eden, though it is not done in the
Old Testament. See Rom. 5:12; John 8:44; 14:30; 16:11;
I John 3:12. Death is the devil's realm, for he is the author
of sin. "Death as death is no part of the divine order"
(Westcott).

15. *And might deliver* (*kai apallaxēi*). Further purpose
with the first aorist active subjunctive of *appallassō*, old
verb to change from, to set free from, in N.T. only here,
Luke 12:58; Acts 19:12. *Through fear of death* (*phoboi
thanatou*). Instrumental case of *phobos*. The ancients had
great fear of death though the philosophers like Seneca
argued against it. There is today a flippant attitude towards
death with denial of the future life and rejection of God.
But the author of Hebrews saw judgement after death
(9:27f.). Hence our need of Christ to break the power of sin
and Satan in death. *All their lifetime* (*dia pantos tou zēin*).
Present active infinitive with *pas* and the article in the
genitive case with *dia*, "through all the living." *Subject to
bondage* (*enochoi douleias*). Old adjective from *enechō*,
"held in," "bound to," with genitive, bond-slaves of fear,
a graphic picture. Jesus has the keys of life and death and
said: "I am the life." Thank God for that.

16. *Verily* (*de pou*). "Now in some way," only here
in N.T. *Doth he take hold* (*epilambanetai*). Present mid-

dle indicative and means to lay hold of, to help, like
boēthēsai in verse 18. *The seed of Abraham* (*spermatos
Abraham*). The spiritual Israel (Gal. 3:29), children of faith
(Rom. 9:7).

17. *Wherefore* (*hothen*). Old relative adverb (*ho* and en-
clitic *then*, whence of place (Matt. 12:44), of source (I John
2:18), of cause as here and often in Hebrews (3:1; 7:25; 8:3;
9:18; 11:19). *It behoved him* (*ōpheilen*). Imperfect active of
opheilō, old verb to owe, money (Matt. 18:28), service and
love (Rom. 13:8), duty or obligation as here and often in
N.T. (Luke 17:10). Jesus is here the subject and the reference is to the incarnation. Having undertaken the work of
redemption (John 3:16), voluntarily (John 10:17), Jesus was
under obligation to be properly equipped for that priestly
service and sacrifice. *In all things* (*kata panta*). Except
yielding to sin (Heb. 4:15) and yet he knew what temptation
was, difficult as it may be for us to comprehend that in the
Son of God who is also the Son of man (Mark 1:13). Jesus
fought through to victory over Satan. *To be made like unto
his brethren* (*tois adelphois homoiōthēnai*). First aorist passive
infinitive of *homoioō*, old and common verb from *homoios*
(like), as in Matt. 6:8, with the associative instrumental case
as here. Christ, our Elder Brother, resembles us in reality
(Phil. 2:7 "in the likeness of men") as we shall resemble him
in the end (Rom. 8:29 "first-born among many brethren";
I John 3:2 "like him"), where the same root is used as here
(*hoiōma, homoios*). *That he might be* (*hina genētai*). Purpose
clause with *hina* and the second aorist middle subjunctive of
ginomai, to become, "that he might become." That was only
possible by being like his brethren in actual human nature.
Merciful and faithful high priest (*eleēmōn kai pistos archiereus*). The sudden use of *archiereus* here for Jesus has been
anticipated by 1:3 and 2:9 and see 3:1. Jesus as the priest-
victim is the chief topic of the Epistle. These two adjectives
(*eleēmōn* and *pistos*) touch the chief points in the function of

the high priest (5:1–10), sympathy and fidelity to God. The Sadducean high priests (Annas and Caiaphas) were political and ecclesiastical tools and puppets out of sympathy with the people and chosen by Rome. *In things pertaining to God (ta pros ton theon).* The adverbial accusative of the article is a common idiom. See the very idiom *ta pros ton theon* in Ex. 18:19 and Rom. 15:17. This use of *pros* we had already in Heb. 1:7f. On the day of atonement the high priest entered the holy of holies and officiated in behalf of the people. *To make propitiation for (eis to hilaskesthai).* Purpose clause with *eis to* and the infinitive (common Greek idiom), here present indirect middle of *hilaskomai,* to render propitious to oneself (from *hilaos,* Attic *hileōs,* gracious). This idea occurs in the LXX (Psa. 65:3), but only here in N.T., though in Luke 18:13 the passive form (*hilasthēti*) occurs as in II Kings 5:18. In I John 2:2 we have *hilasmos* used of Christ (cf. Heb. 7:25). The inscriptions illustrate the meaning in Heb. 2:17 as well as the LXX.

18. *In that (en hōi).* Literally, "In which" (=*en toutōi en hōi,* in that in which), a causal idea, though in Rom. 14:22 *en hōi* means "wherein." *Hath suffered (peponthen).* Second perfect active indicative of *paschō,* permanent part of Christ's experience. *Being tempted (peirastheis).* First aorist passive participle of *peirazō.* The temptation to escape the shame of the Cross was early and repeatedly presented to Christ, by Satan in the wilderness (Matt. 4:8–11), by Peter in the spirit of Satan (Matt. 16:22f.), in Gethsemane (Matt. 26:39), and caused intense suffering to Jesus (Luke 22:44; Heb. 5:8). *He is able (dunatai).* This word strikes the heart of it all. Christ's power to help is due not merely to his deity as God's Son, but also to his humanity without which he could not sympathize with us (Heb. 4:15). *To succour (boēthēsai).* First aorist active infinitive of the old compound verb *boētheō (boē,* a cry, *theō,* to run), to run at a cry or call for help (Matt. 15:25). *Them that are tempted (tois peirazome-*

nois). Dative plural of the articular participle (present passive) of *peirazō*. These Jewish Christians were daily tempted to give up Christ, to apostatize from Christianity. Jesus understands himself (*autos*) their predicament and is able to help them to be faithful.

CHAPTER III

1. *Holy brethren (adelphoi hagioi).* Only here in N.T., for *hagiois* in I Thess. 5:27 only in late MSS. See Heb. 2:11 for same idea. First time the author makes direct appeal to the readers, though first person in 2:1. *Partakers (metochoi).* See Luke 5:7 for "partners" in the fishing, elsewhere in N.T. only in Hebrews (1:9; 6:4; 12:8) in N.T. *Of a heavenly calling (klēseōs epouraniou).* Only here in the N.T., though same idea in 9:15. See *hē anō klēsis* in Phil. 3:14 (the upward calling). The call comes from heaven and is to heaven in its appeal. *Consider (katanoēsate).* First aorist active imperative of *katanoeō*, old compound verb (*kata, nous*), to put the mind down on a thing, to fix the mind on as in Matt. 7:3 and Luke 12:24. *Even Jesus (Iēsoun).* No "even" in the Greek, just like the idiom in 2:9, the human name held up with pride. *The Apostle and High Priest of our confession (ton apostolon kai archierea tēs homologias hēmōn).* In descriptive apposition with *Iēsoun* and note the single article *ton.* This is the only time in the N.T. that Jesus is called *apostolos*, though he often used *apostellō* of God's sending him forth as in John 17:3 (*apesteilas*). This verb is used of Moses as sent by God (Ex. 3:10). Moffatt notes that *apostolos* is Ionic for *presbeutēs*, "not a mere envoy, but an ambassador or representative sent with powers." The author has already termed Jesus high priest (2:17). For *homologia* (confession) see II Cor. 9:13; I Tim. 6:12. These Hebrew Christians had confessed Jesus as their Apostle and High Priest. They do not begin to understand what Jesus is and means if they are tempted to give him up. The word runs through Hebrews with an urgent note for fidelity (4:14; 10:23). See *homologeō* (*homon*, same, *legō*, say), to say the same thing, to agree, to confess, to profess.

353

2. *Who was faithful* (*piston onta*). Present active participle with predicate accusative agreeing with *Iēsoun*, "as being faithful." *That appointed him* (*tōi poiēsanti auton*). See I Sam. 12:6. Dative case of the articular participle (aorist active) of *poieō* and the reference is to God. Note *pistos* as in 2:17. *As also was Moses* (*hōs kai Mōusēs*). The author makes no depreciatory remarks about Moses as he did not about the prophets and the angels. He cheerfully admits that Moses was faithful "in all his house" (*en holōi tōi oikōi autou*), an allusion to Numbers 12:7 (*ean holōi tōi oikōi mou*) about Moses. The "his" is God's. The use of *oikos* for the people (family) of God, not the building, but the group (I Tim. 3:15) in which God is the Father. But wherein is Jesus superior to Moses? The argument is keen and skilful.

3. *Hath been counted worthy of more glory than Moses* (*pleionos doxēs para Mōusēn ēxiōtai*). Perfect passive indicative of *axioō*, to deem worthy, permanent situation described with definite claim of Christ's superiority to Moses. *Doxēs* in genitive case after *ēxiōtai*. For *para* after the comparative *pleionos* see 1:4, 9; 2:7. *By so much as* (*kath' hoson*). A proportionate measurement (common use of *kata* and the quantitative relative *hosos*). *Than the house* (*tou oikou*). Ablative case of comparison after *pleiona*. The architect is superior to the house just as Sir Christopher Wren is superior to St. Paul's Cathedral. The point in the argument calls for Jesus as the builder (*ho kataskeuasas*, first aorist active participle of *kataskeuazō*, to found or build). But it is God's house as *autou* means (verses 2, 5) and *hou* in verse 6. This house of God existed before Moses (11:2, 25). Jesus as God's Son founded and supervised this house of God.

4. *Is God* (*theos*). God is the Creator of all things and so of his "house" which his Son, Jesus Christ, founded and supervises.

5. *And Moses* (*kai Mōusēs men*). "Now Moses indeed on his part" (*men* contrasted with *de*). *In* (*en*). Moses was in "God's house" "as a servant" (*hōs therapōn*). Old word, in LXX, only here in N.T. and quoted from Numbers 12:7f. Kin to the verb *therapeuō*, to serve, to heal, and *therapeia*, service (Luke 9:11) and a group of servants (Luke 12:42). *For a testimony of those things which were afterward to be spoken* (*eis marturion tōn lalēthēsomenōn*). Objective genitive of the articular future passive participle of *laleō*. It is not certain what it means whether the "testimony" (*marturion*) is to Moses or to God and whether it points on to Christ. In 9:9 see *parabolē* applied to the old dispensation as a symbol pointing to Christ and Christianity. *But Christ* (*Christos de*). In contrast with Moses (*men* in verse 5). *As a son* (*hōs huios*). Instead of a *therapōn* (servant). *Over his house* (*epi ton oikon autou*). The difference between *epi* and *en* added to that between *huios* and *therapōn*. It is very neat and quite conclusive, especially when we recall the high place occupied by Moses in Jewish thought. In Acts 7:11 the Jews accused Stephen of speaking "blasphemous words against Moses and God" (putting Moses on a par with God).

6. *Whose house are we* (*hou oikos esmen hēmeis*). We Christians (Jew and Gentile) looked at as a whole, not as a local organization. *If we hold fast* (*ean kataschōmen*). Condition of third class with *ean* and second aorist (effective) active subjunctive of *katechō*. This note of contingency and doubt runs all through the Epistle. We are God's house if we do not play the traitor and desert. *Boldness* (*parrēsian*) *and glorying* (*kai kauchēma*) some had lost. The author makes no effort to reconcile this warning with God's elective purpose. He is not exhorting God, but these wavering Christians. All these are Pauline words. B does not have *mechri telous bebaian* (firm unto the end), but it is clearly genuine in verse 14. He pleads for intelligent confidence.

7. *Wherefore* (*dio*). Probably this inferential conjunction (*dia, ho*, because of which) goes with *mē sklērunēte* (harden not) in verse 8 rather than with *blepete* (take heed) in verse 12 unless the long quotation be considered a parenthesis. The long quotation in verses 7 to 11 is from Psa. 95:7–11. After the quotation the author has "three movements" (Moffatt) in his discussion of the passage as applied to the Jewish Christians (3:12–19; 4:1–10; 4:11–13). The peril of apostasy as shown by the example of the Israelites is presented with vividness and power. *As the Holy Ghost saith* (*kathōs legei to pneuma to hagion*). Just this phrase nowhere else in the N.T., except Acts 21:11 (Agabus), though practically the same idea in 9:8 and 10:15. In I Tim. 4:1 the adjective "Holy" is wanting as in Rev. 2 and 3. But the writer quotes this Psalm as the Word of God and in 4:7 attributes it to David. *If ye shall hear* (*ean akousēte*). Condition of third class with *ean* and first aorist active subjunctive of *akouō*.

8. *Harden not* (*mē sklērunēte*). Prohibition with *mē* and first aorist (ingressive) active subjunctive of *sklērunō*, late verb from *sklēros* (dried up, stiff, hard) as in Acts 19:9; Rom. 9:18. *As in the provocation* (*hōs en tōi parapikrasmōi*). Late compound from *parapikrainō*, late verb to embitter (*para, pikros*), found only in LXX and here and verse 15. It means embitterment, exasperation. For the simple verb *pikrainō*, to make bitter, see Col. 3:19. The reference is to *Meribah* (Ex. 17:1–7). *Like as in the day* (*kata tēn hēmeran*). "According to the day" as in Acts 12:1; 19:23. *Of the temptation* (*tou peirasmou*). The reference is to *Massah* which took place at Rephidim.

9. *Wherewith* (*hou*). Literally, "where" (the wilderness) as in Deut. 8:15. *Tempted me by proving me* (*epeirasan en dokimasiāi*). No word for "me." The Israelites "tested" God "in putting to the proof" (only N.T. use of this word from *dokimazō* and this from the LXX). They were not

content with God's promise, but demanded objective proof (*erga*, deeds) of God.

10. *And saw* (*kai eidon*). "And yet saw." *Wherefore* (*dio*). Not in the LXX, but it makes clear the argument in the Psalm. *I was displeased* (*prosōchthisa*). First aorist active of *prosochthizō*, late compound for extreme anger and disgust. In N.T. only here and verse 17. *Err* (*planōntai*). Present middle indicative of *planaō*, to wander astray, common verb. *They did not know* (*ouk egnōsan*). In spite of God's works (*erga*) and loving patience the Israelites failed to understand God's ways with them. Are we any better? They "cared not to take my road" (Moffatt).

11. *As I sware* (*hōs ōmosa*). "Correlating the oath and the disobedience" (Vincent). First aorist active indicative of *omnuō*, old verb for solemn oath (6:13). *They shall not enter* (*ei eiseleusontai*). Future middle of *eiserchomai* with *ei* as an anacoluthon for the Hebrew *im* (not). Really it is a condition of the first class with the conclusion not expressed, common in the LXX as here (Robertson, *Grammar*, p. 1024). *Into my rest* (*eis tēn katapausin mou*). Old word from *katapauō* (Heb. 4:8), to give rest, in LXX, in N.T. only in Acts 7:49 and Heb. 3:11 to 4:11. Primarily the rest in Canaan and then the heavenly rest in which God dwells.

12. *Take heed* (*blepete*). Present active imperative as in Phil. 3:2 (three times) of *blepō* in place of the more usual *horate*. Solemn warning to the Jewish Christians from the experience of the Israelites as told in Psalm 95. *Lest haply there shall be* (*mē pote estai*). Negative purpose with *mē pote* and the future indicative as in Mark 14:2. But we have in Col. 2:8 *mē tis estai* as in Heb. 12:25; *mē* occurs with the aorist subjunctive, and *mē pote* with present subjunctive (Heb. 4:1) or aorist subjunctive (Acts 5:39). *In any one of you* (*en tini humōn*). The application is personal and pointed. *An evil heart of unbelief* (*kardia ponēra apistias*). A remarkable combination. *Heart* (*kardia*) is common in the LXX

(about 1,000 times), but "evil heart" only twice in the
O.T. (Jer. 16:12; 18:12). *Apistias* is more than mere unbelief, here rather disbelief, refusal to believe, genitive case
describing the evil heart marked by disbelief which is no
mark of intelligence then or now. *In falling away from the
living God* (*en tōi apostēnai apo theou zōntos*). "In the falling
away" [locative case with *en* of the second aorist active
(intransitive) infinitive of *aphistēmi*, to stand off from, to
step aside from (*apo* with the ablative case *theou*) the living
God (common phrase in the O.T. and the N.T. for God
as opposed to lifeless idols)]. "Remember that to apostatize from Christ in whom you have found God is to apostatize from God" (Dods). That is true today. See Ezek.
20:8 for this use of the verb.

13. *So long as it is called today* (*achris hou to sēmeron
kaleitai*). The only instance in the N.T. of this conjunction
(*achri* or *achris* or *achris hou*, etc.) with the present indicative
in the sense of "so long as" or "while" like *heōs*. Elsewhere
it means "until" and with either the aorist indicative (Acts
7:18), the future (Rev. 17:17), or the aorist subjunctive
(Rev. 7:3). *Lest any one of you be hardened* (*hina mē sklērun-
thēi tis ex humōn*). Negative purpose clause with *hina mē*
(that not) and the first aorist passive subjunctive of *sklērunō*, the vivid verb from verse 8. *By the deceitfulness of sin*
(*apatēi tēs hamartias*). Instrumental case *apatēi* (trick,
fraud) as is always the case with sin (Rom. 7:11; II Thess.
2:10). Apostasy (12:4) is their peril and it is a trick of sin.

14. *For we are become partakers of Christ* (*metochoi gar tou
Christou gegonamen*). Second perfect active of *ginomai*,
"we have become," not the equivalent of *esmen* (are). For
metochoi see 1:9; 3:1 and 6:4. We have become partners with
Christ and hence (*gar*, for) should not be tricked into apostasy. *If we hold fast* (*ean per kataschōmen*). The same condition as in verse 6 with *per* (indeed, forsooth) added to *ean*.
Jonathan Edwards once said that the sure proof of election

is that one holds out to the end. *The beginning of our confidence* (*tēn archēn tēs hupostaseōs*). For *hupostasis* see 1:3; 11:1. These faltering believers (some even apostates) began with loud confidence and profession of loyalty. And now?

15. *While it is said* (*en tōi legesthai*). Locative case with *en* of the articular present passive infinitive of *legō*, "in the being said." Thus the author (cf. same phrase in Psa. 42:4) introduces the repeated quotation from verses 7 and 8. Probably it is to be connected with *kataschōmen*, though it can be joined with *parakaleite* in verse 13 (treating 14 as a parenthesis).

16. *Who* (*Tines*). Clearly interrogative, not indefinite (some). *Did provoke* (*parepikranan*). First aorist active indicative of *parapikrinō*, apparently coined by the LXX like *parapikrasmos* (verse 15) to which it points, exasperating the anger of God. *Nay, did not all* (*all' ou pantes*). "A favourite device of the diatribe style" (Moffatt), answering one rhetorical question with another (Luke 17:8) as in verses 17 and 18. There was a faithful minority mentioned by Paul (I Cor. 10:7f.).

17. *With them that sinned* (*tois hamartēsasin*). Dative masculine plural after *prosōchthisen* (cf. verse 10) of the articular first aorist active participle of *hamartanō* (*hamartēsas*, not *hamartōn*). *Carcases* (*kōla*). Old word for members of the body like the feet, in LXX a dead body (Numbers 14:29), here only in N.T.

18. *That they should not enter* (*mē eiseleusesthai*). Negative *mē* (cf. *ei* in verse 11) and the future middle infinitive in indirect discourse. *To them that were disobedient* (*tois apeithēsasin*). Dative masculine plural of the articular first aorist active participle of *apeitheō*, active disobedience with which compare *apistias* in verse 12 and verse 19.

19. *And we see* (*kai blepomen*). Triumphant conclusion of the exegesis of Psa. 95. "So we see."

CHAPTER IV

1. *Let us fear therefore* (*phobēthōmen oun*). First aorist passive volitive subjunctive of *phobeomai*, to be afraid. There is no break in the argument on Psa. 95. This is a poor chapter division. The Israelites perished because of disbelief. We today face a real peril. *Lest haply* (*mē pote*). Here with the present subjunctive (*dokei*), but future indicative in 3:12, after the verb of fearing. For the optative see II Tim. 2:25. *A promise being left* (*kataleipomenēs epaggelias*). Genitive absolute of the present passive participle of *kataleipō*, to leave behind. God's promise still holds good for us in spite of the failure of the Israelites. *Should seem to have come short of it* (*dokei husterēkenai*). Perfect active infinitive of *hustereō*, old verb from *husteros* (comparative of root *ud* like our out, outer, outermost), to be too late, to fail to reach the goal as here, common in the N.T. (11:37; 12:15).

2. *For indeed we have had good tidings preached unto us* (*kai gar esmen euēggelismenoi esmen*). Periphrastic perfect passive indicative of *euaggelizō* (from *euaggelion*, good news, glad tidings) to bring good news, used here in its original sense as in verse 6 of the Israelites (*euaggelisthentes* first aorist passive participle). *Even as also they* (*kathaper kákeinoi*). See verse 6. We have the promise of rest as the Israelites had. The parallel holds as to the promise, the privilege, the penalty. *The word of hearing* (*ho logos tēs akoēs*). As in I Thess. 2:13. Genitive *akoēs* describing *logos*, the word marked by hearing (the word heard). *Because they were not united by faith with them that heard* (*mē sunkekerasmenous tēi pistei tois akousasin*). *Mē*, the usual negative of the participle. A very difficult phrase. The text

is uncertain whether the participle (perfect passive of *sunkerannumi*, old verb to mix together) ends in *-os* agreeing with *logos* or *-ous* agreeing with *ekeinous* (them). Taking it in *-ous* the translation is correct. *Pistei* is in the instrumental case and *tois akousasin* in the associative instrumental after *sun*.

3. *Do enter* (*eiserchometha*). Emphatic futuristic present middle indicative of *eiserchomai*. We are sure to enter in, we who believe. *He hath said* (*eirēken*). Perfect active indicative for the permanent value of God's word as in 1:13; 4:4; 10:9, 13; 13:5; Acts 13:34. God has spoken. That is enough for us. So he quotes again what he has in verse 11 from Psa. 95. *Although the works were finished* (*kaitoi tōn ergōn genēthentōn*). Genitive absolute with concessive use of the participle. Old particle, in N.T. only here and Acts 14:17 (with verb). *From the foundation of the world* (*apo katabolēs kosmou*). *Katabolē*, late word from *kataballō*, usually laying the foundation of a house in the literal sense. In the N.T. usually with *apo* (Matt. 25:44) or *pro* (John 17:24) about the foundation of the world.

4. *Somewhere on this wise* (*pou houtōs*). See 2:6 for *pou tis* for a like indefinite allusion to an Old Testament quotation. Here it is Gen. 2:2 (cf. Ex. 20:11; 31:17). Moffatt notes that Philo quotes Gen. 2:2 with the same "literary mannerism." *Rested* (*katepausen*). First aorist active indicative of *katapauō*, intransitive here, but transitive in verse 8. It is not, of course, absolute rest from all creative activity as Jesus shows in John 5:17. But the seventh day of God's rest was still going on (clearly not a twenty-four hour day).

5. *And in this place again* (*kai en toutōi palin*). The passage already quoted in verse 3 and in 3:11.

6. *It remaineth* (*apoleipetai*). Present passive indicative of *apoleipō*, old verb to leave behind, to remain over. So again in 4:9; 10:26. Here the infinitive clause (*tinas eiselthein eis autēn*) is the subject of *apoleipetai*. This left-over promise

is not repeated, though not utilized by the Israelites under Moses nor in the highest sense by Joshua and David. *Failed to enter in* (*ouk eisēlthon*). "Did not enter in" (second aorist active indicative of *eiserchomai*). It is a rabbinical argument all along here, but the author is writing to Jews.

7. *He again defineth a certain day* (*palin tina horizei hēmeran*). Present active indicative of *horizō*, old verb to set a limit (*horos*, horizon) as in Acts 17:26; Rom. 1:4. *In David* (*en Daueid*). Attributing the Psalm to David or in the Psalter at any rate. *Hath been before said* (*proeirētai*). Perfect passive indicative referring to the quotation in 3:7, 15. *After so long a time* (*meta tosouton chronon*). The time between Joshua and David.

8. *Joshua* (*Iēsous*). The Greek form is Jesus. Condition of the second class (determined as unfulfilled) with *ei* and aorist indicative in the condition and *an* with the imperfect in the conclusion. *He would not have spoken* (*ouk elalei*). Wrong translation, "he would not speak" (be speaking), in the passage in David. Imperfect tense, not aorist.

9. *A sabbath rest* (*sabbatismos*). Late word from *sabbatizō* (Ex. 16:30) to keep the Sabbath, apparently coined by the author (a doubtful passage in Plutarch). Here it is parallel with *katapausis* (cf. Rev. 14:13). *For the people of God* (*tōi laōi tou theou*). Dative case of blessed personal interest to the true Israel (Gal. 6:16).

10. *As God did from his* (*hōsper apo tōn idiōn ho theos*). It is not cessation of work, but rather of the weariness and pain in toil. The writer pictures salvation as God's rest which man is to share and God will have perfect satisfaction when man is in harmony with him (Dods).

11. *Let us therefore give diligence* (*spoudasōmen oun*). Volitive subjunctive aorist of *spoudazō*, old verb to hasten (II Tim. 4:9), to be eager and alert (I Thess. 2:17). The exhortation has a warning like that in 4:1. *That no man fall* (*hina mē pesēi*). Negative purpose with *hina mē* and the

second aorist active subjunctive of *piptō*, to fall. *After the same example of disobedience* (*en tōi autōi hupodeigmati tēs apeitheias*). The unbelief is like that seen in the Israelites (3:12, 18; 4:2). *Hupodeigma* is a late word from *hupodeik-numi* (Matt. 3:7) and means a copy (John 13:15; James 5:10). The Israelites set a terrible example and it is so easy to copy the bad examples.

12. *The word of God* (*ho logos tou theou*). That just quoted about the promise of rest and God's rest, but true of any real word of God. *Living* (*zōn*). Cf. the Living God (3:12). In Philo and the Book of Wisdom the Logos of God is personified, but still more in John 1:1–18 where Jesus is pictured as the Logos on a par with God. "Our author is using Philonic language rather than Philonic ideas" (Moffatt). See John 6:63: "The words which I have spoken are spirit and are life." *Active* (*energēs*). Energetic, powerful (John 1:12; Phil. 3:21; Col. 1:29). *Sharper* (*tomōteros*). Comparative of *tomos*, cutting (from *temnō*, to cut), late adjective; here only in the N.T. *Than* (*huper*). Often so after a comparative (Luke 16:8; II Cor. 12:13). *Two-edged* (*distomon*). "Two-mouthed" (*di-, stoma*), double-mouthed like a river (Polybius), branching ways (Sophocles), applied to sword (*xiphos*) by Homer and Euripides. *Piercing* (*diiknoumenos*). Present middle participle of *diikneomai*, old verb to go through, here only in N.T. *Even to the dividing* (*achri merismou*). Old word from *merizō* (*meros*, part), to partition. *Of soul and spirit* (*psuchēs kai pneumatos*). As in I Thess. 5:23; I Cor. 15:45, but not an argument for trichotomy. Psychology is constantly changing its terminology. *Of both joints and marrow* (*harmōn te kai muelōn*). From *arō*, to join, comes *harmos*, old word, here only in the N.T. *Muelos* (from *muō*, to shut), old word, here only in N.T. This surgeon goes into and through the joints and marrow, not cleaving between them. *Quick to discern* (*kritikos*). Verbal adjective in -*ikos*, from *krinō*, skilled in judging, as the surgeon has to be and

able to decide on the instant what to do. So God's word like his eye sees the secret lurking doubt and unbelief "of the thoughts and intents of the heart" (*enthumēseōn kai ennoiōn kardias*). The surgeon carries a bright and powerful light for every dark crevice and a sharp knife for the removal of all the pus revealed by the light. It is a powerful picture here drawn.

13. *That is not manifest* (*aphanēs*). Old adjective (*a* privative and *phainō*, to show), here only in the N.T. God's microscope can lay bare the smallest microbe of doubt and sin. *Naked* (*gumna*). Both soul and body are naked to the eye of God. *Laid open* (*tetrachēlismena*). Perfect passive participle of *trachēlizō*, late verb to bend back the neck (*trachēlos*, Matt. 18:6) as the surgeon does for operating, here only in N.T. See Rom. 16:4 for the peril of risking one's neck (*trachēlon hupotithenai*). God's eyes see all the facts in our inmost hearts. There are no mental reservations from God. *With whom we have to do* (*pros hon hēmin ho logos*). "With whom the matter or account for us is." There is a slight play here on *logos* of verse 12. Surely every servant of Christ today needs to gaze into this revealing mirror and be honest with himself and God.

14. *A great high priest* (*archierea megan*). The author now takes up the main argument of the Epistle, already alluded to in 1:3; 2:17f.; 3:1, the priestly work of Jesus as superior to that of the Levitical line (4:14–12:3). Jesus is superior to the prophets (1:1–3), to angels (1:4–2:18), to Moses (3:1–4:13), he has already shown. Here he only terms Jesus "great" as high priest (a frequent adjective with high priest in Philo) but the superiority comes out as he proceeds. *Who hath passed through the heavens* (*dielēluthota tous ouranous*). Perfect active participle of *dierchomai*, state of completion. Jesus has passed through the upper heavens up to the throne of God (1:3) where he performs his function as our high priest. This idea will be developed later (6:19f.; 7:26–28; 9:11f., 24f.). *Jesus the Son of God* (*Iēsoun ton huion*

tou theou). The human name linked with his deity, clinching the argument already made (1:1–4:13). *Let us hold fast our confession (kratōmen tēs homologias).* Present active volitive subjunctive of *krateō*, old verb (from *kratos*, power), with genitive to cling to tenaciously as here and 6:18 and also with the accusative (II Thess. 2:15; Col. 2:19). "Let us keep on holding fast." This keynote runs all through the Epistle, the exhortation to the Jewish Christians to hold on to the confession (3:1) of Christ already made. Before making the five points of Christ's superior priestly work (better priest than Aaron, 5:1–7:28; under a better covenant, 8:1–13; in a better sanctuary, 9:1–12; offering a better sacrifice, 9:13–10:18; based on better promises, 10:19–12:3), the author gives a double exhortation (4:14–16) like that in 2:1–4 to hold fast to the high priest (14f.) and to make use of him (16).

15. *That cannot be touched with the feeling (mē dunamenon sunpathēsai).* "Not able to sympathize with." First aorist passive infinitive of *sunpatheō*, late compound verb from the late adjective *sunpathos* (Rom. 12:15), both from *sunpaschō*, to suffer with (I Cor. 12:26; Rom. 8:17), occurring in Aristotle and Plutarch, in N.T. only in Hebrews (here and 10:34). *One that hath been tempted (pepeirasmenon).* Perfect passive participle of *peirazō*, as already shown in 2:17f. *Without sin (chōris hamartias).* This is the outstanding difference that must never be overlooked in considering the actual humanity of Jesus. He did not yield to sin. But more than this is true. There was no latent sin in Jesus to be stirred by temptation and no habits of sin to be overcome. But he did have "weaknesses" (*astheneiai*) common to our human nature (hunger, thirst, weariness, etc.). Satan used his strongest weapons against Jesus, did it repeatedly, and failed. Jesus remained "undefiled" (*amiantos*) in a world of sin (John 8:46). This is our ground of hope, the sinlessness of Jesus and his real sympathy.

16. *Let us therefore draw near* (*proserchōmetha oun*). Present active middle volitive subjunctive of *proserchomai.* "Let us keep on coming to" our high priest, this sympathizing and great high priest. Instead of deserting him, let us make daily use of him. This verb in Hebrews means reverent approach for worship (7:25; 10:1, 22; 11:6). *Unto the throne of grace* (*tōi thronōi tēs charitos*). This old word (*thronos*) we have taken into English, the seat of kings and of God and so of Christ (1:3, 8), but marked by grace because Jesus is there (Matt. 19:28). Hence we should come "with boldness" (*meta parrēsias*). Telling Jesus the whole story of our shortcomings. *That we may receive mercy* (*hina labōmen eleos*). Purpose clause with *hina* and second aorist active subjunctive of *lambanō.* *And find grace* (*kai charin heurōmen*). Second aorist active subjunctive of *heuriskō.* We are sure to gain both of these aims because Jesus is our high priest on the throne. *To help us in time of need* (*eis eukairon boētheian*). *Boētheia* is old word (from *boētheō*, 2:18 which see), in N.T. only here and Acts 27:17. *Eukairos* is an old word also (*eu*, well, *kairos*, opportunity), only here in N.T. "For well-timed help," "for help in the nick of time," before too late.

CHAPTER V

1. *In things pertaining to God (ta pros ton theon).* Accusative of general reference as in 2:17 (Rom. 15:17). The two essential points about any high priest are human sympathy (5:1–3) and divine appointment (5:4). He is taken from men and appointed in behalf of men. *That he may offer (hina prospherēi).* Purpose clause with *hina* and present active subjunctive of *prospherō*, "that he keep on offering (from time to time)." *Both gifts (dōra) and sacrifices (kai thusias).* General term (*dōra*) and bloody offerings, but the two together are inclusive of all as in 8:3 and 9:9 (I Kings 8:64). *For sins (huper hamartiōn).* His own included (7:27) except in the case of Jesus.

2. *Who can bear gently (metriopathein dunamenos).* Present active infinitive of the late verb *metriopatheō (metrios,* moderate, *pateō,* to feel or suffer). It is a philosophical term used by Aristotle to oppose the *apatheia* (lack of feeling) of the Stoics. Philo ranks it below *apatheia.* Josephus (*Ant.* XII. 32) uses it of the moderation of Vespasian and Titus towards the Jews. It occurs here only in the N.T. "If the priest is cordially to plead with God for the sinner, he must bridle his natural disgust at the loathsomeness of sensuality, his impatience at the frequently recurring fall, his hopeless alienation from the hypocrite and the superficial, his indignation at any confession he hears from the penitent" (Dods). *With the ignorant (tois agnoousin).* Dative case of the articular present active participle of *agnoeō,* old verb not to know (Mark 9:32). *And erring (kai planōmenois).* Present middle participle (dative case) of *planaō.* The one article with both participles probably makes it a hendiadys, sins of ignorance (both accidence and

367

sudden passion) as opposed to high-handed sins of presumption and deliberate purpose. People who sinned "willingly" (*hekousiōs*, 10:26) had no provision in the Levitical system. For deliberate apostasy (3:12; 10:26) no pardon is offered. *Is compassed with infirmity* (*perikeitai astheneian*). Present passive indicative of the old verb *perikeimai* here used transitively as in Acts 28:20 (*halusin*, chain). The priest himself has weakness lying around him like a chain. Not so Jesus.

3. *For himself* (*peri heautou*). Note *peri* three times here (*peri tou laou, peri heautou, peri hamartiōn*), but in verse 1 *huper anthrōpōn, huper hamartiōn*. In the *Koiné* this interchange of *peri* (around) and *huper* (over) is common (Matt. 26:28).

4. *Taketh the honour unto himself* (*heautōi lambanei tēn timēn*). Dative case of personal interest (*heautōi*). The priest was called of God. This is the ideal and was true of Aaron. The modern minister is not a priest, but he also should be a God-called man and not one who pushes himself into the ministry or into ecclesiastical office.

5. *So Christ also* (*houtōs kai ho Christos*). Just as with Aaron. Jesus had divine appointment as high priest also. *To be made* (*genēthēnai*). First aorist passive infinitive of *ginomai*. *High priest* (*archierea*). Predicate accusative agreeing with *heauton* (himself) object of *edoxasen*. *But he that spake unto him* (*all' ho lalēsas pros auton*). Ellipsis of *edoxasen* to be supplied from preceding clause. God did glorify Jesus in appointing him priest as we see in Psa. 2:7 quoted already as Messianic (Heb. 1:5). Jesus himself repeatedly claimed that the Father sent him on his mission to the world (John 5:30, 43; 8:54; 17:5, etc.). Bruce holds that Christ's priesthood is co-eval with his Sonship. Davidson thinks it is merely suitable because he is Son. Clearly the Father nominated (Dods) the Son to the Messianic priesthood (John 3:16).

6. *In another place* (*en heteröi*). That is Psa. 110:4. It is this crucial passage by which the author will prove the superiority of Jesus to Aaron as high priest. Only the word priest (*hiereus*) occurs here which the author uses as synonymous with high priest (*archiereus*). The point lies in the meaning of the phrase "After the order of Melchizedek" (*kata tēn taxin Melchisedek*). But at this point the only thing pressed is the fact of the divine appointment of Jesus as priest. He returns to this point (5:10–7:28).

7. *In the days of his flesh* (*en tais hēmerais tēs sarkos autou*). Here (verses 7 to 9) the author turns to the other requirement of a high priest (human sympathy). Since Jesus was "without sin" (4:15) he did not have to offer sacrifices "for himself," yet in all other points he felt the sympathy of the human high priest, even more so by reason of his victory over sin. *Having offered up* (*prosenegkas*). Second aorist active (-*a* form) participle of *prospherō* (cf. verse 3). An allusion to the Agony of Christ in Gethsemane. *Supplications* (*hiketērias*). Socrates, Polybius, Job (40:22) combine this word with *deēseis* (prayers) as here. The older form was *hikesia*. The word *hiketērios* is an adjective from *hiketēs* (a supplicant from *hikō*, to come to one) and suggests one coming with an olive-branch (*elaia*). Here only in the N.T. *With strong crying and tears* (*meta kraugēs ischuras kai dakruōn*). See Luke 22:44f. for a picture of the scene in Gethsemane (anguish and pathos). No doubt the writer has in mind other times when Jesus shed tears (John 11:35; Luke 19:41), but Gethsemane chiefly. *To save him from death* (*sōzein ek thanatou*). A reference to the cry of Jesus in Gethsemane (Matt. 26:39). *Having been heard for his godly fear* (*eisakoustheis apo tēs eulabeias*). Old word from *eulabēs* (taking hold well, Luke 2:25 from *eu, lambanō*, the verb *eulabeomai* in N.T. only in Heb. 11:7), in N.T. only here and 12:28. Fine picture of Christ's attitude toward the Father in the prayer in Gethsemane and in all his prayers.

Jesus in Gethsemane at once surrendered his will to that of the Father who heard his plea and enabled him to acquiesce in the Father's will.

8. *Though he was a Son* (*kaiper ōn huios*). Concessive participle with *kaiper*, regular Greek idiom as in 7:5; 12:17. *Yet learned obedience* (*emathen hupakoēn*). Second aorist active indicative of *manthanō*. Succinct and crisp statement of the humanity of Jesus in full harmony with Luke 2:40, 52 and with Heb. 2:10. *By the things which he suffered* (*aph' hōn epathen*). There is a play on the two verbs (*emathen — epathen*), paronomasia. Second aorist active indicative of *paschō*. He always did his Father's will (John 8:29), but he grew in experience as in wisdom and stature and in the power of sympathy with us.

9. *Having been made perfect* (*teleiōtheis*). First aorist passive participle of *teleioō*, the completion of the process of training mentioned by this same verb in 2:10 "by means of sufferings" (*dia pathēmatōn*) as stated again here in verse 8. *The author of eternal salvation* (*aitios sōtērias aiōniou*). Common adjective from *aitia* (cause), causing, often in Greek with *sōtērias* (Aeschines, Philo), in N.T. only here, Luke 23:4, 14, 22; Acts 19:40. See same idea in Heb. 2:10 (*archēgon*). See Isa. 45:17.

10. *Named of God* (*prosagoreutheis*). First aorist passive participle of *prosagoreuō*, old verb to salute, to address, only here in N.T. Common in Plutarch.

11. *Of whom* (*peri hou*). Or "concerning which," for *hou* can be either masculine or neuter (genitive). It is the likeness of Jesus as high priest to Melchizedek that the author has in mind. He is ready to discuss that but for the fear that the reader may fail to grasp his meaning, for he will run counter to the usual Jewish ideas. Hence he pauses to stir up the interest of the readers (5:11 to 6:20) before going on with the argument (7:1-28). *Hard of interpretation* (*dusermēneutos*). Late and rare verbal compound (*dus, hermēneuō*),

in Diodorus and Philo, here only in N.T. Hard to explain because of the strange (to Jews) line taken, but still more because of their dulness. *Dull of hearing (nōthroi tais akoais).* Old adjective (papyri also), from negative *nē* and *ōtheō*, to push, no push in the hearing, slow and sluggish in mind as well as in the ears. In N.T. only here and 6:12 (slack, sluggish). Plato calls some students *nōthroi* (stupid).

12. *Teachers (didaskaloi).* Predicate nominative after *einai. By reason of the time (dia ton chronon).* Alas, what a commentary on modern Christians. *That some one teach you the rudiments (tou didaskein humas tina ta stoicheia).* Neat Greek idiom, genitive case of the articular infinitive (need of the teaching) with two accusatives of the person (*humas,* you) and the thing (*ta stoicheia,* the rudiments) and the accusative of general reference (*tina,* as to some one). For *stoicheia* see Gal. 4:3, 9; Col. 2:8. *Of the first principles of the oracles of God (tēs archēs tōn logiōn tou theou).* Three genitives linked to each other. *Archēs* (beginning) illustrates *ta stoicheia,* just before, the A B C of Christian teaching like Heb. 6:1f. *Logion* is a diminutive of logos, divine oracles being usually brief, common in the O.T. and Philo for God's words, in N.T. used for the O.T. (Acts 7:38; Rom. 3:2), of God's word through Christians (I Peter 4:11), of the substance of Christian teaching (Heb. 5:12). *Of milk (galaktos).* Because still babes (I Cor. 3:2) and not able to chew "solid food" (*stereās trophēs*), without intellectual and spiritual teeth.

13. *Without experience (apeiros).* Old adjective (alpha privative and *peira,* trial). Inexperienced. The babe (*nēpios,* old word, negative *nē* and *epos,* word like Latin *infans,* infant, not able to talk), not able to chew if one uses only milk and is without teeth. Perhaps moral truth is meant by "word of righteousness" (cf. 1:2; 2:3 for the word spoken by Christ).

14. *For full-grown men (teleiōn).* Predicate genitive. The word is for adults, relative perfection *(teleioi)* in contrast with babes as in I Cor. 2:6; 3:1; 13:11; Phil. 3:15; Eph. 4:4, not absolute perfection (Matt. 5:48). *Their senses (ta aisthē-tēria).* The organs of perception (Stoic term for sense organs) from *aisthanomai* (Luke 9:45), in Plato, Galen, Hippocrates, here only in N.T. *Exercised (gegumnasmena).* Perfect passive participle of *gumnazō,* to exercise (naked, *gumnos*). Galen uses *aisthētēria gegumnasmena* together after *echō* as we have here. For this predicate use of the participle with *echō* see Luke 13:6; 14:19f. "By reason of use" one gains such skill. *To discern (pros diakrisin).* "For deciding between" (from *diakrinō*), old word with ablative *kalou te kai kakou* (between good and evil). See I Cor. 12:1; Rom. 14:1.

CHAPTER VI

1. *Wherefore* (*dio*). Because of the argument already made about the difficulty of the subject and the dulness of the readers. *Let us cease to speak* (*aphentes ton logon*). Second aorist active participle of *aphiēmi*, to leave off or behind. *Of the first principles of Christ* (*tēs archēs tou Christou*). Objective genitive *Christou* (about Christ). "Leaving behind the discussion of the beginning about Christ," another way of saying again *ta stoicheia tēs archēs tōn logiōn tou theou* of 5:12. *And press on* (*kai pherōmetha*). Volitive present subjunctive passive, "Let us be borne on" (both the writer and the readers). The Pythagorean Schools use *pherōmetha* in precisely this sense of being borne on to a higher stage of instruction. Bleek quotes several instances of Greek writers using together as here of *aphentes pherōmetha* (Eurip., *Androm.* 393, for instance). *Unto perfection* (*epi tēn teleiotēta*). Old word from *teleios* mature, adults as in 5:14. Only twice in N.T. (here and Col. 3:14). Let us go on to the stage of adults, not babes, able to masticate solid spiritual food. The writer will assume that the readers are adults in his discussion of the topic. *Not laying again the foundation* (*mē palin themelion kataballomenoi*). The regular idiom for laying down the foundation of a building (*themelion*, Luke 6:48f.). The metaphor is common (I Cor. 3:11) and the foundation is important, but one cannot be laying the foundation always if he is to build the house. There are six items mentioned here as part of the "foundation," though the accusative *didachēn* in apposition with *themelion* may mean that there are only four included in the *themelion*. Two are qualitative genitives after *themelion* (*metanoias* and *pisteōs*). What is meant by "dead works" (*apo nekrōn*

373

ergōn) is not clear (9:14), though the reference may be to touching a corpse (Numb. 19:1f.; 31:19). There are frequent allusions to the deadening power of sin (James 2:17, 26; John 7:25; Rom. 6:1, 11; 7:8; Col. 2:13; Eph. 2:1, 5). The use of repentance and faith together occurs also elsewhere (Mark 1:15; Acts 20:21; I Thess. 1:9).

2. The other four items are qualitative genitives with *didachēn* (*baptismōn, epitheseōs cheirōn, anastaseōs nekrōn, krimatos aiōniou*). The plural *baptismōn* "by itself does not mean specifically Christian baptism either in this epistle (9:10) or elsewhere (Mark 7:4), but ablutions or immersions such as the mystery religions and the Jewish cultus required for initiates, proselytes, and worshippers in general" (Moffatt). The disciples of the Baptist had disputes with the Jews over purification (John 3:25). See also Acts 19:2. "The laying on of hands" seems to us out of place in a list of elementary principles, but it was common as a sign of blessing (Matt. 19:13), of healing (Mark 7:32), in the choice of the Seven (Acts 6:6), in the bestowal of the Holy Spirit (Acts 8:17f.; 19:6), in separation for a special task (Acts 13:3), in ordination (I Tim. 4:14; 5:22; II Tim. 1:6). Prayer accompanied this laying on of the hands as a symbol. The resurrection of the dead (both just and unjust, John 5:29; Acts 24:15) is easily seen to be basal (cf. I Cor. 15) as well as eternal judgment (timeless and endless).

3. *If God permit* (*eanper epitrepēi ho theos*). Condition of the third class with *eanper* (note *per* indeed). See I Cor. 16:7 (*ean ho kurios epitrepsēi*) and Acts 18:21 (*tou theou thelontos*). It is not an idle form with the author. He means that he will go on with the argument and not attempt to lay again the foundation (the elements). Moffatt takes him to mean that he will teach them the elements at a later time (13:23) if the way opens, a less probable interpretation.

4. *As touching those who were once enlightened* (*tous hapax phōtisthentas*). First aorist passive articular participle (the

once for all enlightened) of *photizō*, old and common verb
(from *phōs*) as in Luke 11:36. The metaphorical sense here
(cf. John 1:9; Eph. 1:18; Heb. 10:32) occurs in Polybius
and Epictetus. The accusative case is due to *anakainizein*
in verse 6. *Hapax* here is "once for all," not once upon a
time (*pote*) and occurs again (9:7, 26, 27, 28; 12:26, 27).
Tasted of the heavenly gift (*geusamenous tēs dōreas tēs epouraniou*). First aorist middle participle of *geuō*, old verb
once with accusative (verse 5, *kalon rēma, dunameis*), usually with genitive (Heb. 2:9) as here. *Partakers of the Holy
Ghost* (*metochous pneumatos hagiou*). See 3:14 for *metochoi*.
These are all given as actual spiritual experiences. *And then
fell away* (*kai parapesontas*). No "then" here, though the
second aorist (effective) active participle of *parapiptō*, old
verb to fall beside (aside), means that. Only here in N.T.
In Gal. 5:4 we have *tēs charitos exepesate* (ye fell out of
grace, to law, Paul means).

6. *It is impossible to renew them again* (*adunaton palin
anakainizein*). The *adunaton* (impossible) comes first in
verse 4 without *estin* (is) and there is no "them" in the
Greek. There are three other instances of *adunaton* in
Hebrews (6:18; 10:4; 11:6). The present active infinitive
of *anakainizō* (late verb, *ana, kainos*, here only in the N.T.,
but *anakainoō*, II Cor. 4:16; Col. 3:10) with *adunaton*
bluntly denies the possiblity of renewal for apostates from
Christ (cf. 3:12–4:2). It is a terrible picture and cannot
be toned down. The one ray of light comes in verses 8
to 12, not here. *Seeing they crucify to themselves afresh* (*ana-
straurountas heautois*). Present active participle (accusative
plural agreeing with *tous . . . parapesontas*) of *anastauroō*,
the usual verb for crucify in the old Greek so that *ana-*
here does not mean "again" or "afresh," but "up," *sursum*,
not *rursum* (Vulgate). This is the reason why renewal for
such apostates is impossible. They crucify Christ. *And
put him to an open shame* (*kai paradeigmatizontas*). Present

active participle of *paradeigmatizō*, late verb from *paradeigma* (example), to make an example of, and in bad sense to expose to disgrace. Simplex verb *deigmatisai* in this sense in Matt. 1:19.

7. *Which hath drunk* (*hē piousa*). Articular second aorist active participle of *pinō*, to drink. *Herbs* (*botanēn*). Old word from *boskō*, to feed, green plant, only here in N.T. Cf. our botany. *Meet* (*eutheton*). Old compound verbal (*eu, tithēmi*) well-placed, fit (Luke 9:62). *It is tilled* (*geōrgeitai*). Present passive indicative of *geōrgeō*, old and rare verb from *geōrgos* (tiller of the soil, *gē, ergon*, II Tim. 2:6), here only in the N.T. *Receives* (*metalambanei*). Present active indicative of *metalambanō*, old verb to share in, with genitive (*eulogias*) as here (Acts 2:46) or with accusative (Acts 24:25).

8. *If it beareth* (*ekpherousa*). Present active participle of *ekpherō*, conditional participle. For "thorns and thistles" see Matt. 7:16 for both words (*akanthas kai tribolous*). Roman soldiers scattered balls with sharp iron spikes, one of which was called *tribulus*, to hinder the enemy's cavalry. *Rejected* (*adokimos*). See I Cor. 9:27; Rom. 1:28. For *kataras eggus* (nigh unto a curse) see Gal. 3:10. *To be burned* (*eis kausin*). "For burning." Common sight in clearing up ground.

9. *But we are persuaded* (*pepeismetha de*). Perfect passive indicative of *peithō*, literary plural. Note Paul's use of *pepeismai* in II Tim. 1:12. *Better things* (*ta kreissona*). "The better things" than those pictures in 6:4–8. *That accompany salvation* (*echomena sōtērias*). "Things holding on to salvation" (Mark 1:38), a common Greek phrase *echomena*, present middle participle of *echō*. *Though we thus speak* (*ei kai houtōs laloumen*). Concessive condition of the first class. Explanatory, not apologetic, of his plain talk. *Not unrighteous to forget* (*ou gar adikos epilathesthai*). Second aorist middle infinitive of *epilanthanō* with genitive case (*ergou*,

work, *agapēs*, love). But even God cannot remember what they did not do. *In that ye ministered and still do minister* (*diakonēsantes kai diakonountes*). First aorist active and present active participle of the one verb *diakoneō*, the sole difference being the tense (single act *aorist*, repeated acts *present*).

11. *And we desire* (*epithumoumen de*). Literary plural again like *pepeismetha* (6:9). He is not wholly satisfied with them as he had already shown (5:11-14). They have not given up Christ (6:4-8), but many of them are still babes (*nēpioi*, 5:13) and not adults (*teleioi*, 5:14) and others are in peril of becoming so. *Unto the fulness of hope* (*pros tēn plērophorian tēs elpidos*). For *plērophoria* see I Thess. 1:5; Col. 2:2. *To the end* (*achri telous*). As in 3:6, 14.

12. *That ye be not sluggish* (*hina mē nōthroi genēsthe*). Negative final clause with second aorist middle subjunctive of *ginomai*, "that ye become not sluggish (or dull of hearing)" as some already were (5:11). *Imitators* (*mimētai*). See I Thess. 1:6; 2:14 for this word (our "mimic" in good sense). The writer wishes to hold and develop these sluggards through those who inherit the promises (see 10:19 to 12:3), one of his great appeals later in ch. 11 full of examples of "faith and long-suffering."

13. *Made promise* (*epaggeilamenos*). First aorist middle participle of *epaggellō*. *Could swear by none greater* (*kat' oudenos eichen meizonos omosai*). Imperfect active of *echō* in sense of *edunato* as often with *omosai* (first aorist active infinitive of *omnuō*) and *ōmosen* (he sware) is first aorist active indicative.

14. *Surely* (*ei mēn*). By itacism for *ē mēn* (Deissmann, *Bible Studies*, p. 205). The quotation is from Gen. 22:16f. (the promise renewed to Abraham with an oath after offering of Isaac). *Blessing* (*eulogōn*). Hebraism (present active participle) for the Hebrew infinitive absolute and so with *plēthunōn* (multiplying).

15. *Having patiently endured* (*makrothumēsas*). First aorist active participle of *makrothumos* (*makros, thumos*, long spirit) illustrating *makrothumia* of verse 12. *He obtained* (*epetuchen*). Second aorist (effective) active indicative of *epetugchanō*, old verb with genitive. God was true to his word and Abraham was faithful.

16. *In every dispute* (*pasēs antilogias*). Objective genitive of old word several times in Hebrews (6:16; 7:7; 12:3). Talking back, face to face, in opposition. *Final* (*peras*). Limit, boundary (Matt. 12:42). Men may perjure themselves.

17. *To shew* (*epideixai*). First aorist active infinitive of *epideiknumi*, to show in addition (*epi-*) to his promise "more abundantly" (*perissoteron*). *The immutability of his counsel* (*to ametatheton tēs boulēs autou*). Late compound verbal neuter singular (alpha privative and *metatithēmi*, to change), "the unchangeableness of his will." *Interposed* (*emesiteusen*). First aorist active indicative of *mesiteuō*, late verb from *mesitēs*, mediator (Heb. 8:6), to act as mediator or sponsor or surety, intransitively to pledge one's self as surety, here only in the N.T. *With an oath* (*horkōi*). Instrumental case of *horkos* (from *herkos*, an enclosure), Matt. 14:7, 9.

18. *By two immutable things* (*dia duo pragmatōn ametathetōn*). See verse 17. God's promise and God's oath, both unchangeable. *In which it is impossible for God to lie* (*en hois adunaton pseusasthai theon*). Put this "impossibility" by that in verses 4 to 6. *Theon* is accusative of general reference with *pseusasthai*, first aorist middle infinitive of *pseudomai*. *That we may have* (*hina echōmen*). Purpose clause with *hina* and the present active subjunctive of *echō*, "that we may keep on having." *Strong consolation* (*ischuran paraklēsin*). "Strong encouragement" by those two immutable things. *Who have fled for refuge* (*hoi kataphugontes*). Articular effective second aorist active participle of *katapheugō*, old verb, in N.T. only here and Acts 14:6. The word occurs for fleeing to the cities of

refuge (Deut. 4:42; 19:5; Josh. 20:9). *To lay hold of* (*kra-tēsai*). First aorist active (single act) infinitive of *krateō* in contrast with present tense in 4:14 (hold fast). *Set before us* (*prokeimenēs*). Placed before us as the goal. See this same participle used with the "joy" (*charas*) set before Jesus (12:2).

19. *Which* (*hēn*). Which hope. What would life be without this blessed hope based on Christ as our Redeemer? *As an anchor of the soul* (*hōs agkuran tēs psuchēs*). Old word, literally in Acts 27:29, figuratively here, only N.T. examples. The ancient anchors were much like the modern ones with iron hooks to grapple the rocks and so hold on to prevent shipwreck (I Tim. 1:19). *Both sure and stead-fast* (*asphalē te kai bebaian*). This anchor of hope will not slip (alpha privative and *sphallō*, to totter) or lose its grip (*bebaia*, from *bainō*, to go, firm, trusty). *That which is within the veil* (*to esōteron tou katapetasmatos*). The Holy of Holies, "the inner part of the veil" (the space behind the veil), in N.T. only here and Acts 16:24 (of the inner prison). The anchor is out of sight, but it holds. That is what matters.

20. *As a forerunner* (*prodromos*). Old word used for a spy, a scout, only here in N.T. Jesus has shown us the way, has gone on ahead, and is the surety (*egguos*, Heb. 7:22) and guarantor of our own entrance later. In point of fact, our anchor of hope with its two chains of God's promise and oath has laid hold of Jesus within the veil. It will hold fast. All we need to do is to be true to him as he is to us. *A high priest for ever* (*archiereus eis ton aiōna*). There he functions as our great high priest, better than Aaron for he is "after the order of Melchizedek," the point that now calls for elucidation (5:10f.).

CHAPTER VII

1. *This Melchizedek (houtos ho Melchisedek)*. The one already mentioned several times with whose priesthood that of Christ is compared and which is older and of a higher type than that of Aaron. See Gen. 14:18–20 and Psa. 110 for the only account of Melchizedek in the Old Testament. It is a daring thing to put Melchizedek above Aaron, but the author does it. Moffatt calls verses 1 to 3 "a little sermon" on 6:20. It is "for ever" (*eis ton aiōna*) that he explains. Melchizedek is the only one in his line and stands alone in the record in Genesis. The interpretation is rabbinical in method, but well adapted to Jewish readers. The description is taken verbatim from Genesis except that "who met" (*ho sunantēsas*) is here applied to Melchizedek from Gen. 14:17 instead of to the King of Sodom. They both met Abraham as a matter of fact. For this verb (first aorist active participle of *sunantaō*) see Luke 9:37. *Slaughter (kopēs)*. Old word for cutting (*koptō*, to cut), here only in N.T. These kings were Amraphel, Arioch, Chedorlaomer, Tidal. Amraphel is usually taken to be Khammurabi. *Priest of God Most High (hiereus tou theou tou hupsistou)*. He is called "priest" and note *tou hupsistou* applied to God as the Canaanites, Phoenicians, Hebrews did. It is used also of Zeus and the Maccabean priest-kings. The demons apply it to God (Mark 5:7; Luke 8:28).

2. *A tenth (dekatēn)*. It was common to offer a tenth of the spoils to the gods. So Abraham recognized Melchizedek as a priest of God. *Divided (emerisen)*. First aorist active of *merizō*, from *meros* (portion), to separate into parts. From this point till near the end of verse 3 (the Son of God) is a long parenthesis with *houtos* of verse 1 as the subject of

menei (abideth) as the Revised Version punctuates it. Philo had made popular the kind of exegesis used here. The author gives in Greek the meaning of the Hebrew words Melchizedek (King of righteousness, cf. 1:8) and Salem (peace).

3. *Without father, without mother, without genealogy* (*apatōr, amētōr, agenealogētos*). Alliteration like Rom. 1:30, the first two old words, the third coined by the author (found nowhere else) and meaning simply "devoid of any genealogy." The argument is that from silence, made much of by Philo, but not to be pressed. The record in Genesis tells nothing of any genealogy. Melchizedek stands alone. He is not to be understood as a miraculous being without birth or death. Melchizedek has been made more mysterious than he is by reading into this interpretation what is not there. *Made like* (*aphōmoiōmenos*). Perfect passive participle of *aphomoioō*, old verb, to produce a facsimile or copy, only here in N.T. The likeness is in the picture drawn in Genesis, not in the man himself. Such artificial interpretation does not amount to proof, but only serves as a parallel or illustration. *Unto the Son of God* (*tōi huiōi tou theou*). Associative instrumental case of *huios*. *Abideth a priest* (*menei hiereus*). According to the record in Genesis, the only one in his line just as Jesus stands alone, but with the difference that Jesus continues priest in fact in heaven. *Continually* (*eis to diēnekes*). Old phrase (for the continuity) like *eis ton aiōna*, in N.T. only in Hebrews (7:3; 10:1, 14, 21).

4. *How great* (*pēlikos*). Geometrical magnitude in contrast to arithmetical (*posos*), here only in N.T., "how distinguished." He received tithes from Abraham (verses 4 to 6a) and he blessed Abraham (6b and 7) and even Levi is included (verses 8 to 10). *Out of the chief spoils* (*ek tōn akrothiniōn*). Old word from *akros*, top, and *this*, a heap (the top of the pile). *Patriarch* (*patriarchēs*). LXX word (*patria*, tribe, *archō*, to rule) transferred to N.T. (Acts 2:29).

5. *The priest's office* (*tēn hierateian*). LXX and *Koiné* word from *hiereus*, in N.T. only here and Luke 1:9. *To take tithes* (*apodekatoin*). Present active infinitive (in *-oin*, not *-oun*, as the best MSS. give it) of *apodekatoō* a LXX word (*apo, dekatoō*), to take a tenth from (*apo*). *Brethren* (*adelphous*). Accusative case in apposition with *laon* (people) unaffected by the explanatory phrase *tout' estin* (that is). *Though come out* (*kaiper exelēluthotas*). Concessive participle (cf. 5:8) with *kaiper* (perfect active of *exerchomai*).

6. *He whose genealogy is not counted* (*ho mē genealogoumenos*). Articular participle with negative *mē* (usual with participles) of the old verb *genealogeō* trace ancestry (cf. verse 3). *Hath taken tithes* (*dedekatōken*). Perfect active indicative of *dekatoō*, standing on record in Genesis. *Hath blessed* (*eulogēken*). Perfect active indicative of *eulogeō*, likewise standing on record. Note the frequent perfect tenses in Hebrews. *Him that hath the promises* (*ton echonta tas epaggelias*). Cf. 6:12, 13–15 for allusion to the repeated promises to Abraham (Gen. 12:3, 7; 13:14; 15:5; 17:5; 22:16–18).

7. *Dispute* (*antilogias*). Ablative case with *chōris*. For the word see 6:16. The writer makes a parenthetical generalization and uses the article and neuter adjective (*to elasson*, the less, *hupo tou kreittonos*, by the better), a regular Greek idiom.

8. *Here* (*hōde*). In the Levitical system. *There* (*ekei*). In the case of Melchizedek. *Of whom it is witnessed* (*marturoumenos*). "Being witnessed," present passive participle of *martureō* (personal construction, not impersonal). *That he lives* (*hoti zēi*). Present active indicative of *zaō*). The Genesis record tells nothing of his death.

9. *So to say* (*hōs epos eipein*). An old idiom, here only in the N.T., common in Philo, used to limit a startling statement, an infinitive for conceived result with *hōs*. *Hath paid tithes* (*dedekatōtai*). Perfect passive indicative of *dekatoō*, "has been tithed." This could only be true of Levi "so to speak."

10. *In the loins of his father* (*en tēi osphui tou patros*)·
Levi was not yet born. The reference is to Abraham, the
forefather (*patros*) of Levi. This is a rabbinical imaginative
refinement appealing to Jews.

11. *Perfection* (*teleiōsis*). Abstract substantive of *teleioō*.
More the act than the quality or state (*teleiotēs*, 6:1).
The condition is of the second class, "if there were perfection, etc." The Levitical priesthood failed to give men "a
perfectly adequate relation to God" (Moffatt). *Priesthood*
(*hierosunēs*). Old word, in N.T. only here, verses 12, 24.
Cf. *hieretia* in verse 5. The adjective *Leueitikē* occurs in
Philo. *Received the law* (*nenomothetētai*). Perfect passive
indicative of *nomotheteō*, old compound to enact law (*nomos*,
tithēmi), to furnish with law (as here), only other N.T.
example in 8:6. *What further need was there?* (*tis eti chreia;*).
No copula expressed, but it would normally be *ēn an*, not
just *ēn:* "What need still would there be?" *Another priest*
(*heteron hierea*). Of a different line (*heteron*), not just one
more (*allon*). Accusative of general reference with the infinitive *anistasthai* (present middle of *anistēmi* intransitive).
And not to be reckoned (*kai ou legesthai*). The negative *ou*
belongs rather to the descriptive clause than just to the
infinitive.

12. *The priesthood being changed* (*metatithemenēs tēs hierosunēs*). Genitive absolute with present passive participle of
metatithēmi, old word to transfer (Gal. 1:6). *A change*
(*metathesis*). Old substantive from *metatithēmi*. In N.T.
only in Heb. (7:12; 11:5; 12:27). God's choice of another
kind of priesthood for his Son, left the Levitical line off to
one side, forever discounted, passed by "the order of Aaron"
(*tēn taxin Aarōn*).

13. *Belongeth to another tribe* (*phulēs heteras meteschēken*).
See 2:14 for *metechō*, perfect active indicative here. A differ-
ent (*heteras*) tribe. *Hath given attendance at* (*proseschēken*).
Perfect active indicative (watch perfects in Hebrews, not

"for" aorists) of *prosechō*, old verb, here with either *noun* (mind) or self (*heauton*) understood with dative case (*tōi thusiastēriōi*, the altar, for which word see Matt. 5:23; Luke 1:11).

14. *It is evident* (*prodēlon*). Old compound adjective (*pro, dēlos*), openly manifest to all, in N.T. only here and I Tim. 5:24f. *Hath sprung* (*anatetalken*). Perfect active indicative of *anatellō*, old compound to rise up like the sun (Matt. 5:45).

15. *Yet more abundantly evident* (*perissoteron eti katadēlon*). Only N.T. instance of the old compound adjective *katadēlos* thoroughly clear with *eti* (still) added and the comparative *perissoteron* (more abundantly) piling Ossa on Pelion like Phil. 1:23. *Likeness* (*homoiotēta*). See 4:15, only N.T. examples. Cf. the verb in verse 3. *Ariseth another priest* (*anistatai hiereus heteros*). As said in verse 11, now assumed in condition of first class.

16. *Carnal* (*sarkinēs*). "Fleshen" as in I Cor. 3:1, not *sarkikēs* (fleshlike, I Cor. 3:3). The Levitical priests became so merely by birth. *Of an endless life* (*zōēs akatalutou*). Late compound (alpha privative and verbal adjective from *kataluō*, to dissolve, as in II Cor. 4:1), indissoluble. Jesus as priest lives on forever. He is Life.

17. *It is witnessed* (*martureitai*). Present passive indicative of *martureō*. The author aptly quotes again Psa. 110:4.

18. *A disannulling* (*athetēsis*). Late .word from *atheteō* (alpha privative and *tithēmi*), to set aside (Mark 6:26), in N.T. only here and 9:26. Common in the papyri in a legal sense of making void. Involved in *metathesis* (change in verse 12). *Foregoing* (*proagousēs*). Present active participle of *proagō*, to go before (I Tim. 1:18). *Because of its weakness* (*dia to autēs asthenes*). Neuter abstract adjective with article for quality as in verse 7 with *dia* and accusative case for reason. *Unprofitableness* (*anōpheles*). Old compound (alpha privative and *ophelos*) useless, and neuter singular like *asthenes*. In N.T. only here and Titus 3:9.

19. *Made nothing perfect* (*ouden eteleiōsen*). Another parenthesis. First aorist active indicative of *teleioō*. See verse 11.
And yet law is necessary. *A bringing in thereupon* (*epeisa-
gōgē*). An old double compound (*epi*, additional, *eisagōgē*,
bringing in from *eisagō*). Here only in N.T. Used by Josephus (*Ant.* XI. 6, 2) for the introduction of a new wife in
place of the repudiated one. *Of a better hope* (*kreittonos
elpidos*). This better hope (6:18–20) does bring us near to
God (*eggizomen tōi theōi*) as we come close to God's throne
through Christ (4:16).

20. *Without the taking of an oath* (*chōris horkōmosias*).
As in Psa. 110:4.

21. *Have been made* (*eisin gegonotes*). Periphrastic perfect
active indicative of *ginomai* (perfect active participle of
ginomai) and then *eisin*. The parenthesis runs from *hoi men
gar* (for they) to *eis ton aiōna* (for ever, end of verse 21).
But he with an oath (*ho de meta horkōmosias*). Positive statement in place of the negative one in verse 20.

22. *By so much also* (*kata tosouto kai*). Correlative demonstrative corresponding to *kath' hoson* (the relative clause)
in verse 20. *The surety* (*egguos*). Vulgate *sponsor*. Old word,
here only in the N.T., adjective (one pledged, betrothed),
from *egguē*, a pledge, here used as substantive like *egguētēs*,
one who gives a pledge or guarantee. There may be a play
on the word *eggizō* in verse 19. *Egguaō* is to give a pledge,
eggualizō, to put a pledge in the hollow of the hand. It is not
clear whether the author means that Jesus is God's pledge to
man, or man's to God, or both. He is both in fact, as the
Mediator (*ho mesitēs*, 8:6) between God and man (Son of
God and Son of man).

23. *Many in number* (*pleiones*). Comparative predicate
adjective, "more than one," in succession, not simultaneously. *Because they are hindered* (*dia to kōluesthai*). Articular
infinitive (present passive) with *dia* and the accusative case,
"because of the being hindered." *By death* (*thanatōi*). In-

strumental case. *From continuing (paramenein).* Present active infinitive of the compound (remain beside) as in Phil. 1:25 and in the ablative case.

24. *Because he abideth (dia to menein auton).* Same idiom as in verse 23, "because of the abiding as to him" (accusative of general reference, *auton*). *Unchangeable (aparabaton).* Predicate adjective in the accusative (feminine of compound adjective like masculine), late double compound verbal adjective in Plutarch and papyri, from alpha privative and *parabainō*, valid or inviolate. The same idea in verse 3. God placed Christ in this priesthood and no one else can step into it. See verse 11 for *hierōsunē.*

25. *Wherefore (hothen).* Since he alone holds this priesthood. *To the uttermost (eis to panteles).* Old idiom, in N.T. only here and Luke 13:10. Vulgate renders it *in perpetuum* (temporal idea) or like *pantote.* This is possible, but the common meaning is completely, utterly. *Draw near (proserchomenous).* Present middle participle of *proserchomai,* the verb used in 4:16 which see. *To make intercession (eis to entugchanein).* Purpose clause with *eis* and the articular present active infinitive of *entugchanō* for which verb see Rom. 8:34. "His intercession has red blood in it, unlike Philo's conception" (Moffatt).

26. *Became us (hēmin eprepen).* Imperfect active indicative of *prepō* as in 2:10, only there it was applied to God while here to us. "Such" *(toioutos)* refers to the Melchizedek character of Jesus as high priest and in particular to his power to help and save (2:17f.) as just explained in 7:24f. Moffatt notes that "it is generally misleading to parse a rhapsody" but the adjectives that follow picture in outline the qualities of the high priest needed by us. *Holy (hosios).* Saintly, pious, as already noted. Cf. Acts 2:24; 13:35. *Guileless (akakos).* Without malice, innocent. In N.T. only here and Rom. 16:18. *Undefiled (amiantos).* Untainted, stainless. In the papyri. Not merely ritual purity

(Lev. 21:10–15), but real ethical cleanness. *Separated from sinners* (*kechōrismenos apo tōn hamartōlōn*). Perfect passive participle. Probably referring to Christ's exaltation (9:28). *Made higher than the heavens* (*hupsēloteros tōn ouranōn genomenos*). "Having become higher than the heavens." Ablative case (*ouranōn*) after the comparative adjective (*hupsēloteros*).

27. *First* (*proteron*). Regular adverb for comparison between two, though *prōton* often occurs also (John 1:41), with *epeita* (then) following. *For the sins* (*tōn*). Only the article in the Greek with repetition of *huper* or of *hamartiōn*. *When he offered up himself* (*heauton anenegkas*). First aorist active participle of *anapherō*, to offer up. See same idea in 9:14 where *heauton prosēnegken* is used. Old verb for sacrifice to place on the altar (I Peter 2:5, 24).

28. *After the law* (*meta ton nomon*). As shown in verses 11 to 19, and with an oath (Psa. 110:4). *Son* (*huion*). As in Psa. 2:7 and Heb. 1:2 linked with Psa. 110:4. *Perfected* (*teteleiōmenon*). Perfect passive participle of *teleioō*. The process (2:10) was now complete. Imperfect and sinful as we are we demand a permanent high priest who is sinless and perfectly equipped by divine appointment and human experience (2:17f.; 5:1–10) to meet our needs, and with the perfect offering of himself as sacrifice.

CHAPTER VIII

1. *In the things which we are saying (epi tois legomenois).*
Locative case of the articular present passive participle of
legō after *epi* as in Luke 5:5; Heb. 11:4, "in the matter of
the things being discussed." *The chief point (kephalaion).*
Neuter singular of the adjective *kephalaios* (from *kephalē*,
head), belonging to the head. Vulgate *capitulum*, nominative absolute in old and common sense, the main matter
(even so without the article as in Thucydides), "the pith"
(Coverdale), common in the papyri as in Greek literature.
The word also occurs in the sense of the sum total or a
sum of money (Acts 22:28) as in Plutarch, Josephus, and
also in the papyri (Moulton and Milligan's *Vocabulary*).
Such an high priest (toiouton archierea). As the one described
in chapters 4:16 to 7:28 and in particular 7:26 (*toioutos*) to
28. But the discussion of the priestly work of Jesus continues
through 12:3. *Toioutos* is both retrospective and prospec-
tive. Here we have a summary of the five points of superiority of Jesus as high priest (8:1-6). He is himself a better
priest than Aaron (*toioutos* in 8:1 such as shown in 4:16 to
7:28); he works in a better sanctuary (8:2, 5); he offers a
better sacrifice (8:3f.); he is mediator of a better covenant
(8:6); his work rests on better promises (8:6); hence he has
obtained a better ministry as a whole (8:6). In this resumé
(*kephelaion*) the author gives the pith (*kephalaion*) of his
argument, curiously enough with both senses of *kephalaion*
(pith, summary) pertinent. He will discuss the four points
remaining thus: (1) the better covenant, 8:7-13. (2) The
better sanctuary, 9:1-12. (3) The better sacrifice, 9:13-
10:18. (4) The better promises, 10:19-12:3. One point
(the better high priest, like Melchizedek) has already been

discussed (4:16–7:28). *Sat down (ekathisen)*. Repetition of 1:3 with *tou thronou* (the throne) added. This phrase prepares the way for the next point.

2. *Minister (leitourgos)*. See on Rom. 13:6; Phil. 2:25. *Of the sanctuary (tōn hagiōn)*. "Of the holy places" (*ta hagia*), without any distinction (like 9:8f.; 10:19; 13:11) between the holy place and the most holy place as in 9:2f. *Of the true tabernacle (tēs skēnēs tēs alēthinēs)*. By way of explanation of *tōn hagiōn*. For *skēnē* see Matt. 17:4 and *skēnos* (II Cor. 5:1), old word used here for the antitype or archetype of the tabernacle in the wilderness in which Aaron served, the ideal tabernacle in heaven of which the earthly tabernacle was a symbol and reproduced in the temple which merely copied the tabernacle. Hence it is the "genuine" tabernacle and see John 1:9 for *alēthinos*. *Pitched (epēxen)*. First aorist active indicative of *pēgnumi*, old verb to fasten as the pegs of a tent, here only in the N.T. Cf. Numbers 24:6.

3. *Is appointed (kathistatai)*. As in 5:1. *To offer (eis to prospherein)*. Articular infinitive accusative case with *eis* as is common while *hina prospherēi (hina* with present active subjunctive) for purpose in 5:1, with *dōra te kai thusias* as there. *It is necessary (anagkaion)*. A moral and logical necessity (from *anagkē* necessity) as seen in Acts 13:46; Phil. 1:24. *This high priest also (kai touton)*. "This one also," no word for high priest, accusative of general reference with the infinitive *echein* (have). *Somewhat to offer (ti hō prosenegkēi)*. Second aorist active subjunctive of *prospherō* (verse 3). Vulgate *aliquid quod offerat*. The use of the subjunctive in this relative clause is probably volitive as in Acts 21:16 and Heb. 12:28 (possibly here merely futuristic), but note *ho prospherei* (present indicative) in 9:7. See Robertson, *Grammar*, p. 955.

4. *On earth (epi gēs)*. As opposed to *en tois ouranois* (verse 1). Condition of second class, determined as unful-

filled. *He would not be a priest at all* (*oud' an ēn hiereus*). "Not even would he be a priest." Conclusion of second class condition with *an* and imperfect indicative (*ēn*). *Seeing there are those* (*ontōn tōn*). Genitive absolute with *ontōn* (from *eimi*) and the articular present active participle of *prosphero* (verse 3). Jesus was not of the tribe of Levi and so could not serve here.

5. *Serve* (*latreuousin*). Present active indicative of *latreuō* for which verb see on Matt. 4:10. *A copy* (*hupodeigmati*). Dative case after *latreuousin*. See already on John 13:15 and Heb. 4:11 for this interesting word. *Shadow* (*skiāi*). Dative case. Old word for which see already Matt. 4:16; Mark 4:32; Col. 2:17. See same idea in Heb. 9:23. For difference between *skia* and *eikōn* see 10:1. Here "copy and shadow" form a practical hendiadys for "a shadowy outline" (Moffatt). *Is warned of God* (*kechrēmatistai*). Perfect passive indicative of *chrēmatizō*, old verb (from *chrēma*, business) for which see on Matt. 2:12, 22; Luke 2:26. The word "God" is not used, but it is implied as in Acts 10:22; Heb. 12:25. So in LXX, Josephus, and the papyri. *For saith he* (*gar phēsi*). Argument from God's command (Ex. 25:40). *See that thou make* (*Horā poiēseis*). Common Greek idiom with present active imperative of *horaō* and the volitive future of *poieō* without *hina* (asyndeton, Robertson, *Grammar*, p. 949). *The pattern* (*ton tupon*). The very word used in Ex. 25:40 and quoted also by Stephen in Acts 7:44. For *tupos* see already John 20:25; Rom. 6:17, etc. The tabernacle was to be patterned after the heavenly model.

6. *But now* (*nun de*). Logical use of *nun*, as the case now stands, with Jesus as high priest in heaven. *Hath he obtained* (*tetuchen*). Perfect active indicative of *tugchanō* with the genitive, a rare and late form for *teteuchen* (also *teteuchēken*), old verb to hit the mark, to attain. *A ministry the more excellent* (*diaphorōteras leitourgias*). "A more excellent ministry." For the comparative of *diaphoros* see 1:4. This

remark applies to all the five points of superiority over the Levitical priesthood. *By how much (hosōi).* Instrumental case of the relative *hosos* between two comparative adjectives as in 1:4. *The mediator (mesitēs).* Late word from *mesos* (amid) and so a middle man (arbitrator). Already in Gal. 3:19f. and see I Tim. 2:5. See Heb. 9:15; 12:24 for further use with *diathēkē. Of a better covenant (kreittonos diathēkēs).* Called "new" (*kainēs, neas* in 9:15; 12:24). For *diathēkē* see Matt. 26:28; Luke 1:72; Gal. 3:17, etc. This idea he will discuss in 8:7–13. *Hath been enacted (nenomothetētai).* Perfect passive indicative of *nomotheteō* as in 7:11 which see. *Upon better promises (epi kreittosin epaggeliais).* Upon the basis of (*epi*). But how "better" if the earlier were also from God? This idea, alluded to in 6:12–17, will be developed in 10:19 to 12:3 with great passion and power. Thus it is seen that "better" (*kreissōn*) is the keynote of the Epistle. At every point Christianity is better than Judaism.

7. *That first covenant (hē prōtē ekeinē).* The word *diathēkē* (covenant) is not expressed, but clearly meant by the feminine gender *prōtē. Faultless (amemptos).* Old compound adjective for which see Luke 1:6; Phil. 2:15. The condition is second class and assumes that the old covenant was not "blameless," apparently a serious charge which he hastens to explain. *For a second (deuteras).* Objective genitive with *diathēkēs* understood. The conclusion with *an* and the imperfect passive indicative (*ezēteito*) is clearly a second-class condition. See a like argument in 7:11.

8. *Finding fault with them (memphomenos autous).* Present middle participle of *memphomai* (cf. *amemptos*), old verb, in N.T. only here and Rom. 9:19. The covenant was all right, but the Jews failed to keep it. Hence God made a new one of grace in place of law. Why do marriage covenants so often fail to hold? The author quotes in verses 8 to 12 Jer. 38:31–34 (in LXX 31:31–34) in full which calls for little explanation or application to prove his point (verse 13). *I will make*

(*sunteleso*). Future active of *sunteleo*, old compound verb to accomplish as in Mark 13:4; Rom. 9:28. *A new covenant* (*diathēkēn kainēn*). In 12:24 we have *diathēkēs neas*, but *kainēs* in I Cor. 11:25. *Kainos* is fresh, on new lines as opposed to the old (*palaios*) as in II Cor. 3:6, 14; *neos* is young or not yet old.

9. *In the day that I took them* (*en hēmerāi epilabomenou mou*). Genitive absolute (*mou* and second aorist middle participle of *epilambanō*), "a Hellenistic innovation" (Moffatt) in imitation of the Hebrew after *hēmerāi* in place of *en hēi epelabomen*, occurring also in Barn. 2:28. *By the hand* (*tēs cheiros*). Technical use of the genitive of the part affected. *To lead them forth* (*exagagein autous*). Second aorist active infinitive of *exagō* to denote purpose. *For they continued not* (*hoti autoi ouk enemeinan*). First aorist active indicative of *emmenō*, old verb to remain in (Acts 14:22). The Israelites broke the covenant. Then God annulled it. *I regarded not* (*ēmelēsa*). "I neglected" as in 2:3. The covenant was void when they broke it.

10. *This* (*hautē*). The "new" one of verse 8. *That I will make* (*hēn diathēsomai*). Future middle of *diatithēmi*, "that I will covenant," cognate accusative (*hēn*), using the same root in the verb as in *diathēkē*. *I will put* (*didous*). "Giving," present active participle of *didōmi*, to give. *Into their mind* (*eis tēn dianoian autōn*). Their intellect, their moral understanding, all the intellect as in Aristotle (Col. 1:21; Eph. 4:18). *On their heart* (*epi kardias autōn*). Either genitive singular or accusative plural. *Kardia* is the seat of man's personal life (Westcott), the two terms covering the whole of man's inward nature. *A god* (*eis theon*). Note the Hebraistic use of *eis* in the predicate instead of the usual nominative *theos* as in "a people" (*eis laon*). This was the ideal of the old covenant (Ex. 6:7), now at last to be a fact.

11. *They shall not teach* (*ou mē didaxōsin*). Strong double negative (*ou mē*) with the first aorist active (futuristic)

subjunctive of *didaskō*. *His fellow-citizen* (*ton politēn autou*).
See Luke 15:15; 19:14. *Know the Lord* (*Gnōthi ton kurion*).
Second aorist active imperative of *ginōskō*. In the new
covenant all will be taught of God (Isa. 54:13; John 6:45),
whereas under the old only the educated scribe could understand the minutiae of the law (Dods). See Paul's comparison
in II Cor. 3:7–18. *Shall know* (*eidēsousin*). Future perfect
active, old form of *oida* (note *ginōskō* just before of recognizing God), one of the rare future perfects (cf. 2:13, *esomai
pepoithōs*).

12. *Merciful* (*hileōs*). Old Attic adjective for *hilaos*, common in the LXX, only here in N.T., from which *hilaskomai*
comes (Luke 18:13). *Will I remember no more* (*ou mē mnēsthō
eti*). Double negative *ou mē* with first aorist passive subjunctive (volitive) of *mimnēskō*, to recall.

13. *In that he saith* (*en tōi legein*). Locative case of the
articular present active infinitive of *legō*, "in the saying as to
him." *He hath made the first old* (*pepalaiōken tēn prōtēn*).
Perfect active indicative of *palaioō*, old verb from *palaios*
(in contrast with *kainos*, fresh, new), to treat as old and out
of date. The conclusion is to the point. *That which is becoming old and waxeth aged* (*to palaioumenon kai gēraskon*).
Gēraskō is old verb from *gēras* (age) like *gerōn* (old man)
and refers to the decay of old age so that both ideas appear
here in opposition to *kainos* (*palaios*) and *neos* (*geraios*).
Is nigh unto vanishing away (*eggus aphanismou*). Genitive
case with *eggus* and late word for disappearance (from
aphanizō, Matt. 6:19), here only in the N.T. The author
writes as if the Old Testament legal and ceremonial system
were about to vanish before the new covenant of grace. If he
wrote after A.D. 70, would he not have written "has vanished
away"?

CHAPTER IX

1. *Even the first covenant (kai hē protē). Kai* (even) is doubtful. No word for covenant with *prōtē* (cf. 8:7). *Had (eiche).* Imperfect active, used to have. *Ordinances (dikaiō-mata).* Regulations (from *dikaioō*) as in Luke 1:6; Rom. 5:16. *Of divine service (latreias).* No word for "divine," though worship is meant as in Rom. 9:4; Phil. 3:3. Genitive case. *And its sanctuary, a sanctuary of this world (to te hagion kosmikon).* By *to hagion* the author describes the whole sanctuary (Ex. 36:3; Numb. 3:38) like *tōn hagiōn* in 8:2. *Kosmikon* is a late adjective (Aristotle, Plutarch) from *kos-mos*, relating to this world, like *epi gēs* (upon earth) of 8:4. It is in the predicate position, not attributive.

2. *A tabernacle the first (skēnē hē prōtē).* See 8:2 for *skēnē.* Large tents usually had two divisions (the outer and the inner or the first and the second). Note *prōtē* for the first of two as with the first covenant (8:7, 13; 9:1). The large outer tent was entered first and was called *Hagia* (Holy), the first division of the tabernacle. The two divisions are here termed two tabernacles. *Was prepared (kateskeuasthē).* First aorist passive of *kataskeuazō.* See 3:3. For the furniture see Ex. 25 and 26. Three items are named here: the candlestick (*hē luchnia*, late word for *luchnion*) or lampstand, necessary since there were no windows (Ex. 25:31–39); the table (*hē trapeza*, old word, Matt. 15:27) for the bread (Ex. 25:23–30; Lev. 24:6 of pure gold); the shewbread (*hē pro-thesis tōn artōn*) as in Ex. 25:30; 40:23; Lev. 24:5–9. Probably a hendiadys for the table with the loaves of God's Presence.

3. *After the second veil (meta to deuteron katapetasma).* The first veil opened from outside into the Holy Place, the second veil opened from the Holy Place into the Holy of

Holies (*Hagia Hagiōn*). The word *katapetasma* is from
katapetannumi, to spread down, and we have already had it
in 6:19. Cf. also Matt. 27:51.

4. *Having a golden censer* (*chrusoun echousa thumiatērion*).
The present active participle *echousa* (feminine singular)
agrees with *skēnē* (the Holy of Holies). It is not certain
whether *thumiatērion* here means censer or altar of incense.
In the LXX (II Chron. 26:19; Ex. 8:11; IV Macc. 7:11) it
means censer and apparently so in the inscriptions and
papyri. But in Philo and Josephus it means altar of incense
for which the LXX has *thusiastērion tou thumiatos* (Ex.
30:1–10). Apparently the altar of incense was in the Holy
Place, though in Ex. 30:1–10 it is left quite vague. B puts it
in verse 2. So we leave the discrepancy unsettled. At any
rate the altar of incense was used for the Holy of Holies
("its ritual associations," Dods). *The ark of the covenant*
(*tēn kibōton tēs diathēkēs*). A box or chest four feet long, two
and a half broad and high (Ex. 25:10f.). The Scotch have a
"meal-ark." *Wherein* (*en hēi*). In the ark. There were three
treasures in the ark of the covenant (a pot of manna, Aaron's
rod, the tables of the covenant). For the pot of manna
(golden added in the LXX) see Ex. 16:32–34. For Aaron's
rod that budded (*hē blastēsasa*, first aorist active participle
of *blastanō*) see Numbers 17:1–11. For the tables of the covenant see Ex. 25:16f.; 31:18; Deut. 9:9; 10:5. Not definitely
clear about these items in the ark, but on front, except that
I Kings 8:9 states that it did contain the tables of the
covenant. For *plakes* (tables) see II Cor. 3:3 (only other
N.T. example).

5. *Above it* (*huperanō autēs*). Up above, in local sense as
in Eph. 4:10, with ablative case *autēs* (it, the ark). *Cherubim
of glory* (*Cheroubein doxēs*). Hebrew word (dual form), two
in number, made of gold (Ex. 25:18–22). They are called
zōa (living creatures) in the LXX (Isa. 6:2f.; Ezek. 1:5–10;
10:5–20). *Overshadowing* (*kataskiazonta*). Present active

396 WORD PICTURES IN NEW TESTAMENT

participle of *kataskiazō*, old verb to shadow down on, cover
with shade, only here in the N.T. *The mercy seat (to hilas-
tērion)*. The pinions of the Cherubim spread over the rec-
tangular gold slab on top of the ark termed the mercy seat.
Here the adjective *hilastērios* has to mean mercy seat, the
place, not the propitiatory gift or propitiation, as in Rom.
3:25 (Deissmann, *Bible Studies*, pp. 124–35). *Severally (kata
meros)*. In detail, distributive use of *kata* with *meros* (part).
    6. *These things having been thus prepared (toutōn houtōs
kateskeuasmenōn)*. Genitive absolute with the perfect passive
participle of *kataskeuazō* for which verb see verse 2. A mere
summary has been made of the furniture. *Go in (eisiasin)*.
Present active indicative of *eiseimi*, to go in, old verb, in
N.T. only here, Acts 3:3; 21:18, 26. *Accomplishing (epitel-
ountes)*. Present active participle of *epiteleō* for which see
8:5.
    7. *Alone (monos)*. Predicate adjective with *ho archiereus*.
Once in the year (hapax tou eniautou). Once for each year
(not *pote*, at any time) with genitive of time. *Not without
blood (ou chōris haimatos)*. According to Lev. 16:14f. Not
even he could enter the second tent (Holy of Holies) without
blood. *The errors of the people (tōn tou laou agnoēmatōn)*.
Late word from *agnoeō*, not to know (5:2), only here in the
N.T., but in LXX, papyri, and inscriptions where a distinction is drawn between errors (*agnoēmata*) and crimes
(*harmartēmata*). In Gen. 43:12 *agnoēma* is "an oversight."
But these sins of ignorance (*agnoēmata*) were sins and called
for atonement. See Heb. 10:26 for wilful sinning.
    8. *The Holy Ghost this signifying (touto dēlountos tou pneu-
matos tou hagiou)*. Genitive absolute with present active
participle of *dēloō*, to make plain. Used as in 12:27. *The way
into the Holy place (tēn tōn hagiōn hodon)*. Here as in verses
12, 25 *tōn hagiōn* is used for the very Presence of God as in
8:2 and is in the objective genitive. *Hodon* is the accusative
of general reference with the infinitive. *Hath not yet been*

made manifest (mēpō pephanerōsthai). Perfect passive infinitive of *phaneroō,* to make plain *(phaneros)* in indirect discourse after *dēlountos* with negative *mēpō. While as the first tabernacle is yet standing (eti tēs prōtēs skēnēs echousēs stasin).* Another genitive absolute with present active participle of *echō* (having standing *stasin),* "the first tabernacle still having a place." The veil at the entrance kept the people out of the first tent as the second veil (verse 3) kept the priests out of the Holy of Holies (the very Presence of God).

9. *Which (hētis).* "Which very thing," the first tent *(tēs prōtēs skēnēs,* division of the tabernacle), a parenthesis and explanation. *A parable (parabolē).* Only in the Synoptic Gospels in the N.T. and Heb. 9:9; 11:19. See on Matt. 13:3 for the word (from *paraballō,* to place alongside). Here like *tupos* (type or shadow of "the heavenly reality," Moffatt). *For the time now present (eis ton kairon ton enestēkota).* "For the present crisis" *(kairon,* not *aiōna,* age, not *chronon,* time). Perfect active articular (repeated article) participle of *enistēmi* (intransitive), the age in which they lived, not the past, not the future. See I Cor. 3:22 and Rom. 8:38 for contrast between *enestōta* and *mellonta.* This age of crisis, foreshadowed by the old tabernacle, pointed on to the richer fulfilment still to come. *According to which (kath' hēn).* Here the relative refers to *parabolē* just mentioned, not to *skēnēs.* See 5:1; 8:3. *As touching the conscience (kata suneidēsin).* For *suneidēsis* see I Cor. 8:10; 10:17; Rom. 2:15. This was the real failure of animal sacrifice (10:1-4). *Make the worshipper perfect (teleiōsai ton latreuonta).* First aorist active infinitive (2:10). At best it was only ritual or ceremonial purification (7:11), that called for endless repetition (10:1-4).

10. *Only with meats and drinks and divers washings (monon epi brōmasin kai pomasin kai diaphorois baptismois).* The parenthesis of the Revised Version here is unnecessary. The use of *epi* here with the locative case is regular, "in the matter of" (Luke 12:52; John 12:16; Acts 21:24). What ritual

value these Levitical sacrifices had was confined to minute regulations about diet and ceremonial cleansing (clean and unclean). For "divers" (*diaphorois*, late adjective, in N.T. only in Heb. 1:4; 8:6; 9:10; Rom. 12:6) say "different" or "various." *Baptismois* is, of course, the Jewish ceremonial immersions (cf. Mark 7:4; Ex. 29:4; Lev. 11:25, 28f.; Numbers 8:7; Rev. 6:2). *Carnal ordinances* (*dikaiōmasin sarkos*). But the correct text is undoubtedly simply *dikaiōmata sarkos* (nominative case), in apposition with *dōra te kai thusiai* (gifts and sacrifices). See 9:1 for *dikaiōmata*. *Imposed* (*epikeimena*). Present middle or passive participle of *epikeimai*, old verb to lie upon (be laid upon). Cf. I Cor. 9:16. *Until a time of reformation* (*mechri kairou diorthōseōs*). Definite statement of the temporary nature of the Levitical system already stated in 7:10–17; 8:13 and argued clearly by Paul in Gal. 3:15 to 22. *Diorthōsis* is a late word, here alone in N.T. (from *diorthoō*, to set right or straight), used by Hippocrates for making straight misshapen limbs like *anorthoō* in Heb. 12:12. Here for reformation like *diorthōma* (reform) in Acts 24:2f. Christianity itself is the great Reformation of the current Judaism (Pharisaism) and the spiritual Judaism foreshadowed by the old Abrahamic promise (see Gal. 3 and Rom. 9).

11. *Having come* (*paragenomenos*). Second aorist middle participle of *paraginomai*. This is the great historic event that is the crux of history. "Christ came on the scene, and all was changed" (Moffatt). *Of the good things to come* (*tōn mellontōn agathōn*). But B D read *genomenōn* (that are come). It is a nice question which is the true text. Both aspects are true, for Christ is High Priest of good things that have already come as well as of the glorious future of hope. Westcott prefers *genomenōn*, Moffatt *mellontōn*. *Through the greater and more perfect tabernacle* (*dia tēs meizonos kai teleioteras skēnēs*). Probably the instrumental use of *dia* (II Cor. 2:4; Rom. 2:27; 14:20) as accompaniment, not the local idea

(4:14; 10:20). Christ as High Priest employed in his work the heavenly tabernacle (8:2) after which the earthly was patterned (9:24). *Not made with hands* (*ou cheiropoiētou*). Old compound verbal for which see Mark 14:58; Acts 7:48; 17:24. Cf. Heb. 8:2. Here in the predicate position. *Not of this creation* (*ou tautēs tēs ktiseōs*). Explanation of *ou chieropoiētou*. For *ktisis* see II Cor. 5:17; Rom. 8:19. For the idea see II Cor. 4:18; Heb. 8:2. This greater and more perfect tabernacle is heaven itself (9:24).

12. *Through his own blood* (*dia tou idiou haimatos*). This is the great distinction between Christ as High Priest and all other high priests. They offer blood (verse 7), but he offered his own blood. He is both victim and High Priest. See the same phrase in 13:12 and Acts 20:28. *Once for all* (*ephapax*). In contrast to the repeated (annual) entrances of the Levitical high priests (9:7). *Into the holy place* (*eis ta hagia*). Here, as in verses 8 and 24 heaven itself. *Having obtained* (*heuramenos*). First aorist middle (indirect) participle of *heuriskō*, simultaneous action with *eisēlthen*, and by or of himself "as the issue of personal labour directed to this end" (Westcott). The value of Christ's offering consists in the fact that he is the Son of God as well as the Son of man, that he is sinless and so a perfect sacrifice with no need of an offering for himself, and that it is voluntary on his part (John 10:17). *Lutrōsis* (from *lutroō*) is a late word for the act of ransoming (cf. *lutron*, ransom), in O.T. only here and Luke 1:68; 2:38. But *apolutrōsis* elsewhere (as in Luke 21:28; Rom. 3:24; Heb. 9:15; 11:35). For "eternal" (*aiōnian*, here feminine form) see 6:2. The author now turns to discuss the better sacrifice (9:13–10:18) already introduced.

13. *Ashes* (*spodos*). Old word, in N. T. only here, Matt. 11:21; Luke 10:13. Common in LXX. *Of a heifer* (*damaleōs*). Old word (*damalis*), a red heifer whose ashes mingled with water (*meta hudatos*, verse 19) were sprinkled (*rantizousa*, present active participle of *rantizō*, in LXX, though *rainō*

more common) on the contaminated or defiled ones (Numbers 19) as the blood of bulls and goats was offered for sins (Lev. 16). *Sanctify* (*hagiazei*). First-class condition, assumed as true. This ceremonial ritual does serve "for the cleansing (*katharotēta*, old word here only in N.T.) of the flesh," but not for the conscience (verse 9). The cow was *amōmon*, the individual *katharos*.

14. *How much more* (*posōi mallon*). Instrumental case, "by how much more," by the measure of the superiority of Christ's blood to that of goats and bulls and the ashes of a heifer. *Through the eternal Spirit* (*dia pneumatos aiōniou*). Not the Holy Spirit, but Christ's own spirit which is eternal as he is. There is thus a moral quality in the blood of Christ not in that of other sacrifices. *Offered himself* (*heauton prosēnegken*). Second aorist active indicative of *prospherō* (used so often as in 5:1, 3; 8:3). The voluntary character of Christ's death is again emphasized. *Without blemish* (*amōmon*). Old compound adjective (Col. 1:22; I Peter 1:19) as the sacrifice had to be (Ex. 29:1; Lev. 1:3, 10). *Shall cleanse from conscience* (*kathariei tēn suneidēsin humōn*). Future active indicative of *katharizō*. Some MSS. have *hēmōn* (our). The old Greek used *kathairō*, not *katharizō* (in inscriptions for ceremonial cleansing, Deissmann, *Bible Studies*, pp. 216f.), for cleansing. *From dead works* (*apo nekrōn ergōn*). As in 6:1. "A pause might be made before *ergōn*, from dead — (not bodies but) works."

15. *Mediator of a new covenant* (*diathēkēs kainēs mesitēs*). See 8:6 for this phrase with *kreittonos* instead of *kainēs*. *A death having taken place* (*thanatou genomenou*). Genitive absolute, referring to Christ's death. *For the redemption* (*eis apolutrōsin*). *Of the transgressions* (*tōn parabaseōn*). Really ablative case, "from the transgressions." See verse 12, *lutrōsin*. *Under the first covenant* (*epi tēi prōtēi diathēkēi*). Here there is a definite statement that the real value in the typical sacrifices under the Old Testament system was in the

realization in the death of Christ. It is Christ's death that
gives worth to the types that pointed to him. So then the
atoning sacrifice of Christ is the basis of the salvation of all
who are saved before the Cross and since. *That they may
receive* (*hopōs labōsin*). Purpose clause (God's purpose in the
rites and symbols) with *hopōs* and the second aorist active
subjunctive of *lambanō*.

16. *A testament* (*diathēkē*). The same word occurs for
covenant (verse 15) and will (verse 16). This double sense of
the word is played upon also by Paul in Gal. 3:15f. We say
today "The New Testament" (*Novum Testamentum*) rather
than "The New Covenant." Both terms are pertinent.
That made it (*tou diathemenou*). Genitive of the articular
second aorist middle participle of *diatithēmi* from which
diathēkē comes. The notion of will here falls in with *klēr-
onomia* (inheritance, I Peter 1:4) as well as with *thanatos*
(death). *Of force* (*bebaia*). Stable, firm as in 3:6, 14. *Where
there hath been death* (*epi nekrois*). "In the case of dead
people." A will is only operative then. *For doth it ever avail
while he that made it liveth?* (*epei mē pote ischuei hote zēi ho
diathemenos;*). This is a possible punctuation with *mē pote*
in a question (John 7:26). Without the question mark, it is
a positive statement of fact. Aleph and D read *tote* (then)
instead of *pote*. The use of *mē* in a causal sentence is allow-
able (John 3:18, *hoti mē*).

18. *The first covenant* (*hē prōtē*). Supply *diathēkē* as in 9:1.
Has been dedicated (*enkekainistai*). Stands dedicated. Perfect passive indicative of *enkainizo*, a late verb in LXX, one
papyrus, and in N.T. only here and 10:20. It means to
renew, to inaugurate (I Sam. 11:14; II Chron. 15:8) and in
I Kings 8:63 to dedicate. Note *ta enkainia* (John 10:22) for
the feast of dedication.

19. *When every commandment had been spoken* (*lalē-
theisēs*). Genitive absolute with first aorist passive participle feminine singular of *laleō*. The author uses the

account in Ex. 24:3f. "with characteristic freedom" (Moffatt). There is nothing there about the water, the scarlet wool (*erion*, diminutive of *eros*, *eiros*, old word, here and in Rev. 1:14; for *kokkinos* see on Matt. 27:6, 28), and hyssop (*hussōpou*, a plant mentioned in John 19:29). It had become the custom to mingle water with the blood and to use a wisp of wool or a stem of hyssop for sprinkling (Numbers 10:2-10). *Both the book itself* (*auto te to biblion*). There is nothing in Exodus about sprinkling the book of the covenant, though it may very well have been done. He omits the use of oil in Ex. 40:9f. and Lev. 8:10f. and applies blood to all the details. *Sprinkled* (*erantisen*). First aorist active indicative from *rantizō* (from *rantos* and this from *rainō*), like *baptizō* from *baptō*. Cf. Mark 7:4; Heb. 10:22; Rev. 19:13.

20. *This is* (*touto*). Instead of *idou* of the LXX (Ex. 24:8), just like our Lord's words in Mark 14:24, a possible reminiscence of the Master's words (Dods). The author also has *eneteilato* (he commanded) for *dietheto* of the LXX.

21. *In like manner with the blood* (*tōi haimati homoiōs*). Instrumental case of *haima* (blood). But the use of the article does not necessarily refer to the blood mentioned in verse 19. In Ex. 40:9 Moses sprinkled the tabernacle with oil. It had not been erected at the time of Ex. 24:5f. Josephus (*Ant.* III. 8, 6) gives a tradition that blood was used also at this dedication. Blood was used annually in the cleansing rites on the day of atonement.

22. *I may almost say* (*schedon*). Old adverb, only three times in the N.T., here, Acts 13:44; 19:26. Here it qualifies the entire clause, not just *panta*. *With blood* (*en haimati*). In blood. There were exceptions (Ex. 19:10; 32:30f.; Lev. 5:11f.; 15:5; Numbers 16:46f.; 31:23f., etc.). *Apart from shedding of blood* (*chōris haimatekchusias*). A double compound first found here (coined by the writer) and later in ecclesiastical writers (*haima*, blood, *ek*, out, *cheō*, to pour, like *ekchusis haimatos* I Kings 18:28). "Pouring out of blood." The

author seems to have in mind Christ's words in Matt. 26:28: "This is my blood of the covenant which is shed for many for the forgiveness of sins." The blood is the vital principle and is efficacious as an atonement. The blood of Christ sets aside all other plans for pardon.

23. *The copies* (*ta hupodeigmata*). See 8:5 for this word, the earthly (8:4; 9:1) tabernacle. *With these* (*toutois*). Instrumental case of *houtos*, like the rites above described (verse 19), perhaps with some disparagement. *Themselves* (*auta*). The heavenly realities (8:2, 5; 9:11f.). *With better sacrifices* (*kreittosin thusiais*). Instrumental case again. Point of this section (9:13 to 10:18). *Than these* (*para tautas*). Use of *para* and the accusative case after a comparative as in 1:4, 9. To us it seems a bit strained to speak of the ritual cleansing or dedication of heaven itself by the appearance of Christ as Priest-Victim. But the whole picture is highly mystical.

24. *Made with hands* (*cheiropoiēta*). See verse 11 for this word. *Like in pattern to the true* (*antitupa tōn alēthinōn*). Late compound word, only twice in N.T. (here, I Peter 3:21). Polybius uses *antitupos* for infantry "opposite" to the cavalry. In modern Greek it means a copy of a book. Here it is the "counterpart of reality" (Moffatt). Moses was shown a *tupos* (model) of the heavenly realities and he made an *antitupon* on that model, "answering to the type" (Dods) or model. In I Peter 3:21 *antitupos* has the converse sense, "the reality of baptism which corresponds to or is the antitype of the deluge" (Dods). *Now to appear* (*nun emphanisthēnai*). Purpose clause by the first aorist passive infinitive of *emphanizō* (Matt. 27:53; John 14:21f.). For the phrase see Psa. 42:3. For this work of Christ as our High Priest and Paraclete in heaven see Heb. 7:25; Rom. 8:34; I John 2:1f.

25. *That he should offer himself often* (*hina pollakis prospherēi heauton*). Purpose clause with *hina* and present active subjunctive of *prospherō* (keep on offering himself, like 5:1, 3).

With blood not his own (*en haimati allotriōi*). So-called instrumental use of *en* (accompaniment). *Allotrios* means "belonging to another," "not one's own" (Luke 16:12).

26. *Else must he often have suffered* (*epei edei auton pollakis pathein*). A common elliptical use of *epei* after which one must supply "if that were true" or "in that case," a protasis of a condition of the second class assumed to be untrue. The conclusion with *edei* is without *an* (verbs of necessity, obligation, etc.). See Robertson, *Grammar*, p. 963. The conclusion with *an* occurs in 10:2. See also I Cor. 5:10. "Since, if that were true, it would be necessary for him to suffer often." *Since the foundation of the world* (*apo katabolēs kosmou*). See 4:3 for this phrase. The one sacrifice of Christ is of absolute and final value (I Peter 1:19f.; Rev. 13:8). *At the end* (*epi sunteleiāi*). Consummation or completion as in Matt. 13:39f. which see. *Hath he been manifested* (*pephanerō-tai*). Perfect passive indicative of *phaneroō*, permanent state. See "the primitive hymn or confession of faith" (Moffatt) in I Tim. 3:16 and also I Peter 1:20. Jesus came once for all (Heb. 1:2). *To put away sin* (*eis athetēsin tēs hamartias*). See 7:18 for the word *athetēsis*. "The sacrifice of Christ dealt with sin as a principle: the Levitical sacrifices with individual transgressions" (Vincent).

27. *It is appointed* (*apokeitai*). Present middle (or passive) of *apokeimai*, "is laid away" for men. Cf. same verb in Luke 19:20; Col. 1:5; II Tim. 4:8 (Paul's crown). *Once to die* (*hapax apothanein*). Once for all to die, as once for all to live here. No reincarnation here. *After this cometh judgement* (*meta touto krisis*). Death is not all. Man has to meet Christ as Judge as Jesus himself graphically pictures (Matt. 25:31–46; John 5:25–29).

28. *Once* (*hapax*). "Once for all" (verse 26) as already stated. *Shall appear a second time* (*ek deuterou ophthēsetai*). Future passive indicative of *horaō*. Blessed assurance of the Second Coming of Christ, but this time "apart from sin"

(*chōris hamartias*, no notion of a second chance then). *Unto salvation* (*eis sōtērian*).   Final and complete salvation for "them that wait for him" (*tois auton apekdechomenois*). Dative plural of the articular participle present middle of *apekdechomai*, the very verb used by Paul in Phil. 3:20 of waiting for the coming of Christ as Saviour.

CHAPTER X

1. *Shadow* (*skian*). The contrast here between *skia* (shadow, shade caused by interruption of light as by trees, Mark 4:32) and *eikōn* (image or picture) is striking. Christ is the *eikōn* of God (II Cor. 4:4; Col. 1:15). In Col. 2:17 Paul draws a distinction between *skia* for the Jewish rites and ceremonies and *sōma* for the reality in Christ. Children are fond of shadow pictures. The law gives only a dim outline of the good things to come (9:11). *Continually* (*eis to diēnekes*). See this phrase also in 7:3; 9:12, 14. Nowhere else in N.T. From *diēnegka* (*diapherō*), to bear through. *They can* (*dunantai*). This reading leaves *ho nomos* a *nominativus pendens* (an anacoluthon). But many MSS. read *dunatai* (it — the law — can). For the idea and use of *teleiōsai* see 9:9.

2. *Else they would not have ceased?* (*epei ouk an epausanto;*). Ellipsis of condition after *epei* (since if they really did perfect) with the conclusion of the second-class condition (*an* and the aorist middle indicative of *pauomai*). *To be offered* (*prospheromenai*). Regular idiom, participle (present passive) with *pauomai* (Acts 5:42). *Because* (*dia to*). *Dia* with the accusative of the articular infinitive, "because of the having" (*echein*) as to the worshippers (*tous latreuontas*, accusative of general reference of the articular participle), not "would have had." *No more conscience of sins* (*mēdemian eti suneidēsin hamartiōn*). Rather "consciousness of sins" as in 9:14. *Having been once cleansed* (*hapax kekatharismenous*). Perfect passive participle of *katharizō*, "if they had once for all been cleansed."

3. *A remembrance* (*anamnēsis*). A reminder. Old word from *anamimnēskō*, to remind, as in Luke 22:19; I Cor. 11:24f.

4. *Should take away* (*aphairein*). Present active infinitive of *aphaireō*. Old verb and common in N.T., only here and Rom. 11:27 with "sins." Cf. 9:9.

5. *When he cometh into the world* (*eiserchomenos eis ton kosmon*). Reference to the Incarnation of Christ who is represented as quoting Psa. 40:7-9 which is quoted. The text of the LXX is followed in the main which differs from the Hebrew chiefly in having *sōma* (body) rather than *ōtia* (ears). The LXX translation has not altered the sense of the Psalm, "that there was a sacrifice which answered to the will of God as no animal sacrifice could" (Moffatt). So the writer of Hebrews "argues that the Son's offering of himself is the true and final offering for sin, because it is the sacrifice, which, according to prophecy, God desired to be made" (Davidson). *A body didst thou prepare for me* (*sōma katērtisō moi*). First aorist middle indicative second person singular of *katartizō*, to make ready, equip. Using *sōma* (body) for *ōtia* (ears) does not change the sense, for the ears were the point of contact with God's will.

6. *Thou hadst no pleasure* (*ouk eudokēsas*). First aorist active indicative of *eudokeō*, common for God's good pleasure (Matt. 3:17). God took no pleasure in the animal offering (*thusian*), the meal-offering (*prosphoran*), the burnt-offering (*holokautōmata*), the sin-offering (*peri hamartias*, concerning sin).

7. *Then* (*tote*). When it was plain that God could not be propitiated by such sacrifices. *Lo, I am come* (*Idou hēkō*). The Messiah is represented as offering himself to do God's will (*tou poiēsai to thelēma sou*, the genitive articular infinitive of purpose). *In the roll of the book it is written of me* (*en kephalidi bibliou gegraptai peri emou*). Stands written (*gegraptai*, perfect passive indicative). *Kephalis* is a diminutive of *kephalē* (head), a little head, then roll only here in N.T., but in the papyri. Here it refers "to the O.T. as a prediction of Christ's higher sacrifice" (Moffatt).

8. *Saying above* (*anōteron legōn*). Christ speaking as in verse 5. "Higher up" (*anōteron*, comparative of *anō*, up) refers to verses 5 and 6 which are quoted again. 9. *The which* (*haitines*). "Which very things" (*thusiai*). *Then hath he said* (*tote eirēken*). That is Christ. Perfect active indicative with which compare *tote eipon* (second aorist active) in verse 7 which is quoted again. *He taketh away the first* (*anairei to prōton*). Present active indicative of *anaireō*, to take up, to abolish, of a man to kill (Matt. 2:16). By "the first" (*to prōton*) he means the system of animal sacrifices in verse 8. *That he may establish the second* (*hina to deuteron stēsēi*). Purpose clause with *hina* and the first aorist active (transitive) subjunctive of *histēmi*, to place. By "the second" (*to deuteron*) he means doing God's will as shown in verse 9 (following verse 8). This is the author's exegesis of the Psalm.

10. *We have been sanctified* (*hēgiasmenoi esmen*). Periphrastic perfect passive indicative of *hagiazō*, to set apart, to sanctify. The divine will, unfulfilled in animal sacrifices, is realized in Christ's offering of himself. "He came to be a great High Priest, and the body was prepared for him, that by the offering of it he might put sinful men for ever into the perfect religious relation to God" (Denney, *The Death of Christ*, p. 234).

11. *Standeth* (*hestēken*). Perfect active indicative of *histēmi* (intransitive), vivid picture. *Ministering and offering* (*leitourgōn kai prospherōn*). Present active participles graphically describing the priest. *Take away* (*perielein*). Second aorist active infinitive of *periaireō*, old verb to take from around, to remove utterly as in Acts 27:20.

12. *When he had offered* (*prosenegkas*). Second aorist active participle (with first aorist ending -*as* in place of -*on*) of *propherō*, single act in contrast to present participle *prospherōn* above. *One sacrifice* (*mian thusian*). This the main point. The one sacrifice does the work that the many

failed to do. One wonders how priests who claim that the
"mass" is the sacrifice of Christ's body repeated explain
this verse. *For ever (eis to dienekes)*. Can be construed either
with *mian thusian* or with *ekathisen* (sat down). See 1:3
for *ekathisen*.

13. *Henceforth expecting (to loipon ekdechomenos)*. "For
the rest" or "for the future" (*to loipon*, accusative of extent
of time). The expectant attitude of Christ here is that of
final and certain victory (John 16:33; I Cor. 15:24–28).
Till his enemies be made (heōs tethōsin hoi echthroi autou).
Purpose and temporal clause with *heōs* and the first aorist
passive subjunctive of *tithēmi*. He quotes Psa. 110:1 again.

14. *He hath perfected (teteleiōken)*. Perfect active indicative of *teleioō*. He has done what the old sacrifices failed to
do (verse 1). *Them that are sanctified (tous hagiazomenous)*.
Articular participle (accusative case) present passive of *hagiazō* (note perfect in verse 10) either because of the process
still going on or because of the repetition in so many persons
as in 2:11.

15. *And the Holy Ghost also beareth witness to us (marturei
de hēmin kai to pneuma to hagion)*. *Martureō* is common in
Philo for Scripture quotation. The author confirms his interpretation of Psa. 40:7–9 by repeating from Jeremiah (31:
31ff.) what he had already quoted (8:8–12). *After he hath
said (meta to eirēkenai)*. Accusative case after *meta* of the
articular infinitive perfect active, "after the having said."

16. *With them (pros autous)*. The author changes *tōi oikōi
Israel* (8:10) thus without altering the sense. He also changes
the order of "heart" (*kardias*) and "mind" (*dianoian*) from
that in 8:10.

17. Here again the writer adds "their iniquities (*tōn ano-
miōn*) to "sins" of 8:12 and reads *mnēsthēsomai* (first future passive) with *ou mē* rather than *mnēsthō* (first aorist
passive subjunctive) of 8:12 (the more common idiom). It
is uncertain also whether the writer means verse 17 to be

the principal clause with 15 and 16 as subordinate or the whole quotation to be subordinate to *meta to eirēkenai* of verse 15 with anacoluthon in verse 18. At any rate verse 17 in the quotation does not follow immediately after verse 16 as one can see in 8:10–12 (skipping part of 8:10 and all of 8:11).

18. *There is no more offering for sin* (*ouketi prosphora peri hamartias*). This is the logical and triumphant conclusion concerning the better sacrifice offered by Christ (9:13–10:18). As Jeremiah had prophesied, there is actually remission (*aphesis*, removal) of sins. Repetition of the sacrifice is needless.

19. *Having therefore* (*echontes oun*). The author now gives a second (the first in 8:1–6) résumé of the five arguments concerning the superior priestly work of Christ (10:19–25) coupled with an earnest exhortation like that in 4:14–16, with which he began the discussion, before he proceeds to treat at length the fifth and last one, the better promises in Christ (10:26–12:3). *Boldness* (*parrēsian*). This is the dominant note all through the Epistle (3:6; 4:16; 10:19, 35). They were tempted to give up Christ, to be quitters. Boldness (courage) is the need of the hour. *Into the holy place* (*tōn hagiōn*). That is, the heavenly sanctuary where Jesus is (6:18–20). This is the better sanctuary (9:1–12). *By the blood of Jesus* (*en tōi haimati Iēsou*). This is the better sacrifice just discussed (9:13–10:18).

20. *By the way which he dedicated for us* (*hēn enekainisen hēmin hodon*). This "new" (*prosphaton*, freshly killed, newly made, from *pros* and the root of *phatos*, in the papyri, only here in N.T.) and "living" (*zōsan*) Jesus opened ("dedicated") for us by his Incarnation and Death for us. Thus he fulfilled God's promise of the "New Covenant" (8:7–13) in Jeremiah. The language is highly symbolic here and "through the veil" here is explained as meaning the flesh of Christ, his humanity, not the veil opening into heaven

(6:20). Some do take "veil" here as obscuring the deity of Christ rather than the revelation of God in the human body of Christ (John 1:18; 14:9). At any rate because of the coming of Christ in the flesh we have the new way opened for access to God (Heb. 2:17f.; 4:16).

21. *A great priest* (*hierea megan*). As has been shown in 4:14–7:28. *Over the house of God* (*epi ton oikon tou theou*). As God's Son (3:5f.).

22. *Let us draw near* (*proserchōmetha*). Present middle volitive subjunctive as in 4:16 with which exhortation the discussion began. There are three exhortations in verses 22:25 (Let us draw near, *proserchōmetha*, let us hold fast, *katechōmen*, let us consider one another, *katanoōmen allēlous*). Four items are added to this first exhortation. *With a true heart* (*meta alēthinēs kardias*). With loyalty and fealty. *In fulness of faith* (*en plērophoriāi pisteōs*). See 6:11 for this very phrase. *Having our hearts sprinkled from an evil conscience* (*rerantismenoi tas kardias apo suneidēseōs ponēras*). Perfect passive participle of *rantizō* with the accusative retained in the passive, an evident allusion to the sprinkling of blood in the old tabernacle (9:18–22) and the shedding of Christ's blood for the cleansing of our consciences (10:1–4). Cf. I Peter 1:2 for "the sprinkling of the blood of Jesus Christ." *Our body washed with pure water* (*lelousmenoi to sōma hudati katharōi*). Perfect passive (or middle) of *louō*, old verb to bathe, to wash. Accusative also retained if passive. *Hudati* can be either locative (in) or instrumental (with). See Eph. 5:26 and Titus 3:5 for the use of *loutron*. If the reference here is to baptism (quite doubtful), the meaning is a symbol (Dods) of the previous cleansing by the blood of Christ.

23. *Let us hold fast* (*katechōmen*). Present (keep on holding fast) active volitive subjunctive of *katechō* as in 3:6, 14. *That it waver not* (*aklinē*). Common compound adjective (alpha privative and *klinō*, unwavering, not leaning, here

only in N.T. It is a confession of hope, not of despair. *That promised (ho epaggeilamenos)*. First aorist middle articular participle of *epaggellō*. This is the argument remaining to be discussed (10:26–12:3) and already alluded to (6:13f.; 8:6). The ministry of Jesus rests upon "better promises." How better? God is "faithful," but he made the other promises also. We shall see.

24. *Let us consider one another (katanoōmen allēlous)*. Present (keep on doing so) active volitive subjunctive of *katanoeō*. The verb used about Jesus in 3:1. *To provoke (eis paroxusmon)*. Our very word "paroxysm," from *paroxunō* (*para, oxunō* from *oxus*, sharp), to sharpen, to stimulate, to incite. So here in good sense (for incitement to), but in Acts 15:39 the word is used of irritation or contention as in the LXX and Demosthenes. Hippocrates uses it for "paroxysm" in disease (so in the papyri). *Unto love and good works (agapēs kai kalōn ergōn)*. Objective genitive. So Paul seeks to stir up the Corinthians by the example of the Macedonians (II Cor. 8:1–7).

25. *Not forsaking (mē egkataleipontes)*. "Not leaving behind, not leaving in the lurch" (II Tim. 4:10). *The assembling of yourselves together (tēn episunagōgēn heautōn)*. Late double compound from *episunagō*, to gather together (*sun*) besides (*epi*) as in Matt. 23:37; Luke 17:27. In N.T. only here and II Thess. 2:1. In an inscription 100 B.C. for collection of money (Deissmann, *Light*, etc., p. 103). *As the custom of some is (kathōs ethos tisin)*. "As is custom to some." For *ethos* (custom) see Luke 22:39; John 19:40. Already some Christians had formed the habit of not attending public worship, a perilous habit then and now. *So much the more as (tosoutōi mallon hosōi)*. Instrumental case of measure or degree, "by so much the more as," both with *tosoutōi* and *hosōi*. *The day drawing nigh (eggizousan tēn hēmeran)*. The Second Coming of Christ which draws nearer all the time (Rom. 13:12).

26. *If we sin wilfully* (*hekousiōs hamartanontōn hēmōn*). Genitive absolute with the present active participle of *hamartanō*, circumstantial participle here in a conditional sense. *After that we have received* (*meta to labein*). "After the receiving" (accusative case of the articular infinitive second aorist active of *lambanō* after *meta*). *Knowledge* (*epignōsin*). "Full knowledge," as in 6:4f. *There remaineth no more* (*ouketi apoleipetai*). "No longer is there left behind" (present passive indicative as in 4:9), for one has renounced the one and only sacrifice for sin that does or can remove sin (10:1–18).

27. *Expectation* (*ekdochē*). Usually reception or interpretation from *ekdechomai* (Heb. 11:10), only here in N.T. and in unusual sense like *prosdokia*, like *apekdechomai* (Rom. 8:19, 23, 25), this sense apparently "coined by the writer" (Moffatt) from his use of *ekdechomai* in 10:13. The papyri have it in the sense of interpretation. *A fierceness of fire* (*puros zēlos*). An anger (zeal, jealousy) marked (genitive) by fire. Language kin to that in Isa. 26:11; Zeph. 1:19; Psa. 79:5. See also II Thess. 1:8–10 for a like picture of destined doom. *Devour* (*esthiein*). "To eat" (figuratively), present active infinitive. *The adversaries* (*tous hupenantious*). Old double compound adjective (*hupo, en, antios*), in N.T. only here and Col. 2:14. Those directly opposite.

28. *Hath set at naught* (*athetēsas*). First aorist active participle of *atheteō*, late compound, very common in LXX, from alpha privative and *tithēmi*, to render null and void, to set aside, only here in Hebrews (see Mark 7:9), but note *athetēsis* (Heb. 7:18; 9:26). *Without mercy* (*chōris oiktirmōn*). See II Cor. 1:3. This was the law (Deut. 17:6) for apostates. *On the word of two or three* (*epi dusin ē trisin*). "On the basis of two or three." For this use of *epi* with the locative see 9:17.

29. *How much* (*posōi*). Instrumental case of degree or measure. An argument from the less to the greater, "the

first of Hillel's seven rules for exegesis" (Moffatt). *Think ye* (*dokeite*). An appeal to their own sense of justice about apostates from Christ. *Sorer* (*cheironos*). "Worse," comparative of *kakos* (bad). *Punishment* (*timōrias*). Genitive case with *axiōthēsetai* (first future passive of *axioō*, to deem worthy). The word *timōria* originally meant vengeance. Old word, in LXX, only here in N.T. *Who hath trodden under foot the Son of God* (*ho ton huion tou theou katapatēsas*). First aorist active articular participle of *katapateō*, old verb (Matt. 5:13) for scornful neglect like Zech. 12:3. See same idea in Heb. 6:6. *Wherewith he was sanctified* (*en hōi hēgiasthē*). First aorist passive indicative of *hagiazō*. It is an unspeakable tragedy that should warn every follower of Christ not to play with treachery to Christ (cf. 6:4-8). *An unholy thing* (*koinon*). Common in the sense of uncleanness as Peter used it in Acts 10:14. Think of one who thus despises "the blood of Christ wherewith he was sanctified." And yet there are a few today who sneer at the blood of Christ and the gospel based on his atoning sacrifice as "a slaughter house" religion! *Hath done despite* (*enubrisas*). First aorist active participle of *enubrizō*, old verb to treat with contumely, to give insult to, here only in the N.T. It is a powerful word for insulting the Holy Spirit after receiving his blessings (6:4).

30. *We know him that said* (*oidamen ton eiponta*). God lives and is true to his word. He quotes Deut. 32:35 (cf. Rom. 12:19). For *ekdikēsis* see Luke 18:7f. God is the God of justice. He is patient, but he will punish. *And again* (*kai palin*). Deut. 32:36.

31. *A fearful thing* (*phoberon*). Old adjective (from *phobeō*, to frighten). In N.T. only in Heb. (10:27, 31; 12:21). The sense is not to be explained away. The wrath of God faces wrongdoers. *To fall* (*to empesein*). "The falling" (articular infinitive second aorist active of *empiptō*, to fall in, followed here by *eis*). We are not dealing with a dead or an absentee God, but one who is alive and alert (3:12).

32. *Call to remembrance (anamimnēskesthe)*. Present middle imperative of *anamimnēskō*, as in II Cor. 7:15 "remind yourselves." The former days were some distance in the past (5:12), some years at any rate. It is a definite experience of people in a certain place. Jerusalem Christians had had experiences of this nature, but so had others. *After ye were enlightened (phōtisthentes)*. First aorist passive participle of *phōtizō* in the same sense as in 6:4 (regeneration) and like "the full knowledge of the truth" in 10:26. *Conflict (athlēsin)*. Late word from *athleō*, to engage in a public contest in the games (II Tim. 2:5), only here in the N.T. It occurs in the inscriptions. Cf. 2:10 for the benefit of "sufferings" in training.

33. *Partly (touto men) and partly (touto de)*. Accusative of general reference *(touto)* with *men* and *de* for contrast. *Being made a gazing-stock (theatrizomenoi)*. Late verb to bring upon the stage, to hold up to derision. See Paul's use of *theatron* of himself in I Cor. 4:9. *By reproaches and afflictions (oneidismois te kai thlipsesin)*. Instrumental case. See Rom. 15:3. *Partakers (koinōnoi)*. Partners (Luke 5:10) with those *(tōn* objective genitive). *So used (houtōs anastrephomenōn)*. Present middle articular participle of *anastrephō*, to conduct oneself (II Cor. 1:12).

34. *Ye had compassion on (sunepathēsate)*. First aorist active indicative of *sunpatheō*, old verb to have a feeling with, to sympathize with. *Them that were in bonds (tois desmiois)*. Associative instrumental case, "with the prisoners" (the bound ones). Used of Paul (Eph. 3:1; II Tim. 1:8). *Took joyfully (meta charas prosedexasthe)*. First aorist middle (indirect) indicative, "ye received to yourselves with joy." See Rom. 13:1, 3; 15:7. *The spoiling (tēn harpagēn)*. "The seizing," "the plundering." Old word from *harpazō*. See Matt. 23:35. *Of your possessions (tōn huparchontōn humōn)*. "Of your belongings." Genitive of the articular present active neuter plural participle of *huparchō* used as a

substantive (cf. *humōn* genitive) as in Matt. 19:21. *That ye
yourselves have* (*echein heautous*). Infinitive (present active of
echō) in indirect discourse after *ginōskontes* (knowing) with
the accusative of general reference (*heautous*, as to yourselves), though some MSS. omit *heautous*, some have *heautois*
(dative, for yourselves), and some *en heautois* (in yourselves).
The predicate nominative *autoi* could have been used agreeing with *ginōskontes* (cf. Rom. 1:22). *A better possession*
(*kreissona huparxin*). Common word in the same sense as
ta huparchonta above, in N.T. only here and Acts 2:45. In
place of their plundered property they have treasures
in heaven (Matt. 6:20). *Abiding* (*menousan*). Present active
participle of *menō*. No oppressors (legal or illegal) can rob
them of this (Matt. 6:19ff.).

35. *Cast not away therefore your boldness* (*mē apobalēte oun
tēn parrēsian humōn*). Prohibition with *mē* and the second
aorist active subjunctive of *apoballō*. Old verb to throw away
from one as worthless, only twice in the N.T., here in a
figurative sense and Mark 10:50 in a literal sense (garment
by Bartimaeus). The Jewish Christians in question were in
peril of a panic and of stampeding away from Christ. Recall
katechōmen in verse 23.

36. *Which* (*hētis*). Your boldness of verse 35. *Recompense
of reward* (*misthapodosian*). Late double compound, like
misthapodotēs (Heb. 11:6), from *misthos* (reward, wages) and
apodidōmi, to give back, to pay (repay). In N.T. only here,
2:2 and 11:26. *Of patience* (*hupomonēs*). Old word for remaining under trial (Luke 8:15). This was the call of the
hour then as now. *Having done the will of God* (*to thelēma tou
theou*). This is an essential prerequisite to the exercise of
patience and to obtain the promised blessing. There is no
promise to those who patiently keep on doing wrong. *That ye
may receive the promise* (*hina komisēsthe tēn epaggelian*)
Purpose clause with *hina* and the first aorist middle subjunctive of *komizō*, old verb to carry (Luke 7:37), in the

middle to get back one's own (Matt. 25:27), to receive. See also 11:39. Now the author is ready to develop this great idea of receiving the promise in Christ.

37. *A very little while* (*mikron hoson hoson*). From Isa. 26:20 as an introduction to the quotation from Hab. 2:3f. *He that cometh* (*ho erchomenos*). The article *ho* is added to *erchomenos* in Hab. 2:3 and is given here a Messianic application.

38. *If he shrink back* (*ean huposteilētai*). Condition of third class with *ean* and the first aorist middle subjunctive of *hupostellō*, old verb to draw oneself under or back, to withdraw, as already in Acts 20:20, 27; Gal. 2:12. See Rom. 1:17 for the quotation also of "the just shall live by faith."

39. *But we* (*hēmeis de*). In contrast to renegades who do flicker and turn back from Christ. *Of them that shrink back unto perdition* (*hupostolēs eis apōleian*). Predicate genitive of *hupostolē*, as in 12:11, from *hupostellō* with same sense here, stealthy retreat in Plutarch, dissimulation in Josephus. Here alone in the N.T. *Unto the saving of the soul* (*eis peripoïēsin psuchēs*). Old word from *peripoieō*, to reserve, to preserve (Luke 17:33) to purchase (Acts 20:28). So here preserving or saving one's life as in Plato, but possession in Eph. 1:14, obtaining in I Thess. 4:9. Papyri have it in sense of preservation.

CHAPTER XI

1. *Now faith is* (*estin de pistis*). He has just said that "we are of faith" (10:39), not of apostasy. Now he proceeds in a chapter of great eloquence and passion to illustrate his point by a recital of the heroes of faith whose example should spur them to like loyalty now. *The assurance of things hoped for* (*elpizomenōn hupostasis*). *Hupostasis* is a very common word from Aristotle on and comes from *huphistēmi* (*hupo*, under, *histēmi*, intransitive), what stands under anything (a building, a contract, a promise). See the philosophical use of it in 1:3, the sense of assurance (une assurance certaine, Ménégoz) in 3:14, that steadiness of mind which holds one firm (II Cor. 9:4). It is common in the papyri in business documents as the basis or guarantee of transactions. "And as this is the essential meaning in Heb. 11:1 we venture to suggest the translation 'Faith is the *title-deed* of things hoped for'" (Moulton and Milligan, *Vocabulary*, etc.). *The proving of things not seen* (*pragmatōn elegchos ou blepomenōn*). The only N.T. example of *elegchos* (except Textus Receptus in II Tim. 3:16 for *elegmon*). Old and common word from *elegchō* (Matt. 18:15) for "proof" and then for "conviction." Both uses occur in the papyri and either makes sense here, perhaps "conviction" suiting better though not in the older Greek.

2. *Therein* (*en tautēi*). That is, "in faith," feminine demonstrative referring to *pistis*. *The elders* (*hoi presbuteroi*). More nearly like "the fathers," not the technical sense of elders (officers) usual in the N.T., but more like "the tradition of the elders" (Mark 7:3, 5 = Matt. 15:2). *Had witness borne to them* (*emarturēthēsan*). First aorist passive of *martureō* (cf. 7:8), "were testified to."

418

3. *By faith (pistei).* Instrumental case of *pistis* which he now illustrates in a marvellous way. Each example as far as verse 31 is formally and with rhetorical skill introduced by *pistei.* After that only a summary is given. *We understand (nooumen).* Present active indicative of *noeō*, old verb (from *nous*, intellect) as in Matt. 15:17; Rom. 1:20. The author appeals to our knowledge of the world in which these heroes lived as an illustration of faith. Recent books by great scientists like Eddington and Jeans confirm the position here taken that a Supreme Mind is behind and before the universe. Science can only stand still in God's presence and believe like a little child. *The worlds (tous aiōnas).* "The ages" as in 1:2 (cf. Einstein's fourth dimension, time). Accusative case of general reference. *Have been framed (katērtisthai).* Perfect passive infinitive of *katartizō*, to mend, to equip, to perfect (Luke 6:40), in indirect discourse after *nooumen*. *So that (eis to).* As a rule *eis to* with the infinitive is final, but sometimes as here it expresses result as in Rom. 12:3 (Robertson, *Grammar*, p. 1003). *Hath been made (gegonenai).* Perfect active infinitive of *ginomai*. *What is seen (to blepomenon).* Present passive articular participle (accusative case of general reference) of *blepō*. *Of things which do appear (ek phainomenōn).* Ablative case with *ek* (out of) of the present passive participle. The author denies the eternity of matter, a common theory then and now, and places God before the visible universe as many modern scientists now gladly do.

4. *A more excellent sacrifice (pleiona thusian).* Literally, "more sacrifice" (comparative of *polus*, much). For this rather free use of *pleiōn* with the point implied rather than stated see Matt. 6:25; Luke 10:31; 12:23; Heb. 3:3. *Than Cain (para Kain).* For this use of *para* after comparative see 1:4, 9. For the incident see Gen. 4:4. *Through which (di' hēs).* The sacrifice (*thusia*). *He had witness borne to him (emarturēthē).* First aorist passive indicative of *martureō*

as in verse 2, "he was witnessed to." *That he was righteous*
(*einai dikaios*). Infinitive in indirect discourse after *emarturēthē,* personal construction of *dikaios* (predicate nominative after *einai*) agreeing with the subject of *emarturēthē*
(cf. Rom. 1:22, *einai sophoi*). *God bearing witness* (*marturoun-
tos tou theou*). Genitive absolute with present active participle of *martureō*. *Through it* (*di' autēs*). Through his faith
(as shown by his sacrifice). Precisely why Abel's sacrifice
was better than that of Cain apart from his faith is not
shown. *Being dead* (*apothanōn*). Second aorist active participle of *apothnēskō,* "having died." *Yet speaketh* (*eti lalei*). Cf.
Gen. 4:10 and Heb. 12:24. Speaks still through his faith.

5. *Was translated* (*metetethē*). First aorist passive indicative
of *metatithēmi,* old verb to transpose, to change as in 7:12;
Acts 7:16. *That he should not see death* (*tou mē idein thanaton*). Here again *tou* with the infinitive usually expresses
purpose, but in this case result is the idea as in Matt. 21:
23; Rom. 1:24; 7:3, etc. (Robertson, *Grammar,* p. 1002).
He was not found (*ouch hēurisketo*). Imperfect passive of
heuriskō from Gen. 5:24. Was still not found. *Translated*
(*metethēken*). First aorist active of same verb as *metetethē*
just before. *Translation* (*metatheseōs*). Substantive from
the same verb *metatithēmi,* used already in 7:12 for change.
See also 12:27. Our very word "metathesis." *He hath had
witness borne him* (*memarturētai*). Perfect passive indicative of *martureō,* stands on record still, "he has been testified
to." *That he had been well-pleasing unto God* (*euarestēkenai
tōi theōi*). Perfect active infinitive of *euaresteō,* late compound
from *euarestos* (well-pleasing), in N.T. only in Heb. 11:5f.
and 13:16. With dative case *theōi*. Quoted here from Gen.
5:22, 24. The word is common of a servant pleasing his
master.

6. *Impossible* (*adunaton*). Strong word as in 6:4, 18.
See Rom. 8:8 for same idea with *aresai* (*areskō,* Gal. 1:10).
Must believe (*pisteusai dei*). Moral necessity to have faith

(trust, *pisteuō*). This is true in business also (banks, for instance). *That he is* (*hoti estin*). The very existence of God is a matter of intelligent faith (Rom. 1:19ff.) so that men are left without excuse. *He is a rewarder* (*misthapodotēs ginetai*). Rather, "becomes a rewarder" (present middle indicative of *ginomai*, not of *eimi*). Only N.T. example of *misthapodotēs*, late and rare double compound (one papyrus example, from *misthos* (reward) and *apodidōmi* (to pay back) like *misthapodosia* (10:35; 11:26). *Seek after* (*ekzētousin*). That seek out God.

7. *Being warned of God* (*chrēmatistheis*). First aorist passive participle of *chrēmatizō*, old word for oracular or divine communications as already in 8:5 (cf. Matt. 2:12, 22, etc.). *Moved with godly fear* (*eulabēthē*). First aorist passive indicative of *eulabeomai*, old verb from *eulabēs* (from *eu* and *labein*, to take hold well or carefully), to show oneself *eulabēs*, to act circumspectly or with reverence, here only in N.T. (save Textus Receptus in Acts 23:10), often in LXX. *An ark* (*kibōton*). Gen. 6:15 and Matt. 24:38. Shaped like a box (cf. Heb. 9:4). *Through which* (*di' hēs*). Through his faith as shown in building the ark. *The world* (*ton kosmon*). Sinful humanity as in verse 38. *Heir* (*klēronomos*). In II Peter 2:5 Noah is called "a preacher of righteousness" as here "heir of righteousness." He himself believed his message about the flood. Like Enoch he walked with God (Gen. 6:9).

8. *Not knowing whither he went* (*mē epistamenos pou erchetai*). Usual negative *mē* with a participle (present middle from *epistamai*, old and common verb to put the mind on). Present middle indicative (*erchetai*) preserved in the indirect question after the secondary tense *exēlthen* (went out) from which *epistamenos* gets its time. Abraham is a sublime and graphic example of faith. He did not even know where the land was that he was going to receive "as an inheritance" (*eis klēronomian*).

9. *Became a sojourner* (*parōikēsen*). First aorist active indicative of *paroikeō*, old verb to dwell (*oikeō*) beside (*para*), common in LXX, in N.T. only here and Luke 24:18. Called *paroikon* (sojourner) in Acts 7:6. *In the land of promise* (*eis gēn tēs epaggelias*). Literally, "land of the promise." The promise made by God to him (Gen. 12:7; 13:15; 17:8). *As in a land not his own* (*hōs allotrian*). For *allotrios* (belonging to another) see 9:25; 11:34. *The heirs with him of the same promise* (*tōn sunklēromenōn tēs epaggelias tēs autēs*). Late double compound (*sun, klēros, nemomai*), found in Philo, inscriptions and papyri, in N.T. only here, Rom. 8:17; Eph. 3:6; I Peter 3:7. "Co-heirs" with Abraham.

10. *He looked for* (*exedecheto*). Imperfect middle of *ekdechomai* (see on 10:13) picturesque progressive imperfect, his steady and patient waiting in spite of disappointment. *The foundations* (*tous themelious*). Not just "tents" (*skēnais*, verse 9). Abraham set his steady gaze on heaven as his real home, being a mere pilgrim (*paroikos*) on earth. *Builder* (*technitēs*). Old word from *technē* (craft) or trade (Acts 17:29; 18:3), craftsman, artificer, in N.T. only here and Acts 19:24, 38. *Maker* (*dēmiourgos*). Old word from *dēmios* (public) and *ergon*, a worker for the public, artisan, framer, here only in N.T.

11. *To conceive seed* (*eis katabolēn spermatos*). For deposit of seed. See 4:3 for *katabolē*. *Past age* (*para kairon hēlikias*). Beyond (*para* with the accusative) the season of age. *Since she counted him faithful who had promised* (*epei piston hēgēsato ton epaggeilamenon*). Sarah herself (*autē — Sarra*). Even Sarah, old as she was, believed God who had promised. Hence she received power.

12. *And that as good as dead* (*kai tauta nenekrōmenou*). Accusative of general reference (*tauta*), sometimes singular as in I Cor. 6:8. The perfect passive participle from *nekroō*, late verb to make dead, to treat as dead (Rom. 4:19), here by hyperbole. *By the sea shore* (*para to cheilos tēs thalassēs*).

"Along the lip of the sea" (from Gen. 22:17), *cheilos* here alone in this sense in the N.T. *Innumerable* (*anarithmētos*). Old compound verbal adjective (alpha privative and *arithmeō*, to number), here alone in N.T.

13. *In faith* (*kata pistin*). Here a break in the routine *pistei* (by faith), "according to faith," either for literary variety "or to suggest *pistis* as the sphere and standard of their characters" (Moffatt). *These all* (*houtoi pantes*). Those in verses 9–12 (Abraham, Sarah, Isaac, Jacob). *Not having the promises* (*mē komisamenoi tas epaggelias*). First aorist middle participle of *komizō*, to obtain, as in 10:36; 11:39. And yet the author mentions Abraham (6:15) as having obtained the promise. He received the promise of the Messiah, but did not live to see the Messiah come as we have done. It is in this sense that we have "better promises." *Greeted them* (*aspasamenoi*). First aorist middle participle of *aspazomai*, to salute (Matt. 5:47). Abraham rejoiced to see Christ's day in the dim distance (John 8:56). *Strangers* (*xenoi*). Foreigners. "To reside abroad carried with it a certain stigma" (Moffatt). But they "confessed" it (Gen. 23:4; 47:9). *Pilgrims* (*parepidēmoi*). Late double compound (*para, epi, dēmos*), a sojourner from another land, in N.T. only here and I Peter 1:1; 2:11.

14. *A country of their own* (*patrida*). Land of the fathers (*patēr*), one's native land (John 4:44). Cf. our patriotic, patriotism.

15. *Had been mindful* (*emnēmoneuon*) — *would have had* (*eichon an*). Condition of second class (note *an* in conclusion) with the imperfect (not aorist) in both condition and conclusion. So it means: "If they had continued mindful, they would have kept on having (linear action in both cases in past time). *Opportunity to return* (*kairon anakampsai*). Old verb *anakamptō* to bend back, to turn back (Matt. 2:12), here first aorist active infinitive. Continual hankering would have found a way. Cf. the Israelites in the wilderness yearning after Egypt.

16. *They desire* (*oregontai*). Present middle indicative of *oregō*, old word for stretching out after, yearning after as in I Tim. 3:1. *Their God* (*theos autōn*). Predicate nominative with the epexegetic infinitive *epikaleisthai* (to be called) used with *ouk epaischunetai* (is not ashamed).

17. *Being tried* (*peirazomenos*). Present passive participle of *peirazō*. The test was still going on. *Offered up* (*prosenēnochen*). Perfect active indicative of *prospherō*, the verb so often used in this Epistle. The act was already consummated so far as Abraham was concerned when it was interrupted and it stands on record about him. See Gen. 22:1-18. *He that had gladly received the promises* (*ho tas epaggelias anadexamenos*). *Anadechomai* is old verb to welcome, to entertain, in N.T. only here and Acts 28:7. It seemed the death of his hopes. *Was offering up* (*prosepheren*). It is the imperfect of an interrupted action like *ekaloun* in Luke 1:59.

18. *To whom it was said* (*pros elalēthē*). First aorist passive indicative of *laleō* (Gen. 21:12). God's very words were in the heart of Abraham now about Isaac "his only son" (*ton monogenē*. Cf. Luke 7:12).

19. *Accounting* (*logisamenos*). First aorist middle participle of *logizomai*. Abraham had God's clear command that contravened God's previous promise. This was his solution of his difficult situation. *God is able* (*dunatai ho theos*). God had given him Isaac in his old age. God can raise him from the dead. It was Abraham's duty to obey God. *In a parable* (*en parabolēi*). See already 9:9 for *parabolē*. Because of (*hothen*, whence) Abraham's superb faith Isaac was spared and so he received him back (*ekomisato*) as almost from the dead. This is the test that Abraham stood of which James speaks (James 2:23).

20. *Even concerning things to come* (*kai peri mellontōn*). As told in Gen. 27:28-40 when Isaac blessed Jacob and Esau.

21. *Leaning upon the top of his staff* (*epi to akron tēs rabdou autou*). From Gen. 47:31, but no word for "leaning." The

quotation is from the LXX, the Hebrew having "the head of the bed," but the Hebrew word allows either meaning with different vowel points.

22. *When his end was nigh* (*teleutōn*). Present active participle of *teleutaō*, to finish or close (Matt. 2:19), "finishing his life." *Of the departure* (*peri tēs exodou*). Late compound for way out, exit as here, metaphorically of death as here (Luke 9:31; II Peter 1:15). *Concerning his bones* (*peri tōn osteōn autou*). Uncontracted form as in Matt. 23:27.

23. *Was hid* (*ekrubē*). Second aorist passive indicative of *kruptō*, to hide, as in Matt. 5:14. *Three months* (*trimēnon*). Old adjective used as neuter substantive in accusative case for extent of time, here only in N.T. *A goodly child* (*asteion to paidion*). Literally, "the child was goodly" (predicate adjective). Old adjective from *astu* (city), "of the city" ("citified"), of polished manners, genteel. In N.T. only here and Acts 7:20, about Moses both times. Quoted from Ex. 2:2f. *The king's commandment* (*to diatagma tou basileōs*). Late compound for injunction from *diatassō*, only here in the N.T.

24. *When he was grown up* (*megas genomenos*). "Having become great" (from Ex. 2:11). *Refused* (*ērnesato*). First aorist middle indicative of *arneomai*, to deny, to refuse. He was of age and made his choice not from ignorance. *Son* (*huios*). Predicate nominative with *legesthai* (to be spoken of, present passive infinitive, of *legō*).

25. *Choosing rather* (*mallon helomenos*). "Rather having chosen" (second aorist middle of *haireō*, to take for oneself a position). *To be entreated with* (*sunkakoucheisthai*). Present passive infinitive of the double compound *sunkakoucheō* (from *sun, kakos, echō*), to treat ill with (associative instrumental case), only known example save one in the papyri (second century A.D.), though *kakoucheō* in Heb. 11:37; 13:3. *To enjoy the pleasures of sin for a season* (*proskairon echein hamartias apolausin*). Literally, "to have temporary pleasure

of sin." *Apolausis* is old word from *apolauō*, to enjoy, in
N.T. only here and I Tim. 6:17. *Proskairos* (from *pros*,
kairos) is a common *Koiné* word as the antithesis to *aiōnios*
(eternal) as in Matt. 13:21; Mark 4:17; II Cor. 4:18 (only
N.T. examples). To have been disloyal to God's people
would have brought enjoyment to Moses in the Egyptian
Court for a short while only.

26. *The reproach of Christ* (*ton oneidismon tou Christou*).
See Psa. 89:51 for the language where "the Messiah" ("The
Anointed One") is what is meant by *tou Christou*, here
rightly applied by the writer to Jesus as the Messiah who
had his own shame to bear (12:2; 13:12). There is today as
then (Heb. 13:13) a special reproach (*oneidismos*, already,
10:33) in being a follower of Jesus Christ. Moses took this
obloquy as "greater riches" (*meizona plouton*) than "the
treasures of Egypt" (*tōn Aiguptou thēsaurōn*, ablative case
after comparative *meizona*, for which see Matt. 6:19f.).
Moses was laying up treasure in heaven. *For he looked unto
the recompense of reward* (*apeblepen gar eis tēn misthapodosian*). Im perfect active of *apoblepō*, "for he was looking
away (kept on looking away)." For *misthapodosia* see 10:35.

27. *Not fearing* (*mē phobētheis*). Negative *mē* with first
aorist passive participle of *phobeō* here used transitively with
the accusative as in Matt. 10:26. Moses did flee from Egypt
after slaying the Egyptian (Ex. 2:15), but the author omits
that slaughter and ignores it as the dominant motive in the
flight of Moses. *Thumon* (wrath) is common in the N.T. (Luke
4:28), though here only in Hebrews. *He endured* (*ekarterēsen*).
First aorist (constative) active indicative of *kartereō*, old word
from *karteros*, strong, here only in N.T. Moses had made his
choice before slaying the Egyptian. He stuck to its resolutely.
As seeing him who is invisible (*ton aoraton hōs horōn*). This is
the secret of his choice and of his loyalty to God and to God's
people. This is the secret of loyalty in any minister today
who is the interpreter of God to man (II Cor. 4:16-18).

28. *He kept* (*pepoiēken*).   Perfect active indicative of *poieō*, to make, "he has made," emphasizing the permanent nature of the feast. *The sprinkling of the blood* (*tēn proschusin tou haimatos*).   Rather, "the pouring of the blood" (*proschusis* from *proscheō*, to pour upon), only here in the N.T. (earliest known example). An allusion to the command in Ex. 12:7, 22 but in the LXX *proscheō* is the usual term for the act (Ex. 24:6; 29:16; Lev. 1:5, 11; Deut. 16:6). *That the destroyer of the first-born should not touch them* (*hina mē ho olothreuōn ta prōtotoka thigēi autōn*).   Negative final clause with *hina mē* and the second aorist active subjunctive of *thigganō*, old verb to touch with genitive, in the N.T. only here, 12:20, and Col. 2:21. The articular participle *ho olothreuōn* is from Ex. 11:23. For *prōtotoka* see Luke 2:7 and Ex. 12:29.

29. *Which assaying to do* (*hēs peiran labontes*).   Literally, "of which taking trial" (second aorist active participle of *lambanō*, to take).   The idiom *peiran lambanein* occurs in Deut. 28:56, in N.T. only here and verse 36, though a classical idiom (Demosthenes, etc.).   *Were swallowed up* (*katepothēsan*).   First aorist passive indicative of *katapinō*, to drink down, to swallow down (Matt. 23:24).

30. *Fell down* (*epesan*).   "Fell," second aorist active indicative of *piptō* with first aorist endings as often in the Koiné.   *After they had been compassed* (*kuklōthenta*).   First aorist passive participle of *kukloō*, old verb to encircle (from *kuklos*, circle) as in Acts 14:20.   Antecedent action here.

31. *Having received the spies with peace* (*dexamenē tous kataskopous met' eirēnēs*).   First aorist middle participle of *dechomai*, to welcome (Luke 10:8, 10).   *Kataskopos* is an old compound (*kataskopeō*, Gal. 2:4), used of scout or spy, in LXX, here only in N.T.

32. *And what shall I more say?* (*Kai ti eti legō;*).   Deliberative present active subjunctive (same form as indicative, *legō*).   It is both a literary and an oratorical idiom here. He

feels helpless to go on in the same style as he has done from Abel to Rahab (11:4–31). *Will fail me if I tell about (epileipsei me diēgoumenon peri)*. Literally, "will leave me telling about." Present middle participle of *diēgeomai*, to lead through, carry a discussion through, and masculine (disposing of Priscilla as possible author) with *me*. Vivid and picturesque description of the author's embarrassment of riches as he contemplates the long list of the heroes of faith during the long years in Palestine. He mentions six names (Gideon, Barak, Samson, Jephtha, David, Samuel) and then summarizes the rest under "the prophets" (*tōn prophētōn*, the for-speakers for God) of whom Samuel was the leader.

33. *Through faith (dia pisteōs)*. Change thus from the routine *pistei* used so far. *Subdued kingdoms (katēgōnisanto basileias)*. First aorist middle indicative of *katagōnizomai*, *Koiné* verb to struggle against, to overcome, here alone in the N.T. Used by Josephus of David's conquests. The author has here (verses 33, 34), "nine terse clauses" (Moffatt) with no connective (asyndeton) with great rhetorical and oratorical force (sledge-hammer style). For "wrought righteousness" (*ērgasanto dikaiosunēn*, first aorist middle indicative of *ergazomai*) see Acts 10:35. *Obtained promises (epetuchon epaggeliōn)*. Second aorist active indicative of *epitugchanō*, old verb (already in 6:15) with genitive. But they did not see the fulfilment of the Messianic promise (11:39f.). *Stopped the mouths of lions (ephraxan stomata leontōn)*. First aorist active indicative of *phrassō*, old verb to fence in, to block up. See Dan. 6:18–23.

34. *Quenched the power of fire (esbesan dunamin puros)*. First aorist active indicative of *sbennumi* (Matt. 12:20). See Dan. 3:19–28. *Escaped the edge of the sword (ephugon stomata machairēs)*. Second aorist active indicative of *pheugō*, old verb to flee. "Mouths (*stomata*) of the sword" (Luke 21:24). See I Sam. 18:11; I Kings 19:2. *Were made strong (edunamōthēsan)*. First aorist passive indicative of

dunamoō, late verb from *dunamis* as in Col. 1:11. *Waxed mighty in war* (*egenēthēsan ischuroi en polemōi*). "Became strong in battle" (Psa. 18:34ff.). *Armies of aliens* (*parembolas allotriōn*). Late compound (*para, en, ballō*) for encampment (Polybius, Plutarch), barracks (Acts 21:34, 37), armies in battle line (Rev. 20:9 and here as in LXX and Polybius). Apparently a reference to the campaigns of Judas Maccabeus.

35. *By a resurrection* (*ex anastaseōs*). Cf. I Kings 17:17ff.; II Kings 4:8-37. *Were tortured* (*etumpanisthēsan*). First aorist passive indicative of *tumpanizō*, late verb from *tumpanon* (kettledrum, drumstick), to beat the drum, co beat to death (cf. II Macc. 7 about Eleazar and the Mother and the seven sons), once in LXX (I Sam. 21:13). *Not accepting their deliverance* (*ou prosdexamenoi tēn apolutrōsin*). Offered at the price of disloyalty as in II Macc. 6:21-27. *That they might obtain a better resurrection* (*hina kreittonos anastaseōs tuchōsin*). Purpose clause with *hina* and the second aorist active subjunctive of *tugchanō* to obtain with the genitive case. A "better resurrection" than the temporary ones alluded to in this verse by the women.

36. *Of mockings and scourgings* (*empaigmōn kai mastigōn*). *Empaigmos* is from *empaizō* (Matt. 20:19), late word, in LXX, here alone in N.T. *Mastigōn* (*mastix*, a whip, a scourge) is old and common enough (Acts 22:24).

37. *They were stoned* (*elithasthēsan*). Like Zechariah son of Jehoiada (II Chron. 24:20). "A characteristic Jewish punishment" (Vincent). First aorist passive indicative of *lithazō* (John 10:31). *They were sawn asunder* (*epristhēsan*). First aorist passive indicative of *priō* or *prizō*, old verb (*prion*, a saw). Cruel Jewish punishment (Amos 1:3) said to have been inflicted on Isaiah. *They were tempted* (*epeirasthēsan*). First aorist passive indicative of *peirazō*. The MSS. vary greatly in the text here and the order of these two items. This mild word seems an anticlimax after *epristhēsan*. One

of the seven brothers was fried (II Macc. 7:4) and so *eprēs-thesan* (were burned) from *pimpraō* (Acts 28:6) has been suggested. *With the sword* (*en phonōi machairēs*). "In (by) slaughter of the sword" (Ionic form of the genitive *machaires* as in Ex. 17:13; Numb. 21:24). The fate of unpopular prophets (I Kings 10:10; Jer. 26:23). *They went about* (*perielthon*). Constative aorist active indicative of *perierchomai* (picturesque compound verb). Here the sufferings of the living. *In sheep skins* (*en mēlōtais*). Late word from *mēlon* (sheep), rough garment of prophets as Elijah (I Kings 19:13, 19), here only in N.T. In Byzantine Greek a monk's garb. *In goatskins* (*en aigeiois dermasin*). *Derma*, old word from *derō*, to flay (Matt. 21:35), here only in N.T. *Aigeios*, old adjective (from *aix*, goat), here only in N.T. *Being destitute* (*husteroumenoi*). Present passive participle of *hustereō*, old verb to be left behind, used by Paul of himself (II Cor. 11:9). *Afflicted* (*thlibomenoi*). Present passive participle of *thlibō*, common verb to oppress. *Evil entreated* (*kakouchoumēnoi*). Present passive participle of *kakoucheō*, late compound verb from obsolete *kakouchos* (*kakos* and *echō*), in LXX (I Kings 2:26), in N.T. only here and 13:3. See *sunkakoucheisthai* in 11:25.

38. *Of whom the world was not worthy* (*hōn ouk ēn axios ho kosmos*). Graphic picture in a short parenthetical relative clause (*hōn*, genitive plural with *axios*), a phrase to stir the blood of the readers. *Wondering* (*planōmenoi*). Present middle participle of *planaō*, like lost sheep, hunted by wolves. *Caves* (*spēlaiois*). Old word from *speos* (cavern) as in Matt. 21:13. *Holes* (*opais*). Old word, perhaps from *ops* (root of *horaō*, to see), opening, in N.T. only here and James 3:11. Cf. I Kings 18:4; II Macc. 5:27; 10:6 (about Judas Maccabeus and others).

39. *These all* (*houtoi pantes*). The whole list in verses 5-38. Cf. verse 13. *Through their faith* (*dia pisteōs*). Here rather than *pistei* as so often. *Received not the promise* (*ouk ekomis-*

anto tēn epaggelian). First aorist middle of *komizō.* The Messianic promise they did not live to see (11:13), though they had individual special promises fulfilled as already shown (11:33).

40. *God having provided (tou theou problepsamenou).* Genitive absolute with first aorist middle participle of *problepō,* late compound to foresee, here only in the N.T. *Some better thing (kreitton ti).* "Something better," "the better promises" of 8:6. *That apart from us they should not be made perfect (hina mē chōris hēmōn teleiōthōsin).* Negative purpose clause with *hina mē* and the first aorist passive subjunctive of *teleioō.* But this glorious and gracious purpose (foresight) of God is not due to any special merit in us. It is simply the fulness of the time in God's dispensation of grace of which we are the beneficiaries. But all the same and all the more (*noblesse oblige*), we should prove worthy of our heritage and of God's goodness to us and be loyal to Christ.

CHAPTER XII

1. *Therefore* (*toigaroun*). Triple compound inferential participle (*toi, gar, oun*) like the German *doch denn nun*, a conclusion of emphasis, old particle, in N.T. only here and I Thess. 4:8. There should be no chapter division here, since 12:1–3 really is the climax in the whole argument about the better promises (10:19–12:3) with a passionate appeal for loyalty to Christ. *Us also* (*kai hēmeis*). We as well as "these all" of 11:39 and all the more because of the "something better" given us in the actual coming of Christ. *Compassed about* (*echontes perikeimenon*). Literally, "having (*echontes*, present active participle of *echō*) lying around us" (*perikeimenon*, present middle participle of *perikeimai*, old verb as in Luke 17:2). *Cloud of witnesses* (*nephos marturōn*). Old word (Latin *nubes*), here only in the N.T., for vast mass of clouds. *Nephelē* is a single cloud. The metaphor refers to the great amphitheatre with the arena for the runners and the tiers upon tiers of seats rising up like a cloud. The *martures* here are not mere spectators (*theatai*), but testifiers (witnesses) who testify from their own experience (11:2, 4, 5, 33, 39) to God's fulfilling his promises as shown in chapter 11. *Laying aside* (*apothemenoi*). Second aorist middle (indirect, from ourselves) participle of *apotithēmi*, old verb as in Col. 3:8 (laying off old clothes). The runners ran in the stadium nearly naked. *Every weight* (*ogkon panta*). Old word (kin to *enegkein, pherō*) like *phortos, baros*. Here every encumbrance that handicaps like doubt, pride, sloth, anything. No trailing garment to hinder or trip one. *The sin which doth so easily beset us* (*tēn euperistaton hamartian*). "The easily besetting sin." There are a dozen possible renderings of this double compound verbal from *eu*, well, and *periistēmi*, to place

432

around or to stand around (intransitive). The Vulgate has *circumstans nos peccatum* (the sin standing around us). Probably this is the true idea here, "the easily encompassing (or surrounding) sin." In this case apostasy from Christ was that sin. In our cases it may be some other sin. The verbal adjective reminds one of the ring of wild beasts in the jungle that encircle the camp-fire at night each ready to pounce upon a careless victim. *Let us run* (*trechōmen*). Present active volitive subjunctive of *trechō*, "let us keep on running." *With patience* (*di' hupomonēs*). Not with impatience, doubt, or despair. *The race that is set before us* (*ton prokeimenon hēmin agōna*). Note the article and the present middle participle of *prokeimai*, old compound (already in 6:18, and also in 12:2). Dative case (*hēmin*) of personal interest.

2. *Looking unto* (*aphorōntes eis*). Present active participle of *aphoraō*, old verb to look away, "looking away to Jesus." In N.T. only here and Phil. 2:23. Fix your eyes on Jesus, after a glance at "the cloud of witnesses," for he is the goal. Cf. Moses in 11:26 (*apeblepen*). *The author* (*ton archēgon*). See 2:10 for this word. "The pioneer of personal faith" (Moffatt). *Perfecter* (*teleiōtēn*). A word apparently coined by the writer from *teleioō* as it has been found nowhere else. Vulgate has *consummator*. *For the joy* (*anti tēs charas*). Answering to, in exchange for (verse 16), at the end of the race lay the joy "set before him" (*prokeimenēs autōi*), while here was the Cross (*stauron*) at this end (the beginning of the race) which he endured (*hupemeinen*, aorist active indicative of *hupomenō*), *despising shame* (*aischunēs kataphronēsas*). The cross at his time brought only shame (most shameful of deaths, "yea, the death of the cross" Phil. 2:8). But Jesus despised that, in spite of the momentary shrinking from it, and did his Father's will by submitting to it. *Hath sat down* (*kekathiken*). Perfect active indicative of *kathizō*, and still is there (1:3).

3. *Consider* (*analogisasthe*). First aorist middle imperative of *analogizomai*, old word to reckon up, to compare, to weigh, only here in the N.T. See *katanoēsate* in 3:1. Understanding Jesus is the key to the whole problem, the cure for doubt and hesitation. *Endured* (*hupomemenēkota*). Perfect active participle of the same verb *hupomenō* used in verse 2. *Gainsaying* (*antilogian*). Old word from *antilogos* (from *antilegō*), already in 6:16; 7:7. *Of sinners* (*hupo tōn hamartōlōn*). "By sinners." *Against themselves* (*eis heautous*). Against their better selves if a genuine reading. But *eis heauton* (against himself), against Christ, is far more likely correct. *That ye wax not weary* (*hina mē kamēte*). Negative final clause with *hina mē* and the second aorist active subjunctive of *kamnō*, old verb to be weary as here or sick as in James 5:15. *Fainting in your souls* (*tais psuchais humōn ekluomenoi*). Present passive participle of *ekluō*, old verb to loosen out, to set free, and in passive to be enfeebled, to be tired out (here in soul with locative case), as in verse 5. The rest of the Epistle drives home the argument.

4. *Resisted* (*antikatestēte*). Second aorist active indicative (intransitive) of the double compound *antikathistēmi*, old verb to stand in opposition against in line of battle, intransitively to stand face to face (*anti*) against (*kata*), here only in the N.T. *Unto blood* (*mechris haimatos*). "Up to blood." As was true of Jesus and many of the other heroes of faith in chapter 11. *Striving* (*antagōnizomenoi*). Present middle participle of *antagōnizomai*, old verb with the same figure in *antikatestēte*. *Against sin* (*pros hamartian*). Face to face with sin as in verse 1.

5. *Ye have forgotten* (*eklelēsthe*). Perfect middle indicative of *eklanthanō*, to cause to forget, old verb, here only in the N.T. with genitive case as usual. *Reasoneth with you* (*humin dialegetai*). Present middle indicative of *dialegomai*, old verb to ponder different (*dia-*) things, to converse, with dative. Cf. Acts 19:8f. The quotation is from Prov. 3:11f. *Regard*

not lightly (*mē oligōrei*). Prohibition with *mē* and the present active imperative of *oligōreō*, old verb from *oligōros* and this from *oligos* (little) and *hōra* (hour), old verb, here only in N.T. *Chastening* (*paideias*). Old word from *paideuō*, to train a child (*pais*), instruction (II Tim. 3:16), which naturally includes correction and punishment as here. See also Eph. 6:4. *Nor faint* (*mēde ekluou*). Prohibition with *mē* and present passive imperative of *ekluō* (see verse 3).

6. *Scourgeth* (*mastigoi*). Present active indicative of *mastigoō*, old verb from *mastix* (whip). This is a hard lesson for God's children to learn and to understand. See 5:7 about Jesus.

7. *That ye endure* (*hupomenete*). Present active indicative or present active imperative and so just "endure for chastening." *Dealeth with you* (*humin prospheretai*). Present middle indicative of *prospherō*, but this sense of bearing oneself towards one with the dative here only in the N.T., though often in the older Greek. *What* (*tis*). Interrogative. *Whom* (*hon*). Relative. Cf. Matt. 7:9.

8. *If ye are without chastening* (*ei chōris este paideias*). Condition of first class, determined as fulfilled. Note position of *este* (are) between the preposition *chōris* and *paideias* (ablative case). *Have been made* (*gegonasin*). Perfect active indicative of *ginomai*. *Partakers* (*metochoi*). Partners (3:14). *Then* (*ara*). Accordingly, correspondingly. *Bastards* (*nothoi*). Old word, here only in N.T. Illegitimate.

9. *Furthermore* (*eita*). The next step in the argument (Mark 4:17). *We had* (*eichomen*). Imperfect indicative of customary action, "we used to have." *To chasten us* (*paideutas*). Predicate accusative after *eichomen*, "as chasteners." Old word from *paideuō*, as agent(*-tēs*). Only once in LXX (Hosea 5:2) and twice in N.T. (here and Rom. 2:20). *We gave them reverence* (*enetrepometha*). Imperfect middle of old word *entrepō*, to turn in or at. Here "we turned ourselves to" as in Matt. 21:37, habitual attitude of reverence. *Shall*

we be in subjection (*hupotagēsometha*). Second future passive of *hupotassō*. There is no *de* here to correspond to *men* in the first part of the verse. *Unto the Father of spirits* (*tōi patri tōn pneumatōn*). Rather, "Unto the Father of our spirits" (note article *ton*). As God is.

10. *They* (*hoi men*). Demonstrative *hoi* in contrast (*men*). *Chastened* (*epaideuon*). Imperfect active, used to chasten. *As seemed good to them* (*kata to dokoun autois*). "According to the thing seeming good to them." *Dokoun* is present active neuter singular articular participle of *dokeō*. *But he* (*ho de*). Demonstrative with *de* vs. *men*. *For our profit* (*epi to sumpheron*). Present active articular neuter singular participle of *sumpherō*, to bear together as in I Cor. 12:7. *That we may be partakers* (*eis to metalabein*). Articular second aorist active infinitive of *metalambanō* with *eis* for purpose, "for the partaking." *Of his holiness* (*tēs hagiotētos autou*). Genitive with *metalabein* (to share in). Rare word, in N.T. only here and II Cor. 1:12.

11. *For the present* (*pros to paron*). A classical phrase (Thucydides), *pros* with the accusative neuter singular articular participle of *pareimi*, to be beside. *Not joyous, but grievous* (*ou charas, alla lupēs*). Predicate ablative (springing from) or predicate genitive (marked by). Either makes sense, but note predicate ablative in II Cor. 4:7 (*kai tou theou kai mē ex hēmōn*). *Peaceable fruit* (*karpon eirēnikon*). Old adjective from *eirēnē* (peace), in N.T. only here and James 3:17. Peaceable after the chastening is over. *Exercised thereby* (*di' autēs gegumnasmenois*). Perfect passive participle (dative case) of *gumnazō*, state of completion, picturing the discipline as a gymnasium like 5:14 and I Tim. 4:17.

12. *Wherefore* (*dio*). Because of the chastening. *Lift up* (*anorthōsate*). First aorist active imperative of *anorthoō*, old compound (from *ana, orthos*) to make straight, in N.T. here and Luke 13:13; Acts 15:16. *Hang down* (*pareimenas*). Perfect passive participle of *pariēmi*, old verb to let pass,

to relax, in N.T. only here and Luke 11:42. *Palsied* (*paralelumena*). Perfect passive participle of *paraluō*, old verb to loosen on the side, to dissolve, to paralyze (Luke 5:18, 24).

13. *Straight paths* (*trochias orthas*). Track of a wheel (*trochos*, James 3:6 from *trechō*, to run), here only in N.T. "Straight (*orthas*) wheel tracks." *Be not turned out of the way* (*hina mē ektrapēi*). Negative final clause with *hina mē* and second aorist passive of *ektrepō*, old verb to turn out, to twist, to put out of joint. So I Tim. 1:6. Vivid picture of concern for the lame (*chōlon*, as in Matt. 11:5). Graphic picture of concern for the weak, a good argument for prohibition also.

14. *Follow after peace* (*eirēnēn diōkete*). Give peace a chase as if in a hunt. *With all men* (*meta pantōn*). Like Paul's use of *diōkō* with *eirēnēn* in Rom. 14:19 and his *to ex humōn* (so far as proceeds from you) in 12:18. This lesson the whole world needs including Christians. *Sanctification* (*hagiasmon*). Consecration as in I Thess. 4:7; Rom. 6:19, etc. *Without which* (*hou chōris*). Ablative case of the relative with *chōris* (post positive here). About seeing God compare Matt. 5:8 where we have *katharoi*.

15. *Looking carefully* (*episkopountes*). Present active participle of *episkopeō*, to have oversight, in N.T. only here and I Peter 5:2. Cf. *episcopos* (bishop). *Lest there be any man* (*mē tis*). Negative purpose clause with *ei* (present active subjunctive) omitted. *Falleth short of* (*husterōn apo*). Present active participle of *hustereō* (see 4:1) agreeing with *tis*. Followed here by *apo* and the ablative. *Root of bitterness.* (*riza pikrias*). Quoted from Deut. 29:18. Vivid picture. *Springing up* (*anō phuousa*). Present active participle of *phuō*, to sprout. Pictured here as a quick process. Also from Deut. 29:18. *Trouble* (*enochlei*). Present active subjunctive (in final clause with *mē tis*) of *enochleō*, old verb to trouble with a crowd, to annoy. In N.T. only here and Luke 6:18. *Be defiled* (*mianthōsin*). First aorist passive subjunctive

(in final clause with *mē*) of *mianō*, old verb to dye, to stain, to defile as in Titus 1:15 (the conscience). The contagion of sin is terrible as any disease.

16. *Profane* (*bebēlos*). Trodden under foot, unhallowed (I Tim. 1:9). *For one mess of meat* (*anti brōseōs mias*). Idea of exchange, "for one act of eating" (I Cor. 8:4). *Sold* (*apedeto*). Second aorist middle indicative from Gen. 25:31, 33, and with irregular form for *apedoto* (regular *mi* form). *His own birthright* (*ta prōtotokia heautou*). From Genesis also and in Philo, only here in N.T. From *prōtotokos* (first born, Heb. 1:6).

17. *Ye know* (*iste*). Regular form for the second person of *oida* rather than the Koiné *oidate*. *He was rejected* (*apedokimasthē*). First aorist passive indicative of *apodokimazō*, old verb to disapprove (Matt. 21:42). *Place of repentance* (*metanoias topon*). *Metanoia* is change of mind and purpose, not sorrow though he had tears (*meta dakruōn*) afterwards as told in Gen. 27:38. He sought it (*autēn*, the blessing *eulogian*) with tears, but in vain. There was no change of mind in Isaac. The choice was irrevocable as Isaac shows (Gen. 27:33). Esau is a tragic example of one who does a wilful sin which allows no second chance (Heb. 6:6; 10:26). The author presses the case of Esau as a warning to the Christians who were tempted to give up Christ.

18. *Ye are not come* (*ou proselēluthate*). Perfect active indicative of *proserchomai*. There is no word here in the Greek for "a mount" like *orei* in verses 20 and 22 (and Ex. 19:12f.; Deut. 4:11), but it is clearly understood since the dative participles agree with it unless they be taken as descriptive of *puri* (a palpable and kindled fire" when *puri* would be the dative case after *proselēluthate*). *That might be touched* (*psēlaphōmenoi*). Present passive participle (dative case) of *psēlaphaō*, old verb to handle, to touch (Luke 24:39). *That burned with fire* (*kekaumenoi puri*). Perfect passive participle of *kaiō*, old verb to burn, with instrumental case *puri* (fire), unless the other view (above) is correct.

19. *Unto blackness (gnophōi).* Dative case of *gnophos* (late form for earlier *dnophos* and kin to *nephos,* cloud), here only in N.T. Quoted here from Ex. 10:22. *Darkness (zophōi).* Old word, in Homer for the gloom of the world below. In the Symmachus Version of Ex. 10:22, also in Jude 6; II Peter 2:4, 16. *Tempest (thuellēi).* Old word from *thuō* (to boil, to rage), a hurricane, here only in N.T. From Ex. 10:22. *The sound of a trumpet (salpiggos ēchōi).* From Ex. 19:16. *Ēchos* is an old word (our *echo*) as in Luke 21:25; Acts 2:2. *The voice of words (phōnēi rēmatōn).* From Ex. 19:19; Deut. 4:12. *Which voice (hēs).* Relative referring to *phōnē* (voice) just before, genitive case with *akousantes* (heard, aorist active participle). *Intreated (parēitēsanto).* First aorist middle (indirect) indicative of *paraiteomai,* old verb, to ask from alongside (Mark 15:6), then to beg away from oneself, to depreciate as here, to decline (Acts 25:11), to excuse (Luke 14:18), to avoid (I Tim. 4:7). *That no word should be spoken unto them (prostethēnai autois logon).* First aorist passive infinitive of *prostithēmi,* old word to add, here with accusative of general reference (*logon*), "that no word be added unto them." Some MSS. have here a redundant negative *mē* with the infinitive because of the negative idea in *parēitēsanto* as in Gal. 5:7.

20. *For they could not endure (ouk epheron gar).* Imperfect active of *pherō,* "for they were not enduring (bearing)." *That which was enjoined (to diastellomenon).* Present passive articular participle of *diastellō,* old verb to distinguish, to dispose, to order. The quotation is from Ex. 19:12f. The people appealed to Moses (Ex. 20:19) and the leaders did so also (Deut. 5:23f.), both in terror. *If even (kān).* "Even if." Condition of third class with second aorist active subjunctive of *thiganō* as in 11:28, followed by genitive *orous* (mountain). *It shall be stoned (lithobolēthēsetai).* From Ex. 19:13. Late compound verb from *lithobolos* (from *lithos, ballō*) as in Matt. 21:35.

21. *Fearful* (*phoberon*). As in 10:27, 31, only in Heb. in N.T. *The appearance* (*to phantazomenon*). Present passive articular participle of *phantazō*, old verb from *phainō*, to make visible, here only in N.T. "The manifestation." *I exceedingly fear and quake* (*ekphobos eimi kai entromos*). "I am terrified (*ekphobos*, late compound like *ekphobeō*, to frighten, Mark 9:6) and trembling" (*entromos*, late compound like *entremō*, to tremble at, as in Acts 7:32; 16:29). *Ekphobos* is quoted from Deut. 9:19.

22. *But* (*alla*). Sharp contrast to verse 18 with same form *proselēluthate*. *Unto Mount Zion* (*Siōn orei*). Dative case of *oros*, as with the other substantives. In contrast to Mount Sinai (verses 18-21). Paul has contrasted Mount Sinai (present Jerusalem)· with the Jerusalem above (heaven) in Gal. 4:21-31. *City* (*polei*). As in 11:10, 16. Heaven is termed thus a spiritual mountain and city. *The heavenly Jerusalem* (*Ierousalem epouraniōi*). See 11:10, 16 and Isa. 60:14. *Innumerable hosts of angels* (*muriasin aggelōn*). "Myriads of angels." *Murias* is an old word (from *murios*, I Cor. 4:15) as in Luke 12:1.

23. *To the general assembly* (*panēgurei*). Old word (from *pas* and *aguris*, *ageirō*). Here only in N.T. *Panēgurizō* occurs in Isa. 66:10 for keeping a festal holiday. Possibly to be connected with *aggelōn*, though not certain. *Church of the firstborn* (*ekklēsiāi prōtotokōn*). Probably an additional item besides the angelic host as the people of Israel are called firstborn (Ex. 4:22). The word *ekklēsia* here has the general sense of all the redeemed, as in Matt. 16:18; Col. 1:18; Eph. 5:24-32, and equivalent to the kingdom of God. *Who are enrolled in heaven* (*apogegrammenōn en ouranois*). Perfect passive participle of *apographō*, old verb to write off, to copy, to enroll as in Luke 2:1, 3, 5 (only N.T. examples). Enrolled as citizens of heaven even while on earth (Luke 10:20; Phil. 1:27; 3:20; 4:3; Rev. 13:8, etc.). *To God the Judge of all* (*kritēi theōi pantōn*). All these chief substantives in the dative

case. People should not forget that God is the Judge of all men. *Made perfect* (*teteleiōmenōn*). Perfect passive participle of *teleioō*, perfected at last (11:40).

24. *To Jesus* (*Iēsou*). This great fact is not to be overlooked (Phil. 2:10f.). He is there as Lord and Saviour and still "Jesus." *The mediator of a new covenant* (*diathēkēs neas mesitēi*). As already shown (7:22; 8:6, 8, 9, 10; 9:15) and now gloriously consummated. *To the blood of sprinkling* (*haimati rantismou*). As in 9:19–28. *Than Abel* (*para ton Abel*). Accusative as in 1:4. *Better* (*kreitton*). Comparative of *kalos*. Abel's blood still speaks (11:4), but it is as nothing compared to that of Jesus.

25. *See* (*blepete*). Earnest word as in 3:12. Driving home the whole argument of the Epistle by this powerful contrast between Mount Zion and Mount Sinai. The consequences are dreadful to apostates now, for Zion has greater terrors than Sinai, great as those were. *That ye refuse not* (*mē paraitēsēsthe*). Negative purpose with *mē* and the first aorist middle subjunctive of *paraiteomai*, the same verb used in verse 19 about the conduct of the Israelites at Sinai and also below. *Him that speaketh* (*ton lalounta*). Present active articular participle of *laleō* as in verse 24 (Jesus speaking by his blood). *For if they did not escape* (*ei gar ekeinoi ouk exephugon*). Condition of first class with *ei* and second aorist active indicative of *ekpheugō*, to escape. Direct reference to Sinai with use of the same verb again (*paraitēsamenoi*, when they refused). *Him that warned* (*ton chrēmatizonta*). That is Moses. For *chrēmatizō* see 8:5; 11:7. *Much more we* (*polu mallon hēmeis*). Argument from the less to the greater, *polu*, adverbial accusative case. The verb has to be supplied from the condition, "We shall not escape." Our chance to escape is far less, "we who turn away (*apostrephomenoi*, middle participle, turn ourselves away from) the one from heaven (*ton ap' ouranōn*)," God speaking through his Son (1:2).

26. *Then shook* (*esaleusen tote*). Old verb as in Matt. 11:7. *He hath promised* (*epēggeltai*). Perfect middle indicative of *epaggellō* and it still holds. He quotes Haggai 2:6. *Will I make to tremble* (*seisō*). Old and strong verb (here future active) *seiō*, to agitate, to cause to tremble as in Matt. 21:10. The author applies this "yet once more" (*eti hapax*) and the reference to heaven (*ton ouranon*) to the second and final "shaking" at the Second Coming of Jesus Christ for judgement (9:28).

27. *And this word* (*to de*). He uses the article to point out "*eti hapax*" which he explains (*dēloi*, signifies, present active indicative of *dēloō*). *The removing* (*tēn metathesin*). For this word see 7:12; 11:5. For the transitory nature of the world see I Cor. 7:31; I John 2:17. "There is a divine purpose in the cosmic catastrophe" (Moffatt). *Made* (*pepoiēmenōn*). Perfect passive participle of *poieō*. Made by God, but made to pass away. *That those things which are not shaken may remain* (*hina meinēi ta mē saleuomena*). Final clause with *mē* and the first aorist active subjunctive of *menō*. The Kingdom of God is not shaken, fearful as some saints are about it.

28. *Wherefore* (*dio*). Ground for loyalty to Christ and for calm trust in God. *That cannot be shaken* (*asaleuton*). Old compound with alpha privative and the verbal adjective from *saleuō* just used. In N.T. only here and Acts 27:41. *Let us have grace* (*echōmen charin*). Present active volitive subjunctive of *echō*, "Let us keep on having grace" as in 4:16, though it can mean "Let us keep on having gratitude" as in Luke 17:9. *Whereby* (*di' hēs*). That is *dia charitos*. *We may offer service* (*latreuōmen*). This subjunctive in a relative clause can be volitive like *echōmen* just before (cf. imperative *stēte* in I Peter 5:12) or it might be the futuristic subjunctive as in 8:3 (*ho prosenegkēi*). *Well pleasing* (*euarestōs*). Old compound adverb, here only in N.T. *With reverence and awe* (*meta eulabeias kai deous*). For *eulabeia* see 5:7; 11:7. *Deos*

is apprehension of danger as in a forest. "When the voice and tread of a wild beast are distinctly heard close at hand the *deos* becomes *phobos*" (Vincent).

29. *A consuming fire (pur katanaliskon)*. From Deut. 4:24. Present active participle of *katanaliskō*, old compound verb, here only in the N.T. This verse is to be coupled with 10:31.

CHAPTER XIII

1. *Brotherly love* (*philadelphia*). Late word from *philadelphos* (I Peter 3:8). See I Thess. 4:9. It is always in order in a church. *To show love unto strangers* (*tēs philoxenias*). Old word for hospitality, from *philoxenos* (I Tim. 3:2), in N.T. only here and Rom. 12:3. In genitive case with *epilanthanesthe* (present middle imperative, cf. Heb. 6:10). *Have entertained angels unawares* (*elathon xenisantes aggelous*). Second aorist active indicative of *lanthanō*, old verb to escape notice and first aorist active participle of *xenizō*, old verb to entertain a guest (*xenos*, stranger), according to a classic idiom seen with *lanthanō*, *tugchanō*, *phthanō*, by which the chief idea is expressed by the participle (supplementary participle), here meaning, "some escaped notice when entertaining angels." The reference is to Gen. 18 and 19 (Abraham and Sarah did this very thing).

2. *As bound with them* (*hōs sundedemenoi*). Perfect passive participle of *sundeō*, old verb, here only in N.T. For sympathy with prisoners see 10:34. *As being yourselves also in the body* (*hōs kai autoi ontes en sōmati*). And so subject to evil treatment. See 11:37 for *kakoucheō* and 11:25 for *sunkakoucheō*.

4. *Let marriage be* (*ho gamos*). No verb in the Greek. The copula can be supplied either *estin* (is) or *estō* (let be, imperative). *Had in honour* (*timios*). Old adjective from *timē* (honour) as in Acts 5:34. *Gamos* elsewhere in the N.T., means the wedding or wedding feast (Matt. 22:29; John 2:1). *Undefiled* (*amiantos*). Old compound word (alpha privative and verbal of *miainō*, to defile), already in Heb. 7:26. *Miainō tēn koitēn* is a common expression for adultery. *Fornicators* (*pornous*). Unmarried and impure. *Adulterers*

444

(*moichous*). Impure married persons. God will judge both classes whether men do or not.

5. *Be ye free from the love of money* (*aphilarguros ho tropos*). No copula, but supply *esto:* "Let your manner of life (*tropos*, way, Matt. 23:37), be without love of money" (*aphilarguros*, double compound), once found only in the N.T., here and I Tim. 3:3, but now several times — or the adverb *aphilargurōs* — in papyri and inscriptions (Deissmann, *Light, etc.*, pp. 85f.). Alpha privative and *philos* and *arguros*. The N.T. is full of the peril of money on the character as modern life is also. *Content with such things as ye have* (*arkoumenoi tois parousin*). Present passive participle of *arkeō*, to suffice, to be content as in Luke 3:14. Cf. *autarkēs* in Phil. 4:11. Here in the nominative plural with no substantive or pronoun (anacoluthon, as in II Cor. 1:7) or the participle used as a principal verb as in Rom. 12:16. "Contented with the present things" (*tois parousin*, associative instrumental case of *ta paronta*, present active neuter plural participle of *pareimi*, to be present or on hand). *For himself hath said* (*autos gar eirēken*). God himself as in Acts 20:33 of Christ. Perfect active indicative as in 1:13; 4:3f.; 10:9. The quotation is a free paraphrase of Gen. 28:15; Deut. 31:8; Josh. 1:5; I Chron. 28:20. Philo (*de Confus. Ling.* 32) has it in this form, "a popular paraphrase" (Moffatt). Note the five negatives strengthening each other (*ou mē* with the second aorist active subjunctive *anō* from *aniēmi*, to relax, as in Acts 16:26; *oud' ou mē* with second aorist active subjunctive *egkatalipō* from *egkataleipō*, to leave behind, as in Matt. 27:46; II Tim. 4:10). A noble promise in times of depression.

6. *So that we say* (*hōste hēmas legein*). The usual construction (the infinitive) with *hōste* in the *Koiné* even when the idea is result instead of purpose. The accusative *hēmas* is that of general reference. *With good courage* (*tharrountas*). Present active participle of *tharreō* (Ionic and early Attic *tharseō*, Matt. 9:2) as in II Cor. 5:6, 8. The accusative

agreeing with *hēmas,* "being of good courage." The quotation is from Psa. 118:6. *My helper* (*emoi boēthos*). "Helper to me" (ethical dative *emoi*). *Boēthos* is old adjective (cf. *boētheō,* to help, 2:18), often in LXX as substantive, here only in N.T. *I will not fear* (*ou phobēthēsomai*). Volitive first future passive of *phobeomai.*

7. *Remember* (*mnēmoneuete*). Present active imperative of *mnēmoneuō,* old verb to be *mindful* of (from *mnēmōn,* mindful) with genitive (John 15:20) or accusative (Matt. 16:9). "Keep in mind." Cf. 11:22. *Them that had the rule over you* (*tōn hēgoumenōn humōn*). Present middle participle of *hēgeomai* with genitive of the person (*humōn*) as in verses 17, 24. The author reminds them of the founders of their church in addition to the long list of heroes in chapter 11. See a like exhortation to respect and follow their leaders in I Thess. 5:12f. Few lessons are harder for the average Christian to learn, viz., good following. *The word of God* (*ton logon tou theou*). The preaching of these early disciples, apostles, and prophets (I Cor. 1:17). *And considering the issue of their life* (*hōn anatheōrountes tēn ekbasin tēs anastrophēs*). No "and" in the Greek, but the relative *hōn* (whose) in the genitive case after *anastrophēs,* "considering the issue of whose life." Present active participle of *anatheōreō,* late compound, to look up a subject, to investigate, to observe accurately, in N.T. only here and Acts 17:23. *Ekbasis* is an old word from *ekbainō,* to go out (Heb. 11:15, here only in N.T.), originally way out (I Cor. 10:13), but here (only other N.T. example) in sense of end or issue as in several papyri examples (Moulton and Milligan, *Vocabulary*). *Imitate their faith* (*mimeisthe tēn pistin*). Present middle imperative of *mimeomai,* old verb (from *mimos,* actor, mimic), in N.T. only here, II Thess. 3:7, 9; III John 11. Keep on imitating the faith of the leaders.

8. *Jesus Christ is the same yesterday and today, yea and forever* (*Iēsous Christos echthes kai sēmeron ho autos kai eis*

tous aiōnas). There is no copula in the Greek. Vincent insists that *estin* be supplied between *Iēsous* and *Christos,* "Jesus is Christ," but it more naturally comes after *Christos* as the Revised Version has it. The old adverb *echthes* is rare in the N.T. (John 4:52; Acts 7:28; Heb. 13:8). Here it refers to the days of Christ's flesh (2:3; 5:7) and to the recent work of the leaders (13:7). "Today" (*sēmeron,* 3:15) is the crisis which confronts them. "Forever" (*eis tous aiōnas*) is eternity as well as the Greek can say it. Jesus Christ is eternally "the same" (1:12) and the revelation of God in him (1:1f.) is final and never to be superseded or supplemented (Moffatt). Hence the peril of apostasy from the only hope of man.

9. *Be not carried away* (*mē parapheresthe*). Prohibition with *mē* and present passive imperative of *parapherō,* old verb to lead along (Jude 12), to carry past (Mark 14:36), to lead astray as here. *By divers and strange teachings* (*didachais poikilais kai xenais*). For *poikilos* (many coloured) see 2:4. *Xenos* for guest we have had in 11:13, but here as adjective meaning unheard of (I Peter 4:12) as in older Greek also. The new is not always wrong any more than the old is always right (Matt. 13:52). But the air was already full of new and strange teachings that fascinated many by their very novelty. The warning here is always needed. Cf. Gal. 1:6–9; II Tim. 3:16. *That the heart be established by grace* (*chariti bebaiousthai tēn kardian*). Present passive infinitive of *bebaioō* (from *bainō*) to make stable with the instrumental case *chariti* (by grace) and the accusative of general reference (*tēn kardian*). How true it is that in the atmosphere of so many windy theories only the heart is stable that has an experience of God's grace in Christ. *That occupied themselves* (*hoi peripatountes*). "That walked" in the ritualistic Jewish rules about meats. *Were not profited* (*ouk ōphelēthēsan*). First aorist passive indicative of *ōpheleō,* to help. Mere Jewish ceremonialism and ritualism failed to build up

the spiritual life. It was sheer folly to give up Christ for Pharisaism or for Moses.

10. *We have an altar* (*echomen thusiastērion*). We Christians have a spiritual altar (*thusiastērion*), not a literal one (7:13). This metaphor is carried out. *Whereof* (*ex hou*). Our spiritual altar. *The tabernacle* (*tēi skēnēi*). Dative case with *latreuontes* (serve), *skēnē* being used for "the whole ceremonial economy" (Vincent) of Judaism.

11. *Of those beasts whose blood* (*hōn zōōn to haima toutōn*). The antecedent (*zōōn*) of *hōn* is here incorporated and attracted into the case of the relative, "the blood of which beasts" and then *toutōn* (genitive demonstrative) is added, "of these." Cf. Lev. 4:12f., 21; 16:27 for the Old Testament ritual in such cases. This is the only example in the LXX or N.T. where *zōōn* (animal) is used of a sacrificial victim. See also Ex. 29:14; 32:26f. for burning without the camp.

12. *Wherefore Jesus also* (*dio kai Iēsous*). The parallel is drawn between the O.T. ritual and the better sacrifice of Jesus already discussed (9:13–10:18). The purpose of Jesus is shown (*hina hagiasēi, hina* and the first aorist active subjunctive of *hagiazō,* to sanctify), the means employed (*dia tou idiou haimatos,* by his own blood), the place of his suffering (*epathen,* as in 5:8) is also given (*exō tēs pulēs,* outside the gate, implied in John 19:17) which phrase corresponds to "outside the camp" of verse 11.

13. *Let us therefore go forth to him* (*toinun exerchōmetha pros auton*). Inferential particle (*toi, nun*), usually postpositive (Luke 20:25; I Cor. 9:26) only N.T. examples. Present middle volitive subjunctive of *exerchomai.* "Let us keep on going out there to him." If a separation has to come between Judaism and Christianity, let us give up Judaism, and go out to Christ "outside the camp" and take our stand with him there on Golgotha, "bearing his reproach (*ton oneidismon autou pherontes*) as Jesus himself endured the Cross despising the shame (12:2) and as Moses accepted "the re-

proach of the Messiah" (11:26) in his day. The only decent place for the follower of Christ is beside the Cross of Christ with the reproach and the power (Rom. 8:1f.) in it. This is the great passionate plea of the whole Epistle.

14. *An abiding city* (*menousan polin*). Jerusalem has lost its charm for followers of Christ. Vincent rightly argues that the Epistle must have been written before the destruction of Jerusalem else a reference to that event could hardly have been avoided here. We are now where Abraham was once (11:10).

15. *Through him* (*di' autou*). That is Jesus. He is our Priest and Sacrifice, the only efficient and sufficient one. *Let us offer up* (*anapherōmen*). Present active volitive subjunctive of *anapherō*, "let us keep on offering up." Jesus is living and let us go to him. *A sacrifice of praise* (*thusian aineseōs*). This phrase occurs in Lev. 7:12; Psa. 54:8. The word *ainesis* (from *aineō*, to praise), common in LXX, is only here in N.T. *The fruit of lips* (*karpon cheileōn*). In apposition (*tout 'estin*) and explanation of *thusian aineseōs*. Cf. Hosea 14:3; Isa. 57:19. *Which made confession to his name* (*homologountōn tōi onomati autou*). This use of *homologeō* with the dative in the sense of praise like *exomologeō* is unique, though the papyri furnish examples in the sense of gratitude (Moulton and Milligan, *Vocabulary*).

16. *To do good* (*tēs eupoiias*). Genitive case. Late compound from *eupoios* (*eupoieō*), common in Epictetus, but here only in N.T., a doing good. *To communicate* (*koinōnias*). Genitive case. See II Cor. 9:13 for use for contribution, beneficence. Moffatt notes that the three great definitions of worship and religious service in the N.T. (here, Rom. 12:1f.; James 1:27) are all inward and ethical. *Forget not* (*mē epilanthanesthe*). Prohibition with *mē* and the present middle imperative of *epilanthanō* (6:10; 13:2). Here with the genitive case. *Is well pleased* (*euaresteitai*). Present passive indicative of *euaresteō* (Heb. 11:5). With the associative instrumental case *thusiais* (sacrifices).

17. *Obey* (*peithesthe*). Present middle imperative of *peithō* with dative case. *Submit* (*hupeikete*). Present active imperative of *hupeikō*, old compound to yield under, to give up. Here only in N.T. *They watch* (*agrupnousin*). Present active indicative of *agrupneō* old verb (from *agreō*, to search, *hupnos*, sleep), to seek after sleep, to be sleepless, be watchful (Mark 13:33). *As they that shall give account* (*hōs logon apodōsontes*). Regular Greek idiom with *hōs* and the future participle. For *logon apodidōmi*, to render account, see Matt. 12:36. These leaders as good shepherds recognize keenly their responsibility for the welfare of the flock. *And not with grief* (*kai mē stenazontes*). "And not groaning" (cf. Rom. 8:23). *Unprofitable* (*alusiteles*). Old double compound adjective (alpha privative and *lusitelēs* and this from *luō*, to pay, and *telos*, tax, useful or profitable as Luke 17:2), not profitable, not advantageous, by *litotes*, hurtful, pernicious. Common rhetorical *litotes*, here only in N.T.

18. *Honestly* (*kalōs*). Nobly, honourably. Apparently the writer is conscious that unworthy motives have been attributed to him. Cf. Paul in I Thess. 2:18; II Cor. 1:11f., 17f.

19. *That I may be restored to you the sooner* (*hina tacheion apokatastathō humin*). Purpose clause with *hina* and the first aorist passive subjunctive of *apokathistēmi*, an old double compound as in Matt. 12:13. What is meant by *tacheion* (John 13:27; 20:4) we do not know, possibly sickness. See verse 23 also for *tacheion*.

20. *The God of peace* (*ho theos tēs eirēnēs*). God is the author and giver of peace, a Pauline phrase (6 times) as in I Thess. 5:23. *Who brought again from the dead* (*ho anagagōn ek nekrōn*). Second aorist active articular participle of *anagō* (cf. Rom. 10:7), the only direct mention of the resurrection of Jesus in the Epistle, though implied often (1:3, etc.). *That great shepherd of the sheep* (*ton poimena tōn probatōn ton megan*). This phrase occurs in Isa. 63:11 except *ton megan* which the author adds as in 4:14; 10:21. So here,

"the shepherd of the sheep the great one." *With the blood of the eternal covenant (en haimati diathēkēs aiōniou).* This language is from Zech. 9:11. The language reminds us of Christ's own words in Mark 14:24 (=Matt. 26:28=Luke 22:20=I Cor. 11:25) about "my blood of the covenant." 21. *Make you perfect (katartisai).* First aorist active optative of *katartizō,* to equip, as in 10:5. A wish for the future. See I Cor. 1:10; II Cor. 13:11; II Tim. 3:17. *Working in us (poiōn en hemin).* "Doing in us." Some MSS. read "in you." *Well-pleasing (euareston).* Compound adjective *(eu, arestos).* Usually with the dative (Rom. 12:2), here with *enōpion autou* more like the Hebrew. This is one of the noblest doxologies in the N.T.

22. *Bear with (anechesthe).* Present middle imperative (some MSS. have *anechesthai,* infinitive) of *anechō* with the ablative, "hold yourselves back from" as in Col. 3:13. *The word of exhortation (tou logou tēs paraklēseōs).* His description of the entire Epistle. It certainly is that, a powerful appeal in fact. *I have written (epesteila).* First aorist active indicative (epistolary aorist) of *epistellō,* old word to send a letter *(epistolē)* as in Acts 15:20. *In few words (dia bracheōn).* Common Greek idiom, here only in N.T. (from *brachus,* brief, short). Cf. *di' oligōn egrapsa* in I Peter 5:12.

23. *Hath been set at liberty (apolelumenon).* Perfect passive participle of *apoluō,* to set free, in indirect discourse after *ginōskete.* Possibly from prison if he came to Rome at Paul's request (II Tim. 4:11, 21). *Shortly (tacheion).* Same comparative as in verse 19, "sooner" than I expect (?).

24. *They of Italy (hoi apo tēs Italias).* Either those with the author in Italy or those who have come from Italy to the author outside of Italy.